AN INTRODUCTION TO

America's Music

BY RICHARD CRAWFORD:

Andrew Law, American Psalmodist

William Billings of Boston, with David P. McKay

American Studies and American Musicology

The Civil War Songbook

The Core Repertory of Early American Psalmody

American Sacred Music Imprints, 1698–1810: A Bibliography,
    with Allen Perdue Britton and Irving Lowens

A Celebration of American Music: Words and Music in Honor of H. Wiley Hitchcock,
    co-editor with R. Allen Lott and Carol J. Oja

Jazz Standards on Record, 1900–1942: A Core Repertory,
    with Jeffrey Magee

The Complete Works of William Billings (ed. by Hans Nathan and Karl Kroeger),
    editorial consultant

The American Musical Landscape

Music of the United States of America (MUSA),
    editor-in-chief

America's Musical Life: A History

AN INTRODUCTION TO

America's

Music

RICHARD CRAWFORD

W. W. NORTON
&
COMPANY

NEW YORK

LONDON

For Penelope B. Crawford
wife, mother, musician

The text of this book is composed in Palatino
with the display set in Bernhard Modern
Composition by Matrix Publishing Services, Inc.
Page makeup by Roberta Flechner
Manufacturing by Maple-Vail
Book design by Joan Greenfield

Library of Congress Cataloging-in-Publication Data

Crawford, Richard, 1935–
    An introduction to America's Music / Richard Crawford.
        p.   cm.
    Includes index.
    ISBN 0-393-97409-X (pbk.)
    1. Music—United States—History and criticism.   I. Title.

ML200.C72 2000
780'.973—dc21   00-056859

W. W. Norton & Company, Inc., 500 Fifth Avenue, New York, N.Y. 10110
www.wwnorton.com

W. W. Norton & Company Ltd., 10 Coptic Street, London WC1A 1PU

1 2 3 4 5 6 7 8 9 0

CONTENTS

PART THREE

The Twentieth Century

PREFACE

"WHY WOULD SOMEBODY WHO PLANS TO WRITE A HISTORY OF AMER-
ican music cancel his subscription to the Sunday *New York Times*?" my
colleague asked, surprised by what I had just told her.

"Because the weekly dose of 'all the news that's fit to print' kills most
of a working day and blurs my focus on the past," I replied.

"What about the present?" she shot back. "What about the picture of
where we are now that we get from the Arts and Leisure section and the
book reviews, week by week? Do you really want to give that up?"

"I *live* in the present," I answered, "and so do you and the folks at
the *New York Times*. We all have our own picture of where we are now,
which keeps changing and which we talk about constantly. My question
is how we *got* to where we are now. And to figure that out, I need to im-
merse myself in the past."

"Wait a minute," she replied. "If the destination keeps changing,
won't the route to getting there have to change too?"

"Sure," I said, "which is why history is always being rewritten."

"Well, then, what's the point?"

"The point is that each moment in history has a date, and dates don't
change. Each date points to a musical world with *its* own possibilities and
sounds. As we learn what was possible in, say, 1900 or 1850 or 1620, our
historical imagination takes us into soundscapes different from our own."

"We can find different soundcapes right now by studying the music
of other cultures," she noted.

"That's true," I replied, "but 'the past is also a foreign country.' "

"Aha! A quotation," she responded, "from . . . ?"

"Somebody famous, but I can't remember who," I admitted, realiz-
ing that people who read the Sunday *Times* can usually cite their sources,
but still pretty sure I was doing the right thing.

My embargo ended seven years later, almost to the day. Picking up
the *New York Times* that morning felt self-indulgent, as if I were following breakfast with a gooey dessert. But when I hit the Arts and Leisure
section, I stopped feeling guilty, because I realized that my perspective
on its notions of where we are now had sharpened considerably. I had
spent those last years studying certain trends in music and found that
this particular Sunday's musical news fit right in. The lead article, "Pop

in the 90's: Everything for Everyone," used record-company statistics to make what it claimed as a breakthrough argument: that in the age of the compact disc (which will soon yield to internet distribution, a battle already well under way), the idea that each historical moment has a single, trend-setting style was being challenged by a wave of across-the-board buying. In the preceding nine years, more than one thousand pop CDs, in a wide variety of styles, had sold a million copies or more. (The top-selling album reached 13.5 million!)

In another article, the band Dave's True Story (composed of a female singer and a male guitarist), with 35,000 CDs sold, was said to be "the weirdest and most wonderful lounge act in New York." (This "hard to pigeonhole" duo was described as a cross between Steely Dan and Stephen Sondheim.) Sondheim also showed up, on the theater page, where he and composer Ned Rorem debated the difference between operas and musicals. As Sondheim put it: "An opera is something done in an opera house in front of an opera audience. And a show . . . is something done in either a Broadway or an Off-Broadway theater, in front of that kind of audience." In other words, it's the audience's expectation that really matters.

The letters page carried replies to a recent article about serialism, a technique used by classical composers. And that discussion was continued on the music page in a piece by a *Times* critic, who complained: "The problem of American classical music isn't primarily opportunity, but the mediocrity of its composers. The good people have gone elsewhere"— that is, into pop, rock, and jazz.

The music page also carried an article calling soprano Dawn Upshaw "a shaman disguised as a chanteuse." After noting the variety of Upshaw's recent opera roles, the article announced three New York performances scheduled in the next few weeks: one of early-twentieth-century French art songs, another based on American popular songs, and a third with the Kronos Quartet, centered on "international traditional music." To prepare for the last of these concerts, the article explained,

> David Harrington, the quartet's first violinist had [Upshaw] listen to CD's of traditional music from places as far-flung as India, Egypt, Spain, Portugal, and Latin America. Some of the pieces were arranged for soprano and string quartet. A specially commissioned work by a Mexican composer, Gabriela Ortiz, based on ancient Mayan culture, and Kronos arrangements of songs by Patsy Cline and Stephen Foster round out the program.

On this and the American song evening, the writer commented: "You could call it crossover, but to term Ms. Upshaw a crossover artist is reductive. How can you cross over boundaries that you don't perceive or acknowledge?"

My first reaction to these articles was that I had, by luck, stumbled onto an issue of the *Times* that happened to connect with the main themes of my book. But now I see them as further proof that knowing what happened in the past enriches our understanding of the present. Are the sales of new popular numbers considered news, and does the afterlife of today's hit song make it a force to be reckoned with in tomorrow's marketplace? Does the story of musical life revolve more around performers than composers? Does the infrastructure of American music making support the idea of such categories as classical, popular, and folk music? When a musician stretches or crosses categorical boundaries, do listeners and writers notice and respond? In the current year, the answer to each of these questions is yes. Less obvious is that the same questions would have received the same answer in 1900, as would most of the questions in 1850.

By calling attention to such continuities, this book will help you develop your historical imagination. As you compare examples over time, you will find yourself imagining their impact on yesterday's listeners while retaining an awareness of how their musical world differed from yours.

Let's get back for a moment to the subject of popular music and look at it in historical perspective. The U.S. popular-music trade, which was created to sell sheet music to home customers, became a mass market during the 1840s. The first megahits appeared in the 1890s when publishers on Tin Pan Alley, the center of New York's song industry, discovered that one song could sell several million copies. By the 1920s, thanks to phonograph records, the radio, and the movies (which were always shown with musical accompaniment), music was being distributed both as sound and as notes printed on the page. And after World War II, as teenagers started buying records by the millions, new technologies and media appeared (television, car radios, personal playback equipment, the 45-rpm single, the LP, the cassette tape, the CD), extending the reach of popular music even more. Each of these developments brought new songs in new styles to the public. Yet rather than disappearing, the hits of one era—*Home Sweet Home* (1823), *Old Folks at Home* (1851), *Silver Threads Among the Gold* (1873), *After the Ball* (1892), *Alexander's Ragtime Band* (1911), *The Man I Love* (1924), *Heartbreak Hotel* (1956), *Can't Buy Me Love* (1964)—survived into the next and sometimes much longer, to be sung, played, recorded, remembered, reinterpreted, and sold as so-called standards. Long before the 2000s, yesterday's styles and favorites proved their staying power in the marketplace.

It may seem obvious that in music, performance is "the straw that stirs the drink." But over the past century, most music histories, inspired by classical music, have put composers in the spotlight, while telling us less than we might want to know about the people who have sung and played the music. Since the 1820s, the public has been infatuated by outstanding performers: opera stars such as Maria García Malibran, Jenny Lind, Enrico Caruso, and the Three Tenors; performers of popular music such as Ned Christy, Lillian Russell, Al Jolson, Louis Armstrong, Frank Sinatra, Elvis Presley, Aretha Franklin, and Madonna; conductors such as Theodore Thomas, Arturo Toscanini, and Leonard Bernstein; and also performers who wrote what they sang or played, such as Louis Moreau Gottschalk, John Philip Sousa, Duke Ellington, Woody Guthrie, Bob Dylan, The Beatles, Garth Brooks, and Alanis Morissette. A historical account that overlooked such performers would be missing a vital part of the whole. Yes, composing is what sets Western music making in motion, but the *Times* feature on Upshaw reminds us that a performer's talents and interests can be a historical force—a point that keeps reappearing in this book.

Musical categories are sometimes belittled as marketing tools or as figments of the scholarly mind. Yet no one trying to make sense of American music history can ignore the differences in the way music has been created, performed, and circulated—differences that explain why people often speak of "classical," "popular," and "folk" music. This book uses these labels, linked to something concrete and practical: the role of musical notation. The classical sphere is ruled by composers, who tell performers in a musical score precisely what was intended; the popular sphere is ruled by performers, who shape and alter scores to fit the occasion; and the folk (or traditional) sphere is also ruled by performers, who work from oral tradition and memory rather than notation. Music in the classical sphere strives for *transcendence*, aspiring to outlive the time and place of its creation. Music in the popular sphere pursues *accessibility*, acceptance by the target audience. And folk music seeks *continuity*, performances that respect the original spirit.

Although we take for granted today the existence of separate folk, popular, and classical spheres, classical music did not find a secure place in America until the later 1800s. (The hard, expensive struggle behind that victory is traced in Chapters 12 and 14–19). Once it was established, observers began to see America's musical life as a whole with distinct parts—a hierarchy with classical music at the top and popular music at the bottom. When the boundaries between the spheres were crossed—as in George Gershwin's borrowing of jazz for concert hall works, the Beatles' use of a string quartet in the recording studio, and Dawn Upshaw's exploration of "exotic" folk music—listeners received a jolt of surprise and excitement. As recordings turned performances into permanent works, the classical sphere lost its monopoly on transcendence, and folk music became commercially accessible. Categories are alive and well today, even as their boundaries are constantly being renegotiated. For more than a century, crossovers have been energizing many American works and performances.

So the stories I found that day in the *Times*, newsworthy because they concerned issues and events with a certain buzz, also belonged to history. Reading about these topics in a newspaper confirms that exciting things are taking place in American music. And when we examine our musical past with an eye on performance, musical categories, and economics (how are these musicians earning a living?), as well as composition, we see that a similar kind of excitement has long been percolating through it. We also discover that while the sounds are always changing, many of the patterns behind them are deeply inscribed into the conditions of our musical life.

We don't, of course, need to study music to experience and love it. As listeners and performers, we often hear music that moves us, and only sometimes do we ask why we are moved. Some students have argued that because such questions bring intellect to bear on an emotional experience, they have a distancing effect that dampens the pleasure of listening. To borrow a phrase from an eminent composer, I regret that I cannot give this claim the respect due its advanced age. In my own listening and teaching, I have found that the more fully heart and mind join forces, the deeper the engagement. By following that path, I firmly believe that your pleasure in listening to music will grow.

This book is accompanied by recordings that contain nearly six dozen examples. Chosen from throughout American's music history, each presents a slice of musical experience that is described in a Listening Guide. The guides point to things in the music worth listening for. But rather than complete maps or analyses, they are intended simply as starting points that listeners may use to find their way into the music's sound, structure, and meaning.

Because musical economics forms a major theme of this book, you will also learn something by thinking about the recordings from a financial perspective. Certain key artists, including some who are prominent in the text, are obviously missing from the recordings. Their absence reminds us that in our society, a musical composition is both a work of art and a piece of property. I regret that despite the best efforts of author and publisher, we have been denied permission to include some of the examples that would have told the story best. On the other hand, it is no small lesson to learn that when the desire to present a historical account of music comes into conflict with the desire to control the distribution of that music, the property owner holds the upper hand. In the words of Run-D.M.C. in Listening Guide 70: "It's like that, and that's the way it is."

The stories told on these pages point, however, to something more far-reaching than economics. As a student of American music, you are participating in a centuries-old tradition that is changing even as you study it. Filling in the missing links in our recorded examples will be simple enough, for they are readily available in record stores. More crucial to our goal is that the knowledge and skills you develop during your study will enrich all aspects of your listening life. Through experience and historical imagination, you will find yourself able, I believe, to engage with music that ranges far beyond the examples found here: from music omitted for reasons of space to music yet to be composed—or even imagined.

As for me, I wonder what I'll find in next Sunday's *Times*.

PART ONE

The
First
Three
Centuries

 1

"The First Song"

NATIVE AMERICAN MUSIC

Frank Mitchell, Navaho Singer, on the Blessingway

According to what I learned, a group came up from under the earth—they must have been some kind of supernatural beings. They were given this area of land within the four sacred mountains. It was in this area that the Navajos had their beginnings. . . . And from there the first songs and prayers of the Blessingway had their start. They were for the planting of crops. The first thing the Holy People did was to make a song and a prayer for the plants on the earth so the earth would be fruitful. That was the first song and the first prayer to be performed, and they were the first ones that I learned.

EUROPEAN AND NATIVE AMERICAN OUTLOOKS ON LIFE COULD hardly have been more different. From the time of their arrival in North America, Europeans tended to treat interaction between people as the chief drama of life, played out against the backdrop of nature. American Indians, on the other hand, have traditionally believed that human existence revolves around our place in the natural world. Animals, trees, weather, water, and topography, as well as supernatural beings, all play a role in human life too, because all are related parts of the same whole. Native Americans have tended to experience human life as one strand in a web of interconnectedness. And they judge the worth of their music making by its ability to serve specific functions, not by aesthetics, as Europeans tend to do.

EUROPEANS IN THE NEW WORLD

When individuals meet each other, they notice both differences and similarities. But when members of two completely separate cultures come into contact on a massive scale, with each culture pursuing a different goal, then how people see each other can carry tremendous historical consequences. That was certainly true of the contact between Native peoples and Europeans in North America. And because the history of Indian music making depends heavily on the way Europeans perceived the Natives, the musical information that survives can only be understood in light of those perceptions.

Europeans formed their ideas about Natives during a struggle for land in which they held all the cards. Early on, they reaped a biological advantage, having brought to the New World infectious diseases to which Native Americans had no resistance. In part because of disease, the size of the Indian population declined as the new settlers advanced.

Economics played another part. North America was colonized by imperial powers—Spain, France, and England—eager to tap into New World wealth, whether in gold, furs, farm products, or, eventually, markets for goods from their own countries in the Old World. Yet Natives and Europeans held very different positions in the economics of settlement. The Europeans' urge to expand their influence placed them in the role of aggressors, and those who resisted their invasion were considered enemies. Therefore, an imperial relationship was assumed from the start.

When Europeans encountered the people they hoped to displace, they were struck first by the ways in which the Indians differed from themselves in their manner of life, customs, dress, and behavior. But the settlers also saw similarities, especially in the Natives' capacity for virtue (as the settlers defined it). So the Europeans believed they could supply what Indians needed to reach a "fully human" state: education to civilize them and religious instruction to save their souls. In the Southwest (where the Spanish, moving north from Mexico, had formed settlements) and in the Northeast (where the French had set up trading posts in Canada), Roman Catholic missionaries traveled from the Old World to convert the Natives and to set up mission schools for their education.

The perception of difference, however, suggested that an unbridgeable gulf lay between Natives and settlers. Measured against European values, Indians were found wanting. This attitude fueled contempt, which in disputes gave the settlers an excuse to cheat, brutalize, or kill the Natives, or remove them from land the settlers wanted to occupy. Uninterested in the idea that there might be people truly different from themselves, European settlers tended to equate similarity with good qualities and difference with bad. The so-called good Indians were seen to be friendly, modest, dignified, and brave, and to lead simple lives devoted to their families and closely in tune with nature. It was this idealized perception that inspired European attempts to educate and Christianize Native peoples. Settlers who favored the "bad Indian" image tended, when they thought about the way Indians lived, to see nakedness and sexual

This French engraving of a native couple in Florida, appearing in Alain Manesson Mallet, *Description de l'Univers* (1683), reflects the "good Indian" image.

promiscuity, superstition, laziness, cannibalism and human sacrifice, constant warfare, desire for revenge, and cruelty to captives. And Europeans' observations of Indian cooking and personal hygiene did nothing to raise their opinion of Indian life.

History records the destructiveness that followed when good Indian/bad Indian images took hold. Settlers arrived at these labels without actually trying to understand Native American culture, dress, religion, music, or anything else. These images soon hardened into beliefs that brought about actions, which failed to take either the diversity or the uniqueness of Native cultures into account.

 MUSIC

Our knowledge of the early history of Native American music depends on reports by non-Natives. The character and usefulness of those reports varies, not only with the observers' own musical knowledge but with how they felt about the Indians. One of the earliest observations was made in the 1530s by a Spaniard who, along with three countrymen, had landed years earlier in Florida and undertaken a long journey west, providing medical treatment to several Natives along the way. On reaching an Indian settlement in what is now western Texas near Big Spring, they were greeted by "all the people . . . with such yells as were terrific, striking the palms of their hands violently against their thighs." The Natives' enthusiasm had been inspired by their guests' reputation as healers. They presented the visitors with musical instruments such as "gourds bored with holes and having pebbles in them, an instrument for the most important occasions produced only at the dance or to effect cures, and which none dare touch but those who own them. They say there is virtue in them, and because they do not grow in that country, they come from heaven."

Continuing west, the Spaniards found that their fame as medicine men had preceded them. Natives in the Sacramento Mountains of New Mexico gave them a "jingle bell of copper" and two medicine rattles. Another account from New Mexico in 1540 reaffirms the Indians' use of musical sound for specific functions, this time reporting scenes from near where Albuquerque stands today. When a party headed by Captain Hernando de Alvarado approached a Zuñi pueblo in Pecos, they were welcomed "with drums and flageolets, similar to fifes, of which they had many." One Spaniard also described how music served in the Zuñis' ceremonial grinding of corn. "Three women come in, each going to her stone. One crushes the maize, the next grinds it, and the third grinds it finer.

Before they come inside the door they remove their shoes, tie up their hair and cover it, and shake their clothes. While they are grinding, a man sits at the door playing a flageolet, and the women move their stones, keeping time with the music, and all three sing together."

These reports from the Southwest, written less than half a century after Columbus reached the Western Hemisphere, supply some of the first evidence of Native instruments and uses of music. But they say nothing about its sound. On the other hand, when early observers did mention how Indian music sounded, they were more likely to dwell on their own response—often negative—than on the sound itself. A case in point is the experience of the Jesuit father Paul Le Jeune with a medicine man in the winter of 1634, as told by nineteenth-century American historian Francis Parkman. Parkman's account makes no attempt to treat the music making on its own terms. Nor is it specific enough to show, as we might gather, that the performance's great length came about because the music was repeated many times. But it does testify to the Huron Indians' faith that the physical work of vocalizing and time beating as part of a healing ritual could help cure a lingering illness.

Francis Parkman on Huron Medicine Man Treating Father Paul La Jeune in 1634

The sorcerer believed in the efficacy of his own magic, and was continually singing and beating his drum to cure the disease from which he was suffering. Toward the close of the winter, Le Jeune fell sick, and, in his pain and weakness, nearly succumbed under the nocturnal uproar of the sorcerer, who, hour after hour, sang and drummed without mercy—sometimes yelling at the top of his throat, then hissing like a serpent, then striking his drum on the ground as if in a frenzy, then leaping up, raving about the wigwam, and calling on the women and children to join him in singing. Now ensued a hideous din; for every throat was strained to the utmost, and all were beating with sticks or fists on the bark of the hut to increase the noise, with the charitable object of aiding the sorcerer to conjure down his malady, or drive away the evil spirit that caused it.

Le Jeune later wrote of the Hurons: "All their religion consists mainly in singing."

An Indian Dance of 1670

Admitting that his transcription failed to do justice to the way the music actually sounded, Claude Dablon wrote: "They give their songs a certain turn which cannot be sufficiently expressed by Note, but which nevertheless endows them with all their grace." Dablon did not explain the double bars at the ends of lines 2, 4, and 6 that divide the melody into three sections, but the sections were surely repeated many times in performance.

As transcribed by Dablon, this melody shows a clarity and regularity that can be seen in the notation. The three sections are parallel in certain ways. All begin high and move downward; all seem to take aim on one pitch, which then, through repetition, becomes a resting place for that section; and all, by mixing groupings of three beats with an occasional two-beat pair, achieve a gentle, prose-like rhythm.

Not until later in the 1600s did a musically knowledgeable Westerner write down a Native melody heard within the borders of the present United States and describe the circumstances in which he heard it—and these circumstances were very different from those surrounding the Hurons' efforts to cure Father Le Jeune's ailment. The transcriber was another Jesuit priest, Father Claude Dablon, who was born in France and was said to play several musical instruments well. Dablon and fellow Jesuit Father Claude Allouz had established a mission at Green Bay on Lake Michigan in 1669. In the following year, the two priests visited the present Winnebago County, Wisconsin, where friendly Mascouten, Miami, and Illinois tribes had gathered. Dablon found the Illinois polite and their chief especially kind. Sometimes, he reported, "some of the oldest men would appear, dressed as if for playing a comedy, and would dance to the music of some very tuneful airs, which they sang in excellent accord."

Dablon transcribed music that accompanied a dance honoring the peace pipe, or "calumet." Among the Illinois, men and women with the best voices were chosen to sing for the occasion; berdaches (men who assumed the dress, social status, and role of women), "who are summoned to the Councils and without whose advice nothing can be decided," sang too. According to Dablon, the dancers moved in strict time to the singing, and a mock combat was fought to the slow beat of a drum: "This is done so well—with slow and measured steps, and to the rhythmic sound of the voices and drums—that it might pass for a very fine Entry of a Ballet in France."

During the 1700s, Native music and musical activity were noticed more and more by people who were neither government nor church officials but were fascinated by Indian ways. In 1775, a Euroamerican trader who lived in Indian country for forty years recalled a visit paid him by "an old physician, or prophet," from the Chicasaw nation who entered his house and treated him to a remarkable performance.

A Trader Describes a Chicasaw Medicine-Man Ceremony

When he came to the door he bowed himself half bent, with his arms extended north and south, continuing so perhaps for the space of a minute. Then raising himself erect, with his arms in the same position, he looked in a wild frightful manner, from the south-west toward the north, and sung on a low bass key *Yo Yo Yo Yo*, almost a minute, then *He He He He*, for perhaps the same space of time, and *Wa Wa Wa Wa*, in like manner; and then transposed, and accented those sacred notes several different ways, in a most rapid guttural manner. Now and then he looked upwards, with his head considerably bent backward;—his song continued about a quarter of an hour.

Knowing from experience that the Indians always wanted to keep their religious mysteries secret, the trader was delighted when he learned the purpose of the song: to protect his house "from the power of the evil spirits of the north, south, and west,—and, from witches, and wizards, who go about in dark nights, in the shape of bears, hogs, and wolves, to spoil people."

From the 1700s too come tales of Indian bravery, registered in "death songs" or "war songs." The situation pictured in such songs is grim: after a warrior is captured by members of another tribe, he is tortured and eventually killed. The tormenters seem totally lacking in human sympathy. First, they do all they can to prolong their victim's pain: they tie him to a stake, poke and beat him with torches, and then cool him off with water, allowing "a proper time of respite," the Euroamerican trader writes, "till his spirits recover, and he is capable of suffering new tortures." Second, the tormenting of the prisoner is staged as community entertainment, with women and children participating. "Not a soul, of whatever age or sex, manifests the least pity," according to this account. "The women sing with religious joy . . . and peals of laughter resound through the crowded theater—especially if he fears to die." This last comment suggests the custom's only redeeming feature: the spectacle gives the prisoner a chance to show courage. "The suffering warrior," the trader writes, "is not dismayed; with an insulting manly voice he sings the war-song . . . puts on a bold austere countenance, and carries it through all his pains."

The notion of a dying warrior who sings in the face of torture and imminent death struck a responsive chord with some European Americans in the years following the War of Independence. In fact, a song about such a victim, *The Death Song of the Cherokee Indians*, appeared in Royall Tyler's *The Contrast* (1787), the first play by an American-born writer known to have been produced onstage.

After long contact with Europeans, much of it violently destructive of Native custom, is it still possible at the turn of the twenty-first century to find Indian music that sounds as it did two or three centuries ago? Historians may disagree on the answer, but for many Indians, the question is unimportant. As they see it, they are still making the music that was passed on to them by parents and elders, who in turn learned it from generations before them—and they sing, play, and dance for the same reasons. Their interest lies not in preserving old songs but in maintaining a legacy that connects them to the past and to nature, from which they gain physical and spiritual refreshment.

The Death Song of the Cherokee Indians

First published in England around 1780, the song—with words by Anne Hunter and a melody said to be of Cherokee origin—circulated in this country during the 1780s and 90s. Its strophic form is typical of many songs: several stanzas of text sung to the same music. The version published here is written for a singer supported by an instrumental bass line.

As parlor songs are inclined to do, *The Death Song of the Cherokee Indians* idealizes a real-life event. We are not told why the warrior is bound to the stake in the first place. His tormentors are shadowy figures who cannot provoke a response. The hero, a symbol of superhuman courage, transports himself to a world of memory and devotion to duty. Even as the flames rise around his body, the son of Alknomook "will never complain," as the music maintains a flow of regular two-bar phrases through all four stanzas.

The *Death Song*, however, comes neither from the Cherokees nor any other Indian tribe. It is a product of European culture, inspired by Native imagery of the "good Indian" kind. Its appearance in a stage play of 1787, a collection of published songs in 1789, and sheet music from around 1799 reminds us that by 1800 the new nation called the United States of America had its own means to make and sell cultural products. The Native, or rather the image of the Native, provided material for that industry.

2

European Inroads

EARLY CHRISTIAN MUSIC MAKING

COMMERCIAL AND RELIGIOUS OUTREACH SPURRED EUROPE'S SET-
tlement of North America. The southern arm of the process was controlled
by Spain, whose king and queen, hoping to extract riches from far-off
lands, sponsored the voyage that sent Christopher Columbus to the
Caribbean in 1492. The northern arm of settlement, beginning in the 1530s,
took two different forms. Canada was colonized chiefly as a fur-trading
venture under the direction of the French crown. Working with the Roman Catholic Church, which sent Jesuit priests to make Christians of
American Indians and to minister to white settlers, the French turned the
St. Lawrence River and its waterways into a delivery system for a business profitable in Old World markets. In the meantime, the English, who
soon dominated the continent south of Canada, were far less systematic
in their approach.

North American settlement began an unruly process of give-and-take
among three continents that brought the peoples native to each into
contact—and conflict. We should not think of American history as something that all happened west of the Atlantic Ocean; the territory that is
now the United States was in reality an extension of European empires.
Entrepreneurs in these nations, needing a labor force to extract the "new"
continent's riches, encouraged their own people to settle there. They also
brought slaves from Africa to enhance production and promote the increase in farming. Though geographically separated from Europe, America has for more than four centuries been tied economically, politically,
and culturally to the Old World, forming a vast transatlantic arena in
which the drama of Western expansion has been played out. That fact
looms large in the history of this country's musical life.

For all the violence of the Spanish conquest in 1519 of the Aztecs in
Mexico, the invaders did their work with the blessing of the Roman

Catholic Church, which was vitally interested in converting the Natives to Christianity. Thus, the first Christian sacred music to take root in North America was that of the Roman Catholic liturgy, brought by priests attached to Spanish missions in the New World. Having established their capital in Mexico City, the Spanish created New Spain as a network of settlements ruled from the capital, with each town formed around a central plaza on which stood a church or cathedral. In these churches the people, who gradually came to include more and more *mestizos* (people of mixed blood) as well as Spanish and Indians, came to know the Roman rites of worship.

To make worship services as impressive as possible, the Roman Catholic Church encouraged public display. Monumental church buildings, bright images and flashing color, priestly garments, incense, large spaces within which speech and music could reverberate—all were welcomed into the Catholic tradition. As a part of that heritage, the church also favored musical elaboration, especially vocal polyphony (singing in two or more independent voice parts) and the use of an organ or other musical instruments. Moreover, until the Vatican Council of 1962–65, the Roman Catholic liturgy was carried on throughout the world in Latin, helping to give it an aura of timeless dignity, not to mention the practical advantages of having one liturgy and language for one international church.

By the early 1500s, the Spanish had installed the Roman rite in Mexico and were working to Christianize the Native population. As early as 1528, the Spanish-born Franciscan priest Juan de Padilla was teaching Natives near Mexico City to sing plainsong (Gregorian chant) and to participate in sacred choral part-singing. In 1540, Padilla crossed the Rio Grande into New Mexico and began a similar project among the Moquir Pueblo and Zuñi Indians. Nineteen years later, the Spanish launched a parallel effort in Florida, where the musician and missionary Pedro Martín de Feria taught Natives near the present city of Pensacola how to sing parts of the liturgy in plainsong.

Altogether, it is clear that the Roman Catholic Church used sacred music not only to maintain and bolster the faith of the European settlers but to familiarize the Natives with white settlers' ways. In Texas and especially the territory that is now New Mexico, where the Spanish installed their system of conquest, missions were founded and Natives educated in them to participate in the missions' musical life. Alonso de Benavides noted in 1630 the presence of "schools for reading and writing, singing and playing all instruments," and by 1680 some twenty-five missions existed across the Southwest.

In the latter 1700s, the missionary effort spread farther west. In 1769, the Franciscan Junipero Serra, himself a trained musician, began the colonization of southern California as a part of New Spain. By the 1820s, a network of twenty-one missions existed in California. The Roman Catholic liturgy, with appropriate music, was carried on in these settlements until 1833, when the government in Mexico City secularized the missions, sold their lands, and sent the priests back to Spain. By 1846, musical activity in the settlements had ceased. While it lasted, however, music making in the California missions, rooted in plainsong but with plenty of polyphonic singing as well, displayed the variety of a flourishing colonial practice.

CD 1

LISTENING GUIDE 1

Mass in D Major: Kyrie (Jerúsalem)

The Mass in D major for two choirs and orchestra, discovered recently in a California archive, shows the variety of colonial practice in full bloom. The score, probably composed by Ignacio de Jerúsalem (Italian-born but serving as chapel master of the Mexico City Cathedral from 1749 until his death in 1769), seems to have been carried from Mexico to a mission near present-day Los Angeles by the priest who led the music there. The first movement is in three sections, divided by the words "Kyrie eleison" (Lord, have mercy on us), "Christe eleison" (Christ, have mercy on us), and "Kyrie eleison." Listeners should keep in mind that most of the orchestra and choral parts in this elaborate, festive-sounding sacred work would have been performed by members of the Native American population.

In a parallel development, French Jesuit priests brought Roman Catholic worship to Canada. But the French never tried to install anything like the network of towns that the Spanish introduced to the South. With its long, harsh winters and rough terrain, the northern land proved much harder to settle. So the French in Canada concentrated on setting up commercial outposts. In that arrangement, a trading center in Quebec City served as the chief link to the European market. Agents in France received fox, beaver, and mink furs as products of overseas investment, while in Quebec supervising agents monitored the white and Native trappers who fanned out through the Canadian wilderness to do their work. Jesuits followed the trappers' routes, helping to carry the flag of the French king into the heart of North America. And the sacred music they brought added to the Roman Catholic Church's authority, a trait that proved useful in the settlement of New France.

If the American Southwest and California reflect the northern reach of New Spain, other places—Detroit, St. Louis, and New Orleans are names bearing a French imprint—serve as a reminder of New France's reach southward from Canada. But as important as both of these Roman Catholic realms were to the history of American development, the first Old World settlers to populate what is now the eastern United States were Protestants.

The Protestant Reformation changed the religious, political, and economic face of Europe, leading to conflicts in which all sides remained convinced of their moral superiority. Sacred music seldom plays more than a small role in any such conflict, but as a part of public worship it does reflect fundamental ideas of the religious outlook it represents. In breaking with the Roman Catholic Church, Protestants took issue with some of the main premises of Roman worship.

Protestant reformers challenged two key Catholic beliefs: (1) prescribed rituals fostered true piety, and (2) God was best praised through sacred expression that pleased the senses. Reformers actually split on the role of ritual. German-speaking Protestants, under Martin Luther's leadership, and many in England who joined the state church (Anglican, or Church of England) after King Henry VIII broke with Rome, maintained parts of the Catholic liturgy in translated form. Elsewhere in Europe, however, especially under the leadership of John Calvin, reform went further. Fired by the idea of "the priesthood of all believers," Protestant groups in Switzerland, France, and the Netherlands wanted individuals and congregations to decide on liturgy for themselves. In the same spirit, Reformed Protestants pledged their churchly allegiance to the Holy Bible, not to church tradition. Protestants may have helped advance the cause of literacy by shifting the right to read and interpret Scripture from the church to its members. According to the Reformed vision, no human power should stand between God and the individual believer.

Reformed Protestants scorned the notion that charming the senses in the name of religion could please God. Rejecting the idea that musical skill was worth cultivating in God's service, Calvin and his followers assigned music making to the congregation itself. And they found a style of singing suited to the abilities of most members. In view of the Catholic practice that it countered, it is hard to avoid describing Calvinist sacred music in negative terms: no part singing, no instrumental accompaniment, and no singing of texts outside the psalms, a book in the Hebrew Scriptures (Old Testament). The Calvinist ideal opposed musical professionalism—a stance that Catholics and "liturgical" Protestants, with their priests, choirs, organs, and fondness for elaboration, never took. Many of the English Protestants who settled in North America were driven to immigrate, at least in part, by a desire to worship in an environment where no state church existed. And that helps explain why their favored music was so plain.

PSALMBOOKS IN ENGLISH

Anglicans were enthusiastic congregational singers, using *The Whole Booke of Psalmes, Collected into Englishe Meter* (London, 1562), versified by Thomas Sternhold and John Hopkins. Adopted by the Church of England, that book remained its congregational psalter (book of metrical psalms) until Nicholas Brady and Nahum Tate produced their *New Version of the Psalms of David* in 1696. (The earlier work was then dubbed the *Old Version*.) The *Old Version* turned the psalms into popular poetry, using some of the same simple verse structures as the secular ballads that circulated in oral tradition. These metrical psalms—the texts in the Old Testament Book of Psalms, versified in English and published together in psalters such as the *Old Version*—were to play a key role in American sacred music making through the seventeenth and eighteenth centuries.

The Pilgrims who arrived in 1620 at Plymouth, Massachusetts, sang from a psalter translated by the Reverend Henry Ainsworth, a clergyman who had brought out *The Book of Psalmes: Englished Both in Prose and Metre* in Amsterdam in 1612. Although its verses and tunes differed considerably from those of the *Old Version*, the so-called *Ainsworth Psalter* shared several traits with the earlier book: its pocket size made it easily portable; it printed a tune with each psalm text so that those who read music could sing the tunes directly from the psalter; and it included far fewer tunes (39) than psalms (150). The first and last of these traits are true of all psalters that circulated in New England from then on. Ainsworth didn't need as many tunes as psalms because the psalms were cast in standard verse forms, or meters, so worshipers could sing many different texts to the same tune. *As an art*, then, music played only a secondary role in early New England psalm singing.

The bone-simple OLD HUNDRED is one of the tunes in Ainsworth's psalter. Also found in the Church of England's *Old Version* and many English and American sacred tunebooks since, OLD HUNDRED traces its origin back to the 1550s and early French Calvinist psalm singing. The tune is brief and straightforward enough to be perfect congregational fare, as proved by its continued use in Protestant worship today as the Doxology.

LISTENING GUIDE 2

Old Hundred (Ainsworth Psalter)

No element is more basic to Western music than melody, and centuries of continuous use mark OLD HUNDRED as a good one. The music consists of four phrases of equal length. The shapes of the phrases differ, but their rhythm is almost identical. Melodic movement is neatly balanced between conjunct (stepwise) and disjunct (skipping to a note other than adjacent ones) motion, and between melodic rise and fall. Most of the note-to-note connections are stepwise. But in each phrase, at least one skip occurs: a rising fourth in the first two phrases and a falling third in the next. In the last phrase, three skips of a third take place, two falling and one rising. That phrase, which also begins with an upward leap of a fifth to the melody's highest note, is by far the most active and serves as the melody's climax.

Ainsworth versified Psalm 100 in several stanzas, all sung to the same tune. The excerpt presents only the first stanza.

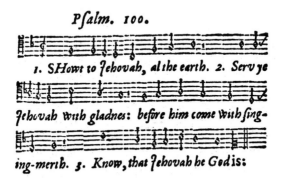

The psalm tune OLD HUNDRED, first published in Geneva in 1561, supplied the music for Henry Ainsworth's version of Psalm 100 in 1612.

The simplicity of OLD HUNDRED is not typical of the tunes in Ainsworth's psalter. Indeed, the difficulty of the book's melodies suggests that the original Pilgrims were accomplished singers. In fact, when the congregation in Salem, Massachusetts, voted in 1667 to give up *Ainsworth*, they cited the difficulty of the tunes, as did the Plymouth congregation itself in 1685.

Early New Englanders were even more troubled, however, by the psalters' faulty translations of the texts. Intent on following God's word faithfully, a group of clergymen from the Massachusetts Bay Colony collaborated on a new psalter that would more closely mirror the scriptural originals. The resulting collection, usually referred to as the *Bay Psalm Book*, was published in Cambridge, Massachusetts in 1640. It was the first full-length book printed in the English-speaking colonies, and in its many revisions and reprints it supplied New England's congregations with texts for psalm singing well into the next century.

If we compare the prose beginning of Psalm 23 in the King James Bible with the versified form in the *Bay Psalm Book*, we can see how metrical psalmody works in practice.

King James Version	*Bay Psalm Book (1651)*
The Lord is my shepherd;	The Lord to me a sheperd is
I shall not want.	Want therefore shall not I.
He maketh me to lie down in	He in the folds of tender grass
green pastures;	Doth make me down to lie.
He leadeth me beside the still waters;	He leads me to the waters still
He restoreth my soul.	Restore my soul doth He;
He leadeth me in the paths of	In paths of righteousness, He will
righteousness for His name's sake.	For His name's sake lead me.

The *Bay Psalm Book*'s translators, following the example of Sternhold and Hopkins, Ainsworth, and others, set the psalm in four-line stanzas so that it could be sung strophically, that is, with all stanzas of text sung to the same music. (Psalm 23 fills five stanzas in the *Bay Psalm Book* version.)

The *Bay Psalm Book*'s translators did all they could to simplify psalmody for congregations. In that spirit, they set 125 of the 150 psalms in common meter, adding 14 in long meter and another 8 in short meter. A congregation singing from the *Bay Psalm Book*, then, needed to know only a handful of tunes. These numbers indicate that tunes in seventeenth-century New England were chosen not to underline the meaning of the words but merely to provide a musical vehicle for their delivery.

Metrical psalmbooks were published to serve worshipers who could
read. But by the 1640s, psalm singing
in some New England congregations
required only one singer to have a
book. That leading singer (sometimes
called the deacon or precentor) would
read the psalm, line by line, to the congregation, who would then sing each
line back in alternation with the leader.
Whether congregations began lining-
out, as this practice came to be called,
because too few worshipers could read
the psalms, buy the books, or sing the
tunes as they were written, the custom
won acceptance as the clergy realized
that without it there would be no con-
gregational singing at all. In 1647, the Reverend John Cotton noted:
"Where all have books and can reade, or else can say the Psalm by heart,
it were needlesse there to reade each line of the Psalm before hand in order to [sing]." But, he continued, the Scriptures made congregational
psalm singing a duty for Christians, not an option, which brought about
the custom of lining-out in places where people lacked "either books or
skill to reade."

Lining-out began, then, as a way of cueing congregation members on
the texts they were to sing. Its impact on psalmody was enormous: first,
it greatly slowed the pace of singing; second, it meant that the repertory
was kept small because tunes had to be chosen from those that the worshipers already knew; finally, the music was entrusted to the leading
singers, who did not necessarily read music themselves. As one observer
of the time wrote, a tune might vary so much from one congregation to
the next that "'tis hard to find Two that Sing [it] exactly alike." Lining-
out gave birth to a singing style in which the tunes were freely elabo-
rated. This style, eventually labeled "the Old Way" of singing, won favor
with many New England worshipers.

But by 1720, some New Englanders were complaining that the Old
Way had departed from the Puritan fathers' psalmody, which had been
governed by the "rule" of musical notation. The Reverend Thomas
Symmes described the process as a movement toward an oral tradition,
and he recommended that "Regular Singing," which carried the authority of notated music, replace the mode of singing called the Old Way. Yet

Symmes understood why people enjoyed singing as they did. In the Old Way, rather than joining others in vocal lockstep, all parishioners were empowered with the freedom—within limits, of course—to decorate their praise of God as the spirit moved them.

Thomas Symmes on Oral Hymn-Singing, 1720

Singing-Books being laid aside, there was no Way to learn; but only by hearing of Tunes Sung, or by taking the Run of the Tune (as it is phrased). The Rules of Singing not being taught or learnt, every one sang as best pleased himself, and every Lead-ing-Singer would take the Liberty of raising any Note of the Tune, or lowering of it, as best pleas'd his Ear, and add such Turns and Flourishes as were grateful to him; and this was done so gradually, as that but few if any took Notice of it. One Clerk or Chorister would alter the Tunes a little in his Day, the next, a little in his and so one after another, till in Fifty or Sixty Years it caus'd a Considerable Alteration.

The clergy's objection to the Old Way of singing inspired a burst of rhetoric on the subject: sermons, pamphlets, newspaper accounts, and Regular Singing meetings. But unlike most theological battles of the time, the published words came from one side only: that of Regular Singing advocates, chiefly ministers condemning a custom of worship that had slipped out of their control. Singers committed to the Old Way made no attempt to justify themselves in writing; they simply continued singing as they liked. In the meantime, the champions of Regular Singing argued that its order and solemnity would help to make public worship more pleasing in the sight of God. And they supported their opinions with references to the Bible.

When seen as a conflict pitting the clergy against the people, rules against customs, and control against freedom, the Regular Singing controversy stands as a colorful episode in New England's cultural history. But in the history of American music, the outcome reached further, touching off a process of singing reform that reshaped New England psalmody. The movement toward Regular Singing brought about the formation of singing schools: instructional sessions devoted to teaching the rudiments of singing and note reading, and focused on sacred music. Organized to improve congregational singing, such schools brought with them the need for books, and in the 1720s publishers in New England began to bring out tunebooks for singing-school use. And as Americans with some musical skill started setting up singing schools of their own, an institution was founded to support musical professionalism—the first chance for native-born American musicians to earn a living through music. Along with the spread of musical learning came a growing taste for music that was more elaborate than unharmonized psalm tunes. By the 1750s, choirs were forming to sing such music in public worship, and by the 1770s, Americans were composing some of the music sung by American choirs.

From Ritual to Art

THE FLOWERING OF SACRED MUSIC

THE REGULAR SINGING CONTROVERSY WAS ONE OF MANY RELI-gious debates that marked early New England life. Cotton Mather, a leading American intellectual of his time, wrote in 1721 on the values of Puritan sacred music making. His eloquent endorsement of biblical texts stresses the importance of words over music. New sacred verses, he believed, should not replace divinely inspired ones merely because they were more up-to-date. While he granted the possible merits of "devout hymns composed by the good men of our own time," they could not match the songs "prepared for us by the Holy Spirit of God."

For Mather and his allies, Regular Singing was a form of prayer. The orderly singing of a sacred text by a whole congregation, they believed, would be pleasing in God's sight. But only a reform of congregational psalmody could lead to that result, because the Old Way lacked such discipline. And indeed, reform began in earnest around 1720, with two developments particularly helpful to the cause: psalm tunes were published to protect them from the whim of oral transmission, and singing instruction became available to congregation members.

In 1721, two books were published in Boston that emphasized sacred *music* over sacred verses and included not only the tunes but instructions on how to sing them. The titles reveal their purpose: John Tufts's *An Introduction to the Singing of Psalm Tunes* and Thomas Walter's *The Grounds and Rules of Musick, Explained.* Both volumes began with an introduction explaining the rudiments of singing: how to use one's voice as part of a congregation, including an explanation of the symbols in which the psalm tunes were written.

The appearance of these two books began a new era in the history of Calvinist psalmody in the New World. Between them they bridged the gap between music as an art with a technical basis and a public ready to

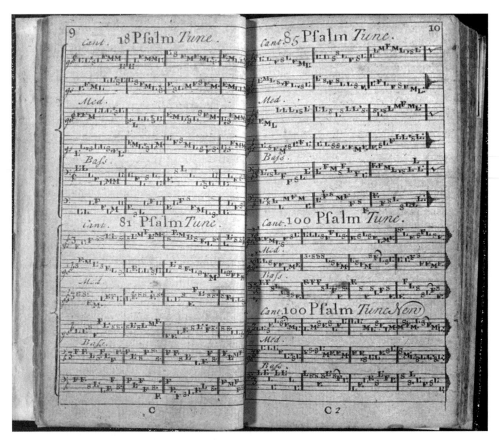

John Tufts's *Introduction*, here in its fifth edition (1726), was an instructional manual with psalm tunes harmonized for three voices. Note that the fourth of the five tunes shown here is OLD HUNDRED.

learn that technique. Those who wished to learn could now attend singing schools, which were aimed at beginners, were taught in the evenings in any available space, and typically lasted three months (a "quarter"). A singing master was not a clergyman but simply a musical individual (always male), perhaps recruited by aspiring singers or perhaps deciding on his own to organize a school and advertise for scholars, who paid a fee. Moreover, though it grew out of the church's needs, the singing school was from the start a social institution distinct from the church.

By the early 1720s, then, the elements of a more disciplined psalmody had been introduced in and around Boston. In some congregations, reform went smoothly. Once a school was formed, the "scholars" persuaded other church members to follow their lead, and Regular Singing replaced the Old Way. But in others, the process could take years, even decades.

With no popes or bishops to hand down decrees, questions about congregational singing and other matters of worship were put to a vote of church members, and the majority ruled. In Farmington, Connecticut, the congregation in 1727 upheld local independence by voting down Regular Singing as a practice "recommended by the Reverend Ministers of Boston."

As it happened, singing schools soon became more than instructional gatherings; they were also social occasions, providing a rare chance for boys and girls to mingle. Supporters praised schools for offering "innocent and profitable recreation" that would help young people do something useful during the long winter evenings, and wean them away from "idle, foolish, yea, pernicious songs and ballads." In the view of others, however, schools encouraged youngsters to be "too light, profane and airy," and to stay out late. Indeed, many who opposed Regular Singing saw it as a secular intrusion into a sacred realm.

Through the agency of singing schools, Regular Singing helped foster musical literacy and independent taste. By the 1760s, these schools had spread widely in the colonies. And by then, too, another organization was taking root: the meeting-house choir, formed not at the prompting of clergy or congregation but by the singers themselves. Choirs brought new energy and musical diversity to the meeting house, but almost from the moment of their appearance they also became targets of complaint—some parishioners found choir members' behavior secular and obnoxious.

The title page of Oliver Brownson's *Select Harmony* (Hartford, 1783) shows choir members in a church gallery.

As early as 1764, an observer described one Boston church choir as "a set of geniuses who stick themselves up in a gallery" and think that they have a right to do all the singing themselves, excluding the congregation. Eager to show off their skill as musicians, they considered the hymns sung by the congregation far too simple, favoring tunes that were more modern, elaborate, and worldly. They would, complained the writer, often perform "a light, airy, jiggish tune better adapted to a country dance" than to "chanting forth the praises of the King of Kings." Here, then, choir and congregation competed rather than complemented each other. The Boston choir confirmed the fear that once musical display won a toehold in the worship service, it would take its own course with little regard for the religious framework in which it had flowered in the first place. *snooty - snobby*

A PHILADELPHIA TUNEBOOK

Given the long history of singing in New England meeting houses, it may seem strange that the first tunebook to address the needs of both congregation and choir was published in Philadelphia. That collection, titled *Urania, or A Choice Collection of Psalm-Tunes, Anthems, and Hymns*, was compiled in 1761 by James Lyon, a Presbyterian born in Newark, New Jersey, and a recent graduate of the College of New Jersey (Princeton). Here one resourceful Philadelphia Presbyterian, apparently working on his own, brought out a sacred tunebook far more ambitious than any that forty years of Regular Singing in Boston had inspired.

Philadelphia was the largest city in the English-speaking colonies, a dynamic settlement that grew steadily larger, unlike Boston, whose population remained the same from the 1740s to 1775. The religious culture of Philadelphia was also more tolerant and more diverse than Boston's, with substantial numbers of Anglicans, Lutherans, Methodists, Baptists, Roman Catholics, and Quakers, as well as Reformed Calvinist "dissenters," including Lyon himself.

Urania was published by subscription, a commercial practice designed to scout the public for customers. Subscription allowed a work to be proposed for publication with a minimum of investment. To enroll subscribers, a publisher would offer copies of the book at a pre-publication discount. Only if enough subscribers were found would the work then be printed, as was Lyon's 198-page volume in June 1762, with a list of subscribers in the front.

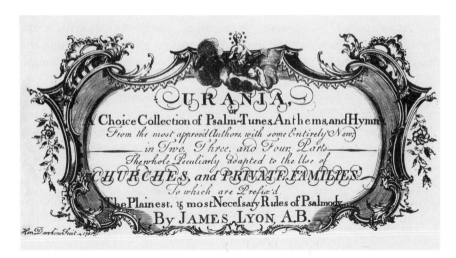

Henry Dawkins engraved this elaborate title page for James Lyon's
Urania (Philadelphia, 1761).

James Lyon's bold act of entrepreneurship lies behind this landmark
of American music history. Not only did Lyon use commercial means to
sell his book, but he compiled a collection designed for broad appeal. For
Urania's musical contents offered something for every sacred singer: standard psalm tunes, left textless so that worshipers could sing them to their
preferred psalter; plenty of choir music (including elaborate psalm tunes
and anthems); and hymn tunes apparently geared to home performance,
as suggested on the title page: "adapted to the use of churches and private families." *Urania* was the first American tunebook to bring psalmody
into the commercial arena, relying on subscription and advertising and
tailoring its contents to attract customers. From a Puritan perspective, the
process bears a distinctly secular flavor, but then, in 1760s Philadelphia
the Puritan perspective carried little weight. *Urania* showed how
psalmody, a mode of sacred expression, could find a niche in a public
marketplace.

The absence in New England of any effort similar to Lyon's suggests
how small a role musical learning had so far played in the tradition of
psalmody. But that would soon change. By the 1760s, singing schools and
Regular Singing were spreading musical literacy and feeding interest in
more elaborate sacred music throughout the region, as suggested by the
roster of church choirs formed in New England after mid-century, especially in Massachusetts. Boston's First Church had a choir by 1758, followed by many others through the next dozen years.

WILLIAM BILLINGS, AMERICAN COMPOSER

america's First composer

In 1770, a young Boston tanner and singing master produced a tunebook reflecting the vitality that had begun to flow into New England sacred music as Puritan restrictions fell away, music literacy spread, and secular attitudes grew more acceptable. *The New-England Psalm-Singer: or, American Chorister*, by William Billings, is a true landmark. Though shorter than *Urania*, it came close to matching that book's variety, with everything from plain congregational tunes to long anthems that would tax the skill of any American choir. In musical content, however, the originality of Billings's book far outstripped Lyon's. Containing 127 compositions, all by Billings himself, *The New-England Psalm-Singer* was the first published collection of entirely American music and the first American tunebook devoted wholly to works by one composer. With its appearance, the number of American sacred compositions in print increased tenfold, and a region that had long fostered psalmody reclaimed leadership in sacred music.

Paul Revere's frontispiece for William Billings's *The New-England Psalm-Singer* (Boston, 1770) encircles a picture of seven singers with a canonic composition: a sacred text apparently performed on a social occasion.

Billings's tunebook reflects changes in New England culture that reached beyond music. By 1770, although some Puritan influence persisted, the region's moral purpose had found a new focus: resistance to Britain's rule of her American colonies.

The state of mind that led in 1775 to war with England could not have been predicted a dozen years earlier. For in 1763, when the Treaty of Paris ended the French and Indian War, many colonists shared a feeling of pride in a hard-won Anglo-American victory. The British, too, looked for a new relationship with this fast-growing part of their empire. But while the Americans saw the departure of the French and Spanish as an opening of fresh opportunities, British officials believed that the time had come for England to receive a higher yield on overseas investments. The first of Parliament's money-raising measures—the Stamp Act of 1764, which increased taxes and duties on imports and exports—began a cycle of escalating grievances. Misunderstandings multiplied. What seemed to the British reasonable steps to govern their colonies were received by some Americans as impositions of external authority. Such responses in turn brought stronger displays of power from the British. Positions gradually hardened, and extremists took over leadership on both sides.

Boston experienced new unrest in 1768, when customs commissioners asked for an armed guard to protect them as they performed their duties. British troops arrived in April. Although an uneasy peace was maintained, some Bostonians viewed the soldiers as an army of occupation. The Boston Massacre of 1770, where British soldiers fired into an unruly mob and killed five colonists, was one of several incidents that inflamed public opinion. During the next several years, conflict simmered as the British troops remained. The American public split into factions: "loyalists" who accepted England's right to rule her colonies as she chose, and "patriots" opposed to British rule. In April 1775, war broke out in Massachusetts between the British soldiers and local minutemen. When the smoke finally cleared in 1781, the colonies had won independence.

Striking an aggressively American note, *The New-England Psalm-Singer* bore the stamp of its time and place. The titles of many tunes refer to Boston and the surrounding area, including Massachusetts counties, cities, and towns, and Boston churches (NEW SOUTH, OLD BRICK). But even more unusual was the glimpse of himself that Billings offered his readers. In the book's introduction, he approached the public as a man of Boston and a musician of the New World. As Billings saw it, composers either were blessed with artistic inspiration or they were not. On "the rules of composition," he wrote: "*Nature is the best Dictator,* for all the hard dry studied Rules that ever was prescribed, will not enable any Person to form an Air [i.e., compose a melody] . . . without a Genius. . . . Nature must inspire the Thought." Confident of the "genius" that linked him with nature's inspiration, Billings then added: "For my own Part, I don't think myself confin'd to any Rules for Composition laid down by any that went before me."

William Billings

Born in Boston in 1746, Billings attended school briefly, then learned the tanner's trade. As a musician, he seems to have been self-taught. By age twenty-three, he was teaching singing schools, an activity he pursued through much of his life. He also held municipal posts. During the 1780s, he served as sealer of leather for the city of Boston, as well as scavenger (street cleaner) and hog reeve (official in charge of controlling roving swine). Billings struggled financially in his later years. The publication of his last tunebook in 1794 was sponsored by local singers as an act of charity toward him and his family. He died in 1800.

Billings also gained historical attention by launching his career on the eve of American independence, in a city that played a key role in the conflict. Far from disguising his own sympathies, Billings celebrated them. The engraver of *The New-England Psalm-Singer*'s frontispiece, for example, was Paul Revere, strongly identified with Boston's patriot faction. Like James Lyon, Billings also published his work by subscription, but he apologized in an advertisement for omitting the subscriber list from his book for want of space. Given Billings's links to Boston's patriots—he was also friendly with the arch-agitator Samuel Adams—it would be interesting to know whether subscribers ran chiefly to like-minded people or included a wider spectrum of Bostonians.

Patriot, composer, vivid personality, William Billings stands as an emblematic figure in American music history. When psalmodists and writers of his own time chose one man to exemplify their tradition, Billings was the natural choice. When later reformers wished to recall the supposedly crude beginnings of American music, Billings served their purposes too. More recently, when music historians have chronicled the origins of American composition, or when choirs have performed music of eighteenth-century Yankees, it is to Billings and his works that both have been most likely to turn. Billings stands foremost among our musical founding fathers, long on talent and historical charisma if short on polish and solemnity.

When Billings died in 1800, William Bentley, a Boston minister who had known him for thirty years, remembered the composer in his diary as "the father of our new England music." Bentley's obituary noted Billings's lack of "a proper education," his disturbing appearance ("a singular man, of moderate size, short of one leg, with one eye . . . & with an uncommon negligence of person"), and the air of defeat that marked his life's end ("He died poor & neglected & perhaps did too much neglect himself"). Yet Bentley could think of no rival who matched the impact of Billings, a man who "spake & sung & thought as a man above the common abilities." And his memory of the psalmodist produced a pungent metaphor: Billings's work showed "inferiour excellence."

LISTENING GUIDE 3

Chester (Billings)

CHESTER, from *The New-England Psalm-Singer*, shows Billings in action as both composer and poet. Written in long meter (8.8.8.8.), the hymn enlists God on New England's side in her quarrel with the mother country. The notion that in 1770 a sacred tunebook could include a piece with a text like CHESTER's shows how far the boundaries of psalmody had stretched since Cotton Mather's day. Then, only divinely inspired texts had been allowed; now, a prophet of rebellion was opening the tradition up to new expressive territory.

Much of CHESTER's appeal lies in a melody (in the tenor part) whose profile is shaped by the dactylic rhythm (long, short-short, or ♩ ♪ ♪) that begins all four of its phrases. Lying high in the voice, the melody reaches the top note F in three phrases, encouraging full volume as the rhythm mandates a fairly brisk pace. It is hard to imagine anyone singing this tune softly or slowly. And the tenor voice holds no monopoly on musical interest. The bass, for example, moves purposefully in all four phrases, supporting the tenor tune. The treble (soprano), whose fourth phrase begins like the tenor's first, sings a melody almost as interesting as the main one. Only the counter voice (alto), whose role is to complete the harmony, lacks tunefulness.

CHESTER thus gave singers a confluence of independent, interlocking melodic lines, tailored to fit metrical verse, a fact important for worshipers and composers alike. But as a musical composition, it points up Billings's lack of artistic polish as well as his talent. Note, for example, that the most strongly stressed syllable in the second phrase falls on "clank," the stanza's least euphonious word. And then there are the parallel fifths between voices, forbidden by

"the Rules of Composition" because they restrict melodic independence. Billings, having sworn to uphold that principle, breaks his
vow in measures 3–4, where treble and tenor move in a chain of
four such intervals. We can imagine the prophet of inferior excellence weighing the alternatives—the sound of the whole versus the
melodic integrity of individual voices—and choosing the first, perhaps because nothing better expressed the inflexibility of Britain's
"iron rod" than the ring of those descending fifths.

Chester suggests how the method of composition Billings describes in one of his tunebooks worked in practice. He began by writing the tenor, or "first part," which he called "nothing more than a flight of fancy" to which other voices were "forced to comply and conform"—that is, to create harmonious "consonances" when sounding with the other voices rather than clashing "dissonances." Billings then composed the rest of the voices so that they would partake "of the same air, or, at least, as much of it as they can get." In other words, Billings tried to infuse voices other than the tenor with melodic interest. But because they were composed *after* the tenor, "the last parts are seldom so good as the first; for the second part [the bass] is subservient to the first, the third part [the treble] must conform to first and second, and the fourth part [the counter] must conform to the other three." By writing voice parts that kept singers musically engaged while still following accepted harmonic practice, Billings strove to reconcile the claims of nature and art—of inspiration and technique.

In his second tunebook, *The Singing Master's Assistant* (1778), Billings added more stanzas to Chester. He also composed anthems paraphrasing Scripture to link the plight of present-day Bostonians with that of the Israelites in Egyptian captivity. The Old Testament Psalm 137 begins: "By the rivers of Babylon, there we sat down, yea, we wept, when we remembered Zion." In his Lamentation over Boston, Billings changed those words to "By the Rivers of Watertown we sat down & wept when we remember'd thee, O Boston." And later in the same piece, he took off from the Lamentations of Jeremiah:

> A voice was heard upon the high places, weeping and supplications of the children of Israel (Jer. 3:21).
> A voice was heard in Roxbury which ecchoed thru the continent weeping for Boston because of their danger (Billings).

Texts like these treated Scripture not only as a guide to spiritual inspiration but as a historical epic that offered timeless parallels to current events.

 OTHER YANKEE PSALMODISTS

For all of Billings's fame, he was just one of many New Englanders who composed and published sacred music in the late 1700s. Like his, their work brings up again the issue of sacredness and secularity. For in eighteenth-century America, psalms and hymns won acceptance as popular poetry, understood and loved by the people. Tunebooks like those of

Billings and his contemporaries, though overwhelmingly sacred in their texts, were too expensive for church use and their music too elaborate for any congregation. They were intended to serve the needs of singing schools (which were not sacred institutions) and musical societies, groups of singers from schools and choirs who banded together for the pleasure of exercising their skills. Rather than church music, then, psalmody was more like popular music.

From the mid-1780s into the early 1800s, tunebooks featured compositions by native-born Americans, including Daniel Read, Lewis Edson, Justin Morgan, Timothy Swan, and others, who hailed from the towns and villages sprinkled across the Massachusetts and Connecticut countryside. In addition to their trades (Read was a comb maker and storekeeper, Edson a blacksmith, Morgan a farmer, schoolmaster, and horse breeder, Swan a hatter), they taught singing schools and wrote music, but without much exposure to the music making of the cities.

New England psalmody lacked the specialization we find in later American music making. The composers, who had acquired their own musical learning in singing schools and through personal experience, were writing essentially for peers, friends, and neighbors. Thanks to subscription and informal interchange, even inexperienced composers could get their music into print. And though the singing was done for the greater glory of God, much of it took place outside public worship. The flexibility of boundaries that were later more sharply drawn—between sacred and secular, professional and amateur, composer and performer, creator and publisher—has led some to call the late eighteenth century a golden age of psalmody. Daniel Read's SHERBURNE was a golden-age favorite.

CD 1
4

LISTENING GUIDE 4

Sherburne (Read)

A band of shepherds are working the night shift. It is a cold evening, the ground is hard, and they are bored. Suddenly they see a flash of light. And there hovers an angel, sent by God to report some startling news about His family. Read's setting, with its homegrown harmony and simple declamation, seems to encourage the performers to sing as people accustomed to sleeping on cold, hard ground themselves, as some of SHERBURNE's early performers doubtless were. For here, commonplace details and world-changing revelation blend into one experience.

SHERBURNE's musical idiom typifies a generation of Yankee

composers. The opening shows two harmonic traits that are
different from anything a European composer of the time
would have written. One is the fondness for "open" sounds—
harmonies that include only the first (root) and fifth notes of a
chord instead of a full triad of root, third, and fifth. That sound
is the simplest of any consonance; thus it resonates well and is
easy to sing in tune. The second unusual trait is greater harmonic freedom, which we can see in measure 3. The first phrase,
instead of following the expected path to a resting point (cadence) on A, the fifth scale degree (or dominant), heads for B, the

sixth. While there is nothing shocking in that move, an ear used
to the formulas of conventional harmony does not expect it.

SHERBURNE is a "fuging tune," an Anglo-American form
beloved of psalmodists and singers of the period. Beginning
with block chords, the texture explodes at its midpoint into a
"fuge," that is, a section where each voice part enters at a different time, so that the text overlaps. The accented quarter notes of
Read's "fuge" subject encourage ecstatic vocal expression that
pushes the rhythm ahead like an engine. As people praising God
by registering joy in the story *and* in the act of singing, it hardly
seems to matter whether they are inside the meeting house or
not. More a piece to be sung than listened to, SHERBURNE offers
its singers plenty of sheer enjoyment.

Yet some religious leaders of the time found the age more gloomy
than golden. Looking back on the years 1770–1800, a singing master in
the 1850s recalled them as "a dark age" because "the tunes were so in-
appropriate." As compositions like SHERBURNE gained favor, he remem-

bered, ministers and "men of correct taste in regard to music, looked on, sometimes grieved and sometimes vexed." But their influence had waned. "They had let go their hold, and the multitude had the whole management of it, and sung *what* and *when* they pleased."

OUTSIDE THE CALVINIST ORBIT

The Church of England supported a musical life on these shores very different from that of the Reformed Calvinists. Anglican worship followed a prescribed church calendar, and the content of many services was specified. The church was also hierarchical, with tiers of officials from the Archbishop of Canterbury on down. In the Anglican system, overseas ministers were licensed to preach by the church's Society for the Propagation of the Gospel in Foreign Parts (SPG), centered in London, which also assigned clergymen to specific churches in the New World. (From 1786 on, American Anglicans called themselves Episcopalians.)

Anglicans in the New World, welcoming visual and musical display, believed that organ music added impressiveness to their worship. As Francis Hopkinson, a prominent Philadelphia Anglican and himself an organist, put it: "I am one of those who take great delight in sacred music, and think, with royal David, that heart, voice, and instrument should unite in adoration of the great Supreme." Indeed, much of the history of early American church music centers on the organ: either the Calvinists' opposition to it or the financial investment needed to buy one. The high cost of importing an organ from overseas was only part of the expense, however, for churches with organs then had to find organists to play them. And that could mean hiring a professional musician with European training.

Francis Hopkinson warned church organists to remember "that the congregation have not assembled to be entertained with [their] performance." But not all organists agreed, as we see in a 1781 description of an Anglican service in Philadelphia that reminded the observer of "a sort of opera, as well for the music as the decorations." Yet an organ could attract a skilled musician to a community, whose musical life might then be enriched by that presence. In 1737, St. Philip's Church in Charleston, South Carolina, hired as its organist Charles Theodore Pachelbel, a native of Germany and son of Johann, composer of the famous *Canon*. Pachelbel played at St. Philip's until his death in 1750. He also performed in public concerts, taught a singing school, and gave private lessons.

Two other Protestant groups led unusually active musical lives. Both were Pennsylvania-based, German-speaking separatist societies that found havens in America, where they pursued their visions of Christian

London organ builder John Snetzler completed this chamber organ in 1762. It is now found in the Congregational Church in South Dennis, Massachusetts.

living. The first formed a cloister in Ephrata, Pennsylvania. Its founder, Conrad Beissel, was a prolific writer who used hymns to present his theological ideas. By the mid-1740s, though more than fifty years old and untrained in music, Beissel had devised a system of composing sacred

Conrad Beissel, founder and leader of the Ephrata Cloister in Pennsylvania, wrote both words and music for many hymns, which were elegantly copied in illuminated manuscripts.

choral music with a soft, otherworldly sound. Conceived for his cloister members alone, Beissel's music was not published. Yet, in a spirit of devotion, it was copied by hand, with elaborate decorations, in beautifully illuminated choral books that have been preserved.

The other group of musically inspired separatists were the Moravians, or Unitas Fratrum, who crossed the Atlantic in the 1740s and 50s to create their own communities in Pennsylvania (Nazareth, Bethlehem) and North Carolina (Salem). Moravians encouraged the singing of elaborate anthems as well as congregational hymns. And as community life grew more settled, organs were introduced into the churches. David Tannenberg, a Moravian born in Saxony but a Pennsylvania resident from 1749, became one of the most important American organ builders, with at least forty-two instruments to his credit. Moreover, choral anthems were sometimes accompanied by orchestras formed by men of the congregation (musical instruments carried none of the secular taint here that disturbed the

This watercolor pictures Moravian bishop Jacob Van Vleck accompanying the singing of girls who may be students at the school in Bethlehem, Pennsylvania, of which he was principal.

Calvinists). Called "collegia musica" (groups of people gathered to make music), instrumentalists also met outside worship services to play chamber and orchestral music, most of it composed in Europe. By 1780, the Bethlehem collegium—four violins, one viola, and pairs of violoncellos, flutes, oboes, French horns, and trumpets—were skilled enough to play symphonies by the day's leading composers: Haydn, Mozart, and the sons of J. S. Bach. Like the singers, collegium members were amateurs who performed to enrich a community life dedicated to God's glory.

Some Moravians—Johann Friedrich Peter, Johannes Herbst, and David Moritz Michael, all born in Europe—also mastered the styles of Continental composers. At a time when few Americans outside the realm of psalmody were capable of composing at all, Moravian communities boasted several who wrote music in an up-to-date European idiom.

LISTENING GUIDE 5

Ich will dir ein Freudenopfer thun (Peter)

"Ich will dir ein Freudenopfer thun," by Johann Friedrich Peter, is a good example of a Moravian anthem, few of which run much longer than two minutes. Peter, a native of Holland who was educated there and in Germany, was an exact contemporary of William Billings. He immigrated to America in 1770 at the age of twenty-four to serve Moravian communities in Pennsylvania. A schoolteacher who also filled several church positions, he directed music for the Salem, North Carolina, congregation between 1780 and 1790, and there he seems to have composed this work for four-voice choir (sopranos I and II, alto, and bass) and orchestra (strings with two French horns). The German text, taken from Psalm 54, may be translated: "I will make a sacrifice of joy to Thee and give thanks unto Thy name, O Lord, for it is good." Peter bases this anthem on one repeated musical figure: the rising ten-note melody to which the first words of the text are set. Played by the violins to start the anthem, this melody is also sung at the choir's first entrance. And from there, it returns often: in the instruments, in the voices, sometimes with the melody changed but the rhythm intact (♩. ♫♩|♩. ♪♩|♩ ♩ ♩|♩), and sometimes in different keys. The natural interweaving of this figure throughout the piece points to the composing skill of Peter, whose six quintets for strings (1789) are the earliest known chamber music written in America.

Each of the traditions touched on in this chapter carried a different significance in its own day. New England psalmody produced a home-grown tradition of composing that served the needs of Puritan-inspired English-speaking Calvinists. Anglican church music created a niche for European-trained professionals. The Ephrata Cloister gave rise to a novel musical style. And the Moravians set up theocratic communities whose life owed much to cosmopolitan styles of music making. The variety of ways that Protestants found to praise God through music reflected the diversity of American Protestantism itself.

4

"Old, Simple Ditties"

COLONIAL SONG, DANCE, AND HOME MUSIC MAKING

A KEY DIFFERENCE BETWEEN MUSIC MAKING IN THE OLD AND NEW Worlds lay in their economic support. In Europe, society's main institutions—the church, the court, and the state—required music for their own purposes, and they paid musicians to supply it. In America, however, no national church existed, nor did any political structure with aristocratic continuity and clout. Lacking such sponsorship, music depended on musicians themselves for much of its support and promotion. The creation of a diverse musical life on these shores has been largely the work of musicians seeking to sell their services.

The number of customers for music grew during the 1700s as the population increased. But professional activity was concentrated in a few cities on the Eastern Seaboard—Boston, New York, Philadelphia, Baltimore, and Charleston—where immigrant musicians practiced what they had learned in Europe. And that fact points to something basic in America's musical life: from the start of European settlement, musicians here have been able to take for granted the ample supply of music from the British Isles and the European Continent, made available through oral tradition and written notation. Given a steady supply from Europe, there was little demand outside church circles for music by American composers. Indeed, it apparently mattered little to singers and players that until long after American independence was won, very few of the songs, dances, or theatrical works they performed were composed here.

BALLADS IN ORAL TRADITION

An ocean separated early English-speaking settlers from the land of their origin, but not from its language, verses, or music. Songs from Great Britain were woven into Americans' lives, as a letter Benjamin Franklin wrote from London in 1765 to his brother Peter back home suggests. Peter had sent Benjamin some original verses, asking that an English composer be hired to set them to music. But in Benjamin's view, the verses called for a simpler tune than a London composer would write. If Peter had given his text "to some country girl in the heart of *Massachusetts*, who has never heard any other than psalm tunes or '*Chevy Chace*,' the '*Children in the Wood*,' the '*Spanish Lady*,' and such old, simple ditties, but has naturally a good ear, she might more probably have made a pleasing popular tune for you than any of our masters here." The songs Franklin names are all ballads: narrative songs in strophic form, with many stanzas of text sung to the same music. All three had originated in Great Britain in the early 1600s or before. That they were still circulating orally in North America in the 1760s testifies to their place in the hearts of the people.

In a version printed in eighteenth-century Massachusetts, *Chevy Chase* tells, in some three dozen eight-line stanzas, a tale of British slaughter. The English nobleman Piercy, Earl of Northumberland, goes deer hunting in Chevy Chase, a wood claimed by a Scot, Earl Douglas. Knowing that a challenge is likely, Piercy takes an army of fifteen hundred with him; Douglas appears with two thousand Scottish soldiers. According to chivalry's code, knights must defend their honor, so Douglas and Piercy join in hand-to-hand combat, each winning the other's respect. Once the two leaders are slain, however, the armies fall upon each other in a bloody struggle that leaves barely a hundred men alive. The widows clean up after the carnage.

The view of society inscribed in *Chevy Chase* could hardly be less democratic. Combat between the earls Piercy and Douglas fills several stanzas, and the death of each is told in detail, while thousands of others are polished off in less than a dozen words. Yet it should be no surprise that a ballad like *Chevy Chase*, with its larger-than-life heroes and gory details, should remain popular. For the concept of honor—that one must fight when challenged to fight—has inspired military effort ever since.

Chevy Chase also points up another trait of balladry: the detachment with which many ballads relate their story. The strophic form itself is partly responsible, parceling out the tale in repeated patterns of verse. And rather than providing commentary on the words, the tune serves as a neutral framework for their delivery, as in psalmody. All the ballad's action-filled events are announced to the same music; the repetitiousness keeps them all on the same emotional level. Sung ballads, then, are no exercise in animated storytelling but a sober, impersonal ritual.

The Children in the Woods, the second ballad named in Franklin's letter, tells a more emotional story. The deaths of a rich man and his wife leave their two young children in the care of an unreliable uncle who stands to inherit the parents' estate if the children die before coming of age. The uncle hires two Russians to take the children into the woods and kill them. But on the journey, the little boy and girl prove so charming that one would-be assassin repents and kills the other instead. He and the children continue to wander, but soon they grow hungry, and the Russian leaves the youngsters to look for food. He never returns, and they lose their way in the forest.

> Thus wandred these two little Babes,
> till Death did end their Grief;
> In one another's arms they dy'd,
> as Babes wanting Relief.

"The Wrath of God" then descends upon the uncle, who eventually dies in prison after the story of his treatment of the children is discovered.

The English poet and critic Joseph Addison admitted that the verse was clumsy but praised *The Children in the Woods* for its authentic feelings. "The Song is a plain simple Copy of Nature, destitute of all the Helps and Ornaments of Art," he wrote in 1711. "Because the Sentiments appear genuine and unaffected, they are able to move the Mind of the most polite Reader with inward Meltings of Humanity and Compassion." The idea that untutored simplicity could touch the depths of the soul grew familiar in eighteenth-century Europe, helping to interest sophisticated observers in songs, sayings, and artifacts of "the folk."

The Spanish Lady deals not with a tragedy but with a romance. British soldiers have invaded Spain and taken prisoners. One captive, a "lovely, young and tender" Spanish woman, falls in love with her English captor. When the English commander orders the release of female prisoners, she is heartbroken. "Leave me not to a Spaniard," she begs. "You alone enjoy my heart." The Englishman insists that he must follow orders, then, after much argument, finally confesses that he is already married. The news transforms her romantic passion into Christian self-sacrifice. Offering the soldier a gold chain to give his wife, she vows to spend the rest of her days in a nunnery, praying for him (and his spouse).

BROADSIDE BALLADS

Oral ballads existed outside any commercial network. But by the early 1700s, songs sung in America to some of the same melodies as the oral ballads were also being bought and sold. Verses commenting on current events might be matched with a familiar tune, printed on sheets called broadsides, and sold in the marketplace, just as sheet music and phonograph records would later make popular songs widely accessible. Broadside ballads, though, lacked the prestige that oral ballads came to enjoy. Their reputation was that of cheap commercial goods. The Reverend Cotton Mather complained in a diary entry in 1713: "I am informed, that the Minds and Manners of many People about the Countrey are much corrupted by foolish songs and Ballads, which the Hawkers and Pedlars carry into all parts of the Countrey."

Almost anything could inspire a broadside ballad: colonial settlement, Indian wars, dissatisfaction with English rule, crime, love, and religion are some of the favorite subjects. In contrast to oral ballads, many broadside ballads show a cartoon-like quality of exaggeration, sometimes coupled with language or images that make later standards of public taste seem prudish.

An example is *The Lawyer's Pedigree*, published in New England in 1755. Rooted in an earthy tradition of English humor, the song denies the legal profession any shred of dignity, prescribing as the tune of choice *Our Polly Is a Sad Slut*, sung in *The Beggar's Opera* (by English author John Gay) by the corrupt Mrs. Peachum, a receiver of stolen goods. And the text taps into the anti–Roman Catholic prejudice that flourished in Protestant Britain and her colonies by parodying an older song called *The Pope's Pedigree*. The tune links lawyers to criminals; the text's background hints that they were also hypocrites, like Catholic clergy whose vows of celibacy did not keep them from enjoying sexual pleasure:

> Thus, as the Story says,
> The pedigree did run;
> The Pope he had a Friar,
> The Friar had a nun:
> The Nun, she was with Child
> And so her Credit sunk.
> The Father was a Friar,
> The Issue was a Monk.

Such ballads were often used for political expression, circulating not only in broadsides but in newspapers. For patriotism—love of one's country and belief in the rightness of its actions—aroused passions well suited to the editorializing that broadside ballads invited. In the years before and during the War of Independence (1775–1781), one claim in particular was trumpeted in song after song, sometimes from an American and sometimes from a British perspective: our side is virtuous and right, your side corrupt and wrong; and if the difference can be settled only through

LISTENING GUIDE 6

The Liberty Song (Dickinson)

John Dickinson's *The Liberty Song*, printed in a Boston newspaper in July 1768, was a takeoff on *Heart of Oak* (1759), a song commemorating an English victory over France during the Seven Years' War. Dickinson, a Pennsylvanian, struck a nerve when he fired a parody of *Heart of Oak* back at the British. Here is the text's first stanza, typeset to resemble the original:

> Come, join Hand in Hand, brave AMERICANS all,
> And rouse your bold hearts to fair LIBERTY'S Call;
> No *tyrannous Acts* shall suppress your *just Claim*,
> Or stain with *Dishonour* AMERICA'S Name.
> > In FREEDOM we're BORN, and in FREEDOM we'll LIVE.
> > Our Purses are ready,
> > Steady, Friends, Steady,
> > Not as SLAVES but as FREEMEN our Money we'll give.

Dickinson's thrust inspired a counterattack. In September 1768, the same Boston newspaper printed a version of *Heart of Oak* upholding the British cause and attacking the patriots:

> *Come shake your dull Noddles, ye Pumpkins and bawl,*
> *And own that you're mad at fair Liberty's Call,*
> *No scandalous Conduct can add to your Shame.*
> *Condemn'd to Dishonour. Inherit the Fame—*
> > In Folly you're born, and in Folly you'll live,
> > To Madness still ready,
> > And Stupidly steady,
> > Not as Men, but as Monkies, the Tokens you give.

combat, then let's fight. In the duel of words that accompanied rising political unrest, two groups of British subjects, the colonizers (loyalists) and
the colonized (patriots), used the same stock of British song to argue for
their cause. The patriotic songs that appeared on broadsides and in newspapers during these years provide their own window on the founding of
the American republic.

Today, the words and music cannot convey the emotional bite that these
text-and-tune combinations must have carried in 1768. Dickinson's pro-
American version takes a familiar, much-loved song and twists its meaning; the loyalist version ridicules the new meaning with antipatriot
venom. Americans and English in Boston then must have been aware of
how each parody transformed the original. The patriot version turns an
anthem of British self-congratulation into an indictment of Britain's poli-
cies. Yet the loyalist version also draws weight from the original, imply-
ing that England, victor over a powerful European rival, could easily dis-
miss a minor family disturbance. In both cases, the melody and its
associations gave an edge to political expression.

Patriotic broadside ballads took their melodies not only from English
songs but from the vast body of dance music that circulated in Britain
and its American colonies. For instance, *The Irishman's Epistle to the Officers and Troops at Boston*, which appeared in the *Pennsylvania Magazine* of
May 1775, only a month after war broke out, was sung to the tune of *Irish
Washerwoman*. In Philadelphia, far removed from the fighting, observers
could look beyond the war's grim side and find humor in an event like
the hasty British retreat from the colonials. In the second stanza, the song's
Irish protagonist taunts the British Regulars, gleefully rubbing salt into
wounds their pride had suffered:

> How brave you went out with muskets all bright,
> And thought to befrighten the folks with the sight;
> But when you got there how they powder'd your pums,
> And all the way home how they pepper'd your bums,
> And is it not, honies, a comical farce,
> To be proud in the face, and be shot in the arse?

DANCING AND DANCE MUSIC

For centuries, dance has been a lightning rod for American public opinion. Two controversial issues have repeatedly surfaced since the 1600s:
(1) dance's erotic dimension and efforts to keep it under control and (2)
dance's connection with social class. Even though dance is being dis-

cussed here as a secular activity, it has long been a matter for debate in American religious life. Moreover, like clothing and manners, dancing has often served as a marker of social trends and fashion.

Before the Civil War (1860s), most social dances came from Europe. More recently, they have originated chiefly on this side of the Atlantic, with new dances tending to be physically freer than the ones they replace. In the story of popular dance's development in America, Puritanism has often been assigned a villain's role. Dances once denounced as instruments of the devil now appear quite proper, making objections raised against them seem quaint. And yet important issues were at stake in the debates that dance has inspired.

The lack of common ground between social dance and the Puritan imagination may be traced to the belief that spirit and flesh are contrary forces locked in a perpetual struggle. Devout Puritans lived their lives believing that they were sinners dependent on the grace of God. Dance that celebrated the human body did so, they believed, at the soul's expense. Yet at the same time, while mistrusting the spirit of dance, Puritans acknowledged that it could be effective as a way to discipline the young. In a tract with a title whose religious passion echoes through the ages— *An Arrow Against Profane and Promiscuous Dancing; Drawn out of the Quiver of the Scriptures* (Boston, 1684)—the Reverend Increase Mather, father of Cotton, wrote that if "the Design of Dancing is only to teach children good Behaviour and a decent Carriage," then he could approve it. To keep "uncleanness" (i.e., sexuality) at bay, however, Mather recommends that girls and boys be taught separately, and by a pious teacher. The one adult Mather refers to in this passage is the dancing master. It was hard for Puritans to believe that grownup men and women could dance together while still honoring and glorifying God.

For non-Puritans, however, dance has not always been considered a secular activity. Many American Indian tribes have relied on music and movement together to establish contact with the spiritual realm. African religions brought to North America by slaves also gave dance a crucial role. Even within Anglo-American culture, the Shakers, a celibate sect founded in late eighteenth-century England that endured in this country into the latter 1900s, were known for their sacred dancing.

Most Anglicans shared the Puritans' view of dancing as secular but not their disapproval of it. In 1714, King's Chapel in Boston hired Edward Enstone from London as its organist, anticipating that his work would include dance instruction. There were also dancing masters in colonial Boston from the 1670s on, whatever the Puritans thought of them. At one end of the dance spectrum were skills taught formally by masters like Enstone that prepared people to attend social functions such as balls. At the other was a casual, informal pastime taking place at home and as part of festive occasions.

Through dance manuals and musical sources, we see that Americans of the colonial era performed both couple dances and so-called country dances. Couple dances, including the gavotte, the bourrée, and especially the minuet, were courtly affairs of French origin that called for precise, schooled movements. To perform such dances well was considered a social accomplishment that was possible only through instruction; those who did so thus had enough leisure time and money for lessons. By 1725, however, group country dancing, a forerunner of square dancing, had come into favor in England and the American colonies. Especially popular were "longways" dances, in which a line of men faced a line of women, and patterns were traced collectively by the whole group.

As an extension of Britain's social structure, colonial society sought to follow Old World models in formal events like balls and banquets. The courtly French minuet, for example, might begin a ball, danced by the most important guests; other dances with prescribed steps might follow. The rest of the evening was often given over to country dances, whose popularity increased on both sides of the Atlantic through the 1700s. But apparently, these dances were not free from implications of class hierarchy either. In 1768, formal balls were discontinued for a time in New York "when consorts of General Gage and Governor Moore could not agree on who should stand first in a country dance."

From its first publication in 1651, Playford's *The Dancing Master* supplied tunes and instructions for several generations of English-speaking dancers. The dance pictured in this 1725 edition's title page is accompanied by three musicians in the gallery at the left.

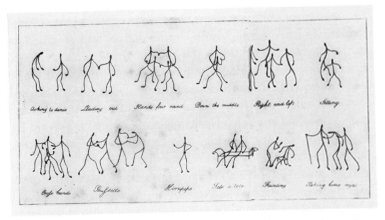

Country dancing remained popular well into the 1800s, as shown by this light-hearted stylization of dancers' behavior from a Philadelphia journal of 1817.

Like the country dances themselves, music for them came from overseas, especially from Anglo-Irish tradition. The music circulated both orally and in written form, including printed collections and manuscripts that musicians copied for their own use. Some of the tunes dated back into the 1600s, and, as already noted, broadside ballads sometimes borrowed their melodies from dance. The tune of *Irish Washerwoman*, for example, survives in many eighteenth-century copies, domestic and foreign, in print and in manuscript; several different longways country dances for the tune have turned up in American sources.

Traits of Dance Music

1. Steady tempo
2. Regular phrases of predictable length (usually four or eight bars)
3. Repeated sections (called strains)

Another favorite country dance tune of the era was *College Hornpipe*, which, like *Irish Washerwoman* and such ballads as *The Spanish Lady*, survived changes of musical fashion. Also known as *Sailor's Hornpipe*, *College Hornpipe* was first published in London in 1766. At least six different American versions were printed in the years 1801–25, and in 1870 thirteen of the twenty American publishers in the Board of Music Trade listed editions for sale. Several decades later, composer Charles Ives, remembering the fiddling at barn dances he had attended as a Connecticut boy in the 1880s, quoted *College Hornpipe* and other dance tunes in the "Washington's Birthday" movement of his *Holidays* Symphony. Today books of fiddle music still carry *College Hornpipe*. And in cartoon films, the appearance of a sailor on the screen is likely to call forth this tune.

Irish Washerwoman

The tune of *Irish Washerwoman* has been traced as far back as Playford's *The English Dancing Master* (1651). The following version, from an American copy of around 1795, is cast in two eight-measure strains.

The second strain resembles the first but occupies a higher range and traces a different melodic curve. Both strains end with the same melodic close. While the melody may be sung, its wide range and frequent leaps point to instrumental origins. The second strain, especially the repeated-note figure near the end, could be played most easily by the fiddle, but players of the flute, the other standard dance instrument of the day, also mastered it.

HOME AND AMATEUR MUSIC MAKING

The main thing we know about music making in early American homes is that it took place. Although documentation is sparse, colonial Boston records show evidence that many citizens owned musical instruments— keyboards (especially harpsichords), plucked and bowed strings, wind instruments, trumpets, and drums—and the painting *A Musical Gathering*, most likely an eighteenth-century American work, depicts a home ensemble in action, with the punch bowl ready to be tapped.

This painting, undated and of unknown authorship but assumed to be North American, shows a punch bowl being brought to a group of players whose instruments include fiddle, oboe, trumpet, cello, and hammered dulcimer.

Since those colonial Americans with cultivated tastes lacked easy access to professional performers, they sometimes made music and held dances in their homes. Like dancing masters, music masters, either itinerant or based in cities, supplied the necessary instruction, giving lessons in singing or on parlor instruments of the day: harpsichord, violin, flute, and guitar. In the years before the War of Independence, amateur music making seems to have increased, with dealers advertising instruments, accessories, and printed music and teachers offering their services in the public press. A musically minded colonial who could pay for lessons had a decent chance to become a competent amateur performer.

In early America, the word "amateur," rather than referring to someone less skilled than a professional, meant one who pursued music simply for love of it, as the Latin root verb (*amare*, to love) suggests. The most illustrious member of that company was Thomas Jefferson, author of the Declaration of Independence and third U.S. president. Jefferson played the violin through much of his life, owned and maintained harpsichords, and collected a large library of music from which he and others performed. In a 1778 letter to an acquaintance in Paris, he called music "the favorite passion of my soul" and told of his aspirations for building musical performance more fully into the life of Monticello, his Virginia country estate. Jefferson saw music in America as standing "in a state of deplorable barbarism" compared with its place in Europe. He invited his correspondent to visit him or to send "a substitute . . . proficient in singing, & on the Harpsichord." To reconcile his "passion for music" with the constraints of his budget, he considered importing from Europe a domestic staff who could double as gardeners, weavers, stonecutters, and instrumental performers. Living in the country, Jefferson imagined a musical environment that would allow him to play and also to retain a "band of music" to gratify his appetite as a listener.

There was no more devoted amateur musician in colonial America, however, than Philadelphia native Francis Hopkinson, the University of Pennsylvania's first graduate, a lawyer and judge by trade, a patriot, and a signer of the Declaration of Independence. Hopkinson began playing the harpsichord at age seventeen, in 1754. He also furthered his musical education by hand-copying arias, songs, and instrumental pieces by European composers favored by mid-century Londoners. By the early 1760s, he was a good enough harpsichordist to join professional musicians in concerts. As an Anglican, Hopkinson was also involved in sacred music, serving for a time as organist of Philadelphia's Christ Church, teaching psalmody, and compiling sacred tunebooks for congregational singing. In contrast to the country squire Jefferson, Hopkinson used home music

Francis Hopkinson of Philadelphia (1737–1791), a prominent patriot during the revolution, was also an active amateur musician who played organ and harpsichord and composed vocal music.

making as a springboard for entry into Philadelphia's musical life, where, given the scarcity of professional performers, his ability and social position made him welcome.

During the War of Independence's last year, Hopkinson produced a patriotic pastiche for solo singers, chorus, and orchestra called *America Independent, or The Temple of Minerva*. The work, for which he wrote his own verses to fit music composed by others, including George Frideric Handel, was performed on March 21, 1781, at the residence of France's minister to the Continental Congress, headquartered in Philadelphia. One stanza praised the Franco-American alliance:

> From the friendly shores of France,
> See the martial troops advance.
> With Columbia's [America's] sons unite,
> And share the dangers of the fight,
> Equal heroes of the day,
> Equal honors to them pay.

In the partisan atmosphere of 1781, what inspired one faction was sure to offend the other. And indeed, *The Temple of Minerva* drew a quick response in the form of a parody. *The Temple of Cloacina* (a cloaca is a sewer or privy), beginning with an instrumental "overturd" and taking an outhouse for its temple, answered Hopkinson's extravaganza in the loyalist press. In one number, Hopkinson's words, addressed to Minerva, were mocked in an indecent "prayer" to Cloacina:

Temple of Minerva	*Temple of Cloacina*
To th'immortal breath of fame,	To the stinking breath of fame,
Give, oh give, her honor'd name.	Give, oh, give the Yankie name,
O'er her councils, still preside,	O'er her close-stools still preside,
In the field her armies guide.	Wipe with nettles her backside.

The goddesses Minerva and Cloacina offer proof that to join the political discourse of the day, even as a gentleman, was to risk involvement in an ideological mud fight.

Francis Hopkinson's musical ambitions reached beyond performances and parodies into the realm of composition. As early as 1759, he was composing songs, cast in two parts—a vocal line with keyboard accompaniment—and modeled on British songs he had copied out on his own.

Three decades later, he published *Seven Songs for the Harpsichord or Forte Piano* (Philadelphia, 1788), dedicated to George Washington, for which he wrote both words and music. A prefatory note declares: "I cannot I believe, be refused the Credit of being the first Native of the United States

My Days Have Been So Wondrous Free (Hopkinson)

Hopkinson's "My Days Have Been So Wondrous Free" (1759) is the first known secular song by a native-born American. Written to a poem by Thomas Parnell, the song reveals both the talent and the inexperience of the twenty-two-year-old composer. Hopkinson's setting of the title phrase shows a feeling for graceful melody and apt text setting. But the rest of the first section ("The little birds that fly / With careless ease from tree to tree / Were but as blest as I") reveals a less sure hand. After the shapely opening, the music seems to lose purpose, hovering for several measures, mostly in running eighth notes, between the dominant and tonic keys. In the second section, the text continues the sunny picture of the singer's state of mind, free of crying and sighing. As the song ends, the melody line moves into the upper reaches of the voice. Rather than full volume, Hopkinson seems here to be encouraging a delicate sound from the singer, an effect picked up by the harpsichord, whose flourishes bring the song to an end.

who has produced a Musical Composition"—a claim referring to the nation born officially in June 1788 when the ninth state ratified the Constitution of the United States of America.

Historical precedence aside, Hopkinson's collection reflects his commitment to the British song tradition, for it surveys the genres that Thomas Augustine Arne, James Hook, Charles Dibdin, and other London composers wrote for comic opera and pleasure-garden performances. Hopkinson tried his hand at a hunting song, a sea song, a "rondo" whose singer scoffs at the notion that love might enslave him, and a pair of pastoral songs in which shepherds vow devotion to idealized maidens. Like his earlier efforts, the music of *Seven Songs* is set on two staves, a vocal line with keyboard accompaniment. Landmark or not, however, the songs seem to have been largely ignored in their own day, though the composer's exchange of letters with Thomas Jefferson in Paris in 1789 shows that Jefferson's daughters, Martha (sixteen) and Polly (eleven), were touched by the "pathos" of one that they played and sang at home.

5

Performing "By Particular Desire"

EARLY MILITARY, CONCERT, AND THEATER MUSIC

MUSICAL INSTRUMENTS HAVE LONG BEEN USED FOR OUTDOOR COM-munication. Drums, for example, played an important signaling role in early American life. In today's sonic world, where music's volume is often boosted by electronics, the sound of fifes and drums being played outside might not strike us as especially loud, but early accounts show that they could seem almost deafening. At a public ceremony to discipline a Continental soldier convicted of thievery in 1775, another soldier wrote that the drums "made such a report in my ears, when accompanied by such screaking of whifes [*sic*] that I could not hear the man next to me."

Military uses for music may be divided into four categories: morale building (or *esprit de corps*), camp duties (which included signaling), public ceremonies, and recreation. On the first count, an eighteenth-century European general noted music's power to impart energy that lifts the spirit. Just as people could be inspired "to dance to music all night who cannot continue two hours without it," he wrote, musical sound could help troops "forget the hardship of long marches."

Music also proved a practical way to regulate camp duties. As armies increased in size, they became more cumbersome to control. Warfare required large groups of soldiers to be moved in an orderly way, and drum cadences worked better than oral commands. By the 1600s, European armies had developed rhythmic and melodic signals such as reveille, retreat, and tattoo. The British military brought these signals to North America, where military leaders used them to communicate quickly with their men, both in and out of battle.

Military life relies a good deal on ceremonies. Parades that feature

56

Hail Columbia (Phile)

Except for *Yankee Doodle*, whose origins are yet to be discovered, the most enduring American instrumental melody of the 1700s was *The President's March*, composed around 1793 by Philip Phile, an immigrant musician who worked in American theaters. In 1798, Philadelphia judge Joseph Hopkinson set patriotic words to the march ("Hail Columbia, happy land"), and from then into the twentieth century the combination of tune and text held a place as a favorite national song.

Phile's melody follows the basic traits of dance music outlined in Chapter 4: steady tempo, regular phrases (four bars in this case), and repeated sections (**AABB**, written ‖:**A**:‖:**B**:‖). The second section, four bars longer than the first (sixteen bars rather than twelve), makes a satisfying connection by using the latter's second phrase as its third (‖:abc:‖:dd'be:‖). The version played here, published in Maine in the 1820s, is an arrangement for a modified band of music playing instruments of the day: pairs of flutes, clarinets, bassoons, and horns, plus a military drum.

uniformed soldiers marching in time to music give the impression of discipline and suggest invincibility. With no risk to life or limb, they contribute to any army's goal: to deter wars as well as to fight them.

Finally, a military unit is both a fighting force and a society, and its musicians have long performed at concerts, meal-time performances, evening entertainments, sports festivals, and riding exhibitions. In fact, the British and American military in the 1700s fostered two different kinds of ensembles, one functional and the other geared more toward aesthetic ends. "Field music"—which involved fifes and drums as in the 1775 ceremony described above—was played by musicians who belonged to the regiments and whose wages were paid out of army appropriations. *Harmoniemusik*, also known as "the band of music" and performed by pairs of wind instruments (oboes, horns, bassoons, possibly clarinets), required more polished players, who were hired by the officers and paid out of their own pockets.

The field music, performed by marching musicians, was portable and loud—an ideal medium for building *esprit de corps*, controlling troop movement, and enhancing ceremonies. The band of music, less loud and portable but with a harmonized sound made by upper-, lower-, and middle-register instruments, offered wider possibilities; it was most useful for recreation, though it could also be an inspirational and ceremonial presence. When colonists formed militia units to fight the War of Independence, they followed British custom, including the two-part division into field music and *Harmoniemusik*.

Taken together, field music and *Harmoniemusik* prefigure the later history of the wind band as it developed on American soil. The latter is a rare early example on this continent of a secular institution's support of music making. Some bands of music played in public concerts and at funerals; some even survived the war. When George Washington toured the United States in 1789, just before taking office as president, bands welcomed him almost everywhere. These ensembles played the full range of the day's music, from marches and patriotic songs to dance tunes. The band's ability to travel and to exist in a variety of forms has made it a uniquely practical ensemble. In that spirit, band performances in early America were given in many different settings, both indoors and outdoors: coffeehouses, taverns, and theaters on the one hand, and parade grounds and pleasure gardens on the other.

 ## CONCERT LIFE

To stage a concert in eighteenth-century America, someone first had to imagine the event and find a place for it. Next, it had to be organized—date fixed, performers secured, music chosen—and advertised. Finally, it had to attract customers. The first step, imagining concerts, was simple, for the musicians who gave them were chiefly immigrants from Europe, where secular assemblies were common; they had only to transplant and adapt to the New World customs already familiar to them from the Old.

Concerts in the 1700s were not necessarily high-toned, formal events, and many were held in modest, often plain rooms with no stage and with temporary arrangements of chairs that might quickly be pushed aside for dancing when the concert was over. The first known public concert in the American colonies took place in Boston in 1729, in a room that a local dancing master used for assemblies. Not until 1754 did the city gain a real concert hall: a room in a building that was refurbished as "an elegant private concert-room." But a room like this made Boston unusual. In most of eighteenth-century America, concert halls were concert halls only as long as the performance lasted.

Benefit concerts, which could be organized quickly, were well suited to the conditions of musical life. The format allowed local organists, traveling professionals, or newly arrived singers in a theater troupe to star in nearly impromptu shows of their own making. The musician who arranged a benefit took the financial risk, paying the expenses and reaping the profits, if any. Benefit concerts were one-time happenings, which distinguished them from most subscription concerts, another eighteenth-century approach. The subscription format allowed organizers to hedge their bets: to issue a public proposal, often for a concert series, and then wait to see whether the response justified going ahead with the plan.

Other types of concerts included the charity benefit given to raise money for a worthy cause, such as aiding residents of the local poorhouse. Concerts were also given by musical societies: organizations formed to promote the art. The St. Cecilia Society of Charleston, South Carolina, for example, brought together amateur and professional musicians on a regular basis. Membership dues acted in effect as a subscription that supported musical performances, some of them open to the public.

The success of public concerts depended on whether their organizers could attract a sizable audience. From the very beginnings of American concert life, audience recruitment called for publicity, and one way to advertise was through handbills, which could be passed from person to person and posted as well. Unlike newspaper announcements, which survive in great numbers, however, few eighteenth-century handbills have been preserved.

The earliest concert ads seldom go beyond the bare facts: Mr. X, for his own benefit, will present a concert at Y hall on date Z; tickets cost U shillings and may be purchased from Mr. V on W Street. After midcentury, however, promoters seem to have lost confidence that a straight factual report would attract an audience. A plea for customers might be framed as a personal invitation, as when a musician in Charleston announced in 1760 that he had "no Doubt, but that it will be in his Power to give the greatest Satisfaction to those Ladies and Gentlemen who shall honor him with their presence." Some announcements implied that public demand, not the organizer's pursuit of the Almighty Shilling, was the reason for a concert. A Philadelphia musician in 1757 headed his ad with the phrase "By particular desire"; and a concert there in 1770 was said to be given "at the request of several Gentlemen and Ladies." Others used flattery, boasts, or even warnings to attract customers. One ad cautioned: "This will positively be the only time of his performing, unless by the particular desire of a genteel company."

Public concerts of the eighteenth century emphasized variety, running more to short pieces than long ones. Most were two-part affairs, each part beginning and ending with as full an ensemble as possible and mixing vocal and instrumental selections. Vocal numbers ranged from solo songs and opera airs to glees (unaccompanied songs for three or more solo singers). Instrumental numbers included solo keyboard pieces, chamber music, and pieces for orchestra, with "Concerto" or "Grand Symphony" meaning one movement, not an entire three- or four-movement work.

The program of a concert given on June 25, 1799, in Salem, Massachusetts, offers a glimpse of how a corps of seasoned troupers might plan a concert. This performance was a joint benefit for Catherine Graupner, a prominent theatrical singer, and Peter Albrecht von Hagen, instrumentalist and orchestra leader, both active in Boston.

A Concert Program of 1799

PART 1ST

Overture, composed by	Pleyel
Song by Mr. Munto	Dr. Arnold
A Sonata on the Grand Forte Piano for 4 hands, by Mrs. Von Hagen and Mr. Von Hagen, jun.	Kozeluch
"By my tender passion," a favourite song in the Haunted Tower, by Mrs. Graupner	Storace
Solo on the Clarinet, by Mr. Granger	Vogel
Lullaby, a favourite Glee for four voices, Mrs. Graupner, Mr. Granger, Mr. Mallet and Mr. Munto	Harrison
Concerto on the Violin by Mr. Von Hagen	Jearnowick

PART 2ND

Concerto on the Piano Forte, by Mrs. Von Hagen	Haydn
Columbia's Bold Eagle, a patriotic song, words by a gentleman of Salem. Music by Mr. Graupner and sung by Mrs. Graupner	
Concerto on the Hautboy, by Mr. Graupner	Le Brun
The Play'd in Air, a much admired Glee in the Castle Spectre, by Mrs. Graupner, Mr. Granger, Mr. Mallet and Mr. Munto	
Quartetto by Messrs. von Hagen, sen. and jun., Mr. Laumont, and Mrs. Graupner.	
"To Arms, to arms," a new patriotic song, written by Thomas Paine, A.M. sung by Mrs. Graupner and music by Mr. von Hagen, jun.	
Finale	Haydn

The program follows the standard two-part format, with orchestra works beginning and ending each part. Soloists supplied variety, and five of the seven belonged either to the Graupner or the von Hagen family. The concert's main singer and co-beneficiary, formerly Catherine Hillier, had immigrated to America in 1794 as part of a London theater troupe. In 1796, she married oboist Gottlieb Graupner, a native of Germany who had moved from there to England, and then to America by 1795. In 1797, the Graupners settled in Boston, where both worked in the city's Federal Street Theater. The von Hagen family—both husband and wife were natives of Holland—had crossed the Atlantic in 1774, living first in Charleston and New York and settling in Boston in 1796. Mrs. von Hagen played keyboard, and her husband worked as an orchestra director as well as a performer on keyboard, wind, and string instruments. Their son, American-born Peter Albrecht von Hagen, Jr., a prodigy on the violin whose public debut took place at the age of eight, was between eighteen and twenty when the Salem benefit concert took place.

With these facts in mind, the Graupner/von Hagen concert may be seen as an event in which Boston's two leading musical families took their act on the road to skim off proceeds from an audience less familiar with their work than Bostonians were. Their program was designed to appeal across a broad range of audience tastes. Instrumental selections by leading European composers of the day testified to their artistic seriousness. Vocal selections, both solo and harmonized, expressed more tender sentiments. And by placing new patriotic numbers on the concert's second half, the performers encouraged Salem's listeners to take pride in their American identity.

 MUSICAL THEATER

Theater companies enhanced the musical lives of their communities beyond the theater's walls. When a company came to town, it arrived with singers and players who were also ready to perform in concerts (as the Salem program shows), participate in church music, and give music lessons. Some company musicians also became involved in publishing and the selling of musical goods.

Like that of Liverpool, York, Edinburgh, and the West Indies, the eighteenth-century American theater was an extension of the London stage. Some foreign performers toured the New World, then returned to the Old. Others settled here. Not until well into the 1800s did any appreciable number of American-born singers or players find a place on U.S.

The New Theater in Chestnut Street, Philadelphia, opened in 1793 and was home to theatrical companies thereafter.

stages. And musical works by Americans had almost no place at all. New World residents whose musical works were produced onstage were all immigrants who had arrived in this country as experienced musicians.

Like dance, the theater provoked strong opposition. In fact, the English language itself reflects deep suspicion of the theater. Most expressions borrowed from the arts convey respect or praise, as in "poetic" justice or the "lyric" beauty of a sunset; in contrast, theatrical terms such as "melodramatic," "putting on an act," or "making a scene" usually do the opposite. The immediate background for American objections, though, lay in English Puritan thought, which treated theater as a generally bad thing, symbolizing a preference for idleness and pleasure over hard work and thrift. For the Puritans, the theater was an institution that lured people away from worthier pursuits, like churchgoing. Actors and actresses were considered vagabonds who threatened the stability of society. Faithful to illusion rather than truth, the theater posed social dangers that made it seem corrupt even to some who were devoted to other forms of art.

Nevertheless, the London-based English-language theater, especially Shakespeare, was the source of enduring theatrical activity in America. English traveling companies first appeared in the colonies in the mid-1700s, in Philadelphia, New York, Charleston, and Virginia (Williams-

NEW THEATRE.

BY PARTICULAR DESIRE. *of President*

George Washington

On *Monday Evening*, Jan. 9, 1797.

Will be prefented, a COMEDY, (in four Acts,) called

THE CHILD OF NATURE.

(From the French of Mad. GENLIS, By the Author of Every one has his Fault.)

Marquis of Almanza,	Mr. Wignell.
Count Valantia,	Mr. Moreton.
Duke Murcia,	Mr. Warren.
Seville,	Mr. Warrell.
Grenada,	Mr. Warrell, jun.
1ft Peafant,	Mr. Cooper.
2d Peafant,	Mr. Mitchell.
Marchionefs, Merida,	Mrs. Morris.
Amanthis,	Mrs. Merry.

To which will be added, (for the third time,) a COMIC OPERA, in two Acts, (as performed at Covent Garden Theatre, upwards of 150 Nights,) called

LOCK AND KEY.

Brummagem,	Mr. Francis.
Cheerly	Mr. Darley, jun.
Captain Vain,	Mr. Fox.
Ralph,	Mr. Harwood.
Laura,	Mrs. Warrell.
Fanny,	Mrs. Oldmixon.
Selina,	Mrs. Harvey.
Dolly,	Mifs. Milbourne.

Box, One Dollar, Twenty-five Cents. *Pit*, One Dollar. And *Gallery*, Half a Dollar.

The Doors of the Theatre will open at 5, and the Curtain rife precifely at 6 o'Clock

Places for the Boxes to be taken at the Office in the front of the Theatre, from 10 till 2 o'clock and from 10 till 4 on the Days of Performance.

Tickets to be had at H. & P. Rice's Book-ftore, No. 50, Market-ftreet, and at the Office adjoining the Theatre.

Ladies and Gentlemen are requefted to fend their Servants to keep places at a quarter before 5 o'clock, and order them, as foon as the Company are feated, to withdraw, as they cannot, on any account be permitted to remain.

No Money or Tickets to be returned nor any perfon, on any account whatfoever, admitted behind the Scenes.

VIVAT RESPUBLICA

This program from Philadelphia's New Theater on January 9, 1797, shows what theatergoers of the time could expect from an evening's entertainment.

burg). New England resisted the effort for a time; between 1750 and 1793, a Boston law prohibited theater entertainments there.

By the 1760s, theaters were being built to accommodate audiences in seats of varying location and price. A typical theatrical evening lasted four or five hours, starting with a long work (a tragedy, comedy, or drama with music) and ending with an afterpiece (a short musical work such as a farce). Musical interludes were common; so were encores of favorite numbers. Straight plays often began with an overture, included music between the acts, and featured songs. Eighteenth- and nineteenth-century Americans seldom formed the silent, respectful gathering of playgoers that we now expect to find in the theater. Early audiences freely shared their opinions with the actors and musicians. The work being performed seems to have been less important to them than the quality of their own experience. If they liked what they saw and heard, they clamored for more; if not, they demanded an end to it.

In other words, the early musical theater in America was a branch of what is called show business today. While the names of the genres—ballad operas, pasticcios, and "operas" whose music was mostly original—may suggest autonomous art forms, all were aimed at audience accessibility. Performers, composers, and impresarios sought most of all to find and please audiences and to increase their size. Toward that end, stage productions featured plots with characters, good or evil, whom spectators could love or hate; players with a talent for comedy, singing, or dancing; a store of melody that was catchy if not already familiar; and a certain amount of spectacle.

Favorite works of the British stage were also popular in America, including *The Beggar's Opera* (1728) by John Gay. Essentially a play whose spoken dialogue alternates with songs, this hugely successful work received its first American performance in New York in 1750. Gay's plot, characters, and lyrics challenged conventional notions of morality with comic precision. The title plays on the idea of high and low. In the first song, Peachum, a seller of stolen goods, ranks his own line of work against others, including politics, law, and the Christian ministry:

> Through all the Employments of Life
> Each Neighbour abuses his Brother
> Whore and Rogue they call Husband and Wife:
> All Professions be-rogue one another:
> The Priest calls the Lawyer a Cheat,
> The Lawyer be-knaves the Divine:
> And the Statesman, because he's so great,
> Thinks his Trade as honest as mine.

When word reaches Peachum and his wife that their daughter Polly has secretly married Macheath, a highwayman, they are horrified, not because of Macheath's profession but because Polly tells them she has married for love. Peachum betrays Macheath to the authorities, then the jailed Macheath betrays Polly by agreeing to marry the jailer's daughter to escape from prison. Macheath is finally brought to the gallows and then freed, because to hang an operatic hero would violate "the Taste of the Town," which demands a happy ending. Mocking operatic customs and blurring the moral distinctions between London society's leaders and its underworld, Gay's work offered a social critique with a bite strong enough to be felt across the Atlantic.

In ballad opera, the songs consist of new words set to familiar tunes. As in the broadside ballad, tunes were chosen not only for their melodies but also for their associations. A good example comes when Polly, pleading with her father to help save Macheath from being hanged, sings a four-line lament in common meter:

> Oh, ponder well! be not severe;
> So save a wretched Wife!
> For on the Rope that hangs my Dear
> Depends poor Polly's life.

The tune for these words is *Now Ponder Well*, familiar through its association with the well-loved ballad *The Children in the Woods*. Gay's intent seems clear: to underline Polly's genuine love for her husband, inviting the audience to perceive her as a pure-hearted character in a drama full of cynicism.

A different kind of association appears when Mrs. Peachum reviles Polly for marrying. The tune Gay borrows for this song is *Oh London Is a Fine Town*, a satirical attack claiming that the city government's officials are totally corrupt. By marrying Macheath, Polly has rejected the career for which she has been groomed. Her parents had looked forward to the day when she would start manipulating the lust of wealthy men, milking their wallets for the Peachum family's enterprise. By trading that prospect for love, she has squandered a family asset, leaving her mother raging at the "sad slut" she has raised:

> Our Polly is a sad Slut! nor heeds what we have taught her.
> I wonder any Man alive will ever rear a Daughter!
> For she must have both Hoods and Gowns, and Hoops to swell her Pride,
> With Scarfs and Stays, and Gloves and Lace; and she will have Men beside;
> And when she's drest with Care and Cost, all tempting, fine and gay,
> As Men should serve a Cucumber, she flings herself away.

Knowing the tunes helped English audiences feel the sting of *The Beggar's Opera*'s social critique, and American audience members must have shared some of that experience.

Ballad operas concentrated on words and ideas, sometimes with society as a target. The pasticcio, another popular theatrical genre of the time, put a higher priority on music. A pasticcio that won great popularity on both sides of the Atlantic was *Love in a Village* (1762), based on a play by Isaac Bickerstaff with music supplied and arranged by Thomas Augustine Arne, first performed in Charleston and Philadelphia in 1766. Rosetta, the heroine, has fled her aristocratic home to avoid a forced marriage, taking a post as chambermaid in a country house. Thomas Meadows has left his home for the same reason and is working as a gardener in the same household. Thomas and Rosetta fall in love. Their connection seems doomed to go nowhere until Thomas's father arrives on the scene and reveals that, from the start, his son's intended bride had been none other than Rosetta. Thus, *Love in a Village* moves from complication to a standard happy ending, obeying the theatrical conventions that *The Beggar's Opera* mocks.

Except for a handful of new pieces, Arne borrowed the music for *Love in a Village* from elsewhere. Most of all, he tapped a vein of lyrical song that flourished at English pleasure gardens from the 1740s on—songs that Francis Hopkinson emulated as a composer. *Love in a Village* proves that lyric melodies sung charmingly to words of romantic love could bring an audience no end of pleasure, no matter how conventional the dramatic situation, the lyrics, or the musical turns of phrase.

By the 1790s, with companies established in Baltimore, Boston, Charleston, New York, and Philadelphia, the theatrical repertory was growing. New works were imported from overseas, while brand-new pieces were created by immigrant composers and playwrights on this side of the Atlantic. Established favorites were sometimes updated by replacing original numbers with newer ones or plugging in popular songs. Thus, English works were routinely transformed in performance into Anglo-American ones.

A favorite comic opera of the time was *The Children in the Wood*, with a libretto by Thomas Morton and music by Samuel Arnold. Premiered in London in 1793, it reached Philadelphia the following year. The story is based on the ballad discussed in Chapter 4, with more characters added, including a heroine—Josephine, the children's governess—and her beloved, a good-hearted carpenter named Walter. Transferred to the stage, the tale lost its tragic ending. The parents, Lord and Lady Alford, have not died but are traveling in India, leaving their two young children in the care of Sir Rowland, Alford's brother. In the last scene, the evil Rowland gets his comeuppance through disgrace and death, and the vir-

John Searle's watercolor of New York's Park Theater in 1822 shows the orchestra pit (with orchestra) and tiered seating that allowed theatergoers from different walks of life to attend without mixing socially.

tuous parents are reunited with their youngsters, restored to health after having been found near death in the forest.

Arnold uses music with dramatic effectiveness in the final scene. Josephine, Walter, and a third character are sitting in a room. Walter, whose role overlaps with that of the ballad's "good" Russian, is troubled because, having lost touch with the children after saving them from assassination, he fears that they have died in the forest. Josephine offers to sing a ballad from a broadside bought "of the old blind pedlar who passed by this morning." She introduces her song as *The Norfolk Tragedy*, about "a ghost, a murdered babe." Walter interrupts her with a cry: "No, don't sing that!" But Josephine goes ahead, laying out the tragedy in three stanzas, which she sings to a folklike melody that Arnold may have borrowed from oral tradition.

> A Yeoman of no mean degree,
> For thirst of Gain and lucre he
> A pretty babe did murder straight.
> By reason of its large Estate.

At least one American Josephine, a Mrs. Marshall who sang the role in Philadelphia in 1795, performed this song unaccompanied, enhancing its archaic quality. In the song's second stanza, the ghost of the dead child knocks at the window. When these words trigger an actual knocking offstage, Walter is terrified. But after Josephine finishes her song, the door bursts open and the rescued children run to Walter's side and embrace him affectionately. Then, in the company of Josephine and Lord and Lady Alford, the true story of his heroism comes out. A brief finale touts the rewards of virtue, and, in fairy-tale fashion, all vow to live happily ever after.

6

Maintaining Oral Traditions

AFRICAN MUSIC IN EARLY AMERICA

FROM SHORTLY AFTER THEIR FIRST ARRIVAL IN VIRGINIA IN 1619, Africans were brought to this country as slaves. Blacks became slaves because certain opportunities in the New World, such as tobacco growing, required a work force that was cheap and dependent. Though most Americans considered it morally wrong, slavery persisted as part of the economic engine that European settlement built on these shores. The Founding Fathers knew that slavery violated the republic's democratic principles, yet the constitutional debates of 1787–88 show that if it had been outlawed, some colonies would never have joined the union.

Slavery's evil touched everyone involved. In regions where blacks outnumbered whites, guilt mingled with fear. Slave rebellions in the Caribbean in the 1790s sent shock waves through North American slaveholders. Revolts were rare in the United States, but the threat of revolt was seldom absent. And when slaves did rebel, panic could lead to tighter repression.

The American slaves came chiefly from West Africa and included peoples with many different languages, religions, and customs. For all their differences, however, these African peoples shared certain similarities in cultural expression. Their sense of community must also have been strengthened by the harshness of their lives in America. Custom and law here treated Africans' differences from each other as insignificant when compared with their differences from (and some believed inferiority to) whites.

AFRICAN ROOTS AND AFRICAN-AMERICAN MUSICIANS

It was once assumed that the forced removal of African Americans from their homeland had destroyed their culture. But that view underrated black culture's hardiness. It now seems clear that Africa-saturated oral traditions were maintained through slavery. Black Africans, for example, were often described as talented musicians. And where there was music there was movement. A European observer in Sierra Leone commented in 1796 that music was "seldom listened to alone, but is generally used as an accompaniment to the dance." Accounts of black singing in America often mention dancing too. Indeed, most of what is known about the slaves' modes of expression confirms their African origins.

Like those of Native Americans, African religions find all of life embued with a sacred spirit. Humankind (including ancestors), nature, and gods make up a sacred whole, which encompasses what Westerners take to be the secular world. This notion of the universe allowed slaves in America to live in a realm of the imagination far more spacious than the one in which they were held as captive laborers. However dehumanizing slavery may have been, customs in the culture they preserved helped slaves to endure, and even leave a legacy of their own.

The African cultural legacy, being oral, is no easier to document than that of the Indians. Yet some observers left comments that allow us to piece together an idea of black music making during the colonial period and in the early republic. Newspapers provide data on black musicians before 1800 in the form of advertisements. Slaves, after all, were part of the American economy; and musical skills could increase a slave's market value, as the following ad from a Virginia newspaper in 1766 confirms: "TO BE SOLD. A young healthy Negro fellow who has been used to wait on a Gentleman and plays extremely well on the French horn." A Boston newspaper in 1745 carried a notice from an owner in Newbury offering a reward for the return of "Cato," who had disappeared a few days earlier: "about 22 Years of Age, short and small, SPEAKS GOOD ENGLISH AND CAN READ AND WRITE . . . has a smooth Face, a sly Look, TOOK WITH A VIOLIN, AND CAN PLAY WELL THEREON." This ad is a reminder that in colonial times slavery was not only practiced in the South. But most of all, it was an attempt to keep Cato from gaining his freedom.

Cato's achievements may have been rare, but learning to play a European instrument was not entirely unusual. Advertisements in the *Virginia Gazette* between 1736 and 1780 carried more than sixty references to black musicians, of whom three-quarters were said to be violin players.

The presence of African-American fiddlers shows acculturation going on, with blacks mastering "white" instruments. It also points to a vocation taking shape: that of the black dance musician. In the North, music for formal dances and for dancing schools was routinely supplied by black musicians. In the South, meanwhile, blacks performed for dancing at their masters' balls, assemblies, and special "Entertainments." Many of these players were slaves, which limited their ability to collect payment. But some were free and may be considered tradesmen of sorts. Already in the eighteenth century, then, black dance musicians were meeting a need in white society. And they must have been skilled, for only their success could explain why an institution as unbending as slavery would allow blacks the role of entertainer.

REGIONAL DIFFERENCES IN BLACK MUSIC MAKING

The Northern United States

Black music making in North America varied with the conditions in which African Americans lived. The most dramatic difference existed between the North, where slavery was sparse, and the South, where it was entrenched. By 1786, Pennsylvania and all states north except New Jersey had either abolished slavery or decided how they would do so. And in the North, blacks formed only a small minority of the population. They worked alongside whites, though seldom accepted as social equals, and were able to enter some skilled trades.

In both North and South, religion loomed large in black-white relations. Whites disagreed about whether blacks should be Christianized, especially if they were slaves. Some believed that religious teaching would help reconcile slaves to their lot and make them more obedient, but others feared such instruction. Generally, however, Christian leaders favored the conversion of blacks. New York's Trinity Church (Anglican) was one place where evangelizing took hold early. In 1741, Trinity's organist, Johann Gottlob Klemm, instructed forty-three Negroes in psalmody. And two years later, the church's minister wrote that when the clerk rose to lead the congregation in psalm singing, "I can scarce express the satisfaction I have in seeing 200 Negroes and White Persons with heart and voice glorifying their Maker."

But the idea of blacks and whites worshiping together was opposed in many other places. Where more than a handful of blacks joined a white religious society, they were often assigned segregated seating. Black

Christians in both North and South most typically worshiped in all-black congregations. The first of these were formed in the South in the 1770s and 1780s under Baptist preachers. In the North, blacks began in the 1790s and early 1800s to establish separate congregations, chiefly under Methodist sponsorship. The founding in 1816 of the African Methodist Episcopal (AME) Church in Philadelphia established a clear racial division in American Protestantism that persists today.

In 1801, the Reverend Richard Allen, one of the AME Church's founders, published a hymnal for Bethel Church in Philadelphia, the first such book assembled by a black author for a black congregation. It followed the format of metrical psalters like the *Bay Psalm Book*: pocket-sized, devoted to multistanza poetry, and without music. Among the more than five dozen items Allen chose for his hymnal are familiar favorites by the British hymn writer Isaac Watts and others. But the hymnal also includes more than twenty texts that cannot be traced to any previous author, suggesting that Allen wrote some or all of them himself.

A few of these texts are printed with refrains: repeated two-line sections, inserted at the end of each stanza, whose text may or may not relate to the subject of the hymn. Being shorter than the stanzas, and normally sung to the same words and music each time they appear, refrains can be learned quickly by ear; they are sometimes sung even by those who do not sing the stanzas. The alternating of a changing four-line stanza with an unchanging two-line response suggests some kind of interaction.

In 1801, the Reverend Richard Allen (1760–1831), an ex-slave, compiled for Bethel Church in Philadelphia *A Collection of Spiritual Songs and Hymns*, the first such book prepared for a black congregation in America.

Perhaps a group might respond to a leader; or one group, bookless and singing refrains only, might respond to another group equipped with books and singing both stanzas and refrains. In any case, Allen's hymnal put into writing the oral practice of responsorial hymn singing.

Holiday celebrations gave African Americans another chance to make music of their own. In some colonies, blacks were given a break from their work schedules during local spring elections, and they staged secular festivals paralleling those of white society. A white observer in Newport, Rhode Island, caught the spirit and sound of the music at an Election Day gathering there in 1756, noting its difference from white musical customs: "Every voice in its highest key, in all the various languages of Africa, mixed with broken and ludicrous English, filled the air, accompanied with the music of the fiddle, tambourine, banjo and drum."

Another holiday for Northern blacks was known as the "Pinkster Celebration," held at Pentecost, seven Sundays after Easter. Pinkster festivities could fill several days. An account of one such celebration in Albany, New York, during the 1770s recalls a dance that lasted from noon until midnight or later. The dancers' movements gradually grew more "rapid and furious," fueled in part by their quaffing of "stimulating potions" that seemed to strengthen "all their nerves and muscular powers" and to make perspiration flow "in frequent streams, from brow to heel," before they dropped out when "extreme fatigue or weariness" set in. The music underlying this riot of physical stamina came from a drum and the drummer's "ever wild, though euphonic cry of *Hi-a-bomba, bomba, bomba*, in full harmony with the thumping sounds," which was "readily taken up and as oft repeated by the female portion of the spectators."

The Reverend Richard Allen's hymns, the Newport Election Day, and the Albany Pinkster festivities are all examples of antiphonal, responsorial, or call-and-response interaction, a trait that shows African influence. Indeed, the refrains in some of Allen's hymns create a responsorial structure that suggests how tenacious the African legacy could be. Even in the North, where the black presence was small, blacks and whites in close contact, and Protestant church singing established as a Euroamerican practice, the African custom of responsorial singing survived.

The Election Day festival of 1756 illustrates a second African trait: what has been called the "heterogeneous sound ideal," a preference for piling up different-sounding lines rather than blending lines into one homogenous sound. In the Newport celebration, singing was accompanied by fiddle, tambourine, banjo, and drum, a combination poorly suited to blending. The Newport example, with "every voice in its highest key," singing a babel of African languages mixed with English and accompanied by instruments, also illustrates a third African trait: the tendency to pack musical events as densely as possible into a relatively short time, thus filling all available musical space.

The Albany Pinkster dance exhibits similar African earmarks. First, it makes bodily motion integral to musical performance: drumming and singing are tied so closely to the dancing they accompany that it is hard to say where music stops and physical motion begins. A second trait lies in the use of the voice. The drummer's repeated cry of *Hi-a-bomba, bomba, bomba*, creating "a full harmony" with the drum, suggests an approach to singing that is more rhythmic than melodic. Moreover, the women who are not dancing repeat this cry, feeding the rhythmic impulse further and illustrating the notion that African musicians tend to approach singing as well as instrumental playing in a percussive manner. Finally, the account illustrates a responsorial interaction among at least three different sound sources: the drumbeat, the drummer's vocal cries, and the vocalizing of the nondancing women.

Greater Virginia

In the mid-1700s, the region known as Greater Virginia, which included parts of today's Maryland and North Carolina, was home to some 400,000 people, of whom 35 to 40 percent were black. Except for the port of Baltimore, Greater Virginia lacked the cities that shaped the economy in the North; it was overwhelmingly rural, with most of the population gathered around the rivers that connected them to the shipping of tobacco, the chief export crop. Though whites in the region imposed one social identity upon blacks, blacks' contact with each other was strong enough to sustain a separate society of their own.

In the 1730s and 40s, a series of religious revivals known as the Great Awakening swept the colonies from Maine to Georgia, making both clergy and slaveowners more inclined to consider slaves as potential Christians. By the 1750s, the Reverend Samuel Davies, a Presbyterian minister in Hanover, Virginia, could point to success in his efforts to bring slaves into the Christian fold. "Ethiopia has also stretched forth her Hands unto God," Davies rejoiced in 1751, going on to explain that congregational singing was helping to attract slaves to his ministry. "The Negroes," he wrote, "above all the Human Species that I ever knew, have an Ear for Musick, and a kind of extatic Delight in Psalmody." A few years later, Davies again praised the singing of black members of his congregation, who, "breaking

This painting shows plantation slaves observing a holiday for dancing, accompanied by banjo and percussion. The painter and date of the picture, which was found in South Carolina, are unknown.

out in a torrent of sacred harmony," could provide a sound powerful enough "to bear away the whole congregation to heaven."

The spread of the Christian faith, however, seems to have done little to restrain the black population's holiday celebrations. In 1774, a Princeton College graduate working as a tutor on a rural Westmoreland County estate contrasted the way Sundays were observed in New Jersey and Virginia. A Sabbath in Virginia did not seem to him to "wear the same Dress as our Sundays to the Northward," which were days of religious solemnity. "Generally here by five o-Clock on Saturday every Face (especially the Negroes) looks festive & cheerful—All the lower class of People, & the Servants, & the Slaves, consider it as a Day of Pleasure & amusement & spend it in such Diversions as they severally choose." The slaves might embrace those diversions wholeheartedly on any day of the week. A visitor to Virginia in 1784 expressed amazement that after a full day of work, a slave might walk several miles to take part in a dance where "he performs with astonishing ability, and the most vigorous exertions, keeping time and cadence, most exactly, with the music . . . until he exhausts himself, and scarcely has time, or strength, to return home before the hour he is called forth to toil the next morning." Perhaps slaves were willing to walk miles to attend dances because dancing for them was both recreational and spiritual—a chance to *perform* their sense of relatedness to community, gods, and ancestors.

South Carolina

Blacks heavily outnumbered whites in South Carolina, which more than any other colony resembled the plantation culture of the West Indies. Outside the capital, Charleston, blacks lived and worked in large isolated groups, many of them on rice plantations. Black-white interaction in South Carolina was limited, but this did not bring slaves any great amount of freedom—especially after the Stono Rebellion of 1739, in which a black revolt left more than twenty whites and even more slaves dead. A report tells how the rebels emboldened themselves with music and dancing, using the drum to recruit other slaves to their cause. They came close to overthrowing their masters, who responded with greater repression. In earlier days, a few slaves had enjoyed the freedom to move from place to place, to earn money, raise food, and learn to read. But now controls were tightened. In hopes of reducing the disproportion of blacks over whites in South Carolina, the importing of new slaves was drastically cut.

Colonial efforts to Christianize South Carolina's slaves reached very few. In 1779, an observer called Negro slaves in South Carolina and Georgia "great strangers to Christianity, and as much under the influence of Pagan darkness, idolatry, and superstition, as they were at their first arrival from Africa." An account written in 1805 by John Pierpont, grandfather of the eminent New York banker J. P. Morgan, reports that on one local plantation different groups of slaves made different kinds of music, depending on the closeness of their ties to Africa.

Louisiana

Louisiana never belonged to the British Empire. Settled first by the French, the territory was controlled by Spain from 1762 to 1800, when it was returned to France, then sold to the United States in 1803 as part of the Louisiana Purchase. With its location and varied political history, Louisiana and its chief city, New Orleans, acquired an ambiance unique in North America. Most of Louisiana's blacks were slaves, but some were not. And the presence of free blacks made legal and social distinctions less sharp and increased the possibilities for a merging of cultures. By

1800, blacks and mulattos in what would become one of America's chief musical centers were found at most levels of society, mixing freely with Europeans, Indians, and mestizos. This multiracial society, while still layered, was less rigidly stratified than anywhere else on the continent.

During the nineteenth century, the relative openness of New Orleans society allowed musicians of mixed blood to participate in white-organized musical activities, including balls and opera performances. Yet as early as the 1750s, blacks were gathering and dancing in public, apparently as a Sunday custom. A witness to these Sabbath revels in 1799 noted the "vast numbers of negro slaves, men, women, and children, assembled together on the levee, drumming, fifing, and dancing, in large rings." And in 1804, another visitor, marveling that stores were open on Sunday mornings, wrote of the black population: "They assemble in great masses on the levee on Sundays, and make themselves glad with song, dance and merriment."

New Orleans was not the only place in North America where blacks carried on such festivities, but nowhere else did the open expression of Africanness become a regular public custom. An 1817 statute limited black dancing to Sundays before sundown, and in Congo Square only, a spacious common known today as Beauregard Square. Two years later, a detailed report of a gathering there was written by architect Benjamin Latrobe, who designed the U.S. Capitol building in Washington, D.C. Working in New Orleans in 1819, Latrobe one Sunday afternoon in February heard "a most extraordinary noise," which sounded to him like "horses trampling on a wooden floor." When he investigated, it turned out to be an assembly of blacks, five or six hundred strong. They had formed themselves into rings, "the largest not 10 feet in diameter." In one ring, two women danced "a miserably dull & slow figure, hardly moving their feet or bodies." Two drums and a stringed instrument provided the music, and there was also singing, which Latrobe recognized as a form of call and response: "The women squalled out a burthen [refrain] to the playing at intervals, consisting of two notes," he wrote, "as the negroes, working in our cities, respond to the song of their leader."

Latrobe found nothing beautiful in the performance. "I have never seen anything more brutally savage," he wrote, nor "at the same time [more] dull & stupid." To his ear, the men's singing was "uncouth," the women's nothing more than a "detestable burthen . . . screamed . . . on one single note." Perhaps it was the strangeness of the whole affair that moved Latrobe to give so full an account, for he guessed that the singing "was in some African language," commenting that "such amusements of Sunday have, it seems, perpetuated here those of Africa among its inhabitants."

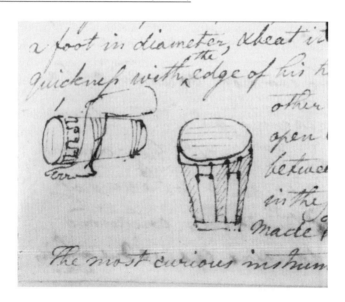

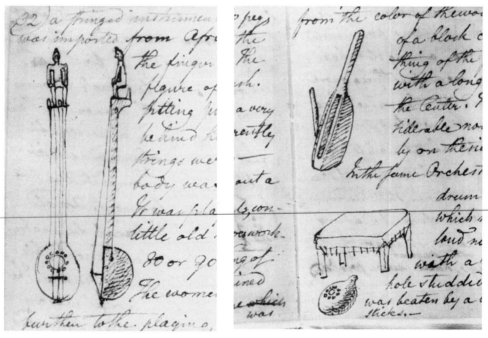

Benjamin Latrobe included sketches of the African instruments he saw played in New Orleans's Congo Square in his journal entry for February 21, 1819.

THE BLACK PRESENCE IN EVANGELICAL CAMP-MEETINGS

The identity of black Americans as a group separate from white Americans was taken for granted until well into the twentieth century. Racial prejudice fed by incomprehension, distrust, and fear defined blacks, socially and legally, as a category of people with no chance of admission into white society. One result was that social activities in which whites and blacks engaged as partners were few and far between. As settlement pushed westward, however, a religious institution took shape that proved more hospitable than most white forums to blacks and their habits of expression: the camp meeting.

The movement from which the camp meeting sprang was the Second Awakening, successor to the Great Awakening of the 1730s and 40s: a surge of religious renewal between the 1780s and 1830 that spread Christianity to the frontier and the back country. Held in the countryside, camp meetings were gatherings at which frontier worshipers camped out for several days of prayer and singing, in an atmosphere of spiritual renewal. Crowds could be large, sometimes numbering in the thousands, and people might travel long distances to attend.

Although camp meetings were usually organized by Methodist and Baptist preachers who were ready to seek out "the plain folk" wherever they happened to live, the meetings were interdenominational and never part of any church's official program of worship. They caught on quickly: a leading Methodist of the day calculated that as many as four hundred camp meetings were held in 1811 alone.

The camp meeting set religion above race and welcomed black participants. Even in slave states, blacks took part, though generally on their own "shouting-ground," where religious meetings were held after the sermon. But while the camp meeting's egalitarianism is generally applauded today, it drew sharp criticism in its own time. In 1819, a tract appeared called *Methodist Error*, written by the "Wesleyan Methodist" John F. Watson, denouncing camp meeting hymns. The music, he writes, consisted of "merry airs, adapted from old songs, to hymns of our composing," and the religious enthusiasm these hymns kindled was no excuse for their shortcomings. "Often miserable as poetry," they were equally "senseless as matter." As for the merry airs, they were "most frequently composed and first sung by the illiterate blacks of the society," proof of their worthlessness.

Watson goes on to note that camp-meeting hymns were often sung "two or three at a time in succession," suggesting that many shared the same mood. Jumping directly from one hymn to another may have reflected the worshipers' wish to maintain momentum, perhaps to encourage rhythmic movement. That possibility is borne out by Watson's shock at something else he had witnessed: some worshipers had actually danced the hymns. "In the blacks' quarter," he writes, "the coloured people get together, and sing for hours together, short scraps of disjointed affirmations, pledges, or prayers, lengthened out with long repetition choruses. These are all sung in the merry chorus-manner of the southern harvest field, or husking-frolic method, of the slave blacks." And when black worshipers sang, bodies moved. "With every word so sung," Watson continues, "they have a sinking of one or [the] other leg of the body alternately; producing an audible sound of the feet at every step, and as manifest as the steps of actual negro dancing in Virginia, &c." At this point, Watson's irritation boils over. Who, he exclaims, "can countenance or tolerate such gross perversions of true religion!"

The traits Watson singles out for attack are African: the reliance on oral transmission, the physical movement, and the responsorial repetitions, choruses, and "short scraps" of tunes. His critique indicates that the camp meeting, rather than establishing a particular kind of hymnody and holding black worshipers to it, allowed them freedom to sing as they saw fit.

What galled Watson most was not the behavior of blacks at camp meetings but their influence. "The example has already visibly affected the religious manners of some whites," he complains. "I have known in some camp meetings, from 50 to 60 people crowd into one tent, after the public devotions had closed, and there continue the whole night, singing tune after tune, (though with occasional episodes of prayer) scarce one of which were in our hymn books." How could so many white worshipers sing hymns all night without hymnbooks? Apparently by following the example of blacks, who did not depend on books in the first place. The hymns they sang relied on short, simple statements of music and text, with plenty of repetition, including call and response. The "endless" stream of hymnody sung by these transported souls seems to have come not from memorizing but from a kind of oral composition they had learned from blacks, using familiar formulas of tune and word.

Watson's criticisms indicate that the camp meeting helped white Protestants learn something that black Protestants' African heritage was always asserting: that the key to sacred expression lay in awakening the proper spirit. The story of the camp-meeting spiritual reflects two complementary processes from which much of the distinctive quality of American music has flowed: blacks infusing Euroamerican practices with African influence, and whites drawing on black adaptations to vitalize their own music making.

Correcting "the Harshness of Our Singing"

NEW ENGLAND PSALMODY REFORMED

AFTER WINNING INDEPENDENCE FROM ENGLAND, AMERICANS RE-alized that the unique circumstances of their lives offered fresh cultural possibilities, including musical ones. The idea of American musical distinctiveness first came to light in the field of New England sacred music. And the earliest musician to make an issue of it was Connecticut-born psalmodist Andrew Law.

Law's career revolved around three innovations, all related to nationality. First, when he began his work as a compiler, he included compositions by American psalmodists in a repertory that until then had been mostly European. Second, after experiencing a conversion in taste, he advanced the idea that European sacred music was superior to American. And third, Law struggled later in life to popularize the music he favored by simplifying musical notation. All three of these innovations took hold during Law's lifetime: the music of American composers did win wide circulation; a taste for European psalmody was embraced by many Americans; and a new system of notation akin to Law's did gain wide success. Law's changing view of nationality provides a window on a key period of American musical development.

Though a devout Calvinist and ordained minister, Law never followed a clergyman's career. Instead, not long after graduating from Rhode Island College (now Brown University) in 1775, he took up the trade of singing master and followed it for nearly half a century, spending much of his life as an itinerant. His search for schools took him up and down the Eastern Seaboard, from Vermont to South Carolina, and his work as a tunebook compiler spread his reputation further. The image of Law that endures is that of a religious entrepreneur whose zealous ambition centered on sacred music and the singing school. To judge from Law's letters, the main disappointment of his career was that he failed to profit financially from changes that he helped to introduce.

In 1778, despite wartime unrest, inflation, and the scarcity of paper, the twenty-nine-year-old Law and his brother William set up a tunebook-printing business in Cheshire, Connecticut. From then until he died in 1821, his career in psalmody followed two complementary tracks: the singing schools he taught and the tunebooks he compiled and published. The first tunebook Law compiled, *Select Harmony* (1779), reveals him as a champion of American composers, at a time when the notion that Americans could compose music at all was still new. In the summer of 1778, he announced a subscription for a new "Collection of Psalm-Tunes and Anthems, from the most celebrated authors in Great Britain and America." By placing the music of Oliver Brownson, Amos Bull, Abraham Wood, and other unknown Americans side by side with that of William Billings and British psalmodists, Law implied that the Americans and the British were creative peers, giving a boost to fellow New Englanders just starting to try their hand at composition.

In 1794, Law published under the general title *The Art of Singing* a new repertory of sacred music that revealed his conversion in musical taste. "A considerable part of American composition is in reality faulty," Law writes. "European compositions aim at variety and energy by guarding against the reiterated use of the perfect chords"—presumably open fifths and octaves. American composers, on the other hand, dwelled on such chords until their tunes were "all sweet, languid and lifeless," chiefly because the singing was so deficient that "perfect chords" were the only ones that could be sung in tune. *The Musical Primer* announced a program of reform: "The harshness of our singing must be corrected. Our voices must be filed. Every tone must be rendered smooth, persuasive and melting: and when a number of voices are joined together they must all . . . be in the most perfect tune."

Once Law declared himself against American composition, he maintained that stance for the rest of his life, systematically replacing American music in his tunebooks with British. Having endorsed an Old World approach to composition, Law moved the melody line in his tunebooks from the tenor to the treble (soprano) voice, where it could be heard more easily. After Law died, he was given credit in some circles for having championed the cause of "correct taste" in sacred singing. Yet from the mid-1790s on, his tunebooks lost ground in the marketplace to others that blended American and European favorites, as he himself had been the first to do. Not until the early 1800s did his Europeanized ideal of taste begin to take hold in New England psalmody.

Shortly after the turn of the century, Law made the most radical change of his career. He abandoned standard musical notation, copyrighted his own system, and in 1803 began to publish in shape notes—a practice he continued for the rest of his life. But by the time Law entered the marketplace with his shape notation, a tunebook called *The Easy Instructor*, compiled by William Little and William Smith and published in Philadelphia, had already been circulating for two years. Setting its own shape notes on a staff, in contrast to Law's staffless version, *The Easy Instructor* proved highly successful in regions west and south of New England, remaining in print well into the 1820s. Again, Andrew Law was unable to capitalize on an idea that, in other hands, proved both popular and profitable.

The anonymous British psalm tune MEAR, as printed in shape notes in William Little and William Smith, *The Easy Instructor* (Philadelphia, [1801]). The shapes represent singing syllables *fa*, *sol*, *la*, and *mi*.

OLD HUNDRED as printed in shape notes in Andrew Law, *The Musical Primer*, 4th ed. (Philadelphia, 1803). Law's staffless notation won few customers and is not known to have been used by other compilers.

Solmization

Since the Middle Ages, the technique of solmization, which assigns a particular syllable to each pitch in a scale, has been used to teach singers how to sing from notation. In modern form, a major scale is sung on seven syllables: *do, re, mi, fa, sol, la, ti,* [*do*].

do   re   mi   fa   sol   la   ti   do

In early America, singing masters taught note reading according to a four-syllable system in which a major scale was sung *fa, sol, la, fa, sol, la, mi,* [*fa*].

fa   sol   la   fa   sol   la   mi   fa

Once singers knew their major and minor scales, could find the keynote *fa* and the leading tone *mi* on the page, and had the intervals between syllables ingrained in their voices and memories, they were ready to read music.

Shape notes assigned a different-shaped notehead to each of the four singing syllables.

fa   sol   la   fa   sol   la   mi   fa

Singers who could coordinate shapes with syllables were spared having to figure out which note to sing.

"ANCIENT MUSIC" AND REFORM

Musical reform, which promoted a "correct" Europeanized taste over the music that had gained currency in public worship—much of it American composed—was centered in New England. The clearest account of reform was written in the 1850s by a participant, Nathaniel D. Gould. According to Gould, in the "dark age" ushered in around 1770 by Billings, people eager to hone musical skills for their own sake had wrested the control of singing away from the clergy and the people. By 1800, public worship was plagued by nonsinging congregations, outspoken choir members, and a sprightliness in choral singing that encouraged competitiveness and pride. In that state of crisis, true Christians realized that the time had come to regulate and desecularize the singing in worship services. Beginning in mid-decade in Massachusetts, clergymen and other community leaders joined forces with "prominent singers" to advocate "ancient music," which they found ideal for kindling a genuine religious spirit among congregation members.

By ancient music, Gould meant European tunes composed decades, even centuries, earlier and newer tunes whose simple style resembled that of the older favorites. Whereas American-composed psalmody was a recent creation, ancient music had already stood the test of time. Whereas self-taught locals had composed the newer psalmody, ancient music was the work of Europeans with Old World training. Whereas some New England psalmody exhibited an infectious rhythmic snap, ancient music moved with a gravity better suited to the decorum of public worship. And whereas New England psalmody often revealed its composers' ignorance of proper harmony, ancient music embodied true musical science at work.

OLD HUNDRED was the quintessential piece of ancient music. "I have been informed," Andrew Law wrote in an essay, "that Handel said, he would give all his oratorios, if he might be the author of OLD HUNDRED." Although Handel is not known to have said any such thing, Law's statement carries a figurative truth. The pious sentiments of Handel's oratorios required many skilled musicians for their expression, but such sentiments lay open to anyone who sang or listened to OLD HUNDRED.

As of 1805, then, ancient music, embodied in OLD HUNDRED and other tunes like it, gave reformers a rallying point. New Englanders of that era often formed associations devoted to certain causes. Debating societies, missionary societies, professional societies, and societies for moral improvement flourished throughout the region. So did sacred music societies—the Essex Musical Association in Salem and the Middlesex Musical Society, for example—and these groups helped reformers win more public attention and support than an individual like Andrew Law could ever hope to match.

Gould names two tunebooks as spearheads of reform: *The Salem Collection of Classical Sacred Musick* (Salem, 1805) and *The Middlesex Collection of Church Musick; or, Ancient Psalmody Revived* (Boston, 1807). Between them, they contain a total of 185 compositions, and all but 3 are European in origin; in fact, almost the whole repertory harks back to the 1770s or earlier. And most of the music is harmonized in block chords, as are OLD HUNDRED and the "common tunes" of the early Protestant Reformation.

In contrast to most earlier American tunebooks, which were published under a compiler's name and whose introductions address readers on a more-or-less personal basis, *The Middlesex Collection* was compiled by the anonymous "Middlesex Musical Society," and *The Salem Collection*'s contents chosen by a committee "whose names, were we at liberty to mention them, would add authority to the work." *The Salem Collection* apologizes for the current "general and most deplorable corruption of taste in our church musick," and *The Middlesex Collection* takes a similar approach. "The tunes here introduced," its preface intones, "are recommended by their antiquity, and more by their intrinsic excellence . . . for the spirit and flavor of old wine are always depressed by the commixture of new." Claiming to represent right-thinking Christians through the ages, the compilers imply that the best of all possible sacred repertories had already been in existence for generations.

The forces marshaled by reformers, including the clergy, influential laymen, and societies devoted to the cause, proved successful. Sacred tunebooks published in the Northeast after 1805 show a quick drop-off in American musical content and a corresponding rise in European. Addressing the public as an unnamed "we" and making pronouncements that brooked no argument, ancient music advocates won their purpose by launching a reform process in the name of religion.

The reformers' approach raises a basic question: To what audience is sacred music addressed? The main goal of Christian sacred music until the mid-1700s was to praise God, and praise could be delivered in many forms. In a Handel oratorio, God is praised through the composer's artifice and the performers' skill. At the other end of the spectrum is the congregational hymn, which requires no great skill to perform but is deemed worthy because of the spirit in which it is sung. Such a spirit, whether confessing sin or making "a joyful noise unto the Lord," was certainly alive among New England choirs and singing schools, for all the criticisms that reformers leveled at them. William Billings's paraphrase of Psalm 148, which urges all creatures to find their own way of praising God, is set to music calculated to push singers and listeners into a mood of wholehearted involvement (see Listening Guide 10).

In Handel's oratorios, congregational hymns, and Billings's anthems, the singing is directed "out there," toward the ear of God. The reform of early nineteenth-century New England psalmody partakes of a different spirit—one centered not on praise but on edification. Rather than God, its main recipients were the people who worshiped God. It is this fact, more than nationality, that beginning in the early nineteenth century divided Protestant music making into two distinct branches.

LISTENING GUIDE 10

Thanksgiving Anthem (Billings)

Billings's Thanksgiving anthem "O Praise the Lord of Heaven," whose text is based on Psalm 148, appeared in a sacred tune-book he published in 1794. The work, set for four-part chorus, falls into six sections, the last one repeated. Billings begins in a stately 3/4 time, with dialogue among the voice parts. The second section starts with the basses singing "Praise him, sun and moon and blazing comets" and ends with an injunction to "admire, adore." Section three, faster than anything heard so far, is based on four lines of poetry: "Ye dragons whose contagious breath / People the dark abodes of death, / Change your dire hissings into heavenly songs, / And praise your maker with your forkéd tongues." Here Billings repeats the last two words often, enlivening "forkéd" with melismas (many notes on one syllable), and then vaulting out of the dragons' den by bringing back the title line sung to the opening music. Section four relaxes the intensity, starting a new list of praising agents with "Fire, hail, and snow," chiefly in quarter-note motion. Section five ("Join creation") quickens the syllables' delivery to eighth-note motion. And Section six offers an ecstatic musical outpouring on the word "Hallelujah." Perhaps no composition of Billings demonstrates better his gift for varying momentum to create musical excitement.

Sections 4–6

Fire, hail and snow, wind
   and storms,
Beasts & cattle, creeping
   insects, flying fowl,
Kings & princes, men &
   angels,
Praise the Lord.
Jew & gentile, male &
   female, bond & free,
Earth & heaven, land &
   water,
Praise the Lord.

Young men & maids,
   old men & babes,
Praise the Lord.
Join creation, preservation,
And redemption join in one;
No exemption, nor
   dissention,
One invention, and intention,
Reigns through the whole,
To praise the Lord.
Hallelujah.
Praise the Lord.

EDIFICATION AND PRAISE

Edification means intellectual, moral, or spiritual improvement. And sacred music that was considered a way of "improving" those who used it grew out of a sensibility different from any discussed so far in this chronicle. Praise, based on faith, needed no explanation; edification, based on reason, thrived on explanation, as shown by the rhetoric of the reformers, who always had a rationale to support their program. Praise tended to accept current practice; edification was more inclined to argue for change, appealing to outside authorities whose opinions were presumed superior.

Early in the 1800s, a split opened up in Protestant sacred music that was to have lasting reverberations in America. Those who made edification their ideal believed that worship was a solemn affair deserving its own kind of music, separate from secular music in sound, idiom, and style of performance. But Christians who held to praise as an ideal were more inclined to understand sacred expression, music included, as an extension of everyday life than something separate from it. The God they worshiped was more attuned to what was in the hearts of His worshipers than to the piety of their manner or the particular sounds with which they praised Him.

As long as Protestant sacred music was ruled by an attitude of praise, questions of moral and spiritual improvement remained secondary. The New England sacred music reform, as a move away from praise toward edification, shifted the focus toward human authorities and away from God. Since the early 1800s, these two attitudes have persisted. Traditions centered on praise, from shape-note hymnody to African-American spirituals and gospel, have resisted the notion that a split between the two was possible, let alone desirable. But in the early 1800s, the idea that edification could be effectively pursued through a musical style became a driving force in American sacred music. Its appeal in the churches and meeting houses of the urban Northeast matched the vigor with which evangelical revivalism's music of praise reached out to "plain folk."

PART TWO

The
Nineteenth
Century

8

Edification and Economics

THE CAREER OF LOWELL MASON

IN *DEMOCRACY IN AMERICA* (1835), A CLASSIC ANALYSIS OF AMERI-
can institutions and "habits of the heart," French writer Alexis de Tocqueville noted a key difference between France and the United States. "In
France I had seen the spirits of religion and of freedom almost always
marching in opposite directions," but in America, "I found them intimately linked together in joint reign over the same land." Although religion "never intervenes directly in the government of American society,"
he observed, it should nevertheless "be considered as the first of their political institutions."

Early in the 1820s, a figure appeared on the musical scene whose work
illustrates Tocqueville's claim. Lowell Mason is remembered as the "father" of public school music teaching and also as a sacred music reformer
and composer of hymn tunes. While both are true, Mason's grasp of how
sacred and secular music were linked proved an even greater contribution.

In the early 1800s, group singing was widely accepted as a Protestant
way to praise God and edify congregation members. But group singing
of secular music was rare. It was here that Mason saw new possibilities.
Having begun his career as a psalmodist in the 1820s, he perceived that
secular singing, like psalmody, could also be organized around instruction and tunebooks. Without dropping his work in psalmody, Mason began in the 1830s to teach secular music. From then on, he worked to make
organized musical participation, sacred *and* secular, available to Americans on as wide a scale as possible.

Mason approached secular singing with a purpose similar to that of
psalmody: to improve the singers intellectually, morally, and spiritually.
To his way of thinking, the improvement that edification offered could

be a force for freedom; it could break the bonds of ignorance, just as Christian conversion freed sinners from the bonds of ungodliness.

The free institution of public schooling into which Mason moved was itself marinated in the religious spirit. And given that fact, his involvement in both church and public school music seemed natural and complementary. When Mason enlarged his sphere of activity beyond sacred music, he vastly increased his range of potential customers. He also became rich. As the first American musician to recognize common ground between religion and free institutions, Mason discovered that edification could be big business.

 LOWELL MASON, PSALMODIST

Born in Medfield, Massachusetts, in 1792, Mason attended singing school as a youngster, and he also learned to play a variety of instruments, including the organ. In 1812, he left home and spent the next fifteen years in Savannah, Georgia, where he worked as a bank clerk, led church choirs, and studied harmony and composition with a German-born musician who had immigrated to Savannah. It was also in Georgia, while still in his late twenties, that Mason compiled his first tunebook.

Mason found most of the music for his book in other publications, especially a London collection called *Sacred Melodies, from Haydn, Mozart, and Beethoven*, which adapted melodies by European masters to English hymn texts. Seeking a publisher, he traveled north to Boston in 1821, for no printer in the South then owned a font of music type. In a letter to a friend, Mason described his manuscript as a book with enough hymn tunes for congregations to sing in public worship, plus some "longer pieces for Country Choirs." He took pride in the musical know-how his collection displayed. He had harmonized the melodies correctly, "and I trust every false relation, and every forbidden progression will be avoided." American reformers since Andrew Law had maintained that harmonic correctness separated the sheep from the goats: musicians who understood the principles behind consonance, dissonance, and proper chord progressions and musicians who did not—i.e., Yankee psalmodists. The word signaling the distinction was "science." Scientific music was based on theoretical knowledge rather than simply talent or practical experience.*

---

*Nineteenth-century American writers often described music grounded in theoretical expertise as "scientific." An earlier British source reflects that meaning: "The word science is usually applied to a whole body of regular or methodical observations or propositions . . . concerning any subject of speculation."

Mason chose the right sponsor for his tunebook when he approached the Boston Handel and Haydn Society. This group had been founded in 1815 to improve "the style of performing sacred music" and to promote more American performances of music by "Handel and Haydn and other eminent composers." Appearing in 1822, the *Boston Handel and Haydn Society Collection of Church Music* won resounding success. It lasted through nearly two dozen editions, and money from its sales helped support the society's activities for years to come. As for Mason, the financial arrangement he worked out—profits were split equally between compiler and publisher—proved to be the cornerstone on which he built his career. By 1839, when the last edition was published, Mason's share of the proceeds had reached approximately $12,000.

After arranging to publish his book, Mason returned to Savannah and his job in the bank, but in 1827 he moved to Boston as the leader of music in several churches and president of the Handel and Haydn Society. Thus, until he was thirty-five years old, Mason's professional life was centered outside the field of music. Through shrewd planning, talent, and energy, he entered his new calling at a level of income and prestige unprecedented for a newly professed American musician.

By 1832, just five years after assuming a key role in Boston's sacred music scene, Mason had embarked on the teaching of secular music. He also remained involved as a church musician, compiler, and hymn tune composer. Showing great talent in the last of these roles, he produced more than 1,100 tunes for congregations to sing. The line between Mason's compositions and his arrangements is not always clear, however, as shown by ANTIOCH, the tune to which Isaac Watts's text "Joy to the World" is now sung as a Christmas carol.

When Mason first published ANTIOCH in 1836, he attributed the tune to Handel, although the melody has never been found in this form in Handel's compositions. Those who know Handel's *Messiah*, however, will hear echoes of it in the hymn tune. The tune begins with a four-note motive, descending stepwise (Joy to the World), that shares both melody and text declamation with the *Messiah* chorus "Lift up your heads." Later in ANTIOCH, the melody sung to the words "And heav'n and nature sing" is close to the one played by violins at the start of *Messiah*'s opening tenor recitative, "Comfort ye, my people." From these fragments, Mason composed a new tune for Watts's text. Mason's tune starts high, with a burst of energy underlining the text's rapturous mood. His closing is also vivid. Its repetition of the last line (And heav'n and nature sing) suggests an image of the whole world rejoicing at the birth of Jesus. In fact, with its word repetition, the dividing of text between upper and lower voices, and the tom-tom effect of the repeated notes, Mason's setting of the last line recalls the fuging tune, a form long scorned by New England reformers.

During the 1830s, Mason and his fellow reformer Thomas Hastings took the lead in creating a style of hymnody that preserved some traits of the preceding generation's ancient music, while also appealing to the taste of worshipers in their own day. In a letter of 1837, Hastings wrote with satisfaction: "Europe has no style *strictly devotional* that compares at all with what we are cultivating in this country." OLIVET (1831), a setting of Ray Palmer's text "My Faith Looks Up to Thee," embodies that devotional style.

LISTENING GUIDE 11

Olivet (Mason)

Among the voice parts, only the soprano melody has a clear profile. The harmony follows European scientific principles at their simplest, emphasizing tonic and dominant chords. As with ancient music, Mason's setting poses no competition for the text and invites congregational singing.

Yet the rhythm and structure of OLIVET are not those of ancient music. Instead of a succession of half or quarter notes, OLIVET features a rhythmic motive in five of its seven poetic lines. And the rhythmic pattern and harmony are coordinated to serve a highly subjective set of words. In the second half of Palmer's text, the worshiper pleads with God: "Now hear me when I pray. / Take all my sins away. / Oh, let me from this day / Be wholly thine." The second line, sung to the same music as the first, seems more imploring, for the bass remains static, increasing the expectation that it will soon move. The third line is even more urgent, calling out on the highest note in the whole melody ("*Oh*, let me from this day"). By the time a cadence relieves the tension, eighteen consecutive G's have sounded in the bass, giving OLIVET a rising dramatic curve that supports the text's self-dramatizing demands.

LOWELL MASON, TEACHER OF CHILDREN

Like psalmodists before and after him, Mason taught singing schools in hopes of improving teenagers' and adults' musical taste through performance. Around the time that he moved to Boston, however, the tax-supported public school was just being established there. The rise of public schools placed new attention on children, whose potential for making music had never received much notice. Convinced that reform was the road to edification, Mason grasped the advantages of teaching young children to sing *before* their taste was formed, so they could learn to appreciate "good music" as they developed their singing skills.

Around 1830, Mason formed the earliest known singing school for children, which he taught free of charge. The class grew quickly: from six or eight at the start to five or six hundred a few years later. And after a year of teaching gratis, he began to collect fees and to devote more of his energies to secular teaching, especially of children.

In 1832, in collaboration with George James Webb, an immigrant musician from England, Mason helped to found the Boston Academy of Music, which taught both sacred and secular singing. Soon he was offering teachers' classes through the academy, and published his *Manual of the Boston Academy of Music* (Boston, 1834; eleven more printings by 1861) to serve them. The introduction of vocal music into public schools had been one of the academy's main objectives from the start, and in 1837, with three assistants, Mason approached the Boston school board and offered free singing classes in the city's public schools for the coming year. The

Lowell Mason (1792–1872)
not long after he moved from
Savannah, Georgia, to
Boston.

success of that volunteer experiment led the board to declare vocal music a regular school subject in 1838 and to hire Mason and his associates as teachers. He taught music in the Boston schools until 1855.

A key to Mason's economic success was that as he moved from one pioneering project to the next, he compiled, composed music for, and published new tunebooks. Through this entire period, for example, the *Boston Handel and Haydn Society Collection* came out in a new edition virtually every year. And to that sacred collection Mason steadily added others, each aimed at a different clientele.

By all accounts, Mason was an outstanding teacher with a commanding personality. But what gave him authority as a teacher of other teachers was a systematic method of instruction. In honing his teaching techniques, Mason learned much from William Woodbridge of Boston, who in the 1820s had studied the educational methods of the Swiss educator Johann Heinrich Pestalozzi. Pestalozzi's principles, adopted to music, appealed to Mason:

1. teach children to sing before they learn written notes;

2. make students active learners, by having them imitate sounds;

3. teach one subject at a time, such as rhythm, melody, or expression, and practice each separately;

4. help students master each step through practice before moving to the next; and

5. teach principles and theories *after* the practice.

According to George F. Root, one of Mason's associates in the Boston public school venture, Woodbridge made Mason a promise: "If you will call together a class, I will translate and write out each lesson for you . . . as you want it, and you can try the method; it will take about twenty-four evenings." Mason agreed, and the class was assembled. "Speaking to Dr. Mason once about this remarkable class," Root relates, "I asked him what those ladies and gentlemen paid for that course of twenty-four lessons. 'Oh, they arranged that among themselves,' he replied. 'They decided that five dollars apiece would be about right.' 'And how many were there in the class?' He smiled as he answered: 'About five hundred.' " Mason was sometimes attacked for being mercenary, overpaid, or both. Root denied that he was either: "I do not believe he ever made a plan to make money, unless when investing his surplus funds. In his musical work it was . . . a clear case . . . of seeking first what was right."

LOWELL MASON'S ECONOMICS

Mason seems to have been the first American musician who made a profit from musical work. How he managed that remarkable feat is worth our attention.

To earn a living in music, you have six basic choices: composing, performing, teaching, distributing (or publishing), writing about music, and manufacturing musical instruments and other goods. Mason's career was striking in that he took part in all of these occupations except the last. Yet while he was an active composer, performer (as church organist and choir leader), and writer on music, teaching music and distributing it were the keys to his financial success and his widespread influence.

Long before Mason came on the scene, teaching was the foremost American musical profession. But the notion that it could also be profitable seems to have been Mason's invention, at least on this side of the Atlantic. The key lay in the large scope of the projects he tackled, which were often too big to handle alone. From the time he began children's classes, Mason used assistants, and by 1844–45 he was teaching singing in six Boston public schools, while supervising ten assistants who taught in ten others. Mason's aides taught from his methods, used his books, and were paid by him from funds he collected from the school board. It seems likely that he took a cut of those funds for himself.

When Mason entered the book trade, profit was linked not to authorship but to financial risk. Hence, only publishers stood to reap substantial capital from successful books. Mason was never a publisher. Yet in view of the deal he worked out for the *Boston Handel and Haydn Society Collection*, he seems to have found ways to collect a larger share of the proceeds from his books than did other authors. Indications are that he earned substantial rewards as an author without taking a publisher's risk—good reason to avoid that role in an enterprise that already served his interests so well.

How wealthy did Mason become? In 1837, he was sufficiently well-off to manage a European trip of several months that took him to England, Germany, Switzerland, and France. An 1848 list of Boston taxpayers valued his estate at $41,000, making him by far the richest musician in town. And *The Rich Men of Massachusetts*, a book published in 1852, set his worth at $100,000. Mason's tunebooks were regularly updated, and many of them continued to sell for years—especially *Carmina Sacra: or Boston Collection of Church Music* (1841), which logged sales of 500,000 by 1858. Mason traveled to Europe for a longer stay at the end of 1851, remaining there until the spring of 1853. When he returned to the United States, it was not to Boston but to New York, where he set up new headquarters while he and his family settled in Orange, New Jersey. In 1869, three years before Mason's death, the plates of his copyrighted works alone were said to be worth over $100,000.

If Mason's publications produced a fountain of profit that flowed abundantly, he supplemented that income by taking part in conventions and so-called normal institutes for the training of music teachers. Moreover, after mid-century, the name Mason stood not only for Lowell but also for a substantial family enterprise. By the mid-1850s, Mason Brothers publishers, set up by sons Daniel Gregory and Lowell, was flourishing. And son Henry was a founding partner in Mason and Hamlin, a firm of reed-organ makers established in 1854, which later entered the piano-making business (1883). By looking to the musical needs of a wide range of Americans, Mason and his family prospered.

Lowell Mason's career traces a path from scarcity to abundance, achieved by targeting new customers while holding on to older ones: first singing schools and congregations, then children, adult secular singers, and finally teachers, courted as potential users of his books. In the 1830s, he broadened the framework of psalmody to include secular edification, and by the 1850s, Mason commanded a growing network of trade that he himself had partly invented.

MASON'S RIVALS, COLLABORATORS, AND LEGACY

Once Lowell Mason began exploring Americans' appetite for edification, other musicians recognized that a burgeoning market stood ready to be tapped. Thomas Hastings, an established psalmodist before Mason came on the scene, served the cause of scientific sacred music in the 1810s and 20s, through tunebooks and a treatise on musical taste; he also composed hymn tunes. In 1832, he moved to New York City, where he worked as a choir leader and tunebook compiler. Despite their sometime collaboration and complementary goals, Hastings in his later years considered Mason a rival and came to resent his success. A letter he wrote in 1848 sarcastically described Mason's idea of doing good as being in a position to "multiply and sell books."

While Hastings's promotion of scientific sacred music helped to carry forward that branch of Mason's musical endeavor, two younger men, both students of Mason's, rang fresh changes on his legacy of organized musical participation. William B. Bradbury, a native of Maine, enrolled in the Boston Academy of Music and sang in one of Mason's church choirs in the early 1830s. After teaching music in Maine and New Brunswick (1836–40), Bradbury took a post as organist and choir leader in a New York Baptist church. There he established classes for children similar to Mason's in Boston. His first tunebook, *The Young Choir* (1841), continued that emphasis, and it was followed by others aimed at Sunday schools. The sales of Bradbury's tunebooks reached more than two million copies. Among the popular hymn tunes he composed are WOODWORTH ("Just as I am") and CHINA ("Jesus loves me! this I know"), the latter published in 1862. Bradbury also showed something of Mason's knack for business. In 1854, he helped to found a piano-making firm in New York, and in 1861 his publishing company opened in the same city.

Another musician who carried Mason's message in new directions was George Frederick Root. Born in 1820 on a Massachusetts farm, Root grew up hoping to be a musician. Yet he never played organ or piano until, at age eighteen, he moved from his hometown of Sheffield to Boston, where he was ordered by his first mentor to begin teaching an even ranker beginner. And after a brief struggle to make his "clumsy fingers" negotiate a keyboard, he was playing the last hymn in church services, apparently so the regular organist could leave to play another service. Root later explained his quick acceptance into professional ranks as more a matter of opportunity than talent. Lowell Mason had "just commenced what proved to be a revolution in the 'plain song' of the church and of the people," he recalled. And Mason's "methods of teaching the elementary principles of music were so much better . . . than anything . . . seen [before] that those who were early in the field had very great advantage.

In Root's autobiography, Mason is his respected mentor, model, and eventually colleague. Root sang in the Boston Academy Chorus in 1838, and by 1840 he was teaching as one of Mason's assistants in the Boston public schools. The following year, Mason hired him as an instructor in one of his teacher-training conventions, and three years later Root moved from Boston to New York, where he led a church choir and taught from Mason's books in various schools, including "young ladies'" academies and the New York State Institution for the Blind. In 1853, Root enlisted Mason to be one of his collaborators at the first of several three-month normal institutes in New York City.

Root granted that a hierarchy of musical genres existed, with European masterworks at the top. Indeed, he was a lover of the classics, especially Handel's *Messiah*, Mendelssohn's *Elijah*, and the works of Beethoven and Wagner. But he was also a practical man who had a clear sense of his own abilities, and early in the 1850s he realized that he had a choice to make. "A majority of the music-loving world," he knew, enjoyed only an "elementary" state of musical knowledge. Would he be selling out if he turned his efforts toward serving the majority, rather than the art of music?

Mason convinced Root that he would not. In the first place, beginners' love for music was no less genuine than that of connoisseurs, and in the second, beginners' taste ought not to be despised. As Root came to understand, "all must pass" through the same hierarchy of musical genres, and very few reached the top. Moreover, the journey need not be one from bad to good music but from simple music to more complex and scientific compositions. Root later wrote: "I am simply one, who, from such resources as he finds within himself, makes music for the people, having always a particular need in view." Root's idea of himself as a musician of the people eventually led him to compose popular songs, something that Mason never attempted.

Edification, in whose name Root toiled throughout his career, was a dynamic ideal in the first half of the nineteenth century. Yet not everyone believed in it. In sacred music, edification's opposite number was "praise": the belief that the Almighty—*not* fellow human beings—was the proper recipient of sacred expression. It is therefore time to trace that impulse as it developed in different regions of the United States before the Civil War.

9

Singing Praises

SOUTHERN AND FRONTIER DEVOTIONAL MUSIC

IN 1933, GEORGE PULLEN JACKSON, A NEW ENGLAND–BORN PROFES-
sor of German at Vanderbilt University in Nashville, Tennessee, published
a book—*White Spirituals in the Southern Uplands*—about a remarkable tradition he had encountered among "plain folk" in the region. Gathering
on weekends, groups of Southerners staged all-day "singings" of sacred
music, and they brought their own books: oblong volumes of psalm and
hymn tunes, fuging tunes, and anthems set mostly for four-part chorus
with the melody in the tenor voice. They seated themselves according to
voice part—soprano (treble), alto (counter), tenor, and bass—in a rectan-
gle with an open space in the middle. Into that space stepped a succession of singers from the ranks, each leading the group in two or three
pieces. Typically, before adding the words to a piece, the group would
sing the notes on four syllables: *fa, sol, la,* and *mi.* Jackson, who found the
singers' note-reading ability astounding, learned that most of them had
attended singing schools. They tended to vocalize full blast, paying little
heed to voice quality and making no attempt to blend, but with no audience in sight, such things didn't seem to matter.

While the singing promoted by Lowell Mason and his disciples always
included a human audience, which it tried to please, singers in Jackson's
Southern tradition made music to glorify God; theirs was an attitude of
praise. According to their understanding, the power of the music and the
absorbed concentration they brought to their singing made it worthy of
the recipient, no matter *how* it sounded. Neither self-awareness nor an audience played any role, for when human judgments of musical quality
began to be made, Jackson warned, "at that moment, this singing of, for,
and by the people loses its chief characteristic."

Conversations at the singings he attended helped Jackson understand
what these gatherings meant to the singers. "Every time I go to one of

This photograph was taken on August 9, 1930, in Mineral Wells, Texas, at the convention of the Texas Inter-State Sacred Harp Musical Association.

these singings," one veteran confided, "I feel that I am attending a memorial to my mother"; when one of her favorite pieces was sung, it was "as if heaven itself hovers over the place." Pleasure in making music was also part of the attraction. But in the end, the spiritual environment seems to have left the deepest impression. Many of the people imagined heaven as "a place where they will meet again those beloved singers who have gone before, and sing again with them, endlessly."

SHAPE NOTES AND SOUTHERN HYMNODY

Jackson's research revealed these singings to be the tip of a historical iceberg. Rather than keeping pace with religious and musical change, people in the Upland South (which includes the Shenandoah Valley and parts of Maryland, Virginia, West Virginia, Kentucky, Tennessee, North and South Carolina, and Georgia, but not the coastal areas) had preserved a tradition dating back to New England in the 1700s.

With historical perspective, the Southern practice looks more like a transformation than a simple survival of the Northern practice. Psalmody was sung in New England during the latter 1700s by rural people, city dwellers, college students, and Calvinist churchgoers of all ages, singing in the name of art as well as praise. In the Southern uplands, however, psalmody took root among rural plain folk with stern views of religion and generally old-fashioned ways. And perhaps nothing marks the Southern branch of sacred singing as a countrified tradition more clearly than the musical notation in which it circulated.

Many Southern tunebooks used the four-shape notation that William Little and William Smith's *The Easy Instructor* had introduced in the early 1800s. Indeed, soon after shape notes were invented, musical reformers branded them a crutch needed only by ignorant or rural singers. (In 1835,

Thomas Hastings called them "dunce notes.") Reform took its stand with musical science, and where science was valued, shape notes came to symbolize the unscientific.

That attitude did not stop their spread, however, especially in regions where the reformers' message went unheard, such as New York State, New Jersey, Pennsylvania, and the Ohio River Valley. After 1810, as the frontier pushed westward, new shape-note collections began to appear in cities and towns farther and farther from Boston and Philadelphia. And while favorites from New England at first dominated the shape-note repertory, new tunes by local composers were also welcomed. The new pieces were seldom scientific. IDUMEA, written in the 1810s, shows one way that Southern psalmodists set their stamp on American sacred music.

Composed by Virginia-born Ananias Davisson, IDUMEA contains many open fifths, sounded on the strong downbeat of its three-beat measures. In contrast, the weak upbeats (third beat of each measure) are often sung to quarter notes that involve harmonic collisions. Such dissonances, Davisson writes in *Kentucky Harmony*, "answer a similar purpose to acid, which being tasted immediately before sweet, give the latter a more pleasing relish." In that spirit, IDUMEA alternates the two flavors.

IDUMEA was a new composition added by a local psalmodist in 1816 to the repertory as the New England tradition moved south. But the sacred repertory also grew through other means. MORALITY, from a Pennsylvania shape-note collection of 1813, sets religious words to a tune borrowed from a secular song; this composition is a "folk hymn," a term coined by Jackson to describe "songs with old folk-tunes which everybody could sing and with words that spoke from the heart of the devout in the language of the common man."

In 1805, Vermont composer and compiler Jeremiah Ingalls had brought out *The Christian Harmony*, a tunebook especially rich in folk hymns. One, called INNOCENT SOUNDS, set to words by English Methodist Charles Wesley, relates how the devil long ago took over the domain of good tunes, only because the religious faithful were too timid to claim them for their own. It was time to recapture the best tunes for God by replacing their secular words with sacred ones.

> Who, on the part of God, will rise,
> Innocent sounds recover;
> Fly on the prey, and seize the prize,
> Plunder the carnal lover:
> Strip him of every moving strain,
> Of every melting measure;
> Music in virtue's cause retain,
> Risk the holy pleasure.

The music to which Ingalls set Wesley's stanzas is as sprightly as the title of the borrowed melody suggests: *Merrily Danc'd the Quaker*.

Ingalls's book, however, was not a success. Perhaps it failed in the marketplace because it appeared in New England at the very time the ancient music reform was taking shape, a movement that could hardly have differed more in spirit from the democratic cast of folk hymnody. Yet if folk hymns were out of step with the North's prevailing religious mood, they were welcomed in the hinterlands to the south when in 1813 MORALITY appeared in *Wyeth's Repository, Part Second*. A "duetto" for melody and bass rather than a setting for four voice parts, MORALITY is a blend of the urban and the rural: the melodic style of a popular song, with harmonies that twice slip into successions of parallel fifths. The setting demonstrates that whatever a melody's origin, the way it is harmonized has much to do with determining its character. For we have already seen this melody in a parlor arrangement, sung to the words of *The Death Song of the Cherokee Indians*, or *Alknomook* (Chapter 1). In *Wyeth's Repository*, the text is a six-stanza religious ballad that meditates on the transcience of human affairs.

PLAIN FOLK, PRAISE, AND *THE SACRED HARP*

Three regions of shape-note singing emerged after 1810. The first stretched westward from Pennsylvania and the Shenandoah Valley to Cincinnati and St. Louis. The second, carried on by Germans, sometimes in their native language and sometimes in English, lay between the Shenandoah Valley and Philadelphia. The third was farther south, chiefly South Carolina and Georgia. Regional differences aside, however, the Southern shape-note tradition bore the stamp of revivalism, a religious impulse embodied in the Second Awakening (see Chapter 6) that touched many regions of the country in the early 1800s. In fact, the shape-note tradition reveals the power of revivalism, not only because it encouraged the kind of worshipful singing that qualifies as praise, but because it indicates a leveling of class consciousness. Revivalism opened the medium of print to any American who had a message to deliver.

The idea of author and book buyer (i.e., singer) as social peers is reflected in the two tunebooks that brought shape-note hymnody to the deep South: William Walker's *The Southern Harmony* (New Haven, Conn., 1835), and Benjamin Franklin White and Elisha J. King's *The Sacred Harp* (Philadelphia, 1844). Both were printed in the North for lack of music-printing facilities in the regions where their authors lived. The earlier book, compiled in South Carolina, sold 600,000 copies by 1866. And *The Sacred Harp*, compiled in Hamilton, Georgia, has been one of the great successes in American publishing history. Although co-compiler King died before the book appeared in print, it went through three revisions and several editions under White's supervision, was revised further after his death, and is still in print today, used at singings around the country. The stories that circulated about the authors reveal *The Sacred Harp* as an icon of Upland Southern culture, a book "of, for, and by the people," as Jackson put it.

Elisha J. King, a Georgia native and Baptist singing-school master, was a talented musician who has lived in memory through his association with the book. Benjamin Franklin White, the senior partner, was a native South Carolinian who moved to Harris County, Georgia, around 1840. The youngest of fourteen children, White received only three months of formal schooling, yet still managed to become editor of *The Organ*, the official newspaper of Harris County. Having begun to study music on his own, White "would sit for hours at a time," a sympathetic observer wrote in 1904, "and would watch and listen to birds as they sang from the branches of the trees, and learned as much or more from these observations than he did from other men's works."

A surge of interest in local history and biography took place in the United States after 1850, as the evangelical temperament combined with a respect for elders. Biographers related the life stories of early Americans as tales of virtue in action. B. F. White's life fit this mold. Prominent as a singing master and editor, he also became a civic leader despite his lack of schooling. As White lay dying at seventy-nine, he was said to have "recounted all the mistakes as well as the good that had followed him throughout his life. He summed it all up in the words, 'The end has come and I am ready,'" departing from this world only after singing the melody of SOUNDING JOY, which he had composed to words by Isaac Watts.

These recollections reflect the evangelical belief that a well-lived life deserves a fitting end, with the chief actor teaching one final lesson. Perhaps the lesson taught by White's life was that he achieved eminence in the Upland South as a typical figure, not an innovative one. A 1904 account of the book's history confirms that point by explaining how he and King relied on their friends' and neighbors' taste in singing. Between White's house and the street, the writer recalls, "there was a beautiful grove of oak, hickory and other large trees, and in the yard was an old-fashioned well of pure water." People would gather there and "in this grove, veranda and house sing the songs long before they were published in book form."

The Sacred Harp emphasizes old favorites over new pieces. Familiar numbers in the third edition (1859) include OLD HUNDRED, Daniel Read's SHERBURNE, and the folk hymns MORALITY and PLENARY, the latter a setting of Watts's funeral hymn "Hark! from the tombs a doleful sound" to the tune of *Auld Lang Syne*. A more recent favorite is NEW BRITAIN, a three-voice harmonization of the hymn *Amazing Grace*. Although the tune's composer is unknown, it seems to have originated in the Shenandoah Valley, appearing first in print in 1831. The *Sacred Harp*'s third edition also contains WONDROUS LOVE, a Southern folk hymn whose secular antecedent was a song about the pirate Captain Kidd.

LISTENING GUIDE 12

Wondrous Love

WONDROUS LOVE shows a certain kinship with the camp-meeting spiritual (see Chapter 6). Although it lacks a separate refrain, repetitions of text and music saturate the piece with a refrain-like spirit. The form is unusual, scanning poetically as 12.9.6.6.12.9. The first stanza's many incantations of "Oh! my

soul" and "for my soul" to the same short-short-long rhythmic
motive creates an exclamatory, awestruck mood. Just as important is the way the melody begins: with the first five words sung
three times, each at a higher pitch, and climaxing on the highest
note of the piece—precisely at its midpoint—which is sustained
for emphasis. The tenor melody's downward movement in the
second half of the piece balances the first half's trajectory. That
shape allows the text's main argument to unfold over a whole
stanza, while hammering home, measure by measure, an

emotional response to the miracle of Christ's sacrifice. By the stanza's end, only one phrase—"that caused the lord of bliss"—has gone unrepeated.

Also striking is the way the three voices move, often locking together in parallel fifths and octaves, forfeiting the independence that makes earlier New England and Southern psalmody satisfying to sing and listen to. But if the effect of intertwining voices is lost, a rugged power is gained, especially in the second phrase (repeated as the last phrase), where every interval between tenor and bass except the final one is a fifth. The impact is heightened by the sound of Southern singers' voices. WONDROUS LOVE endures as part of a singing tradition that distilled the attitude of religious praise into an untutored, heartfelt utterance.

HYMNODY OF NORTHERN REVIVALISM

Revivalism formed the core of American Protestantism before the Civil War, whether on the frontiers of Kentucky or in New York's high society. Old-line Calvinism, harking back to the Protestant Reformation, had held that only a certain number of Christians were actually predestined for salvation, while other souls burned in hell for their sins. The Second Awakening of the early 1800s introduced the alternative of "free grace," opening the possibility of salvation to all sinners and granting human effort a place in religious life. With the rise of revivalism in the North came a sense that the standard hymns were no longer enough to speak for new religious sensibilities. And as Protestants searched for new hymns, their first step was to shift the emphasis from an intimidating God to joyous salvation, substituting welcome for dread.

Revivalism in the North left a mark on two 1831 tunebooks: *The Christian Lyre*, compiled by Joshua Leavitt, a Congregational minister in New York City, and *Spiritual Songs for Social Worship*, compiled by Thomas Hastings and Lowell Mason. Leavitt's collection was the first American tunebook to take the form of a modern hymnal, with music for every hymn and the multistanza texts printed in full with the music. Some of the music was original; the rest came from a variety of sources—New England psalm tunes, rural folk hymns, revival songs, and even popular songs in sacred makeovers, including *Home, Sweet Home*. Leavitt's book sold in the tens of thousands, and its format and contents were copied by other songsters and hymn collections for the next several decades.

In borrowing Leavitt's format, Hastings and Mason's *Spiritual Songs* managed also to compete with it successfully. The book contained four hundred hymns and tunes, many of them original, including a number by Hastings himself. The texts, by Isaac Watts as well as later writers, summarized the main evangelical themes of the day (including millennialism) more fully than any earlier revival hymnal.

Sacred tunebooks, from Lyon's *Urania* to *The Sacred Harp*, were published to serve singing schools, musical societies, singing conventions, and even meeting-house choirs, but not worshiping congregations. The oblong shape, vocal instruction, and varied musical forms separate such books from hymnals used by congregations. Well into the 1800s, most congregational hymnals were word books: metrical psalters or hymn collections printed without music. Some congregations still relied on a small stock of tunes learned by rote; some turned worship music over to a choir or organist. In either case, there was no need for tunes in hymnals. Leavitt's *The Christian Lyre* and Mason and Hastings's *Spiritual Songs*, however, *were* intended for congregations. Their success shows that revivalism brought fresh democratic energies into religious life. One who embodied that process in the 1820s and 30s was Charles Grandison Finney, the day's leading revivalist preacher.

A lawyer by trade, Finney devoted himself to Christian evangelism from the time of his conversion in 1821. He began preaching in towns along the Erie Canal in New York, the region he called the "burned-over district." In Finney's image, Methodist circuit riders had swept through the territory like forest fires whose heat left spiritual desolation behind: "souls hardened," as he put it, against religious teaching. Finney forged his preaching style to reach such spiritual hard cases. (His powers of persuasion must have been awesome; the Presbyterian Church ordained him in 1824, even though he refused formal training as a minister and admitted that he had never read the Westminster Confession, which laid out the heart of Presbyterian doctrine.) Finney drew simple parables from his experience as a horseman, marksman, and sailor. He was also a talented singer. Determined to make religious life congregation-centered, Finney preached in a lively, colloquial style that drew his listeners in, and the result was a harvest of converts and a growing reputation.

As Finney and others brought the appeal of revivalism to middle-class Americans, Leavitt, Mason, and Hastings were ready with a fresh supply of congregational music. (Leavitt, in fact, once wrote Finney that *The Christian Lyre* had been inspired by his preaching and urged him to scatter copies through his congregation.) Hastings, a staunch advocate of musical science and a writer of hymn texts himself, gave special attention to fashioning a musical style that would encourage congregational performance. His hymn tune TOPLADY, sung to the text "Rock of ages, cleft for me," shows how an arch musical reformer responded to the challenge of revivalistic worship and its drive for more participation.

Like Mason's OLIVET, TOPLADY reflects the devotional style Hastings and Mason had worked out by the early 1830s. Repetition is the tune's lifeblood, both in overall structure (**aba**) and in smaller details. The middle section is simply a two-bar melodic figure sung twice. Both **a** and **b** sections are based on the same two-bar rhythmic motive, with only one tiny change. From a rhythmic point of view, one stanza of TOPLADY consists of the same two-bar motive repeated five times; over three stanzas, the motive is sung eighteen times.

TOPLADY, OLIVET, and other new numbers in *Spiritual Songs* lack the air of religious ecstasy that was sought in revival song. Indeed, the congregation-centered ideal that Hastings and Mason pursued was far removed from the God-centered one emphasized in this chapter. But the style of hymnody they created, blending European science with American revivalism, has endured in Protestant hymnals to this day. Its success proves that in American religious life, music with an edifying rationale can carry a middle-class appeal missing from music devoted to praise, whose advocates, rather than explaining themselves, simply sing.

10

"Be It Ever So Humble"

THEATER AND OPERA, 1800–1860

THE GLAMOUR OF THEATER IN THE UNITED STATES WAS AN ILLUSION created by players (most of whom were English by birth) at work in a blue-collar vocation. A typical stage performer made an annual salary of around $300. By way of comparison, an American workman in the 1790s could expect a yearly wage of $300 to $375. Stage players enjoyed one economic advantage over laborers, however. In addition to salaries, they were rewarded with benefits: performances whose beneficiary kept whatever proceeds topped expenses. A star's benefit might net as much as $500 or more; a decent yield for nonstarring players was $100—one-third of a typical yearly salary.

Female actors were paid less than males. In an age when most theater works idealized the virtues of their heroines, an actress could not count on being treated with respect, onstage or off. No matter how important her role, her name always followed those of male actors on the bill. She was fair game for comments on her personal life and appearance, and was expected to perform as long as possible during pregnancies. Only actresses who played leading roles received a benefit night of their own; the rest shared the proceeds of their husbands' or male companions' benefit.

Company managers leased theaters from local proprietors. In turn, the manager ran the company's day-to-day operations, took the financial risk, and reaped the profits if any. Responsible for both artistic results and the financial bottom line, company managers led hectic lives. It was their job to decide the length of each evening's entertainment and the assignments of individual players, and they could be sure that their decisions would be debated and sometimes denounced by performers, critics, and audience members.

The chief American companies spent the season in cities like Boston, New York, Philadelphia, Baltimore, Charleston, and New Orleans.

111

Smaller companies were formed from their ranks for summer touring, which gave players year-round work. A memoir by actor-dancer John Durang describes what life was like in such an outfit. Between 1808 and 1816, Durang toured with a small company to towns in Pennsylvania and Maryland where regular theatrical performances were unavailable. Preparing seven or eight nights of entertainment, Durang's troupe ran through the repertory, then moved on to the next town, where they repeated it. They adapted the regular season's "tragedys, comedys, farces, and operas" for smaller forces, and also offered their audiences dancing, pantomimes, acrobatics, and even plays in German.

MUSIC IN THE THEATER

Into the 1810s and 20s, stock companies in America were still playing such venerable English works as *The Beggar's Opera* and *Love in a Village*. But newer works by the likes of Henry Rowley Bishop, music director at a famous London theater, were also entering the repertory: the melodrama *Clari, the Maid of Milan*, which Bishop composed to a libretto by the American actor and writer John Howard Payne, was one. First performed in London in 1823, *Clari* opened six months later at New York's Park Theater and held a place on the American stage into the 1870s. One of the songs sung in the show may explain its public appeal more than its plot. For Bishop and Payne's *Home, Sweet Home*, written to catch the heroine's emotion as she returns home after being abducted, became one of the most popular songs of the nineteenth century.

LISTENING GUIDE 13

Home, Sweet Home (Bishop)

The music of *Home, Sweet Home* is simple: a melodic range of an octave; a repetitive structure of four-bar phrases (**aabbcb**); harmony limited to basic chords in the key of E major (especially the tonic and dominant). These simple elements combine with the words to create a feeling of stability that manifests the idea of home.

Rhythmic motion is one of the song's many stable features. The accompaniment flows in sixteenth notes, interrupted only by the **c** phrase ("Home, home, sweet, sweet home") and the final vocal flourish. The harmony supports that continuity. The bass

sounds the tonic pitch on more than half of the forty-eight beats in this twenty-four-bar song. And the harmonic rhythm—the rate and pattern of change in harmony—could hardly be more regular. All **a** and **b** phrases begin with two bars over a tonic bass note, move to the dominant for one bar, and then return to the "home" pitch (E).

The melody riding the surface of this harmonic foundation is hardly more adventurous. In fact, one of the tune's chief traits is its gravitation toward G-sharp, the third scale degree. Harmonized by the bass's E, this restful tenth becomes the song's home sonority. Bishop's melody also makes clever use of the tonic note E. In phrases **a** and **c**, it is the bottom note, the point where **a** begins and ends. In the **b** phrase, it is the top note, marking the song's only surge of melodic energy. Like the walls of a house, the pitch E provides both the melody's upper and lower boundaries and the harmony's bedrock, domesticating any hint of restlessness that the accompaniment's sixteenth-note flow might suggest.

The single-mindedness of *Home, Sweet Home* makes the **c** section stand out. Payne's words, turning from explanation to eulogy, trigger a contrast in which musical time, strictly metered to this point, suddenly becomes free. Bishop's melody invites the singer to linger over "home," drawing out the "o" vowel and the double "e" on "sweet," as though enraptured. Payne's last line, rather than trying for poetic eloquence, makes a simple statement of fact: "There's no place like home."

The recording heard here was made in 1928 by Italian-born operatic soprano Amelita Galli-Curci, who takes the languid approach she used when singing this song as a recital encore.

Many Americans found *Home, Sweet Home* an apt reflection of their feelings. And because, as a piece of music originating in England, the song could not be copyrighted in the United States, many American music publishers rushed their own editions into print. By 1870, American performers of virtually every stripe could buy a sheet-music version tailored to their own needs. Pianists could choose from among dozens of fantasies, variations, waltzes, polkas, marches, and arrangements for four hands. Singers interpolated the song into stage performances, seeking to touch the hearts of audience members for whom it was already a kind of anthem.

Home, Sweet Home won a popularity in its day parallel to that of more recent recorded hits. It was performed in most of the settings that made up America's musical landscape: the operatic and concert stage, the parlor, the dance hall, the parade ground, the battlefield, the campfire. From the early 1800s to the recent past, Americans have treasured songs especially for their melodies, and no melody was more loved in the nineteenth century than this one.

 ITALIAN OPERA IN AMERICA

On the night of November 29, 1825, New York's Park Theater witnessed a performance of Rossini's *The Barber of Seville*, marking the debut of a newly arrived opera troupe headed by the tenor Manuel García. The audience that had gathered to hear Count Almaviva serenade his beloved—"In the smiling sky / The lovely dawn was breaking"—actually heard "Ecco ridente in cielo / Spunta la bell'aurora," and the implications of this fact reverberate through the later history of music in the United States.

When we consider the new things the García troupe brought to New

York, it becomes clear why their visit was a landmark event. The Park Theater was the first in the United States to offer opera sung by European-trained singers in the original Italian. In mezzo-soprano Maria García, the troupe also introduced New York's first star female singer. Though only seventeen, "the Signorina," as she came to be called, was already a commanding performer; since that day, star performers have loomed large on the American scene. A lively discussion in the press followed the García troupe's arrival. More than a new musical form, foreign-language opera was received as a social phenomenon that raised questions about economics, manners, and social class.

García rented the theater for two nights a week, sharing the stage with an English stock company already in residence. An orchestra of twenty-six accompanied the performances. By all accounts, the Garcías' opera season was neither a smashing success nor a failure; rather, it marked the start of a long struggle (lasting almost three decades) to establish Italian opera in New York. And on the eve of the Civil War, New York and New Orleans were still the only American cities with resident opera companies of their own. Nevertheless, it is no exaggeration to call opera the most potent force to hit the American musical world in the nineteenth century. One reason lies in the musical and dramatic nature of opera itself. Another was that the operatic stage provided a showcase for star singers.

Italian opera relies on the drama inherent in the notion of larger-than-life characters, with strong, sometimes beautiful voices, pouring out their emotions—love, rage, grief, exultation—on a grand scale, to music suited for such displays. Singers like Maria García earned adulation and moved audiences by making public spectacles of themselves. Their skill at communicating the human passions with utter conviction surely helped opera cut across social and class lines, attracting a wide range of listeners.

Another factor in opera's popularity was the environment in which performances took place. By most accounts, audiences of the period were anything but silent and passive. "We (the sovereigns) determine to have the worth of our money when we go to the theatre," a Boston correspondent wrote in 1846. "Perhaps we'll flatter Mr. Kean [tonight] by making him take poison twice." Rather than mere spectators, audience members were participating witnesses who cheered favorite performers on, abused others, and expected calls for encores to be obeyed.

Opera is both a form uniting drama, spectacle, and music *and* a bundle of elements that can be pulled apart and changed. The programs given around 1840 at New York's Olympic Theater reflect opera's adaptability. *The Roof Scrambler*, a parody of Bellini's *La sonnambula*, was a particular hit there, not to mention *Fried Shots* (a parody of Carl Maria von Weber's

Der Freischütz). In works like these, performers twisted operatic dramas for comic effect, adapting music freely from the original scores. Offstage, the melodies, titles, subjects, leading characters, and plot elements of famous operas supplied hit musical numbers for the sheet-music trade, for home performers to sing and for pianists and wind bands to play. (Bishop's *Home, Sweet Home* was an example from the English tradition.) As a theatrical form, opera struggled for a toehold on these shores. But as a frame of reference and a cornucopia of song, it enriched the theater and the musical scene as a whole.

The poet Walt Whitman celebrated opera's adaptability in "Italian Music in Dakota," a poem picturing a regimental army band stationed at the edge of a vast Western wilderness, playing operatic songs. Whitman fancies nature listening "well pleas'd" to the band's twilight performance. His recognition of the power of melody provides another illustration of how Italian opera won a place in the lives of nineteenth-century Americans.

OPERA STARS AND COMPANIES

In March 1826, on the night before her eighteenth birthday, Maria García married a merchant in New York. Several months later, the rest of the company left for an engagement in Mexico, and she, as Madame Malibran, stayed behind. Her performances had already received high praise; but now the young mezzo-soprano made the leap from singer to full-

Maria García (1808–1836), Spanish mezzo-soprano, came to the United States with her father's opera troupe in 1825, married Eugéne Malibran in 1826, and returned to Europe in 1827, having achieved stardom on these shores. Highly acclaimed in Europe, she died from injuries suffered in a riding accident.

fledged star and won New Yorkers' hearts. With her chance to sing Italian operas gone, she learned English ones, showing skill as both actress and singer whenever she stepped onstage. Early in 1827, a critic wrote: "She not only knew her own part perfectly, but prompted the others, and directed the whole stage arrangement." Malibran was lauded for good taste, dignity of deportment, lack of exaggeration, charm, simplicity, ease, and grace—the first woman of the stage whom the American public accepted as "respectable." By the time she left for Europe in 1827, she was earning $500 per night in New York while still turning a profit for theater owners and managers.

A charismatic star like Malibran could make audience members feel that she was playing directly to them. Stars overshadowed other players—a fact that stock companies tried to minimize by passing lead roles around. Before Malibran, singers of star quality on the American stage had remained within the company's hierarchy, receiving higher pay than lesser players but still under the manager's control. The audience appeal of a star like Malibran, however, shifted public attention toward herself and away from the company. As a result, the power of managers declined, and that of public opinion grew.

From the 1820s on, theatrical performance revolved more and more around stars, which meant that finding and presenting them became a key part of a manager's business. One could write the history of musical performance in America by tracing variations on the category of star: a singing actress like Malibran; an operatic tenor like Enrico Caruso; a jazz musician like Louis Armstrong; a rock-and-roll singer like Elvis Presley. All of these individuals managed in performance not only to connect with audiences but to fill them with wonder and hence to assume a public image that was larger than life. In the nineteenth and early twentieth centuries, no other star-producing forum equaled that of the operatic stage.

PROMOTING A STAR: JENNY LIND'S AMERICAN TOUR, 1850–52

Star making requires not only a talented, charismatic performer but also imaginative promotion. And one of the great selling jobs in history took place in 1850 when the impresario P. T. Barnum presented Swedish soprano Jenny Lind to the American public. Believing that a concert tour of the United States could be lucrative for both him and Lind, Barnum first courted her through transatlantic correspondence. When Lind resisted his overtures, Barnum opened his pockets. Perhaps in hopes of discouraging him, she set the figure for a concert tour at the then-astronomical sum of

Swedish soprano Jenny Lind (1820–1887) made her first American appearance under the sponsorship of P. T. Barnum before a packed
house at New York's Castle Garden.

$187,000, paid in advance. Barnum managed to raise the money; then,
having secured her services, he set about creating a demand for them.

Well before Lind's arrival, Barnum launched a publicity campaign
that stressed the singer's virtuous Christian character and the prestige of
opera singing. The campaign succeeded. Lind's ship from Europe was
greeted by a crowd of thirty thousand when it landed in New York Har-
bor on September 1, 1850. And that was only the first of a series of mob
scenes, orchestrated by Barnum and his agents, that greeted her arrival
wherever she went. From reports of huge, enthusiastic gatherings, Barnum created the impression that Jenny Lind tickets were always at a
premium. He auctioned off, with great public fanfare, the first pair of ad-
missions to Lind's first concert in a city. Thus, cities as well as individuals competed to show their devotion to Lind and her art.

In another masterstroke, Barnum fed "Lindomania" by announcing
that she would donate to charity her share of the receipts from her first
American concert. It is hard to imagine better testimony that Lind was
the kind of woman that Barnum's publicity claimed: in the midst of fever-
ish excitement, here was a great star thinking of people who needed the
money more than she did! Thus Lind's arrival, her persona, travels, deeds,
and perhaps most of all, Americans' embrace of her visit, were received
not simply as an artistic enterprise or a commercial venture. They were
news, reported throughout the country. Avid expectation, a certain
amount of curiosity, and more than a hint of competitiveness—Can *we*

appreciate Jenny Lind as well as others who have heard her?—were among the feelings that moved people to buy tickets and that also helped shape their reactions to her performances.

Once in the hall, what did Jenny Lind's audiences actually hear? Her concerts followed a standard format whose key ingredient was variety. After an overture by the orchestra, another operatic vocalist warmed up the crowd. When Lind finally did step onto the stage, it was usually to sing an Italian aria that showed some aspect of her vocal technique. An instrumental solo might follow, providing more contrast while perhaps also suggesting a parallel between vocal and instrumental virtuosity. Then Lind returned to wind up the first half with another selection.

The second half showed even more diversity: another overture, more arias by Lind and others, and perhaps a second instrumental solo. But the main difference was the presence of songs that most audience members already knew. *Home, Sweet Home,* for example, appeared on a Washington concert program in December 1850, which closed with *Hail Columbia,* offering patriotic sentiments to a gathering that included President Millard Fillmore. Lind's audiences eagerly anticipated her simpler numbers. A Boston critic wrote that people "who would sit unmoved during the exercise of her matchless powers in the scientific productions of Mozart, Bellini, etc.," went into raptures of delight when she sat down at the piano and rendered the "folk songs."

P. T. Barnum convinced many Americans that a powerful experience

During Lind's stay in the United States (1850–52), her picture was used to advertise a variety of products, most notably sheet music.

lay in store for them; then, through Lind's artistry and his own planning, he met their expectations. By peddling recitals of a foreign opera singer, he created a cultural sensation that was also a commercial bonanza, involving not only concert tickets, sheet music, and pianos, but such Lind-endorsed products as gloves and stoves. Having taken a major financial risk, Barnum saw it pay off handsomely: he turned a profit of more than $500,000 from his connection with Lind.

OPERA IN NEW ORLEANS AND SAN FRANCISCO

Between 1827 and 1833, almost the only non-English operas sung in New York, Philadelphia, Boston, and Baltimore were presented by the company of the Théâtre d'Orléans from New Orleans, under manager John Davis's leadership. The company's summer tours brought to Northern audiences operas by French composers and carried on a tradition that could trace its roots back to 1796, when a performance of a French opera was given in a local theater. New Orleans, Louisiana's first city, was home to many French and Spanish citizens—often called Creoles in these years, whatever their race—whose cultural ties to the United States were tenuous and whose scorn for Americans fed their desire to remain culturally distinctive. In New Orleans, presenting French operas in their original language was a way to assert a French identity.

John Davis's company set a standard of high quality and lavish expense. In 1822, Davis traveled to France and brought back with him actors, singers, instrumentalists, and dancers, the latter for the ballets that French opera required. From the 1822–23 season on, opera in the Théâtre d'Orléans was played by a resident company whose personnel were imported; the orchestra impressed Northerners on the company's summer tours. Davis also sought out fresh repertory, giving American premieres of many stellar works, chiefly French. To meet the expenses such an ambitious program required, the company took to touring: first to Havana, Cuba, in 1824 and later to the Northeast. When Davis retired in 1837, he was succeeded by his son, who kept the troupe in a flourishing condition into the 1850s. The theater closed after the Civil War.

One reason Davis maintained an excellent company at the Théâtre d'Orléans is because he had a competitor. James Caldwell, an English immigrant and erstwhile actor, had arrived in New Orleans in 1820 as head of a touring company from Virginia. In 1824, Caldwell began to play English-language opera at the 1,100-seat Camp Street Theater in the city's new American section. Compared with Davis's audiences, Caldwell's could be rough and ready. As time passed, however, Caldwell's audience learned to behave with more restraint as he offered them a wider range of works. In 1835, Caldwell built the new St. Charles Theater and began to present traveling troupes there.

Local opera, then, flourished in New Orleans in both foreign language and English forms until after the Civil War. Managers used the population's love for social dancing to attract audiences. The Théâtre d'Orléans had its own ballroom, and a ticket to the opera might also entitle the holder to attend a ball after the performance. A newspaper notice in 1836 reported: "Spectacles and operas appear to amuse our citizens more than any other form of public amusement—except balls." As well as enticing customers into the theater, social dancing gave members of the opera orchestra more professional work.

Meanwhile, opera also gained a foothold on the continent's western edge. Thousands of miles separated San Francisco from the cities of the Midwest. Communication by railroad, transcontinental telegraph, even regular overland mail was established only after 1859, making the region until then a maritime colony of the East as well as a western frontier settlement. Until the mid-1860s, the "colony" could be reached most easily from the East by two seagoing routes, both long and expensive: across the isthmus of Panama or around Cape Horn. With the sea as their lifeline to goods and information, San Franciscans doted on shipping news. By local custom, when any sizable ship reached the wharf, a cannon was fired from Telegraph Hill—a sound disruptive to theatrical life because it sent most customers scurrying for the exit.

Early San Francisco's population was unique, for men greatly outnumbered women. In the 1850 census, only 8 percent of California's population was female, many of those said to be women of ill repute. This state of affairs is explained by the discovery of gold in northern California early in 1848, when San Francisco was a village of 500. By 1851, 30,000 people lived there, most of them men drawn by the prospect of getting rich quick. Thus, San Francisco changed overnight from backwater to boomtown, a place where an expensive cultural form like opera could flourish.

The city's first theater opened in October 1850. By the beginning of 1853, though fires had already burned three theaters to the ground, four more were open and operating. The man most responsible for establishing opera as an enduring local presence was Thomas Maguire, a New York native who moved to San Francisco in the late 1840s. He made his fortune in the West not by striking gold, but by running a successful saloon and gambling parlor and by building and renting out theaters. In

1856, Maguire opened the elegant new Maguire's Opera House, and four years later an Italian troupe took up residence there. Interested more in the power of what could happen onstage than the financial bottom line, Maguire set his prices low: $1 and 50 cents at a time when the going local price for opera tickets ranged from $3 to $1. He later calculated that during the 1860s, he lost $120,000 on opera.

In 1860, Maguire replaced his resident troupe with a new organization: the Maguire-Lyster Company, fashioned out of the traveling Lyster English Opera Company and a complement of Italian singers or English singers who performed Italian opera in its original tongue. This company featured two "wings," one Italian and the other English; Maguire provided an orchestra of twenty-five players for both wings. Instead of being alternated with minstrels, acrobats, and other popular entertainment, as opera usually was, the Maguire-Lyster Company played opera every night, and to substantial crowds.

That year, 1860, in San Francisco has been termed an *annus mirabilis* (year of wonders) in the annals of opera. A total of 145 performances were given in Maguire's Opera House, which seated 1,700. It has been estimated that attendance averaged 1,500 per performance, making a total of 217,000 seats sold in a city of 60,000. By comparison: in New York City today (population 8 million), the Metropolitan Opera, whose house seats 3,800, would have to build an additional fifty-two houses to accommodate a similar audience over 145 evenings. No American city, at any time, has shown a passion for operatic performance equaling that of San Francisco in 1860.

Blacks, Whites, and the Minstrel Stage

IN THE EARLY 1850s, SAMUEL CARTWRIGHT, A LOUISIANA PHYSI-cian, wrote an essay on diseases that were said to afflict black slaves, including "rascality," "drapetomia" (running away), and "dysaesthesia aethiopica," which caused sufferers to "break, waste, and destroy everything they handle." These words could suggest that the writer was describing clever slaves who avoided work by convincing the master they were too dumb for the job. But Cartwright intended no such irony. Proclaiming the theory of "polygenesis," he argued that each race was a separate and distinct *genus* rather than a variety of one species. In the southern United States, some accepted that theory as proof that Africans were biologically inferior to Caucasians, and that being slaves was their natural destiny.

It is obvious today that polygenesis was simply a bit of fake science to support racial prejudice. But its existence also points to deep conflicts in the feelings Americans held about race. In the early and middle 1800s, white Americans were fascinated with the image of the African-American slave. And that fascination—a mixture of curiosity, fear, love, and loathing—formed a key ingredient of blackface minstrelsy, the era's most popular form of entertainment.

Minstrelsy, which originated with white performers pretending on-stage to be black, has been called racist and exploitative entertainment. There is no question that race was fundamental to the minstrel show. Taking for granted the superiority of Euroamerican culture, white minstrels relied on black-influenced song, dance, and humor to give their performances vitality. And there is no evidence that white minstrels shared profits with the black Americans whom they imitated. Yet neither racism—the belief that one's own ethnic stock is superior—nor economic exploitation fully explains minstrelsy's impact. For while entertaining audiences with jokes, skits, and music, minstrels also played on social issues. A black stage character could appear stupid one moment and cunning the next, able to frustrate the white man's designs. On one level, the black mask enabled white stage minstrels to amuse audiences by imitating black ways of talking, moving, dancing, laughing, singing, and playing musical instruments. On another, white minstrels learned that blacking up freed them to behave onstage in ways that polite society found uncivilized. They could also comment critically not just on black-white relations but on society in general: on politics, culture, and social class.

The spectacle of performers freed from social restraint could delight audience members. In 1843, H. P. Grattan, an English actor, visited Buffalo, New York, and there, as part of an audience filled with boatmen, he watched a minstrel troupe perform. "So droll was the action, so admirable the singing, so clever the instrumentation, and so genuine was the fun," Grattan later wrote, "that I not only laughed till my sides fairly ached, but . . . I never left an entertainment with a more keen desire to witness it again."

The freedom enjoyed by performers included behavior not to be found in other kinds of theater. An English observer in 1846 described minstrels as "animated by a savage energy," their "white eyes roll[ing] in a curious frenzy." The frenzy was widely believed to have been inspired by black slaves themselves, who, as another observer wrote in 1857, were apt to "let themselves go" in "dervish-like fury . . . all night long, in ceaseless, violent exertions of frenetic dancing." In their unbuttoned manner, blackface minstrels of the 1840s and early 1850s hold traits in common with rock-and-roll musicians from the 1950s on.

Three elements, then—the black mask, the chance for social commentary, and the creation of a zone of unbridled pleasure—combined to give blackface minstrelsy its appeal. Minstrelsy's main subject was not really whites' views of African Americans but whites' responses to the conditions of their own lives, delivered from behind a mask fashioned out of their notions about African-American culture.

The late 1820s and early 1830s saw the creation of two stage characters who enjoyed a long life: Jim Crow and Zip Coon. Around 1828, an actor named Thomas D. "Daddy" Rice made theatrical history when, after noticing a crippled black stable groom's singing and weird dancing in Cincinnati, he memorized the first and tried to copy the second. He then bought clothes like those the stablehand wore, and finally, blacked up as "Jim Crow," he began doing an impersonation between acts of the play in which he was appearing. Audiences loved it, and Rice soon won fame as an "Ethiopian delineator." The Jim Crow character became a pushy Southern plantation hand who strutted the stage, unaware that his raggedy naïveté made him a buffoon.

The character Zip Coon was as urban and stylish as Jim Crow was rural and rough. Like Jim Crow, Zip Coon was boastful, and he appeared in garishly fancy clothes. The adventures outlined in the song *Zip Coon*—sung by singing actor George Washington Dixon—include romance:

Among the blackface characters found onstage before the 1840s, when the minstrel show became a full evening's entertainment, one of the most prominent was the stylish, sophisticated Zip Coon.

O its old Suky blue skin, she is in lub wid me
I went the udder arter noon to take a dish ob tea;
What do you tink now, Suky hab for supper,
Why chicken foot an posum heel, widout any butter.
O ole Zip Coon he is a larned skolar,
O ole Zip Coon he is a larned skolar,
O ole Zip Coon he is a larned skolar,
Sings posum up a gum tree an coony in a holler.

But this romance has more obstacles to overcome than the unsavory
supper Suky puts on the table. One is that Zip seems too wrapped up in
himself to be a serious lover. Another is that the music of *Zip Coon*, the
two-strain fiddle tune known as *Turkey in the Straw*, fails to evoke even a
hint of love's tenderness.

THE FIRST MINSTREL SHOWS

The first full-length minstrel show was given in Boston in 1843 by Dan
Emmett (fiddle), Billy Whitlock (banjo), Dick Pelham (tambourine), and
Frank Brower (bones), billing themselves as the Virginia Minstrels. Their
performing customs were followed by many of the minstrel companies
that sprang up in the wake of their success.

The Virginia Minstrels arranged four chairs onstage in a semicircle,
with tambourine and bones at either end and fiddle and banjo in between,
and filled their programs with short musical numbers. They divided an
evening's entertainment into two parts, the first including a would-be topical speech, delivered in dialect. It soon was customary for a minstrel
show's first part to concentrate on the Northern urban scene, with the second shifting to the South and closing with a lively plantation number.
But however standardized the overall form, the flow of events in any
given minstrel show lay with the performers. Each skit, song, and dance
was a self-contained act. Ad-libbing and topical comments were part of
the format, giving customers and players a sense of collaboration.

Within a few months of their debut, the Virginia Minstrels toured the
British Isles, where audiences also welcomed blackface shows. And by
the mid-1840s, minstrelsy was sweeping the United States. In 1844, a
troupe called the Ethiopian Serenaders was invited to play at the White
House. Spurred by popular demand, countless minstrel troupes were
formed: the African Melodists, the Congo Minstrels, the Gumbo Family,
the New Orleans Serenaders. Companies appeared especially along the
Mississippi and in the cities of the Northeast, and the growing railroad
system made touring easier. But the center of blackface entertainment was
New York City; by the 1850s, at least ten minstrel houses were open there,

and a few companies enjoyed consecutive runs of several years or more.

Minstrelsy was the first musical genre to reverse the east-to-west transatlantic flow of performers to North America. Until Americans began to perform on stages in styles invented here, a vast majority of stage performers were immigrants, chiefly from the British Isles. Minstrelsy, however, had no need for European-trained performers. What it required were those who, like the four Virginia Minstrels, could step into the voice and the character of an "Ethiopian" stage darky and entertain an audience with comic turns, dancing, and the singing and playing of popular music.

Minstrel skills could not be gained through formal study, and this is confirmed by the makeup of the original minstrel band: violin, banjo, tambourine, and bones. Only the violin was an instrument with established methods of instruction and a repertory of composed music. Yet the violin led a double life. As the fiddle, this bowed string instrument stood at the heart of Anglo-American dance music, with its jigs, reels, and hornpipes and its characteristic ways of playing them. Like their country counterparts, minstrel fiddlers like Dan Emmett held their instrument loosely and more or less in front of themselves, rather than clamping it between chin and shoulder. As a minstrel-band fiddle, the violin was less a singing, lyric voice than a wiry, rhythmic one, played with little or no vibrato.

The early banjo originated in Africa and was made from materials found in nature: a large hollow gourd with a long handle, strung with catgut. West African slaves were playing banjos in the New World before 1700. No record of white banjo playing exists, however, before Joel Sweeney began learning from slaves in Virginia, probably in the late 1820s; by the 1830s, Sweeney was passing on their playing techniques to other white performers, such as Billy Whitlock. The early minstrel banjo, which gave the ensemble its distinctive character, did not sound like a modern banjo. Its body was larger, the fingerboard had no frets, and its five gut strings were tuned well below the modern pitch. The sound was therefore fuller and suited to its role as a melody instrument.

That two of the early minstrel band's four members played small, portable percussion instruments testifies to the group's emphasis on rhythm, sound, and body movement over melody and harmony. The sound of the bones, which resembles that of castanets, is made by holding a pair in either hand and clicking them together with the fingers, allowing a skilled player to produce complex rhythmic patterns. The tambourine, an ancient percussion instrument of Near Eastern origin, is a combination idiophone (the metal jingles) and membranophone (the drum head, which makes sound through the vibration of a membrane). It could be struck with the fingers for accents and also shaken to provide a layer of shimmering sound.

SONGS OF THE MINSTREL SHOW

The advent of the minstrel show brought a need for a new songs. *Old Dan Tucker*, attributed to Dan Emmett, illustrates one way in which early minstrels translated raw energy into music.

LISTENING GUIDE 14

Old Dan Tucker (Emmett)

This song sounds like a stomping Anglo-American dance laced with black elements. Rather than a harmonized melody, the tune seems more like a musical framework in which words are delivered to a strict, driving beat. In its published sheet-music form, *Old Dan Tucker* fills twenty-eight bars: an eight-bar introduction and a four-bar tag frame a sixteen-bar vocal statement split equally between verse and refrain.

The introduction sets a raucous mood. Although arranged here for piano (i.e., for home use), the music was clearly not conceived with a keyboard instrument in mind. The right-hand melody is better suited for banjo or fiddle, and the constant repetition of the opening four-note figure signals that rhythm will overshadow melody in this song. The return of that figure after each refrain suggests a stage performance where two different sounds are pitted against each other: the twanging, minstrel-band timbre of the introduction and coda, perhaps backing dance movements, and the more conventional, songlike sound of the vocal sections.

The verse of *Old Dan Tucker* seems designed for singers who are also playing instruments while jumping around onstage. Nearly three-quarters of its syllables are sung on the same note: text declamation, not tune, is the priority here. Rhythmic drive is so important that the phrase endings are given no time to settle in. Verse leads directly into chorus; the refrain ends on its last bar's last eighth note so that the instrumental coda can start with a clean entrance on the next bar's downbeat.

In contrast to the published version, the recorded performance we hear is by folksinger Pete Seeger, accompanying himself on five-string banjo.

First page of Daniel Emmett's *Old Dan Tucker*. The cover notes that the song is "arranged for the piano forte by Rice," suggesting that Emmett himself lacked experience in the world of parlor music.

Stephen C. Foster (1826–1864), born near Pittsburgh on July 4, the nation's fiftieth anniversary, wrote more songs that won enduring popularity than any other American songwriter of the nineteenth century.

The character Dan Tucker seems like a blackface version of the pioneer frontiersman. Independent and disrespectful, Dan Tucker holds genteel standards in contempt. It seems to have been his independent spirit that moved a New York journalist in 1845 to nominate him along with blackface characters Jim Crow, Zip Coon, and Sambo as this country's national poets. Granting that black slaves were the originators and white minstrels the imitators, this writer marveled at Americans' reception of "negro" songs, which invited respectable folk to flaunt social niceties.

At about the time Emmett and the Virginia Minstrels were starting out on the East Coast, a teenage youth in Allegheny, Pennsylvania, was getting together with friends to stage amateur minstrel shows for fun. And at twenty-four, with several hits already to his credit, Stephen C. Foster embarked on a songwriter's career, one of the most significant in this country's history. *Gwine to Run All Night*, or *De Camptown Races* (1850), was one of Foster's early minstrel show hits.

LISTENING GUIDE 15

De Camptown Races (Foster)

This song, also in verse-and-refrain form, resembles *Old Dan Tucker* in several other ways, as if Foster took the earlier song as a model. Foster follows Emmett's suggestion of the minstrel

band sound by contrasting the registers of the instrumental (high) and vocal (lower) sections. His song is also full of comic exaggeration. And, like Emmett's song, *De Camptown Races* features both call and response and syncopation.

But Foster wrote his song in a different melodic idiom. If the music of Emmett's song is driven and aggressive, Foster's is jaunty and tuneful. In contrast to Emmett's introduction, chiefly sound and rhythm, Foster's is melodic, beginning with the shapely tune that dominates the verse and ends the refrain. Foster's melodies bear up well under repetition. The opening tune is one of three catchy melodic bits, the others being the syncopated response in the verse ("doo-dah!") and the five-note ascending figure that starts the refrain ("Gwine to run all night"). Foster's song also offers a wider range of sound than Emmett's, including a four-voice chorus in the refrain section (not heard on our recording).

Though we might take the differences between *Old Dan Tucker* and *De Camptown Races* as a matter of different composing styles, they also reflect changes in minstrelsy between 1843 and 1850. *Old Dan Tucker* represented the dominant voice of early minstrelsy: the black mask, linked with tough, unlyrical, folklike music, that invited white entertainers to mock genteel social customs with fierce intensity. In the next few years, however, blackface minstrels vastly increased their audience, in part by broadening their musical repertory. Rip-roaring comic songs like *Old Dan Tucker* were still sung, but so were sad songs, love songs, sentimental songs, and even opera parodies. By mid-century, the noisy, impromptu entertainments cooked up by Dan Emmett and the Virginia Minstrels were becoming a thing of the past. Moving into the center of American show business, minstrelsy evolved toward a more restrained kind of spectacle. A song like *De Camptown Races*, with a tune written to hold performers to the prescribed notes, helped to channel unruliness into a more controlled mode of expression.

One who worked to widen minstrelsy's audience appeal was the impresario and performer E. P. Christy. Born in 1815 in Philadelphia, he perfected his blackface imitation as a comic singer in the 1830s, then founded his own troupe in the early 1840s. Acting as the group's manager, he also performed as interlocutor (master of ceremonies), played banjo, and sang. Christy's Minstrels toured for several years before opening in April 1846 in New York City, where a critic complimented them for "chaste, refined, and harmonious" singing. Offering family entertainment at cheap prices, Christy's Minstrels took up residence at New York's Mechanics' Hall for a seven-year run (1847–54).

Christy's Minstrels came to be the most successful minstrel band in America. The company embraced a wide variety of vocal music, solo and choral, including sentimental songs, glees, and arrangements of opera numbers. They came on the scene at about the same time Stephen Foster was publishing his first songs. Christy must have recognized that Foster's songs would appeal to the audiences his company was trying to attract, and Foster knew there was no better way to promote sales of his songs than to have them sung onstage by a famous company like Christy's. Thus, though they seem not to have met in these years, Christy and Foster became collaborators of a sort.

In 1850, when Foster became a full-time songwriter, he entered into an agreement that gave Christy's Minstrels exclusive first-performance rights to his new songs. In 1851, Foster allowed Christy to claim authorship of *The Old Folks at Home*, a song of huge popularity. The following year, though, he wrote Christy asking permission to restore his own name to its rightful place on the song's cover. "I find that by my efforts I have

Edwin P. Christy (1815–1862) led one of the nation's most successful minstrel troupes and introduced many of Foster's songs to the public.

done a great deal to build up a taste for the Ethiopian songs among re-fined people," Foster told Christy. "I have concluded to reinstate my name on my songs and to pursue the Ethiopian business without fear or shame and lend all my energies to making the business live." We know that Christy refused Foster's request because until the copyright expired in 1879, sheet-music printings of *Old Folks at Home* continued to name Christy as author and composer. Moreover, Christy scrawled an epithet on the back of Foster's letter: "vacillating skunk"!

Foster has often been portrayed as the injured party in this matter: a young composer seeking only to be recognized for his achievements. But Christy's response is understandable. After benefiting for more than a year from Christy's fame and his plugging of the song (whose royalties Foster was receiving), here was Foster, who in an earlier letter had called himself "a gentleman of the old school," proposing to renege on a done deal.

The song that prompted this exchange reaches into new expressive territory. Foster's character, a displaced slave, sings of loneliness and longing, having no apparent plan to return to the home for which he yearns. Together the words and tune convey the emotional weariness that isolation can bring.

Foster's songs signaled the direction in which minstrelsy was headed by mid-century. Unlike Emmett, Foster played piano and conceived his songs at the keyboard. And in songs like *De Camptown Races* and *Old Folks at Home*, he showed a knack for writing minstrel music suited to the talents and tastes of parlor performers. In the early 1840s, Dan Emmett brought songs drawn from the countryside and circus into urban theaters. Now, around 1850, Foster had found an idiom that seemed equally at home in the parlor and on the stage.

Foster's *Old Folks at Home* (1851) shows his reliance on a single four-measure melody and the simplicity of the piano accompaniment, accessible to inexpert players.

BLACKFACE MINSTRELSY IN THE 1850s

Through the minstrel show's early years, as antislavery sentiment grew in the North, Southerners hardened their allegiance to slave ownership. As the frontier moved west, bitter fights took place over whether slavery would be allowed in newly settled territories, which might then become states of the Union. Against this background, minstrelsy, which had often cultivated a gray area between black and white extremes, retreated from controversy. Black characters were portrayed sentimentally, with contented Negroes fondly recalling the good old days on the plantation. Restless or unhappy blacks gradually disappeared from minstrel stages. By the mid-1850s, the minstrel show was built around the notion that the plantation was blacks' rightful home, the only place they would be truly happy and well cared for.

Politics, the economy, regional pride, and religion were all involved in the rising tension between North and South. And from 1852 on, so was literature. For in that year, Harriet Beecher Stowe's novel *Uncle Tom's Cabin: or, Life Among the Lowly* was published. Stowe tried in her work "to awaken sympathy and feeling for the African race, as they exist among us; to show their wrongs and sorrows, under a system so necessarily cruel and unjust as to defeat and do away the good efforts of all that can be attempted for them." A huge literary success in the North, *Uncle Tom's Cabin* was banned as subversive literature in some parts of the South. Abraham Lincoln, on meeting Stowe for the first time in the 1860s, is supposed to have greeted her as "the little lady who started the war."

Within weeks of its publication, plays based on Stowe's book began to appear on American stages, bringing characters like Uncle Tom, the saintly, trustworthy slave, and Simon Legree, the hard-fisted, hardhearted slave driver, to life in the theater. And in 1854, Christy and Wood's Minstrels used Stowe's characters in a plantation sketch they called "Life Among the Happy." By all accounts, this performance featured plenty of dancing, singing, and high spirits. It made little use of Stowe's plot and omitted any reference to the cruelty and suffering of slavery, which had moved Stowe to write her novel in the first place. It simply capitalized on the vogue for Uncle Tom and Company by borrowing their names, attaching them to stereotyped characters, and conducting business as usual on a carefree Southern plantation.

A symbol of the new landscape in which black characters moved can be found in the career of ex–Virginia Minstrel Frank Brower. In 1854, Brower began playing Uncle Tom in blackface, complete with a charac-

This early advertisement for Harriet Beecher Stowe's *Uncle Tom's Cabin* (1852) marks it as one of the great publishing successes of the era.

teristic dance called the "Uncle Tom jig," and he made that role a personal specialty. In the novel, Tom's master introduces him as "a good, steady, sensible, pious fellow. He got religion at a camp-meeting, four years ago; and I believe he really *did* get it. I've trusted him, since then, with everything I have." In contrast, the character Brower played in a stage sketch of 1863 was aging, hard of hearing, and stupid. To Stowe's readers, and indeed to many Americans in this year of Emancipation, Uncle Tom was a powerful symbol of humanity. But on the minstrel stage, at least as played by Frank Brower, he was a simple, feeble old man who came to dancing life at the sound of banjo music.

Home Music Making and the Publishing Industry

BY THE MID-1800s, A SUBSTANTIAL MUSIC BUSINESS EXISTED IN THIS country to meet the desires of women and men, playing and singing at home, for recreation and entertainment as well as edification. The spread of home music making belonged to a larger trend in the early 1800s, which saw a growing middle class seek refinement and gentility. But home music making was a business from the start, built around sheet music: not costly to publish or purchase, tailored to the skills and tastes of buyers, and hence an ideal artifact for a democracy.

The sheet-music trade required several agents: composers (and arrangers) to create the music; publishers to produce and circulate it; teachers to give lessons in performing it (and also sell it to their students); and manufacturers of musical instruments to play it. Each filled a necessary role, but publishers were the chief architects.

ALEXANDER REINAGLE AND THE MUSIC BUSINESS

We can trace the beginnings of the home-music-making business to a specific year in the life of one immigrant musician: the English-born composer and performer Alexander Reinagle in 1787. When the thirty-year-old Reinagle arrived in the New World in the spring of 1786, no such thing as an American *music* publisher existed. Virtually all the composers then working in America were psalmodists whose music reached the public in tunebooks brought out by book publishers. Until 1787, all secular sheet music music was imported. In that year, however, the first American-published sheet music issued from the Philadelphia shop of

Alexander Reinagle (1756–1809), a native of Portsmouth, England, came to America in 1786, settled in Philadelphia, and during fifteen years with the New Company directed musical productions there and in Baltimore. Most of his music was destroyed by a fire in 1820.

engraver and metalsmith John Aitken. During the next five years, Aitken published sixteen items and had no competitors. But in 1793, musical artisans in New York, Boston, and Baltimore began to publish sheet music, and the United States from then on had its own music-publishing trade.

Signs point to Alexander Reinagle as the instigating partner in Aitken's publishing venture. For one thing, twelve of Aitken's sixteen publications were composed by, arranged by, or printed for Reinagle. For another, when Reinagle took the post of music director for the New Theater in Philadelphia's Chestnut Street in 1793, Aitken stopped publishing sheet music. Reinagle's interest in the music business had surfaced soon after he landed in the New World. A newspaper notice from mid-1786 advertised for pupils "in Singing, on the Harpsichord, Piano Forte, and Violin" and proclaimed Reinagle's readiness "to supply his Friends and Scholars with the best instruments and music printed in London." Within a year, Reinagle had begun to take part in all four of the professional roles involved in the sheet-music trade. He composed and arranged music for home use; he gave lessons to singers and players; he involved himself in the distribution of music; and he plugged the work of London instrument builders. His activity indicates that the American music business in the mid-1780s was still so elementary that one musician could take on almost the whole enterprise himself.

Two of Alexander Reinagle's works show that by the early 1790s he was already distinguishing music that could be sold to home buyers from music that could not. The first is a piano sonata he composed in Philadelphia, probably between 1786 and 1794. This work, most likely written for Reinagle himself to play in public concerts, reveals a command of the keyboard idiom of eighteenth-century European masters such as C. P. E. Bach and Joseph Haydn. The second piece, a song called *America, Commerce, and Freedom,* was sung in a stage work of 1794 (see p. 141).

Reinagle, Sonata No. 1 for fortepiano (Philadelphia, 1786–1794?), page 1. This work was not published until 1978.

Reinagle's song was published soon after it was composed, while nearly two centuries elapsed before the piano sonata saw publication. Why would a song go straight into print and a piano sonata by the same composer stay in manuscript? Because when this music was written, there was a market for songs and almost none for piano sonatas. Songs—short, melodious, simple to perform, and carriers of verse—combined traits that appealed to amateur performers, especially when they heard the songs sung onstage. But mastering a sonata required a good deal more skill, practice, and most likely lessons. Besides, good players could buy imported music by Old World composers. Who needed a piano sonata by Alexander Reinagle? Reinagle's own answer remains elusive; there is no sign that he tried to get his sonatas into print.

In Reinagle's two compositions we can see the divided heritage of composing as an occupation in the United States. In writing the sonata, Reinagle was acting as a member of the composing *profession*, whose ideal is tied not to economic outcome but to intellectual control, including a composer's right to control performances through written scores. In contrast, Reinagle's role in *America, Commerce, and Freedom* was more like that of a tradesman working to please customers. Composed for the theater, the song was expected also to appeal to amateur performers at home.

Some have considered the notion of a Great Divide between so-called classical and popular music a device used by critics and historians to impose an aesthetic hierarchy supporting their own classical preferences. Indeed, by calling Reinagle's sonata more impressive than his song, I may seem to have endorsed such a hierarchy. I make the comparison, however, not to to assign value but to point to the different relationship each piece creates between the composer, the performer, and the written score.

NOTATION, THE GREAT DIVIDE, AND AMERICAN MUSICAL CATEGORIES

Before the advent of the phonograph, musical notation was the key to musical commerce. Not until a piece was written down and printed could it become a commodity to be bought and sold. But musical notation also embodies the authority of the composer. Performers who played pieces like Reinagle's sonata followed the composer's instructions closely. In contrast, the score for Reinagle's song is less prescriptive. From the song's beginning to the instrumental tag at the end, the top line of the keyboard part does nothing but double the voice; and the lower line is a stripped-down, elementary bass whose only flash of independence is the eighth-

Reinagle, *America, Commerce, and Freedom*, from *The Sailor's Landlady*
(Philadelphia, 1794?) in its original sheet-music printing.

note motion in the next-to-last system. Not a single chord appears until
the last two beats of the piece, a curious way to write for an instrument
with chord-playing ability.

It is hard to imagine many players performing the keyboard part of
America, Commerce, and Freedom exactly as written. Some would surely
add chords, decorate the melody, or enrich the bass. Others might double the bass line with a cello if one were available, or substitute guitar for
keyboard, or extend or cut out the instrumental tag. Still others might
sing the song unaccompanied, at a fast or slow clip, or move it to a different key. Significant departures from the score would be unacceptable
in the sonata, but expected in the song. The score of *America, Commerce,
and Freedom* was published and sold as an outline to be filled in and realized by performers according to their abilities, tastes, and moods.

Given where the authority lies, Reinagle's piano sonata may be called
a piece of *composers' music* and his song a piece of *performers' music*. Performers' music, while offering composers little control over performances,
gave them access to customers in the marketplace. Composers' music offered artistic control but few if any customers, at least in Reinagle's day.

From an economic standpoint, early American writers of composers' music were strictly on their own, while writers of performers' music worked at the behest of theater managers and publishers. By writing both kinds of music, Alexander Reinagle exercised the full range of his artistic and economic opportunities.

The field of opera offers a clear delineation between musical categories. Although many Americans in the antebellum (pre–Civil War) years took opera to their hearts, most of them encountered operas not as integral works of art, faithful to a composer's score, but in altered form: as arrangements, pastiches, excerpts, and single numbers. Adaptation—the tailoring of the music to suit particular audiences and circumstances—was the key to opera's popularity in America. Composers' authority counted for little in the musical theater, for there the key to success lay in capturing an audience's attention. Opera and theatrical music in the first half of the nineteenth century, therefore, must be considered performers' music.

Until after the Civil War, the idea of accessibility dominated the public performance of virtually *all* music in the United States. Indeed, perhaps no development in musical performance was more important than the appearance of a new attitude, which may be called "authenticity." Authenticity valued composers above performers, works over occasions, and placed ultimate authority in written scores. Performers who followed the ideal of authenticity took audience enjoyment as secondary and judged performances on their faithfulness to the work as the composer was thought to have conceived it.

For composers, then, the Great Divide lay in deciding whether to write composers' music, with authoritative scores, or performers' music, intended more as a springboard for the interpretations of singers and players. For performers, the divide was similar but not identical: opera performers seeking accessibility, for example, were not obliged to approach the music they sang with authenticity in mind. For both composers and performers, the attitude toward a work's notation was all-important. To what extent did composers expect deference to what they wrote down? Were performers more determined to seek a work's essence in the composer's notation or in communicating it to listeners? The answers to these questions reflected the existence of different kinds of musical works, which came to be grouped under such labels as "classical" and "popular."

Composers' music constitutes the classical sphere, built around an ideal that may be called *transcendence*: the belief that musical works can achieve a permanent artistic stature; that such works form the basis for a worthwhile musical life; and that performers have a duty to sing and play them by following the composer's notation closely. Performers' music, in contrast, constitutes the popular sphere, whose chief premise is *accessibility*, giving authority most of all to the audience.

While the classical and popular spheres both depend on notation, a great deal of music in U.S. history has relied on oral transmission. This unwritten folk music makes up a separate domain: the "traditional" sphere. Music making in the traditional sphere tends to be connected with particular customs and ways of life. In its drive to preserve linguistic, cultural, and musical practices, the traditional sphere is ruled by a commitment to *continuity*.

Many musicians have pursued transcendence, accessibility, or continuity separately and for its own sake. Yet it is striking how often these goals have collided, intersected, coexisted, or blended. What kind of cultural transaction is taking place when a composer in the classical sphere "borrows" from the popular or the traditional sphere? or when a traditional melody is notated and performed as if it were a composed piece? or when a widely accessible popular genre sustains itself until it enters the performing arena of the classical sphere? or when a recording makes a performance a candidate for transcendence? Circumstances like these have been commonplace in American music history. In fact, much of the music thought to be most fully American plays on the boundaries of the spheres—evidence that for musicians who make the music, the boundaries really do exist.

SHEET MUSIC AND HOME MUSIC MAKING

Earlier in this chapter, sheet music was described as inexpensive and thus ideal for a democracy. That statement holds true for the years after 1845, but earlier in the century sheet music was a luxury. Perhaps it would be better to say that having started out as a costly enterprise, home music making by the mid-1800s was a pastime accessible to many Americans. In the late 1820s, the trade was turning out 600 titles per year, but the number grew to 1,600 annually in the early 1840s and 5,000 in the early 1850s. The threefold leap between 1840 and 1850 reflects a burgeoning of demand.

The economics of sheet-music publishing depended on a variety of factors, including copyright law. As first written, the law protected only authors who were American citizens or residents. A foreign hit like *Home, Sweet Home* was issued by many different publishers because no American edition of the song could be copyrighted. Therefore, it was cheaper for publishers to print foreign music than American music, which required them either to purchase rights from the composer or pay a royalty on copies sold. We should not overlook this fact of economics when we consider nineteenth-century musical taste. The American appetite for European music owed much to the notion that Old World culture was superior, but the dollars-and-cents advantage to publishers was also a factor.

While money could be made in the sheet-music trade, publishers complained that the business was risky. Indeed, all but a few of its products lost money. A notice of 1859 from Oliver Ditson & Co., a highly successful firm, painted a bleak picture: "Not one piece in ten pays the cost of getting up; only one in fifty proves a success." Success in the trade depended on these exceptions: the composer whose name helped to sell copies; the stage hit that transferred well to the parlor; the vocal or instrumental number that the public took to its heart. When one of their pieces struck pay dirt, publishers did all they could to exploit it, packaging the title and melody in as many different arrangements as possible. The enormous outpouring of sheet music during the century's second half testifies that, whatever the risks, publishing it could be lucrative.

MEN, WOMEN, AND PIANOS

By the 1820s, the piano was on its way to becoming *the* parlor instrument of the nineteenth and twentieth centuries, in varied shapes and sizes: square pianos, uprights, spinets, consoles, and grands.

The pattern of growth in keyboard manufacturing paralleled that of the sheet-music trade. At first an import and a luxury reserved for the few, keyboard instruments over the years became accessible to more and more people. Jonas Chickering of Boston began in the 1830s to mass-produce metal-framed instruments. By 1851, some 9,000 pianos per year were being made in the United States, with Chickering, the leading firm, producing 10 percent of that total. It has been estimated that one out of 4,800 Americans bought a new piano in 1829; in 1910, a year in which 350,000 pianos were produced, one out of 252 bought one.

Pianos were solo as well as accompaniment instruments, and a great deal of sheet music was published for piano alone. Between 1820 and the Civil War, three kinds of piano pieces dominated the repertory:

(1) variation sets, based on the melodies of popular songs, hymn tunes, or opera arias (from the 1830s on);

(2) dances, including waltzes, polkas, galops, cotillions, marches, and quicksteps; and a small amount of

(3) abstract music, especially rondos.

When Americans began to publish sheet music in the late 1700s, customers came from the ranks of the wealthy. The activity of a well-ordered house involved a mixture of business and pleasure, including music. A change took place in the nineteenth century, however, when business moved out of the house. The process began when governors and other officials began conducting their business affairs in state capital buildings. Even more dramatic was the shift of commerce and industry to office buildings. As power once dispersed among private dwellings was concentrated elsewhere, the home became more a center for family and cultural activity. Husbands left home in the morning, spent their days in the competitive marketplace, then returned in the evening to domestic sanctuaries prepared by their wives. In removing their own work from the home, men gave up their involvement in much that happened there, while domestic affairs came to be considered women's work. Home music making was deeply influenced by the change.

Women in this social setting were responsible for raising children, managing household affairs, and beautifying their surroundings. The

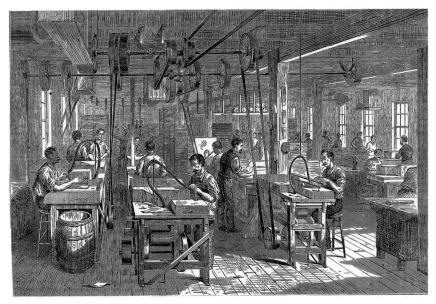

This engraving from 1887 depicts the Action Room of the Chickering Piano Manufactory in Boston.

sheet-music and piano trades thus came to assume that parlor piano was a female activity, and piano music published from the 1840s on was shaped by the trade's view of women's musical taste and capacities. Was this an accurate view? It is impossible to tell; the publishers and composers who dominated the sheet-music business were all male. But we do have a good idea of the female sensibility that this music was tailored to please.

One guidebook from the 1700s distinguished women from men "by that *Delicacy*, express'd by *Nature* in their *Form*." Another claimed that "natural softness and sensibility" made women generally agreeable and disposed them toward a taste for beauty. That theme was repeated in countless nineteenth-century writings. An attraction to certain objects of beauty, such as flowers, was widely held (and not only by men) to be part of women's nature; something had to be wrong with women who did not feel it.

Piece after piece of piano sheet music testifies that women were emotional creatures, and seeks to touch the player's or listener's emotions or imagination, primarily through familiar melodies. Publishers squeezed their song hits for all they were worth. For example, the *Board of Trade Catalogue* (1871) lists forty-nine different piano versions of *Home, Sweet Home* under "Rondos, Fantasies, Variations, &c." While dressing up and repackaging familiar tunes may now seem less artistic than industrial, it allowed people in a society where all music was "live" music the real pleasure of rehearing favorite melodies. Also, in the nineteenth-century parlor, music's purpose was more social than artistic, and touching the heart was among the highest social purposes of all. Composers and arrangers, fully allied with the popular sphere's credo of accessibility, were far more concerned with the feelings of players and listeners than with any concept of artistic originality or integrity.

Dance music, the second large category of piano composition, stressed rhythm over melody. Each popular dance had its own tempo, meter, and way of moving. As in later times, the advent of new dances sometimes signaled social changes: the rise of an ethnic group, for example. If the new dance caught on, money could be made by tapping its popularity, as happened with the polka. A dance apparently originating among Bohemian peasants, the polka was introduced to America in 1844 on a New York stage and for a time enjoyed considerable vogue. One reason Stephen Foster's *Oh! Susanna* (1848) caught the spirit of its time so well is that it borrowed the still-fresh polka rhythm. The *Board of Trade Catalogue* reports that some 3,600 different polkas were published between the mid-1840s and 1870. Only ten of these are called simply *Polka*; the rest bear headings like *Polka brilliante*, *Polka fantastique*, *Polka militaire*, *Polka senti- mentale*, and other fanciful names. Female names abound among the ti- tles, from Ada to Zenobia, with nine different titles referring to Jenny Lind. There are polkas named after every conceivable blossom (especially the rose), as well as precious metals and jewels, birds, places, and moods; now and then, titles with industrial or masculine associations crop up, such as the *American Petroleum Polka*, the *Ninety-Seventh Regiment Polka*, and *Uncle Tom's Polka*. All these titles (and perhaps their title-page de- signs) were intended to catch the attention of the prospective buyer.

LISTENING GUIDE 16

Papageno Polka (Stasney)

Parlor piano music was published not only in sheet music but in musical anthologies such as *The Home Circle* (Boston, 1856). And the title of one of that collection's numbers, *Papageno Polka*, is no mystery: it is based on melodies associated with Papageno, a character in Mozart's well-known opera *The Magic Flute* (1791). Attributed to "Stasney" (perhaps the German band director Lud- wig Stasney, 1823–1883), this piece weaves several Mozartean snippets into a three-part **ABA** form, testifying that parlor com- posers took familiar, catchy tunes from any source they could find.

The Magic Flute predates the advent of the polka by almost half a century. Yet two of its melodies—Papageno's first song in the opera and a tune he hums after his mouth is locked shut for excessive talking—feature rhythms close to the characteris- tic polka rhythm that emerged in dance music of the 1840s: 2/4 ♫ ♫ | ♩ ♪ ↱|. It appears that after noticing that link, the composer mixed the Mozart quotations with music of his own, and poured the result into a standard form based on four-bar phrases and eight-bar sections.

It is not easy to find *musical* grounds for calling a piano dance piece *Griselda Polka* instead of *American Petroleum Polka*. But nineteenth-century parlor culture was not much concerned with issues of art or musical sub- stance. Publishers were anxious above all to sell their products. With the help of the piano industry, they tailored a growing repertory of sheet mu-

This political cartoon capitalizes on the advent of the polka in 1844 to comment on the prospects of Democratic presidential candidate James K. Polk, who won election later that year.

sic for what they took to be the taste of female amateur pianists. Yet for all the piano's prominence, the singing voice was the favorite home instrument of all, and the heart of the sheet-music trade lay in the solo song with keyboard accompaniment. And, from early in the century through the Civil War, songs written for parlor performance provide insight into the way Americans viewed themselves.

13

Star Spangled banner - tune from England

From Jeanie to Dixie

PARLOR SONGS, 1800–1865

ON THE EVENING OF SEPTEMBER 13, 1814, WASHINGTON LAWYER Francis Scott Key was onboard ship during a naval battle. The United States and Great Britain were at war, and the British fleet was bombarding Fort McHenry, which guarded the city of Baltimore. Key later recalled the moment when the firing stopped and spending the rest of the night in suspense, unsure whether the fort had surrendered or the British had given up their attack. Finally, "in the dawn's early light," he saw the American flag, still flying over the fort.

Key wrote a poem about the experience, and his verses were published in a Baltimore newspaper. As the national anthem (since 1931), *The Star-Spangled Banner* now carries a ritual status that makes it hard to view objectively. But the song did not begin life as a national anthem. First of all, it was a response to an event, appearing in a newspaper, then on a broadside, then in sheet music. Like many songs of its kind, it borrowed a familiar tune: a drinking song composed in the 1770s for a London men's club. Key's borrowing reflects the shared heritage of language and culture that linked the United States to Great Britain.

The Star-Spangled Banner embodies a patriotic state of mind into which singers are invited to step. The Americans in Key's song have thrown off the yoke of monarchy and are now defending themselves against more oppression. As people of a nation dedicated to freedom, citizens can musically perform their belief in that ideal. A patriotic song is thus a hymn addressed not to God, but to fellow citizens.

Patriotic songs were one of several genres that found their way into the nineteenth-century home circle. Another was centered on a mythic view of love harking back to the Middle Ages, when love between knights and ladies was ruled by a courtly code. Songs based on the lore of medieval chivalry began to appear early in the 1800s. John Hill Hewitt,

149

The Star-Spangled Banner (Baltimore, 1814) in its first sheet-music edition.

born in New York in 1801 to a family of immigrant musicians, took this approach in *The Minstrel's Return'd from the War* (composed 1825 in Greenville, S.C.; published around 1833 in New York). Choosing as his main character a minstrel-knight of yore (a minstrel was a medieval entertainer; blackface performers later appropriated the name), Hewitt wrote a text that seems inspired by the Christian crusades. Hewitt's music begins like a march, then becomes more serenade-like as the knight woos his fair lady. In the fourth stanza, the hero lies mortally wounded on the battlefield.

By the mid-1830s, Anglo-American songwriters were matching another kind of music to the imagery of archaic romance: an Anglo-Italian style similar to Henry R. Bishop's in *Home, Sweet Home.* The influence of Italian opera brought to Anglo-American song a new source of grace and intensity, as well as a higher (but still accessible) tone. The gently arched shape of its melodies lent itself well to even vocal production as well as turns, trills, and other kinds of ornamentation.

Why would songs featuring brave knights and protected damsels have such appeal for Americans? Part of the answer is that both courtly medieval love and nineteenth-century courtship were based on separation of the sexes. Within courtly love's idealized realm, men and women acted as virtually different species, each governed by its own rules. In fact, chivalric courtship songs grew popular in America at a time when business was separating itself from home life. The distancing of men from women and the redefining of their roles made an impact on the language and decorum of romance. It now became possible to imagine men as gladiators who jousted in the public arena by day, then returned to domestic "bowers," where they sang and were sung to.

As early as the 1820s, songwriters had begun adapting the courtship song for democratic customers, taking separation, not medieval romance, as their main subject. Male lovers and their ladies might be separated by shyness (the love might be secret), the social code, physical distance (journeys often sparked love songs), or death, the ultimate separation. Almost all of these songs take a man's point of view, and they dwell on the pain of separation. Elevated speech, Italianate melody, and an image of pure, nonfleshly love became standard ways to express a yearning for the beloved. The songs do *not* show lovers coming together, touching, freely conversing, or developing an erotic attachment.

Stephen Foster was a leading American master of the translated courtly love song. His first published composition, *Open Thy Lattice, Love* (1844), for example, is a serenade, a song type originating in the Middle Ages. The melody traces a graceful curve in 6/8 time, and the rhythm, as in some Italian arias, invites the singer to be flexible. The accompaniment suggests the strumming of a guitar. In the text, the man camps at the woman's window while she stays protected inside. And that tension feeds the singer's romantic fantasy. He pictures a nighttime seaside scene with the two lovers sailing off into the sunrise, the stars keeping vigil just for her.

LISTENING GUIDE 17

Jeanie with the Light Brown Hair (Foster)

One of Foster's classic songs of courtship, *Jeanie with the Light Brown Hair*, deals with permanent separation: Jeanie has either gone away for good or died. In the text, which Foster himself wrote, her admirer is left with only memories of the look, the grace, and the sound of Jeanie to sustain him.

> I dream of Jeanie with the light brown hair,
> Borne, like a vapor, on the summer air;
> I see her tripping where the bright streams play,
> Happy as the daisies that dance on her way.
> Many were the wild notes her merry voice would pour.
> Many were the blithe birds that warbled them o'er:

> Oh! I dream of Jeanie with the light brown hair,
> Floating, like a vapor, on the soft summer air.

The lover goes on to recall Jeanie's smile, but he reports nothing that she ever said or thought. Jeanie trips through meadows singing, dancing, and plaiting flowers, apparently all but oblivious to her suitor's presence.

But Foster's music makes this flimsy scenario work. The first section (lines one and two of the text) is strong enough to bear plenty of repetition. And Foster takes advantage of it, using a well-worn principle of musical form: statement, restatement, contrast, and return, or **aaba**. The tune begins high in the singer's range, with "I *dream*" capturing in one stroke the sense of fantasy that the song portrays. The accompaniment's repeated quarter-note chords act as a rhythmic foil for the vocal line, which, after emphasizing "dream," pushes ahead in eighth notes, then falls into phase with the piano on "light brown hair." Foster's next gesture neatly matches music and words: the upward leap on "vapor" encourages the singer to try for a lighter-than-air sound while reinforcing the dreaming mode of the first line.

Jeanie's first four bars show a grace that Foster at his best could command. By starting measure 3 on the downbeat, Foster gives "borne" the emphasis due the song's first active verb—an emphasis he supports with the first chord change since the voice entered. That chord begins a harmonic progression that moves away from the tonic, just as the summer air carries the dream of Jeanie. And the phrase-ending melodic cadence ("on the summer air") is sung to harmonies that change every beat. Thus, in just four bars of singing, Foster has taken a familiar premise—a suitor dreaming of his absent lover—and set it to music so memorable that both performers and listeners are eager to learn what will happen next.

I   dream   of   Jea - nie   with   the   light   brown—   hair,

Borne,   like   a   va - por,   on   the   sum - mer   air;

Cover art such as the winsome portrait on Stephen Foster's *Jeanie with the Light Brown Hair* (1851), rare before the 1830s, was by mid-century a regular feature of sheet music.

OTHER SONGS OF SEPARATION AND YEARNING

While songs of the later nineteenth century praise the triumphs of technology—steam engines, bicycles, balloons, and automobiles—many pre–Civil War songs tend to prefer the past. Stephen Foster's *The Voice of By Gone Days* (1850), for example, announces that then was better than now and claims the sound of that older voice as a tonic for the "weary hearted." The reason is that the singer's beloved has died—or, as the lyrics say, "beloved of angels bright," she has gone to join "their bless'd and happy train."

Poets and songwriters searched for subjects that would trigger yearning, and one device was to focus on inanimate objects rather than people. Henry Russell's *Woodman, Spare That Tree* (1837), set to a text by George Pope Morris, is an example. The English-born Russell was both a songwriter and a performer of his songs, perfecting his art in the United States during the 1830s. An accomplished keyboard player, Russell accompanied his singing on a small upright piano, which allowed him to face the audience. In his autobiography, he named the statesman Henry Clay, known for his power to hold an audience spellbound, as his main inspiration.

Morris's poem for *Woodman, Spare That Tree* is written in the voice of a man hailing a woodcutter who is ready to swing into action:

> Woodman spare that tree!
>   Touch not a single bough;
> In youth it shelter'd me,
>   And I'll protect it now;
> 'Twas my forefather's hand
>   That placed it near his cot,
> There, woodman, let it stand,
>   Thy ax shall harm it not!

Russell directs that the song be sung "With much feeling and Expression." After a long piano introduction, the melody is cast in four sections, **aabc**. We can imagine Russell performing this song in public, his face miming emotions during the intro to prepare the audience for his vocal entrance.

The threat of loss hangs over *Woodman, Spare That Tree*: the prospect that an ancient, majestic thing, the site of family memories, will be destroyed. Russell apparently milked the song for all it was worth, sometimes offering a spoken prologue tying it to a real-life incident. The text

Lith.ª of Endicott N.Y.

THE WORDS COPIED FROM THE   NEW YORK MIRROR, WRITTEN BY

GEORGE P. MORRIS,

BY WHOM THIS SONG IS RESPECTFULLY DEDICATED TO

BENJAMIN M. BROWN, ESQ.

THE MUSIC BY

Henry Russel.

New York, Published by FIRTH & HALL, Nº 1, Franklin-Sq

George P. Morris's melodramatic tale of a threatened oak is suggested by the cover of this 1837 song by Henry Russell, though the tree looks a bit undernourished above its trunk.

leaves the tree's fate unresolved, and Russell used that uncertainty to create suspense in concerts. After one performance, he wrote, an audience member, "in a very excited voice, called [out] 'Was the tree spared, sir?' 'It was,' I said. 'Thank God for that,' he answered, with a sigh of relief."

The theme of yearning and loss also pervades some blackface minstrel songs, including *Carry Me Back to Old Virginny* and *Old Folks at Home*.

Favorite parlor songs on the same subject include *I'll Take You Home Again, Kathleen, Silver Threads Among the Gold,* and *When You and I Were Young.* But operatic numbers were also sung in American parlors, and so were religious, comic, and topical songs. Moreover, during the early and middle 1800s, movements took shape to abolish slavery and to reform the way Americans worshiped, their drinking habits, and the treatment of women in society. And popular song was enlisted in support of these movements.

THE HUTCHINSON FAMILY AND SONGS OF SOCIAL REFORM

The leading singers of activist songs in the pre–Civil War years were the Hutchinsons of Milford, New Hampshire, who began singing together for pleasure and then found that they could make a career out of it. Their reform music has caught recent historians' attention, partly because it anticipates the work of such later folk protest singers as Woody Guthrie and the young Bob Dylan. But first and foremost, the Hutchinsons were entertainers who made their mark singing music of the day for paying audiences.

The Hutchinsons were inspired in 1840 to enter the public arena after attending a concert of the Rainer family, a traveling troupe from Europe who performed in native costume. In 1842, the Hutchinson Family Singers, a quartet made up of brothers Judson, John, and Asa and their young sister Abby, launched a career as a touring ensemble. Their travels, beginning in New England, took them down the Eastern Seaboard to New York, Philadelphia, and Washington, where in 1844 they sang in the White House for President Tyler. In 1845–46, they performed in the British Isles, then returned and continued to tour the United States. Their heyday ended in 1849 when Abby married and left the troupe.

Entering a field dominated by foreign musicians, the Hutchinsons stressed their American origins. They seemed to play themselves onstage: members of a small-town New England family. A New York critic in 1843 praised their singing as "simple, sweet, and full of mountain melody."

The Hutchinsons' first reform-minded goal was to help reduce American consumption of alcohol, which in 1830 stood at nearly three times the per capita rate measured in 1975. During the 1830s, reformers mounted an antidrinking campaign, connecting drink to poverty, immorality, lack of family responsibility, and neglect of women and children. Their cam-

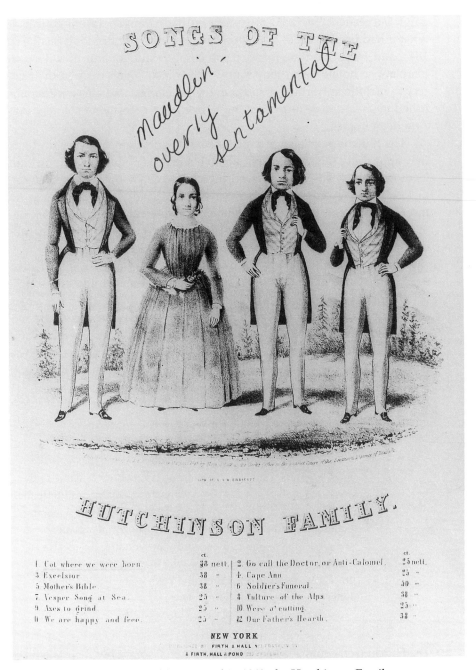

From 1842 until sister Abby married in 1849, the Hutchinson Family singers toured the United States and Great Britain, entertaining and edifying audiences with their songs.

paign succeeded: by 1845, consumption had dropped to one-fourth of what it had been in 1830. John Hutchinson took a nondrinking pledge in 1841, and from that time forward the family made a point of staying in temperance hotels when they toured. They also began early in their career to include antidrinking songs in their concerts, and a few were published in sheet-music form, helping to bring the message of sobriety into American homes.

The Hutchinsons also plunged into the fight against slavery. In 1843, they appeared at an antislavery rally in Boston's Faneuil Hall, joining with leading abolitionists, including ex-slave Frederick Douglass, who became a close friend. According to one eyewitness, slavery that day found no more forceful foe than the Hutchinson Family Singers. "Speechifying, even of the better sort," he wrote, "did less to interest, purify and subdue minds, than this irresistible Anti-Slavery music."

One of the group's most effective rallying cries was *Get Off the Track!*, sung to the tune of *Old Dan Tucker* and trading on that minstrel song's rough appeal. The sheet music, published in 1844, billed the piece as "A song for Emancipation." When sung by the Hutchinsons, the song's impact could be overwhelming. An account written after the New England Anti-Slavery Convention in May 1844 leaves the impression that the Hutchinsons' performance was the emotional climax of the entire event.

The Hutchinsons Sing at a Boston Antislavery Rally, 1844

And when they came to that chorus-cry, that gives name to the song, when they cried to the heedless pro-slavery multitude that were stupidly lingering on the track, and the engine "Liberator" coming down hard upon them, under full steam and all speed, the Liberty Bell loud ringing, and they standing like deaf men right in its whirlwind path, the way they cried "Get off the track," in defiance of all time and rule, was magnificent and sublime. . . . It was the cry of the people.

The Hutchinsons published a number of original songs, but their talent lay especially in public performing. When singing for an audience, they convinced spectators of the emotional truth of what they were hearing. Yet none of the compositions bearing their name gained lasting popularity.

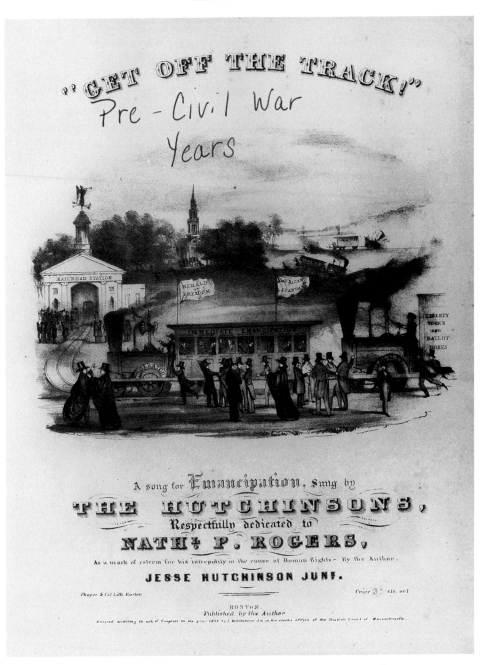

The Hutchinsons' emancipation song *Get Off the Track*, sung to the tune of the minstrel hit *Old Dan Tucker*, made an especially strong impression at abolitionist meetings and rallies in the North.

 SONGS OF THE CIVIL WAR

When war erupted in 1861 between the Northern and Southern states, the sheet-music industry responded with vigor. The songs of the Civil War, fueled by patriotic feelings and commerce, brought together in a new cause many of the elements discussed so far in this chapter: myth making, sentimentality, yearning, reform, and loss.

After war broke out in April 1861, song provided a way for North (the Union) and South (the Confederacy) to define their ideals. Just two days after Virginia left the Union, a pro-secessionist mob in Baltimore attacked a regiment of Union troops from Massachusetts, and in the fighting that followed, lives were lost on both sides. The incident inspired one of the first enduring songs of the war. James Ryder Randall, native Baltimorean, wrote the words just after the attack:

> The despot's heel is on thy shore,
>   Maryland!
> His torch is at thy temple door,
>   Maryland!
> Avenge the patriotic gore
> That flecked the streets of Baltimore,
> And be the battle-queen of yore,
>   Maryland! My Maryland!

Randall's poem, immediately published in newspapers, urges fellow Marylanders to resist federal tyranny. His appeal is cast in elevated language familiar from the earlier courtship song, with some biblical diction mixed in:

> For life and death, for woe and weal,
>   Thy peerless chivalry reveal,
>   And gird thy beauteous limbs with steel,
>   Maryland! My Maryland!

In October 1861, Randall's words appeared in a sheet-music version, set to the German Christmas song *O Tannenbaum.*

Maryland, My Maryland is less patriotic than chauvinistic. Patriotic expressions reflect a love of country and concern for its well-being, but Randall's song is short on love and long on vengeance. Expressing total allegiance to one side and implacable hatred of the other, it calls fellow countrymen names—"tyrants," "vandals," "Northern scum"—that undercut the two sides' common ground. Its tone, found in both Northern and Southern songs, surely helped to create an emotional climate in which all-out war could be waged.

In a parallel vein, the pro-Union *Battle Cry of Freedom* denounces the southern "traitor," while the *Battle-Hymn of the Republic*, with words by Julia Ward Howe, preaches how glorious it is to fall in step beside an om-

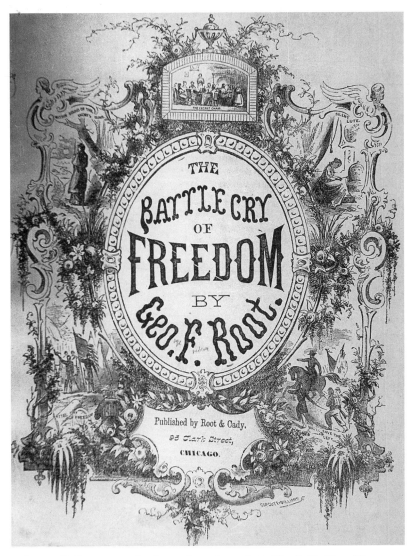

George F. Root wrote both words and music to *The Battle Cry of Freedom* (Chicago, 1862), whose cover offers a variety of wartime vignettes while also plugging other Root and Cady Civil War hits.

nipotent God, marching into battle at the head of a virtuous (Northern) army. Howe's poem, which celebrates the birth and sacrifice of Jesus while also conveying the unforgiving tone of Old Testament prophecy, was published in January 1862. A few months later, these words, with the "Glory, Hallelujah" refrain added, were published in sheet-music form, sung to a Methodist hymn tune of the late 1850s. The music's character and the added refrain take the edge off the harsh message of Howe's words, and the cry of joy at the end of each stanza emphasizes camaraderie and high spirits over revenge. Like many enduring American songs, this one was made by several hands—poet, composer, arranger—some of them unknown.

LISTENING GUIDE 18

The Battle Cry of Freedom (Root)

The Battle Cry of Freedom (1862) was written by George F. Root as a recruiting song for the Union army.

Root's song offers a mix of soul-stirring ingredients: the flag, a collective cheer, the notion of fighting for a high ideal, a blunt statement of the Union's goal in less than ten words ("Down with the traitor, / Up with the Star"), and a refrain that, like "Glory, Hallelujah," could easily be learned on the spot.

Written in march time, *The Battle Cry of Freedom* presents three memorable ideas: "Yes, we'll rally round the flag," "Shouting the battle cry of Freedom," and in the refrain, "The Union forever, / Hurrah, boys, hurrah!"

Yes we'll ral - ly round the flag, boys, we'll ral - ly once a - gain,

Shout - ing the bat - tle cry of Free - dom.

The Un - ion for - ev - er, Hur - rah boys, hur - rah!

Every musical phrase in the song is a statement or variant of one of the three, keeping melodic energy at a high level. Dotted rhythms tie the melodic phrases together; and the syncopation in the chorus on the song's highest pitch (G) casts the word "forever" into relief with a climactic jolt. When these musical details, supported by purposeful harmony, are linked to the resonant phrases in the text, there is little mystery why *The Battle Cry of Freedom* became popular. It was also taken over by the Confederates and adapted for their use. Originally published for solo voice and mixed chorus, Root's song is recorded here by a men's chorus.

marching song

> Yes we'll rally round the flag, boys, we'll rally once again,
> Shouting the battle cry of Freedom,
> We will rally from the hillside, we'll gather from the plain,
> Shouting the battle cry of Freedom.
> The Union forever, Hurrah, boys, hurrah!
> Down with the Traitor, Up with the Star;
> While we rally round the flag, boys, Rally once again,
> Shouting the battle cry of Freedom.

The signature song of the Confederacy also originated in the North. *Dixie*, attributed to Ohio-born minstrel Dan Emmett and introduced on a New York stage in 1859, found its way the following year to New Orleans, where it caused a sensation. Thus, even before the Civil War broke out, *Dixie* was a favorite Southern song. Here are the first stanza and refrain as they appeared in the original sheet music:

> I wish I was in de land ob cotton,
> Old times dar am not forgotten,
>   Look away! Look away! Look away! Dixie Land.
> In Dixie Land whar I was born in,
> Early on one frosty mornin,
>   Look away! Look away! Look away! Dixie Land.
>
>   Dan I wish I was in Dixie,
>   Hooray! Hooray!
>   In Dixie Land, I'll take my stand,
>   To lib an die in Dixie.
>   Away, Away, Away down south in Dixie,
>   Away, Away, Away down south in Dixie.

dancing song

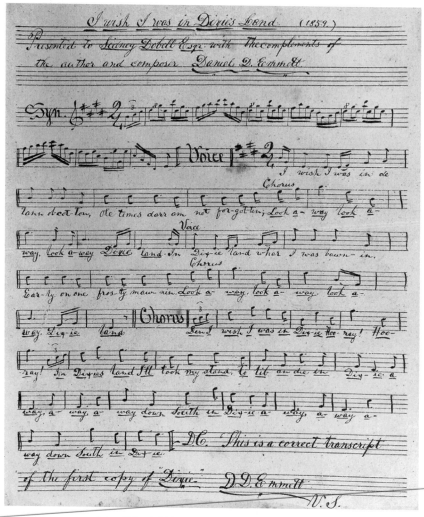

This manuscript of Daniel Emmett preserves *Dixie* (1859) in the composer's own hand.

What made *Dixie* a Southern favorite? Why would white people fighting to preserve slavery express their solidarity in the comic dialect of a minstrel-show slave? And why would a song without standard patriotic trappings command such allegiance? While these questions may not yield definite answers, Emmett's song seems to have offered a myth of the South so inviting that Southerners wholeheartedly embraced it.

The words and images of *Dixie* picture the South as a place to love, supporting that view with homey details. The tune, however, is probably most responsible for the song's electric appeal. Neither a march nor a hymn, *Dixie* is a dance written to accompany the jaunty strut of a minstrel-show walkaround—where performers cavorted in what was taken to be the manner of Southern plantation hands. When combined with its words, the tune kindles the kind of enthusiasm that has long made Southerners want to hoot and holler, wave banners, and throw hats in the air. The day after the South's military surrender in April 1865, President Abraham Lincoln was serenaded at the White House by jubilant citizens and several bands. After bantering with the crowd, Lincoln asked the bands

The cover of Will S. Hays's *The Drummer Boy of Shiloh* (1863) pictures the final prayer of a wounded noncombatant on the brink of death.

to play *Dixie* because the North had recaptured it, and besides, he said, it was "one of the best tunes I have ever heard." But *Dixie* was never included in the North's spoils of war. By 1865, it was so firmly linked to the South and the mood of defiance that lingered long after the Confederate army surrendered that it could not be reclaimed by the nation as a whole.

As well as centering on inspiration, patriotism, and revenge, many songs also took the human tragedy of the Civil War as their theme. Some were set on the battlefield. Others dwelled on the feelings of those who remained at home. Among the most popular was *Weeping, Sad and Lonely, or When This Cruel War Is Over*, with words by Charles C. Sawyer and music by Henry Tucker.

LISTENING GUIDE 19

Weeping, Sad and Lonely (Tucker)

This song is sung by the beloved of a Northern soldier who is away at the front. She addresses him as if in a letter:

> Dearest love, do you remember
> When we last did meet,
> How you told me that you loved me,
> Kneeling at my feet?
> Oh! how proud you stood before me,
> In your suit of blue,
> When you vow'd to me and country,
> Ever to be true.
> Weeping, sad and lonely,
> Hopes and fears, how vain (yet praying)
> When this cruel war is over,
> Praying! that we meet again.

The singer goes on to confess that "many cruel fancies" haunt her. She imagines her soldier wounded, worrying that no one will comfort him. In the last stanza, however, she decides that, fighting in a noble cause, he will receive the protection of angels.

Tucker's music is simple and straightforward, with six sung four-bar phrases (**aabcda**) and a unity stronger than that diagram may suggest. The rhythmic pattern of **a** (♩. ♪ ♫♫ ♩ ♩) also appears in phrases **b** and **c**. That pattern thus appears in every phrase except **d**, which Tucker makes the climax of the song by starting the refrain with it.

Imagine a parlor performance of the time, with singers gathered around a piano or a guitar player, as in this recording. One singer or perhaps the whole group in unison might sing the stanzas. But when phrase **d** arrives, they divide into four-part harmony to declaim "Weeping, sad, and lonely" in a new quarter-note tune. It is here, where vocal harmony replaces unison, and a new rhythm supplants the one heard in every previous phrase, that the words of an individual to her soldier boyfriend turn into a collective lament of families, households, and larger communities. The return of the **a** melody to end the refrain then offers hope to all who count themselves victims of the war's cruelty: this terrible conflict will not last forever.

Few songs of the Civil War try to deal with the connection between patriotic glory and the price that soldiers pursuing it are asked to pay. But one exception, *Tenting on the Old Camp Ground* by Walter Kittredge, looks beyond the standard language of heroism. Union General William Tecumseh Sherman once wrote: "War, like a thunderbolt, follows *its* laws and turns not aside even if the beautiful, the virtuous and charitable stand in its way." And the primary law of war, in Sherman's words, was "to produce results by death and slaughter." The soldiers in *Tenting on the Old Camp Ground* are pictured not as agents of war's thunderbolt but mourners of their own fate.

The center of gravity in *Tenting on the Old Camp Ground* is the refrain, where, rather than raising their voices in ecstatic, comradely shouts, soldiers sing in four-part harmony about war weariness. The arrangement adds a layer of drama. It opens with reveille in the piano (four bars), followed by a loud, jaunty, four-bar "tempo di marcia" (march time), which is repeated. But after the voices enter, that mood gradually loses steam. The piano now plays two rather than four chords per measure, as in a slow march; brief fills between phrases suggest military signals from the field, as if in the distance. The final lines are sung quietly to rolled, sustained piano chords. Imagination combines here with the idiom of the sentimental song to create a mood of numb resignation: an authentic human response to the Civil War.

Testifying to the war's mindless brutality, a Rhode Island volunteer recalled what happened when several Union soldiers entered the house of a Confederate family in Fredericksburg, Virginia, and listened as a private played "really fine music" on the piano. "As he ceases playing, another says, 'Did you ever see me play?' and seizing his rifle, he brings it down full force upon the keyboard, smashing it to splinters." That action signaled the soldiers to go on a rampage, destroying the remaining furniture in the house. It was in response to incidents like this one, as well as to battles in the field, that a song like *Tenting on the Old Camp Ground* explored the gap between the heroic and the sentimental, pondered what war could lead decent men to do, and thus reached a level of understanding that neither standard approach could manage.

14

Of Yankee Doodle and Ophicleides

BANDS AND ORCHESTRAS, 1800 TO THE 1870s

AS THE 1800s DAWNED, THE AMERICAN MILITARY WAS STILL USING wind instruments according to customs borrowed from the British army, with fifes and drums performing field music, while bands of music (oboes, clarinets, French horns, and bassoons) played so-called *Harmoniemusik* for listening (see Chapter 5). After the revolution, the size of the army had been drastically reduced. But in 1792, Congress passed an act ordering every able-bodied white male citizen between eighteen and forty-five to join his state militia. Field music was required for each battalion, and bands of music were also maintained, though these were essentially civilian groups.

The wind band's public appeal is fundamental to its history. Indeed, the idea of a band that only connoisseurs can appreciate seems a contradiction in terms. For two centuries and more, American bands have been stoking enthusiasm by playing tunes that listeners already know in ways they can readily appreciate.

Bands have courted audiences through sound as well as repertory. And the addition of two new instrumental families transformed the sound of the nineteenth-century wind band. The first was the percussion, especially the so-called Janissary instruments of triangle, tambourine, cymbals, and bass drum, which by the 1830s were standard in American ensembles. The second was the brass. In the 1700s, brass instruments were nothing more than long coiled tubes; players could sound a limited number of pitches by changing lip pressure. In 1810, Joseph Halliday of Dublin, Ireland, found that by cutting holes in the side of a bugle and fitting them with keys, he could change the tube's effective length. The result was a brass instrument that could play any note in any scale. Halliday's bugle helped to inspire the making of ophicleides, a family of keyed brass. And within a few years, German instrument makers introduced valves rather

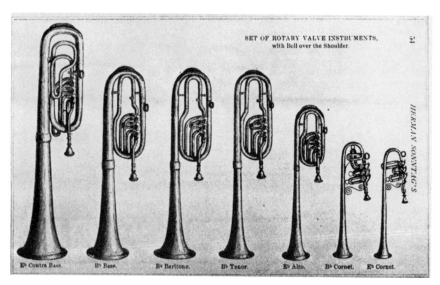

The instruments of the saxhorn family were advertised in dealers' catalogs beginning about the middle of the nineteenth century.

than keys, taking fuller advantage of the brass tube's natural resonance. By the 1820s, many brass instruments—the keyed bugle, bass ophicleide, cornet, trumpet, and French horn—were capable of playing melodies. And by mid-century, the brass band was the typical American wind ensemble.

Adolphe Sax's invention of the saxhorn, modeled after the upright tuba, in Paris in the early 1840s furthered the brass band's vogue. A brass band with cornets, percussion, and saxhorns ranging from alto down to bass could achieve a uniform blend. By the time of the Civil War, saxhorns formed the core of the typical band, but not everyone found them an improvement. A veteran bandsman writing in 1893 after sixty years in the business admitted that recent band instruments were "much better made and easier to learn" than those of his youth. Yet he missed the sound of bands in the pre-saxhorn age, with their sharply contrasting instrumental colors. Instruments of varied construction offered a palette of different tone qualities more interesting, to this musician's ear, than the blend that prevailed in the later 1800s.

 ## MUSIC PLAYED BY BANDS

By the middle 1800s, bands in America were serving functions that had nothing to do with the military. Bands might be heard in theaters, private halls, hotels, resorts, parks, hospitals, or churches; they were hired to perform at sporting events, fairs, store openings, dinner parties, club meetings, and even funerals. In all these settings, music served as an adjunct to some other purpose. But bands also played concerts, and here they followed the long-standing custom of varying the sound from number to number.

During the 1850–51 season, for example, the American Band of Providence, Rhode Island, presented a series of concerts in a local hall. The group numbered sixteen: a bugle in E-flat and a bugle in B-flat, cornet in E-flat, post horn, trumpet, three percussionists (side drum, bass drum, and cymbals), and eight saxhorns (two alto, two tenor, one baritone, and three bass). On one surviving program, the band offered a concert in two parts with six numbers on each. The first half consisted of a march, a vocal song, a cornet solo (with orchestra), a dance piece, another song, and an overture, in that order.

A concert at Western Reserve College in Ohio (1858) featured "A. James, The Great English Harpist," singer W. Milton Clark, and the Tallmadge Cornet Band and Orchestra in a performance whose first half included the following:

Prairie Flower Quickstep	Band
Akron Gallopade	Orchestra
Blue Bells of Scotland—Harp	A. James
Song	W. Milton Clark
Passage from Verdi	Orchestra
Solo—Harp	A. James
Song	W. Milton Clark
Zitti Zitti	Orchestra
Mountain Echo	Band

Like the Providence concert, this one offered a variety of sound, even including an orchestra. Indeed, nineteenth-century band concerts embraced virtually all the musical genres that audiences of the time were likely to hear: marches, patriotic songs, popular songs, programmatic pieces, solo pieces, transcriptions of orchestra works, and dance pieces. Except for programmatic pieces, each type is represented on the two programs noted here.

It is obvious that the band's military background links it to the march, and that band instruments are well suited to the march's character. When the sheet-music business began in the 1790s, marches were among its standard issues—in arrangements for keyboard, upon which the parlor trade in sheet music depended. Stately grand marches, many of them with fanfare-like melodies and a characteristic dotted-rhythm motive

($\sqrt{}$), dominated the form through the 1820s. In the 1830s, the quickstep came into prominence, its sprightlier, more flowing melodic style reflecting the brass's new aptitude for playing melody. Both the Rhode Island and Ohio programs began with marches, a rousing way to open a concert.

Bands were also a natural medium for such patriotic favorites as *The Star-Spangled Banner*, *Yankee Doodle*, the French *La marseillaise*, and *Hail Columbia*, a favorite patriotic lyric from around 1800. In the 1860s, band performances of such Civil War numbers as *The Battle-Hymn of the Republic*, *The Bonnie Blue Flag*, *The Battle Cry of Freedom*, and *Dixie* popularized their melodies and enhanced the band's inspirational role.

Band arrangements of popular parlor songs were common: new hits like Foster's *My Old Kentucky Home* and James Pierpont's *Jingle Bells*; older favorites like *Auld Lang Syne* and *Home, Sweet Home*; and medleys of Irish and Scottish songs (*The Last Rose of Summer*, *Annie Laurie*). The harp rendition of *Blue Bells of Scotland* on the Tallmadge Band's concert provides one example. And the second half of that concert ended with the band playing the *Gentle Annie Quickstep*, featuring a tune Stephen Foster wrote in 1856—a reminder that quicksteps, made up of several strains, might borrow a popular song melody for one of them.

Bands also played works intended to be descriptive or narrative. Under such titles as *The Night Alarm* or *An Alpine Storm*, such program music appealed to both European and American audiences. *The Battle of Prague* was a perennial favorite in the United States. Written in the 1780s by Bohemian composer Franz Kotzwara, this work was still well enough known a century later for Mark Twain to call it a "venerable shivaree." A number of American composers modeled battle pieces of their own on *The Battle of Prague*, with short movements depicting different scenes in the conflict: camp maneuvers, the call to arms, the cavalry charge, the moans of the dying, the victory call. Program music could also be inspired by less dramatic events; for example, John Holloway's *Wood Up Quickstep* (1834) is said to represent the refueling of a wood-burning steamboat.

Solo pieces like *Wood Up*, written to exhibit a star performer's virtuosity, formed another staple of the band repertory. In the Providence concert, a cornet solo with orchestra accompaniment provides an example. The presence of A. James on the Tallmadge concert also implies that some virtuoso display was unveiled there, at least enough to justify the label "The Great English Harpist." No fewer than five instrumental soloists were featured in an 1835 "Grand Concert" by the Boston Brass Band: a trombonist, flutist, violinist, clarinetist, and cornet (keyed bugle) player. The cornet soloist was often the wind band's star performer.

Bands also performed arrangements of classical orchestra works.

Overtures by Rossini and eventually Wagner were common, as were selections from operas and symphonic works by Mozart, Verdi, Mendelssohn, and Bellini, included on programs to balance lighter fare. In later years, bands were often credited with raising public taste. John Philip Sousa, who for several decades led America's most famous wind ensemble, claimed in 1910 that bands had helped make Wagner "less of a myth to the people at large than Shakespeare."

Dance music held a key place in the band's repertory. A group that played marches in a parade one day might serve as a dance ensemble the next. Bands that played for dancing were expected to accompany new dances as they found their way into American ballrooms. But dance music also lent variety to concert performances. The second half of the Tallmage Band's concert included three quicksteps, a waltz, and a set of quadrilles, the latter played by an orchestra.

CD 1
20

LISTENING GUIDE 20

Helene Schottische (Dignam)

Helene Schottische, based on a popular dance form, is heard here in an arrangement for a twelve-member brass band: two E-flat cornets, two B-flat cornets, seven saxhorns (three E-flat altos, two B-flat tenors, a B-flat and an E-flat bass), and drums. The arrangement survives in a manuscript written out during the Civil War (1863–64). It was made by Walter Dignam, born in England (1827) but an American resident from 1844, and leader of the Second and Fourth New Hampshire Regiment Band in Virginia during the conflict. Himself a skilled player of the instrument, Dignam intended the demanding first E-flat cornet part for himself. Played on instruments from the 1800s, the recording shows the delicacy, restraint, and beauty of sound possible from this kind of ensemble, which was formed more for functional than for artistic purposes.

The Rhode Island and Ohio concert programs reveal common ground between bands and orchestras of the time. Except for the New York Philharmonic Society, which numbered around sixty and played only a few concerts per season, and orchestras that accompanied operas in the theater, most mid-century ensembles, known as "social orchestras," consisted of five or fewer players and accompanied dancing or played in domestic settings. In the mid-nineteenth century, Elias Howe of Boston published social-orchestra music for two violins (one for melody and the other for rhythmic background), a cello, and a fourth instrument that could be a clarinet, flute, cornet, harp, or piano. *The American Collection of Instrumental Music* (1856) offered marches, quicksteps, waltzes, country dances, quadrilles, and polkas arranged for a similar ensemble.

Bands enjoyed more public appeal than orchestras and a broader institutional base. That point is confirmed by an 1856 program of the Manchester Cornet Band of New Hampshire, which shared the concert with an orchestra, several vocalists, and a pianist. The band's prominent place on the program, leading off and ending each half, is proof of its local prestige. It was clearly under band sponsorship that Manchester's citizens heard the music on this ambitious concert, most of it composed originally for orchestral and theatrical performance.

CLASSICAL MUSIC AS ENTERTAINMENT

In the mid-nineteenth century, American concert life was transformed when European impresarios recognized in the United States a market for concert performers. Customers would be plentiful, these entrepreneurs realized, if musical artistry could be packaged as entertainment. Canals and railroad lines now connected distant cities, making a touring circuit possible. The telegraph, invented in the mid-1830s, simplified communication. The growth of leisure time and the rise of the music-teaching profession encouraged the making of music in middle-class homes. As more Americans were taught to play and sing, the audience for music grew. Concert halls, opera houses, and assembly rooms appeared in more and more cities.

The 1840s saw these elements fused into a network for marketing entertainment, which might be anything from a lecturer or concert pianist to a minstrel troupe or a team of acrobats. Before Jenny Lind's landmark tour in 1850–51, solo violinists and pianists had traveled the United States in search of monetary gain. Most were managed by European-born impresarios.

Typically, a manager contracted with a star performer (as did Barnum with Jenny Lind) to give a specified number of concerts for a specified amount of money. Thus performers worked under the artistic control of the manager, who was ready to do whatever necessary to round up an audience. In a country where many potential concertgoers had never attended a concert, adversarial feelings between managers and their artists were common. Some impresarios were sophisticated music lovers and even musicians, but their role invited a thoroughly commercial approach to concert giving. Asked, for example, by a New Orleans concertgoer what kind of music his artists were going to perform, impresario Bernard Ullman replied: "Financial music."

By the 1840s, impresarios like Ullman had seized power in the entertainment network and were giving audiences what they liked: virtuoso display, wide variety, compositions based on familiar tunes, descriptive instrumental music (program music), established favorites, and dance music, especially dances currently in vogue. As customers applauded their use, these elements hardened into a formula that governed concert programming. Performers on the circuit seldom took artistic risks. Many grew weary of repeating the same pieces, but as long as customers seemed to respond to them, managers held performers to standard routines.

# ORCHESTRAS ON TOUR

Soon after the American concert circuit was set up, orchestras joined soloists as touring attractions. Among the first was the Austrian Steyermark ensemble, which arrived in Boston in 1846, twenty men strong. Recalling the group's visit a half century later, a Boston musician wrote that they performed "mostly light dance music, overtures, potpourris, and solos." The picturesque "Steyermark country uniform" and a certain amount of stage business enhanced their appeal; their playing seems to have been no less impressive. In December 1847, a New York critic commented: "Even the Philharmonic might learn from these Styrians."

In October 1848, a twenty-five-man ensemble from Berlin, the Germania Musical Society, arrived in New York. Performing for audiences of up to three thousand in the principal American cities, the Germanians played more than nine hundred concerts in North America before disbanding in 1854. The Germanians' concert programs during their first two months in New York were devoted mostly to dance music by Johann Strauss and others, sprinkled with overtures by Mozart and Rossini and their specialty, Mendelssohn's Overture to *A Midsummer Night's Dream*. Some selections were intended as crowd pleasers. For example, *Up Broadway*, composed by the group's leader, offered a tone portrait of sounds encountered on a journey along that New York thoroughfare. Mixed with Beethoven symphonies, Strauss waltzes, and the Mendelssohn overture,

GERMANIA MUSICAL SOCIETY.

This unusually detailed lithograph shows twenty-one of the twenty-five original players in the Germania Musical Society, which toured the United States from 1848 until it disbanded in 1854.

a novelty like *Up Broadway* was a repertory staple for all audiences that, together with polished ensemble playing and frequent tours, helped to make the group successful. Even after the orchestra broke up, its influence continued, for many of the members settled in American cities. Ex-Germanian Carl Bergmann led the New York Philharmonic for two decades, and Carl Zerrahn conducted the Boston Handel and Haydn Society from 1854 until 1898.

Another landmark orchestral tour began in the summer of 1853, when French-born conductor Louis Jullien sailed with twenty-seven instrumentalists from England to the United States. When he reached New York, he recruited another sixty players. Then, at the helm of this large orchestra, he began a series of New York concerts that lasted into the fall. Size was not the only unusual thing about Jullien and his orchestra. For he himself was the star performer: a conductor who had spent nearly twenty years in Paris and London polishing his charisma and charming audiences through instrumental performance.

Jullien had enrolled at the Paris Conservatory in 1833, then dropped out three years later and began to organize popular concerts—promenade concerts, as they came to be known in England—that featured overtures, instrumental solos, and plenty of dance music, well played and at a cheap ticket price. The atmosphere at these concerts was informal; audience members were free to sit, stand, or stroll while the music was being heard. With Philippe Musard in Paris and Johann Strauss in Vienna, Jullien belonged to the first generation of conductors who succeeded by making themselves into intriguing public figures.

Around 1840, Jullien moved from Paris to London, where he won an immediate following. One feature of Jullien's programs was their reliance on quadrilles: popular four-couple contradances consisting of five sections in 2/4 or 6/8 time. The dance's foursquare phrases provided molds into which familiar melodies could be fitted: popular songs and operatic numbers. Thus the quadrille was both a dance form and a musical form, with the finale sometimes used to create a colorful climax.

Jullien's orchestra successfully imported his London formula to the United States, playing more than two hundred concerts in ten months. The conductor made a vivid impression wherever he appeared. One New York writer likened him to a military hero: "Have we a Napoleon amongst us?" he asked. "Yes—the Napoleon of music, who, after conquering Eu-

Conductor Louis Jullien's New York concerts created an enthusiasm that, as these fanciful cartoons show, stopped short of artistic reverence.

rope, has invaded the realms of Yankee Doodle and Hail Columbia, with fiddles, fifes, trumpets, drums." Another journalist described how the conductor mimed the musical sounds. "Talk of descriptive music!" he exclaimed. "Why, here, the very whisk of the horses' tails, as they rush into the fight, is perceptible; and if you are not bright enough to understand all this musical language—look at the index, M. Jullien, who acts it out."

Even those who criticized Jullien granted that his orchestra played well. The critic John Sullivan Dwight warmly praised a New York performance he heard in October 1853: "To hear the great works of the masters brought out in the full proportions of so large an orchestra, where all the parts are played by perfect masters of their instruments, is a great privilege and great lesson." Jullien also performed compositions of his own on the tour, including the *American Quadrille*, based on *Yankee Doodle*, *Hail Columbia*, *Hail to the Chief*, and *The Old Folks at Home*. In a "monster concert" given just before the orchestra's return to Europe, the New York audience heard his *Fireman's Quadrille*, whose final section featured a real blaze, complete with clanging bell and a battalion of firefighters rushing in to quench the flames.

PATRICK S. GILMORE, BANDMASTER

Wind bands never wavered in their commitment to performers' music and audience accessibility, even while raising their level of artistry and professional status. A key figure in steering the wind band's course after 1850 was Patrick S. Gilmore, a bandmaster who proved that the band could cut loose from military affiliation and succeed as an independent ensemble in the public arena.

Born in Ireland in 1829, Gilmore immigrated to the United States in 1849 as a cornetist. He settled in Boston and began in the early 1850s to lead bands, including the Salem Brass Band, which he took over in 1855. The next year, Gilmore engaged the keyed-bugle virtuoso Ned Kendall in a public competition. Neither was judged to have won the contest, but with a shrewd gift for promotion, Gilmore parlayed his challenge into public recognition for himself and the cornet.

In 1858, Gilmore resigned from the Salem Brass Band and founded Gilmore's Band, which made its debut at the Boston Music Hall in April 1859. The group was a professional ensemble, with the leader in charge of both its artistic and business sides. Gilmore conducted the band, supplied uniforms for his thirty-two players, chose the music, booked engagements, and handled all other details. He also collected the profits.

Patrick Sarsfield Gilmore
(1829–1892), Irish-American bandmaster.

The outbreak of the Civil War in April 1861 interrupted the successful routine of Gilmore's Band, which became part of a Massachusetts regiment. When all volunteer military bands were mustered out of the Union
army in August 1862, Gilmore and his musicians returned to Boston, playing concerts to sustain public morale. In 1864, he accompanied a band to
New Orleans, where he staged a giant musical event celebrating the in-
auguration of a new governor: a "Grand National Band" boasting some
500 players and a chorus of 5,000 schoolchildren.

Gilmore's grandiose streak was soon to find an even grander focus.
In June 1869, mindful that the war's end had not soothed the bitterness
between North and South, he organized a National Peace Jubilee in
Boston, a musical event of unprecedented scope. Gilmore assembled vast
forces: an orchestra of 500, a band of 1,000, a chorus of 10,000, and many
famous soloists. Over a five-day span, an ambitious program of concerts
took place, including symphonic music, oratorio excerpts, band music,
and the singing of schoolchildren. The program for one of the concerts
reveals that, for all his emphasis on gargantuan effects, Gilmore took care
to vary his selections. The concert began with a huge orchestra featuring
some four dozen trumpeters on the solo part of a French operatic overture. A choral hymn followed, and then a newly composed march for
band and orchestra combined. Next came a soprano aria, which scaled
down the volume so that the following number—Verdi's "Anvil" Chorus, with a hundred Boston firefighters socking real anvils—could roar
forth in all its splendor. Gilmore then relied on the patriotic familiarity
of *Hail Columbia* to avoid anticlimax.

Testimony to the jubilee's success came from one who had first opposed it: the Boston critic John Sullivan Dwight, editor of *Dwight's Journal of Music* and a champion of music as edifying art. Dwight began his
review by admitting his initial reservations about the whole endeavor. As
Dwight saw it, Gilmore had seemed determined "to 'thrust' greatness
upon us by sheer force of numbers." And that approach had made "dis-

interested music-lovers" like himself anxious about "the honor and the modesty of Art." Yet he acknowledged that the bandleader had caught the public's attention. And he had lined up the support of local businesses to sponsor the vast undertaking, including the building of a coliseum big enough to hold 50,000 people. The spectacle of "so many beings met and held together there in full sight of each other, and in perfect order" formed the most indelible memory of all.

Dwight found the choral singing an impressive demonstration of "the musical resources of our people." Gilmore's jubilee gave "tens of thousands of all classes (save, unfortunately, the poorest)" the chance to experience music and to esteem it, perhaps "for the first time . . . as a high and holy influence" and "the birthright of a free American," and not "a superfluous refinement of an over-delicate and fashionable few."

The National Peace Jubilee of 1869 testifies to the wind band's key place in American life. For it was a bandleader who conceived and organized this event, an artistic and financial success for which an entire region pooled its musical resources. While the sheer numbers of musicians involved was remarkable, so was the participation of all manner of music makers: European-born conductors, solo singers and players, church musicians, whole choirs, public school teachers, orchestra players, bandsmen, and children—not to mention the Boston Fire Department. Gilmore, the only musician in Boston with ties to such a wide community, was the catalyst that made the enterprise work.

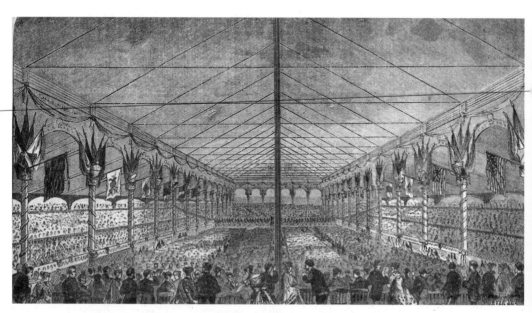

The Coliseum for Gilmore's National Peace Jubilee of 1869 was built specially for the event and dismantled after it was over.

15

From Church to Concert Hall

THE RISE OF CLASSICAL MUSIC

ON CHRISTMAS NIGHT IN 1815, A CONCERT TOOK PLACE IN BOSTON'S Stone Chapel that marks a new stage in Americans' recognition of music as an art. Some months earlier, the Boston Handel and Haydn Society had been formed to improve sacred music performance and promote the sacred works of eminent European masters. And now the society was giving its first public performance. Attended by an estimated one thousand, the program included excerpts from Haydn's *The Creation* and Handel's *Israel in Egypt*, as well as the "Hallelujah" Chorus from Handel's *Messiah*. According to a Boston newspaper report, the concert "electrified" the crowd, adding: "The excitements to loud applause were frequently irresistible."

This concert was a landmark event in the role it gave to composers. Reformers of psalmody had long been praising European musical science, but their interest lay in congregational singing, not in the complexities of oratorio: large-scale religious works for chorus, solo singers, and orchestra. The Boston Handel and Haydn Society set out to establish a place for Handel and Haydn *as composers of oratorios*, placing fresh emphasis on the music itself. Boston audiences could now experience the evocative power of musical sound that was artistic as well as sacred.

The society's first concert was also unusual in the way it brought sacred music to listeners who paid their way into the church, listened rather than sang, and responded by clapping rather than praying. Thus began a tradition of oratorio performances that laid the groundwork for a concert life new to the United States.

CONGREGATIONS, CHOIRS, AND ORATORIOS

In 1821 (as noted in Chapter 8), Lowell Mason approached the Handel and Haydn Society with a manuscript tunebook he had compiled in Georgia, proposing that the society publish the book, with the proceeds split equally between author and publisher. Appearing in seventeen editions in as many years, *The Boston Handel and Haydn Society Collection of Church Music* (1822) proved a financial windfall for the partners, enriching each by about $12,000. The book's success helped the society continue its concerts for chorus and orchestra while also expanding its repertory. By 1827, when Mason moved to Boston as the society's president, the Handel and Haydn Society was Boston's foremost musical organization.

By publishing Mason's tunebook, the society was helping to raise the standard of singing in public worship, the era's main form of democratic music making. But in its concerts, the Handel and Haydn Society also showed Bostonians how far sacred choral singing could reach. The singers performing Handel's and Haydn's scientific music were amateurs, most likely drawn to oratorio by the sacred subject matter. Once enlisted, however, choristers were asked to sing demanding voice parts artistically and on pitch, with decent vocal quality and clear pronunciation.

In chapter 7, we saw how reformers of psalmody took up the cause of European standards and "correct taste." Some also linked a European musical standard to refinement and gentility. But in the Handel and Haydn Society, composers were more than symbols of refinement; they were the authors of works that singers and listeners were coming to know through experience. Members of the chorus could seek religious exaltation—praise directed to the ear of God—while trying to improve their singing and learning great music. Thus the society promoted artistic skills in the name of religion, not refinement. Sacred subject matter, citizen involvement, and self-financing grounded what might have been an elite enterprise in democratic values.

Like oratorio societies, church choirs also brought the aesthetic pleasure of sacred choral music to singers and listeners alike. But psalmodists remained wary of sacred choral singing's aesthetic side. If choirs strove only for a pleasant sound, Thomas Hastings wrote, "why, then, let us have at once the *prima-donnas* of the drama for our leading singers." Indeed, by the time of the Civil War, many urban churches employed "quartet choirs": usually a soprano, alto, tenor, and bass, some of them opera or concert singers. Professional singers brought into churches a mastery that amateurs could not match. But some, evangelical leaders warned, also displayed an insincerity that could blunt the religious impact of performances during public worship.

CHURCH ORGANS AND ORGANISTS

In the early 1800s, more and more congregations bought organs—the largest financial investment in music that Americans of that era were ready to make. Organ playing in church was considered a ritual offering to God, yet organ playing, like oratorio singing, carried its own aesthetic force. "Perhaps no work of man's," an enthusiast wrote in the mid-1830s, "can claim equal power of exciting and arresting the feelings." The organ's sound and its power to affect the emotions complicated church leaders' efforts to control its expression.

The eighteenth-century practice of Episcopal churches hiring their organists from England continued in the nineteenth. Many of the most active composers in America during the early years of independence were organists. Before the Civil War, those performing in larger city churches were also mostly immigrants, but after the war the most illustrious organist–composers were native born: John Knowles Paine, Horatio Parker, George W. Chadwick, Arthur Foote, Dudley Buck, and Charles Ives.

As affluence grew in America, so did the grandeur of organs. In 1846, a Brooklyn builder completed a large instrument for New York City's Trinity (Episcopal) Church at a cost of $10,500. The Trinity organ, then

Trinity Church on New York City's Wall Street.

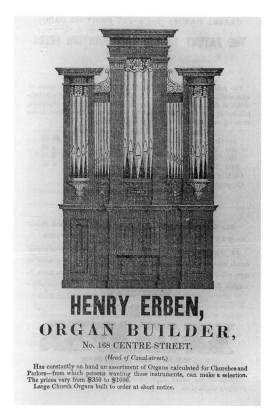

HENRY ERBEN,
ORGAN BUILDER,
No. 168 CENTRE-STREET,
(Head of Canal-street,)
Has constantly on hand an assortment of Organs calculated for Churches and Parlors—from which persons wanting these instruments, can make a selection. The prices vary from $350 to $1000.
Large Church Organs built to order at short notice.

The business card of Henry Erben (1800–1884), one of New York's leading organ builders of the nineteenth century.

the largest in the United States, impressed both ear and eye. One description noted the instrument's majestic height, "60 feet above the pavement of the church." An observer who found the lowest pipes "big enough for a small family and room for boarders" wondered whether the organist intended "to save house rent" by living in one of them.

In the 1820s and 30s, as more meeting houses and churches acquired organs, finding qualified people to play them was not always easy. Yet organists were as likely to draw criticism for showing off as for being incompetent. In the view of Thomas Hastings, organists often became virtual "dictators" over public worship. Hastings complained especially about the way some organists buried hymns in "massive peals of legato harmony." And for some, he lamented, the end of each hymn stanza brought a "moment of liberation," when the instrument was "allowed to burst forth in all the rhapsody of execution, as if exulting in its emancipation from an unwilling captivity!"

The opening of Trinity Church's giant instrument brought the organ's dual function of worship and artistry into conflict. Two days were set aside for a public display in which local organists were invited to play anything they chose. The invitation, a local newspaper reported, brought a "suffocating jam" of people flocking to the church gates. When the doors were opened, the crowd streamed into the church with "such a buzz and a chatter" as had never been seen before. Not everyone was there for the music, though: inside the church, "the organ was in full blast, and the audience in full march, examining the various parts of the building, most being busily engaged in conversation upon various topics, with only here and there a group listening to the organ." The music included opera arias, "marches from military bands, and waltzes from the ballroom." Dismissing the display as "a farce," the report charged that the house of God had been turned into "an exhibition room."

Like choral singing, organ playing was more than a means of sacred expression; it fostered both performing skill and an aesthetic sense. By the 1840s, thanks partly to opera and partly to the church, the idea of music as an art was beginning to take hold in concert life.

CLASSICAL INSTRUMENTAL MUSIC COMES TO BOSTON

Just as sacred music flourished in churches, other kinds of music were linked to the theater, the military, the school, and the parlor. But one kind of Old World music had no tie to entertainment, religion, education, or the home: classical instrumental music. Originating in the latter 1700s, this music followed the design of a sonata: written for certain combinations of instruments, in three or four movements, and with no descriptive program. Haydn, Mozart, and Beethoven, for example, raised the symphony, a sonata for orchestra, to prominence in the concert hall; for more intimate settings, they wrote string quartets (sonatas for four string instruments), duo sonatas for violin and piano, and solo sonatas for piano alone.

In the hands of these masters, the sonata exemplified composers' music: a serious, discursive form, with themes presented, repeated, and developed over long stretches of time. A growing appreciation in Europe for instrumental music eventually carried over to the United States. But in the early 1800s, this music was still new to America, and it posed problems for performers and listeners alike.

By the 1830s, a few American musicians and writers were starting to recognize Beethoven as a master, but explaining why, given his music's lack of words and programmatic reference, was difficult. Before Americans could embrace Beethoven's works, reasons for listening to them were needed, and so was a framework to support their performance. We can observe how Bostonians overcame these obstacles by tracing the path that led to the first performance of Beethoven's First Symphony there in 1841.

One leader in the effort was John Sullivan Dwight (later the city's chief music critic), an ardent music lover whose interest in philosophy combined with a passion for German poetry. In 1838, he published an English translation of poems by Johann Wolfgang von Goethe and Friedrich von Schiller, finding in their work a spiritual quality that convinced him "how life, and thought, and poetry, and beauty, are the inheritance of [humankind], and not of any class, or age, or nation." Dwight also saw certain musical works as universal. By 1837, he was convinced that Beethoven was a thinker on a par with Socrates, Shakespeare, and Newton. And he found instrumental music "a language of feeling" that had reached its peak in works for orchestra. In 1841, Dwight described Beethoven's slow movements as uniquely eloquent music that was able "to hallow pleasure, and to naturalize religion." With such pronouncements, Dwight helped pave the way for classical instrumental music.

Institutional support came first from the Boston Academy of Music. Founded in 1833 to teach singing, the academy boasted Lowell Mason as its first professor and soon caught on with the public. Revenues from membership dues, classes for children and adults, and contributions were enough by 1835 to refurbish a local theater, supply it with a new organ, and set up academy headquarters there. An instrumentalist was hired to teach instrumental music, and singing instruction then became merely

John Sullivan Dwight (1813–1893), a member of Harvard College's class of 1832 and an 1836 graduate of Harvard's Divinity School, became Boston's leading writer on music with the founding of *Dwight's Journal of Music*, which he edited from 1852 until 1881.

one stage in a farther-reaching project to enrich and diversify Boston's musical life. At the end of the decade, an orchestra was assembled, and it was this orchestra of the Boston Academy of Music that gave the local premiere of Beethoven's First Symphony on February 13, 1841.

The concert seems to have created no particular stir, but other orchestra performances followed. In 1842, a local newspaper reported that only a few years earlier the music of Haydn, Mozart, and Beethoven "would hardly have drawn an audience of fifty persons. Now, we see the hall filled an hour before the commencement of the performances . . . which speaks well for the increase of correct musical taste in our good city." The same article praised the Academy of Music's role in bringing about "this great revolution in musical taste." The academy's 1843 report even suggested a link with personal virtue. Calling classical orchestra music "an intellectual and social enjoyment" of a high order, the report warned that rejecting such a worthwhile force would be a "discouraging and painful symptom of the character of our population."

This last comment and others like it have led some scholars in recent years to conclude that, even more than a love of art, the force that stood behind the establishment of some nineteenth-century musical institutions was a wish to exercise social control by excluding others because of their class or ethnic background. That charge, however, does not apply to the Boston Academy of Music, an organization financed by its hundreds of members and devoted chiefly to work in which they participated: sacred singing, choir music, and elementary musical learning. The academy's involvement in the whole range of music making, from simple to complex, reflected a political outlook that has been described as republicanism in Thomas Jefferson's mold. That view saw society as both hierarchical, in that the best-qualified citizens held authority, *and* egalitarian, in that all members of society were free to earn the position they deserved. A specialized cultivation of classical instrumental music would have contradicted the principle of wholeness the academy had embraced.

The Boston Academy of Music's sponsorship of classical instrumental music complemented the ideas of John Sullivan Dwight, who believed "in the capacity of all mankind for music," because music supplied "a genuine want of the soul." Just as the Handel and Haydn Society had given local citizens a chance to hear oratorios, the academy was now introducing the symphonies of Mozart and Beethoven to the public. In the early 1840s, with Dwight's idealistic notions in the air and an appetite for instrumental music apparently growing, there seemed reason to hope that American listeners of all stripes would come to embrace "music of the highest class."

NEW YORK AND THEODORE THOMAS, CONDUCTOR OF THE CLASSICS

In April 1842, a number of New York's leading musicians gathered to discuss the founding of an orchestra whose members would be permanent. The constitution that resulted called for a structure of "actual" and "professional" members who performed and associate members who attended rehearsals and concerts. The new ensemble, named the New York Philharmonic Society, was founded, therefore, as a cooperative venture whose playing members were less interested in financial gain than in the chance to play the best symphonic music. The United States's oldest professional orchestra, the society gave its first concert in December 1842.

The new orchestra sought to edify players and audiences alike. Playing only four programs per season, the Philharmonic could be no more than a complement to any musician's livelihood. Yet its survival shows that it filled a need on the local scene. Moreover, the Philharmonic's early history is intertwined with the careers of many influential musicians, including Theodore Thomas, the premier American conductor of the nineteenth century.

Thomas, whose family immigrated from Germany in 1845, was recruited in 1853, at age eighteen, to play in Louis Jullien's orchestra, which was then taking New York by storm. The following year, he joined the first-violin section of the New York Philharmonic Society. Within a few years, he also was serving as concertmaster of the Italian opera orchestra at New York's Academy of Music. Although Thomas played violin in public into his fourth decade, a talent for leadership set him apart from the beginning. His musical outlook was also distinctive. First and foremost, Thomas took it as his mission to help raise musical standards so that the symphony orchestra's place in the United States would be secured. "Throughout my life," he wrote in 1874, "my aim has been to make good music popular." Where most performers were obliged to respect audience taste enough to gratify it, Thomas worked to elevate public taste to the point where it would be worth gratifying. He trusted that audiences would come to understand things his way. As a contemporary put it: "He was sure that he was right, and he was sure that the people would see he was right."

Thomas mastered not only the artistic but the business side of his trade. In May 1862, he conducted his first professional orchestra concert in New York's Irving Hall, an event for which he took the financial risk himself. Soon he also began to conduct the Brooklyn Philharmonic Soci-

Theodore Thomas (1835–1905), German-born American conductor and one of the most powerful classical musicians in the nineteenth-century United States.

ety, formed in 1857 as a parallel to New York's. But it was as conductor of the Theodore Thomas Orchestra (1865–90) that he accomplished one of the more complex balancing acts in the history of American music, by controlling both its artistic and economic arms. In fact, Thomas's career challenges the notion that art and economics are separate things, for without a musical marketplace the Thomas Orchestra could never have survived. His great achievement was to discover within that marketplace an audience for the symphony orchestra.

Thomas found his audiences by blending idealism with a strong pragmatic streak. Three related concerns dominated the Thomas Orchestra's early years: how the ensemble played, what it played, and where it played. The quality of the playing demonstrated the conductor's pragmatic idealism in action. On the podium, Thomas strove for precise, polished performances. Since much of the music he programmed was hard to play, good performances relied on skilled players and time to rehearse them. In an age of makeshift ensembles, however, the best players were the most in demand; and to recruit them, Thomas had to pay good wages, which hinged on the quantity of work he could provide them. Thus, as well as performing the classics in concert halls, from 1865 on the orchestra also made a specialty of outdoor concerts (a summer series in Central Park Garden proved especially popular): mixing symphonic movements with overtures, dances, and lighter selections in settings where customers felt relaxed and comfortable—snacking, drinking, and socializing. Such "concessions" to public taste, Thomas believed, chipped away at barriers between audience and orchestra. At the same time, the frequency of performances enabled the Thomas Orchestra to improve until it outstripped all other American ensembles.

Yet Thomas was able to stay in business only by touring. In 1869, the

Thomas Orchestra made the first of many cross-country journeys, and through the early 1870s the orchestra sometimes spent more than half the year on the road. While the touring life was difficult, the quality of the playing remained high. Russian pianist and composer Anton Rubinstein testified after an 1873 tour with Thomas that only the orchestra of the National Conservatory of Paris was the Thomas Orchestra's equal in personnel—"but, alas, they have no Theodore Thomas to conduct them."

Thomas's belief in the superiority of certain classical works never wavered. Performers and listeners alike, he believed, were tested and measured by the great symphonic compositions. In listening to music by Beethoven and other great composers, Thomas wrote, "faculties are called into action and appealed to other than those [the listener] ordinarily uses," absorbing attention and freeing listeners "from worldly cares." Recognizing that "the complexities of symphonic form are far beyond the grasp of beginners," Thomas planned the Central Park Garden concerts of the 1860s and early 70s for just such beginners: the concerts, featuring music with "very clearly defined melody and well-marked rhythms, such . . . as is played by the best bands," were meant to prepare novice listeners "for a higher grade of musical performances." But when the audience gave a symphony orchestra its attention, the impact could be breathtaking, even for inexperienced listeners. In 1877, the Thomas Orchestra paid a visit to a Mississippi River town, playing works by Mendelssohn, Charles Gounod, Camille Saint-Säens, Robert Schumann, Hector Berlioz, and Liszt. "Life was never the same afterward," a writer who heard that concert as a boy later recalled, for audience members had been shown that "there really existed as a fact, and not as something heard of and unattainable, this world of beauty, wholly apart from everyday experiences."

In Europe, most orchestras were local organizations financed by local resources and addressed to local audiences. But before a similar situation could arise in the United States, three elements had to come together: (1) a belief in the artistic importance of the symphony orchestra; (2) civic pride, centered in the feeling that an orchestra enriched community life; and (3) wealth, donated in recognition that the marketplace could not support an orchestra of the first rank. The first of these elements ranked classic orchestral works among the supreme human achievements, and took music to be a composer-centered art. Thomas was a prime mover in establishing the ritual elements in a symphony concert: an atmosphere of attentive restraint; a code of behavior and dress; and an assumption that performers spare no effort to honor the composers' artistic intentions. Just as liturgy ruled the worship of a God whose presence, though unseen, was always felt, so musical scores stood in for composers who, though most likely absent, were celebrated in concert performances.

The Music Hall in Cincinnati, Ohio, opened for the city's third May
Festival in 1878, under the direction of Theodore Thomas.

Beginning in the 1880s, orchestras were formed where money was
available to free them from dependency on the marketplace. But Thomas,
still at the helm of his own ensemble, continued to dream of a permanent
orchestra: one that offered its musicians full-time employment, with funding independent of the marketplace and not supplied by Thomas himself. When asked by Chicago businessman Charles Norman Fay if he
would consider moving to Chicago for such a post, Thomas is said to
have replied: "I would go to hell if they gave me a permanent orchestra."
In response, Fay organized a group of financial backers who then invited
Thomas to become the new Chicago orchestra's music director, with complete control over its artistic affairs.

And so, from 1891 to the end of his life, Thomas had his orchestra
and the autonomy he had long desired. Although he faced such obstacles
as the continuing need to tour and the lack of a suitable concert hall, the
orchestra succeeded. On December 14, 1904, Thomas conducted the in-
augural concert in Orchestra Hall, the ensemble's new home, built under
his supervision. But influenza immediately overtook him. Ten days later,
he laid down his baton after a concert for the last time, and he died on
January 4, 1905.

By the time of Thomas's death, a classical sphere based on composers' music was established in America, and a number of cities boasted symphony orchestras. Musical life in centers like New York, Boston, Philadelphia, and Chicago seemed to be catching up with that of European cities, where an infrastructure of musical activity existed: performing groups, concert halls, conservatories, and enough public interest in these institutions to support them financially. And long before, American composers had begun to arrive on the scene. Their careers show that the classical sphere defined by advocates of the European masters had been too narrow to contain the new democracy's musical energies in the earlier 1800s.

16

From Log House to Opera House

ANTHONY PHILIP HEINRICH AND WILLIAM HENRY FRY

AMONG THE MUSICIANS WHO PLAYED IN THE NEW YORK PHILHAR-monic Society's first concert in December 1842, one member of the viola section could lay claim to being the nation's chief composer of orchestral music. Anthony Philip Heinrich, a sixty-one-year-old Bohemian-born American, had by 1842 written at least a dozen such works, most of them still unperformed. We might guess that a new ensemble like the Philhar-monic would have been eager to play new American compositions, but that was not the case. Indeed, the New York Philharmonic Society was founded and grew to its early maturity almost entirely apart from any engagement with music by American composers.

THE LOG-HOUSE COMPOSER OF AMERICA

Born near the German border of northern Bohemia in 1781, Heinrich be-gan his life in prosperity, thanks to a family business. Learning to play violin and piano as a boy, he became a merchant and part-time musician. Heinrich visited the United States in 1805 and returned in 1810, hoping to establish his business here. After the Napoleonic Wars abroad wiped out his family's fortune, Heinrich, at the age of thirty-six, decided to embark on a musical career—in the West, rather than in the cities of the Eastern Seaboard. From Philadelphia, where he had played in a theater orchestra, he traveled in 1817 to Pittsburgh, then down the Ohio River as far as Kentucky, where he decided to settle. Apparently under the spell of this encounter with the American wilds, Heinrich made a decision that shaped the rest of his life. Not only would he seek his fortune in music; he would be a composer.

Heinrich has often been linked with the Romantic spirit that appeared in European music in the early 1800s: a preference for the original, unique, extreme, expressed in rich harmonies and innovative textures and tone colors. Indeed, Heinrich was a true original. Living alone in a log cabin near Bardstown, Kentucky, and with no access to formal musical learning, he had only his own intuition to rely on when he began to compose. Romantic artists also drew inspiration from nature, and so did Heinrich in such orchestra works as *The Wild Wood Spirits' Chant* (1842) and *Manitou Mysteries* (1845).

Heinrich's prose adds to his image as a colorful character, "vegetating in my Bardstown log house" and living on "roots, milk and bread, quite solitary." Occasionally his isolation was broken. Late one evening, Heinrich was "playing on the violin a dead march in honor of my poor departed wife," when suddenly "a negro prowling about" burst into his cabin. The startled composer was asked to keep playing, for the music had drawn the guest there in the first place. Heinrich repeated the dirge, "which pleased him amazingly." This adventure, he recalled, "at dead of night, in the lonely forest, seemed to me rather poetical."

Heinrich left no account of how he learned to compose. But in the spring of 1818, a young Bardstown man brought him an original poem and asked him to set it to music. "I took pencil and instantaneously reciprocated," Heinrich recalled, suggesting a mind stocked with musical ideas that needed only to be written down. From then on, music poured out of him: songs and music for violin and piano, then more piano pieces, and from the 1830s on, music for orchestra. In 1820, he published *The Dawning of Music in Kentucky* (Op. 1), a collection of vocal and instrumental pieces. In a review, the editor of a Boston music journal registered amazement at the result. An ex-businessman nearing forty years of age had suddenly declared himself a composer, and had then written music that showed "originality of conception" and "classical correctness," not to mention "boldness and luxuriance of imagination."

In 1823, Heinrich left Kentucky for Boston. Now a composer of some experience, he served briefly as a church organist, probably played in theater orchestras, did some teaching, and published a new collection of his work: *The Sylviad, or Minstrelsy of Nature in the Wilds of N. America* (Op. 3). The Boston journal that had praised Opus 1 also endorsed this latest offering. All the composer's works, the reviewer wrote, "abound in boldness, originality, science, and even sublimity; and embrace all styles

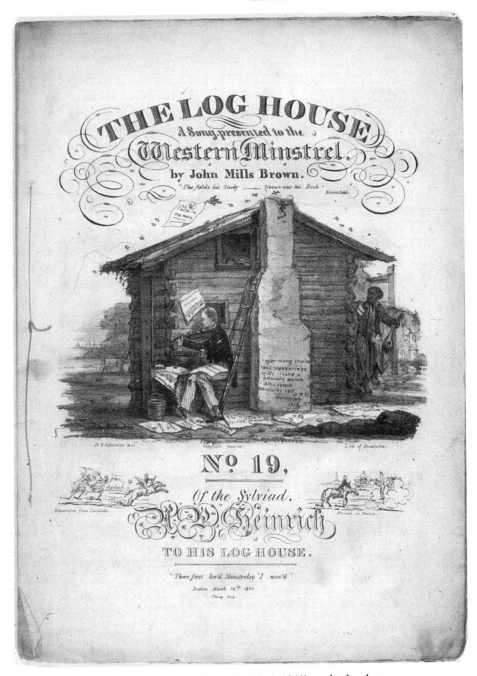

This image of Anthony Philip Heinrich (1781–1861) as the Loghouse Composer of Kentucky is found in his *The Sylviad*, Op. 3, a collection of pieces for keyboard, voice, and other instruments.

of composition, from a waltz or song up to the acme of chromatic frenzy." Heinrich, the review concluded, "may be justly styled the *Beethoven of America.*"

Heinrich reveled in the homespun image of "loghouse composer." His music often quotes national tunes, and many instrumental works were inspired by an image or story found in the American landscape. Heinrich was also the first American composer to celebrate the customs of North America's native peoples. Beginning in 1831 with *Pushmataha, a Venerable Chief of a Western Tribe of Indians,* he tried to depict Indian life in a series of works for large orchestra. Still, the technical difficulty of his works put them beyond the reach of most performers and made it hard for him to find an audience.

What did the notion of Heinrich as the Beethoven of America mean in the 1820s? To John Rowe Parker, who gave him that label, Beethoven took a nonconforming, exploratory approach to composing that seemed to "anticipate a future age." His symphonies were "romances of the wildest invention," in which he crowded "zig zag notes" even "into subservient parts," caring little for the performer's convenience. For Parker, Beethoven was a genius whose music could be unpredictable, even sometimes overloaded. And that is where he found parallels with Heinrich, who "seems at once to have possessed himself of the key which unlocks to him the temple of science and enables him to explore with fearless security the mysterious labyrinth of harmony."

Heinrich lived for almost forty years after these words were published, still composing but receiving few performances and meager public recognition. After an 1846 benefit concert for the composer in New York, a critic reflected: "Heinrich is undoubtedly ahead of the age; and we believe that his music will be far more popular long after he is dead than now." In a letter written the same year, the composer described himself as an artist striving not to please audiences but to serve the art of music: "I hope there may be some method discoverable, some beauty, whether of regular or irregular features. Possibly the public may acknowledge this, when I am dead and gone. I must keep at the work with my best powers, under all discouraging, nay suffering circumstances."

As concert repertories in the early 1800s were formed around works by composers both living and dead, the idea took hold that the true worth of a composition could only be judged at a chronological distance. Composers unappreciated today might be perceived differently tomorrow. By mid-century, as works by Beethoven and other long-dead authors still spoke to present-day audiences, a composer like Heinrich had reason to feel that his own music's fate lay in the hands of posterity.

WILLIAM HENRY FRY: AMERICAN COMPOSER

No American composer of the nineteenth century wrote an opera that entered the standard repertory. In fact, with few exceptions, opera in America before the Civil War revolved around works that London audiences favored. English companies performed English operas or adaptations of foreign ones, and stars of other nationalities came to the United States by way of London. Nevertheless, from the 1790s on, composers in this country did add works of their own to the stage repertory: Benjamin Carr's *The Archers* (1794), John Bray's *The Indian Princess* (1808), and Rayner Taylor's *The Ethiop* (1813), all by immigrants from England. An opera from the 1840s looms larger, not only as a through-composed work in the grand-opera manner but because it was a home-grown effort: *Leonora* (1845), with music by Philadelphia-born William Henry Fry.

One of four sons of a Philadelphia newspaper publisher, Fry was born in 1813. He attended Mount St. Mary's Academy in Emmitsburg, Maryland, then studied music with French-born Leopold Meignen, said to be a graduate of the Paris Conservatory, who had settled in Philadelphia. In 1833, an opera orchestra in Philadelphia played an overture composed by the twenty-year-old Fry. And soon he embarked on his life's main vocation: writing about music, which he did between 1837 and 1841 for his father's newspaper, the Philadelphia *National Gazette*. He also continued to compose.

In the early 1840s, Fry concentrated his musical energies on opera, leading up to the premiere of *Leonora*, which took place in Philadelphia in 1845. *Leonora* was a Fry family enterprise: William wrote the music and brother Joseph the libretto, brother Edward acted as impresario, and the family covered half the production costs. The Frys intended *Leonora*, based on an English play, for the Seguin Opera Company, headed by English singers Anne and Edward Seguin. The Seguins had arrived in America in the late 1830s, formed a troupe in 1841, and watched it blossom into a company that dominated English opera performance in the United States for almost a decade. Soprano Anne Seguin sang the role of Leonora, Edward Seguin sang the lead bass role, and company singers took the other parts. Leopold Meignen, Fry's first composition teacher, conducted the performance.

The *New York Herald* sent a correspondent to Philadelphia for *Leonora*'s premiere. Headlines in his breezy account set the tone: "Grand Opera by Fry and Brother—Excitement among the Quakers—Great rush to the

Theater . . . The commencement of the new musical revolution—Awful commotion among the flats and sharps." The review mocked Fry's effort. "The long agony is over," it announced. "The child is christened, and 'Alleghania' has at last an opera of its own—musical taste is on the ascendant, and native Mozarts yet unborn shall lisp with gratitude, in after ages, the mighty name of Fry." After a summary of *Leonora*'s plot and its musical underlining, the writer continued: "All were delighted with the music, it was so much like an old acquaintance in a new coat . . . a warm 'hash' of Bellini, with a cold shoulder of 'Rossini,' and a handful of 'Auber' salt—whilst others congratulated Mr. Fry upon his opera being so much like *Norma*, an evident proof that the same grand idea may consecutively strike two great minds."

The *Herald* review also quoted from a post-performance speech Fry delivered in front of the curtain. As a boy, he confided, he had already decided to compose an opera. Under Meignen's instruction, "I studied every great composer, from Palestrini up to Rossini, and then I stopped. I then wrote an opera, and since then I have written several"—*Leonora* was Fry's third—"which circumstances or ill luck, it matters not, has prevented them from being brought out." Fry made no excuses for his work. "This opera," he proclaimed, "has been written according to the highest rules of art, and is to be judged by the severest criticisms of art."

Fry was thus challenging the musical form that had long dominated the American stage. English operas, with their combination of sung numbers and spoken dialogue, seemed to him corruptions of true operatic form. Following the model of Italian composers, Fry had composed *Leonora* as a grand opera with every word "sung throughout, and accompanied by the orchestra." Fry saw his own work as drawing on "the genius of melody as a universal dialect, which claims, indeed, supremacy over words." His continuously sung opera, he believed, opened a place for English-language works in the true operatic tradition.

Fry's project as an American opera composer, then, was to master European techniques of opera writing so that audiences could experience them in the English language. Thus, he made no attempt to disguise his models. *Leonora* in 1845 received twelve performances at the Chestnut Street Theater and four more by the Seguins in Philadelphia the following year. It was then laid aside until 1858, when a revised version was sung in New York City—this time, ironically, in an Italian translation.

In 1846, Fry moved to Paris, where he worked as a foreign correspondent. He returned to the United States in 1852, settling in New York as the *Tribune*'s music critic and making his presence felt in a series of lectures on music, with illustrations by an orchestra, a chorus, a band, and vocal soloists. The lectures were quoted widely in New York's news-

Fry is pictured here (top row, standing at the left) in a daguer-
rotype from the 1850s with other members of the staff of the
New York Tribune, for which he wrote.

papers, and they drew large crowds—an average of two thousand, according to one estimate.

Fry's last lecture, given early in 1853, closed with a tirade on American musical life. As Fry saw it, the United States faced two major problems: the ignorance of audiences and the weak presence of American
composers. Because of the first, musical appetites were being satisfied by
inferior forms. The second resulted from the absence of financial support
for composers. Even in the largest cities, barely one or two composers
could be found, and outside the cities there were none at all. Furthermore,
the few who did exist lacked creative boldness. Having long ago won political freedom, Fry argued, the United States now needed "a Declaration
of Independence in Art." "Until American composers shall discard their
foreign liveries and found an American school" of musical forms favored
by concert hall and opera house, he warned, "art will not become indigenous to this country, but will only exist as a feeble exotic."

Fry's raising of the issue of musical nationalism introduces a subject
that has long been debated: what constitutes "American music"? Twentieth-century composer and critic Virgil Thomson once said that to create
American music, one needed only to be an American and to compose. In
other words, American music is defined by nationality, not by style. Fry's

idea of musical nationalism resembled Thomson's: he insisted that American composers deserved a hearing in this country simply because they were Americans.

On Christmas Eve 1853, Louis Jullien conducted the premiere of Fry's new *Santa Claus* Symphony, whose title page reads: "Written expressly for Jullien's orchestra, and performed with the greatest applause." The symphony contained several movements, but rather than following classical sonata principles, it was structured by a narrative program that interpreted the musical sounds. A bassoon, for example, represented Santa Claus himself. When a New York critic called Fry's symphony a good Christmas piece but undeserving of serious attention, the composer fired off a long, heated reply, sparking a controversy that continued for months in local newspapers and music journals. The controversy invited Americans, perhaps for the first time, to think of concert life as a form of national expression. Was it enough for them simply to hear the music of European masters? Or should a place also be reserved for home-grown talent?

No one at the time was better equipped to argue on behalf of American composers than Fry, who denounced the Philharmonic Society for never having "asked for or performed a single American instrumental composition during the eleven years of its existence." The attack drew a quick rebuttal from a Philharmonic member, which was then answered sarcastically by George Frederick Bristow, himself an American composer, an officer of the orchestra, and one of its violinists. Bristow backed up Fry's charge:

> As it is possible to miss a needle in a haystack, I am not surprised that Mr. Fry has missed the fact, that during the eleven years the Philharmonic Society has been in operation in this city, it played once, either by mistake or accident, one single American composition, an overture of mine. . . . This single stray fact shows that the Philharmonic Society has been as anti-American as if it had been located in London during the Revolutionary War, and composed of native-born British tories.

From the time of its founding, Bristow claimed, the Philharmonic Society's directors and players had carried on "little short of a conspiracy against the art of a country to which they have come for a living." In Bristow's view, some immigrant members of the orchestra, especially the Germans, were biting the hand that fed them. "What is the Philharmonic Society in this country?" he asked. "Is it to play exclusively the works of German masters, especially if they be dead? . . . Or is it to stimulate original art on the spot?" Bristow himself wrote symphonies inspired by Mendelssohn; but with Mendelssohn's own symphonies available and

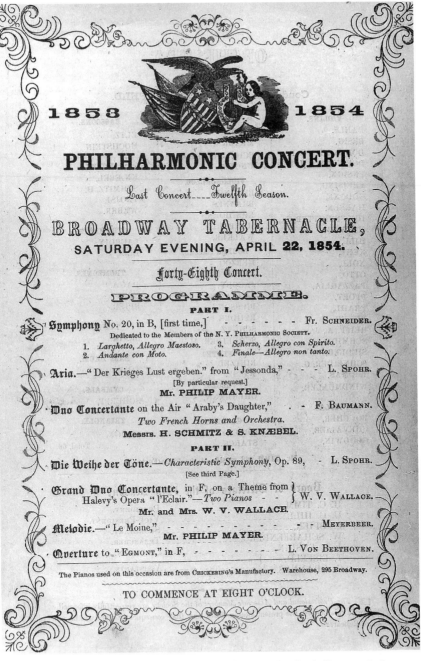

This program from an 1854 concert by the New York Philharmonic Society shows what the group's concerts were like in the mid-nineteenth century, when Fry and Bristow were arguing for more American music.

still unfamiliar, the Philharmonic found no reason to perform Bristow's. Fry and Bristow advocated *American* orchestra music on ideological grounds, but their appeal made little headway against the Philharmonic's cycle of supply and demand. Rooted in an ample supply of European masterworks, the orchestra created a demand for performances of more of the same.

A present-day observer of this debate can hardly help but take the side of Fry and Bristow. Yet in the mid-nineteenth century, to perform untested music was risky, and the fragile economic status of orchestras argued against such risks. It was not until later in the century that American composers began to find a place in the concert hall.

17

A New Orleans Original

GOTTSCHALK OF LOUISIANA

IN JUNE 1857, NEW ORLEANS–BORN COMPOSER AND PIANIST LOUIS
Moreau Gottschalk was bound by ship from Cuba to St. Thomas when
his vessel passed within sight of the island of Santo Domingo. Gottschalk's
first-ever glimpse of the Haitian coast brought to mind stories he had
heard as a child. His mother was descended from an official of the French
colonial regime that ruled Santo Domingo until the slave rebellion of the
1790s overthrew it. "When very young," Gottschalk recalled in his journal, "I never tired of hearing my grandmother relate the terrible strife that
our family, like all the rest of the colonists, had to sustain" when the slaves
overwhelmed them. That memory led to another from Gottschalk's boyhood. "In the evening, the Negroes, myself, and the children of the house
formed a circle around my grandmother. We would listen, by the trem-
bling fire on the hearth, under the coals of which Sally, the old Negress
[the Gottschalks' longtime slave], baked her sweet potatoes. . . . We
listened to Sally so well that we knew all of her stories by heart, with an
interest that has lasted till today." For Gottschalk, the "picturesque language," "exquisite originality," and "simple and touching melody" of
Creole ballads he had learned in his youth went "right to the heart" and
conjured up a "dream of unknown worlds."

Not only did Gottschalk remember his past; he relied on it as an artistic source. The son of an English-Jewish father and a mother who was
culturally French by way of Haiti, raised Roman Catholic in a household
where blacks and whites mingled freely, Gottschalk recognized the artistic possibilities in his cultural background. In the annals of American composition, he is known for bringing indigenous, or folk, themes and
rhythms into music written for the concert hall. His shipboard reflections
show that this practice was rooted in respect for the unique appeal of
these supposedly primitive forms.

GOTTSCHALK AND HIS MUSIC

Born in 1829 into a family that valued his musical talent, Gottschalk also had the good fortune to grow up in a lively musical environment. The population of New Orleans stood at forty-six thousand in 1830, supporting several full-time theaters and half a dozen dance halls—a mecca for musicians seeking employment. Local music stores sold instruments and sheet music, and they published the work of local composers. A touring circuit that connected New Orleans with New York and Havana, Cuba, brought many performing musicians to town. The city's streets and sa-

Louis Moreau Gottschalk (1829–1869) was painted by French artist J. Berville around 1843, shortly after he arrived in Paris to continue his musical training there.

loons were home to such informal music makers as fiddlers and banjo pickers, and minstrel troupes began to appear in the 1840s. Organists played and choirs sang in Roman Catholic churches. And army bands offered a range of music from military to recreational. Thus, New Orleans, with its mingling of Spanish, French, and free black residents, enjoyed a highly diverse musical life, from artistically elegant to functional and homespun.

Gottschalk's career was rooted in this musical richness. His mother took him to the opera, and he also picked up his musical vernacular in front of the hearth and around the city. He began playing piano at three and was soon taking lessons from a member of a local opera company. He also learned to play violin. Gottschalk sailed for France just after turning thirteen, ready for further musical education in Europe. His father had hoped that he would study at the Paris Conservatory, but the director rejected Gottschalk without an audition on the grounds that "America is only a land of steam engines." Soon, however, the boy was accepted as a piano pupil by a respected teacher. As the center where the world's leading pianists displayed their art, Paris proved the ideal place for Gottschalk to prepare for a virtuoso's career. When he made his own debut as a pianist in Paris shortly before his sixteenth birthday, the great composer and pianist Frédéric Chopin was in the audience.

Gottschalk's playing won approval, and he had also begun to compose. Starting with dance-based pieces, he paid homage to Chopin in a series of mazurkas and waltzes. Then in 1849, he based four new compositions on melodies he had learned in America: *Bamboula*, *La savane* (The Tropical Plain), *Le bananier* (The Banana Tree), and *Le marcenillier* (The Manchineel Tree), all published in Paris under the name "Gottschalk of Louisiana." These pieces established Gottschalk as a musical representative of the New World in the Old. And they provide a glimpse of a young American artist, discovering an approach suited to his talents as a composer who played his own works in public. Throughout his career, Gottschalk wrote music that was difficult for the player but easy on the listener.

By the end of 1852, Gottschalk was ready to leave Europe, and the first concert he played after landing in New York took place in February 1853. Together with works by Liszt, Verdi, and others, plenty of Gottschalk's own music appeared on this program, including *La bananier* (Op. 5) and a "Grand Caprice and Variations" for two pianos on *The Carnival of Venice*. As with other pianists of the time, Gottschalk's concerts seldom took the form of solo piano recitals, except where other skilled musicians were unavailable. He was joined in his American debut by a flute soloist, several singers, a pianist, and an orchestra.

LISTENING GUIDE 21

The Banjo (Gottschalk)

A different side of Gottschalk appears in *The Banjo*, published in New York City in 1855. Again, seeking material with immediate impact, he chose two attention-grabbing elements: the sound of the banjo and Stephen Foster's well-known minstrel song *De Camptown Races*.

Formally speaking, *The Banjo* is an unbalanced piece. Its brief introduction, based on Foster's tune (8 bars), is followed by a long section that imitates the banjo's sound (162 bars), then a shorter section presenting Foster's tune and ending in a noisy burst of pianistic effort (54 bars). If Gottschalk had wanted balance, he could have brought back the banjo imitation in a three-part form (**ABA**) or expanded the second section of his two-part form. But neither would have produced so much sheer excitement.

The beginning of *The Banjo*'s longest section is also unconventional. Gottschalk introduces his banjo sound in measure 9. As a plucked instrument with gut strings, capable of rhythmic energy but not much volume, the banjo of Gottschalk's day called for close listening. And here it is as if the audience is invited to lean toward the music, concentrating on the details of Gottschalk's hushed imitation. Instead of a melody, he offers a sound.

Though *The Banjo* was separated by distance, time, and a host of artistic conventions from direct African influence, the piece's African-American lineage, with its emphasis on rhythm and sound over melody, is unmistakable.

The Banjo's overall form may be unusual, but its phrase-by-phrase unfolding is straightforward. Indeed, on that level, Gottschalk's piece is rooted in the conventions of dance music: a strict tempo, regular phrase structure, and lots of repetition. The beat and the four-bar phrases carry listeners comfortably ahead. And the music is at once familiar (Foster's song), novel (the banjo imitation), and ingenious enough (the variety of banjo sounds) to hold their attention. Finally, the contrast between *The Banjo*'s last roar and the delicacy of its picking sections dramatizes the vastly different capabilities of the grand piano—a technological marvel of the age—and the banjo itself, still in some quarters a homemade instrument in 1855.

Seven banjos, a tambourine, several pairs of bones, and a free-flowing pennant spell out the title of Gottschalk's piano piece *The Banjo* in its first edition (New York, 1855).

GOTTSCHALK AND THE CLASSICS

Gottschalk's artistry was rooted in the sound of the piano. Explaining why he favored instruments made at the Boston factory of Jonas Chickering, he wrote: "I like their tone, fine and delicate, tender and poetic," adding that Chickering pianos allowed him to achieve "tints more varied than those of other instruments." These words point to the heart of Gottschalk's musical philosophy, which held sound to be as important to a piece of music as were colors to a painting. Technique, though essential, was never enough. "Many pianists whose thundering execution astonishes us still do not move us," he wrote, because "they are ignorant of sound"—the surest means of touching listeners' hearts. Painters could learn to draw and musicians to play the right notes, if they worked hard enough. But a command of sound, which carried music's spiritual side, depended on intuition. "Color and sound are born in us," Gottschalk thought; they were "the outward expressions of our sensibility and of our souls."

Gottschalk's belief in the primacy of sound distanced him from the outlook of Theodore Thomas and the Boston critic John Sullivan Dwight, which he considered Germanic. Dwight once advised performers to play with "no show or effect" so that "the composition is before you, pure and clear . . . as a musician hears it in his mind in reading it from the notes." In other words, music is a composer's art; it should not be judged by the way it sounds but by the way the composer has conceived it on paper. Though performance always involves interpretation, the Germanic outlook directed performers to look to the score, not their personal whims or the mood of the audience, for interpretive guidelines.

In Dwight's first review of a Gottschalk concert (1853), he admitted that the pianist's tone was "the most clear and crisp and beautiful that we have ever known." But he then dismissed Gottschalk as an artist. "Could a more trivial and insulting string of musical rigmarole," he asked about one of the pieces, ever "have been offered to an audience of earnest musical lovers?" Dwight may never have asked the question posed years later by composer Charles Ives—"My God, what has sound got to do with music?"—but he shared Ives's attitude. For him, the sonic beauty of Gottschalk's playing was an attempt to hide artistic emptiness.

In this clash of priorities, Gottschalk knew exactly where he stood. In 1862, he wrote: "Music is a thing eminently sensuous. Certain combinations move us, not because they are ingenious, but because they move our nervous system in a certain way." In other words, for all the inge-

This photograph of Gottschalk and admirers was taken at Saratoga, New York, during a concert tour in 1862.

nuity preserved in composers' scores, music does its work in performance, occasion by occasion. Performers and composers can have no worthier goal than to form emotional links with their listeners.

From his New York debut in 1853 until early 1857, Gottschalk traveled the United States, establishing himself as a charismatic presence in concert life and a prominent American composer. He also negotiated a fee for endorsing Chickering pianos, and he signed a contract to publish new piano works through a New York firm. Gottschalk thus profited not only from concert performances but also from the selling of musical goods. Complaints in his journal, however, suggest the price he and other stars paid for the rewards that came their way, including schedules crammed too full of concerts and train rides; hotels that roused guests with an alarm bell and served indigestible food; bizarre audience behavior; and constant demands that popular numbers be endlessly repeated.

But these were hazards of the profession. More frustrating to Gottschalk was the disparagement he received for being both a performer and a composer. Some critics took the pianist to task for playing his own compositions in public. But, Gottschalk replied, if he had not been a composer at all, any musician "who had manufactured a polka or a valse would have thrown it in my face that I played only the music of others." Or, if his compositions had been less catchy and original, he might have been accused of copying. Whatever his detractors might say, composing was fundamental to both Gottschalk's musical nature and his career, and the public *liked* his music. Being "cast in an original mold," he could hardly "abdicate his individuality," even if he tried.

As Gottschalk saw it, critics who championed the classics placed living composers, especially American, at a disadvantage. He knew, for example, that the very idea of classic works depended on who was defining them and how. In any discussion of the subject, Gottschalk wrote, he would insist on "reserving the right to ask you what you understand by the classics," for the label could be used as a "convenient club with which you knock on the head all those who annoy you." Aware also that a preoccupation with the classics threatened musical diversity, he asked, "If because the apple is a fruit less delicate than the pineapple, [would you] wish that there should be no apples?" And in another food analogy: "There are some individuals who like only dried fruit," he wrote. "They even like it a little moldy, and if they find dust in it they are transported." In contrast, Gottschalk likened new compositions—works not yet classified or categorized, and with sound their only credential—to a "fruit in flower," free of mold and dust, and exuding "the perfume that opens to the sun and betrays a young and vigorous growth." But just as the flavor of a freshly picked plum comes without the guaranteed sweetness or shelf life of a prune, so the aesthetic reward of a new composition, unlike that of a classic, is unknown.

GOTTSCHALK'S LATER CAREER

Sixteen years of life remained to Gottschalk after he returned in 1853 from Europe, and, although he never left the Western Hemisphere again, he spent less than half of that time in North America. After touring the United States and Canada until 1857, he passed the next several years in the Caribbean, with long stays in Puerto Rico, Martinique, Guadeloupe, and especially Cuba, where he played many concerts, staged festivals, and even for a time managed the opera in Havana. Early in 1862, he returned to his native land, winning a warm reception for his second New York debut performance on February 11. A strenuous tour followed, with Gottschalk calculating at one point that he had given eighty-five concerts in four and a half months and traveled fifteen thousand miles by train in a country where long-simmering sectional conflict had erupted into civil war. (An ardent foe of slavery, he supported the Northern cause.) Among at least a dozen new compositions he introduced in 1862 was *The Union*

Gottschalk in full maturity.

(Op. 48), a war-inspired fantasy on national songs, featuring *The Star-Spangled Banner*, *Hail Columbia*, and *Yankee Doodle.**

Gottschalk toured eastern North America until early 1865, when he sailed for California by way of Panama. Arriving in San Francisco in April, he played concerts there and in Oakland, San Jose, Sacramento, and Stockton. The month of June found him inland, performing in the mining towns of Nevada, including Virginia City, where he stayed eleven days and which he declared "the saddest, the most wearisome, the most inhospitable place on the globe." Not long after his return to the coast, however, Gottschalk was involved in an incident whose outcome made San Francisco seem even less hospitable than Nevada. That it involved a

---

*John G. Doyle has traced Gottschalk's itinerary for 1862, starting with "the principal cities of the East: Philadelphia, Newark, Baltimore, Washington, Worcester, Providence, Portsmouth, Portland, Salem, Springfield, Burlington, New Haven, and Boston; in New York State he appeared in Lockport, Ogdensburg, Watertown, Batavia, Rochester, Auburn, Canandaigua, Geneva, Elmira, Oswego, Rome, and Utica; in the West he was heard in Cincinnati, Louisville, St. Louis, Chicago, Milwaukee, Toledo, Cleveland, Detroit, Erie, Sandusky, Zanesville, Columbus, Madison, and Indianapolis; in Canada, Kingston, Hamilton, Montreal, Quebec, Ottawa, and Toronto. There was a concert in August for wounded soldiers in Saratoga. In October Gottschalk played with Theodore Thomas in chamber concerts in New York and met the young prodigy Teresa Carreño."

young woman will surprise no reader of his journal, which confesses that, from time to time during performances, his eyes might sweep the audience in search of feminine beauty. In September 1865, the pianist failed to return a local schoolgirl to her residence on time after an outing with another couple, and offended local propriety to the point that vigilante justice was threatened. Though Gottschalk stoutly denied any wrongdoing, he took the precaution of fleeing by sea to South America, and there he spent the rest of his life, performing in Lima, Peru (1865–66); Santiago and Valparaiso, Chile (1866–67); Montevideo, Uruguay, and Buenos Aires, Argentina (1867–68); and Rio de Janeiro, Brazil. He died in 1869 in Rio of pneumonia, aggravated by extreme exhaustion, after organizing and performing in a monster concert involving some 650 musicians. His death was marked by a hero's funeral.

No other American-born musician of the 1800s matched Gottschalk's impact, which continued after he died at the age of forty. Biographies were written, and his journal was edited and published. With the composer no longer alive to perform it, his music sustained a life of its own. Editions of his works were published in North and South America, Europe, and Cuba. But in the twentieth century, his music dropped out of

According to this Rio de Janeiro cartoon, when Gottschalk died in Brazil in December 1869, he was mourned on three continents.

the concert repertory, and Gottschalk was gradually forgotten. In the 1970s, when dance impresario Lincoln Kirstein suggested that the New York City Ballet stage a work called *Cakewalk* using Gottschalk's music, the only one in the company who had even heard of the composer was George Balanchine, the great choreographer, who recalled hearing this music in his native Russia.

Gottschalk poses a challenge for historians and students of American music. On the one hand, there is no denying the wide swath that he cut in the international musical life of the 1850s and 60s and later. Acknowledged as a superior pianist, he also won praise as a composer from both critics and listeners in Europe, South America, the Caribbean, and North America. His music delighted and moved audiences then, and it still sounds original today. On the other hand, Gottschalk is not widely performed nowadays, when the repertory of the concert hall and the teaching studio is believed to render the true verdict on musical quality. According to this line of thinking, whatever may be admired in Gottschalk's personality or approach to composition, the music has simply not been good enough to survive.

A case may also be made, however, that Gottschalk's eclipse has had more to do with historical fashion than the worth of his music. His artistic pedigree is unique, blending the grass-roots flavor of New World rhythms and melodies with the elegant sounds and textures of French pianism. That blend, however, went unappreciated by those who shared the Germanic outlook that gained strength after the Civil War. Once Gottschalk was no longer around to play it, his staunchly non-Germanic music lost its place in an American concert hall wary of music that, in the composer's own words, was "not yet consecrated."

18

Two Classic Bostonians

GEORGE W. CHADWICK
AND AMY BEACH

THROUGH MUCH OF THE NINETEENTH CENTURY, AMERICAN CLAS-
sical works were written by isolated figures such as Heinrich, Fry, and
Gottschalk. But during the latter 1800s, in and around Boston, the first
real group of American composers since the Yankee psalmodists or the
Moravians took shape. Several deserve to be remembered, including John
Knowles Paine, George W. Chadwick, Arthur Foote, Horatio Parker, and
Amy Cheney (Mrs. H. H. A.) Beach, all native New Englanders. And to
that group may be added New York–born Edward MacDowell, who lived
and worked for a time in Boston.

A 1907 article by Chadwick, looking back to the 1890s, recalled how
it had felt to belong to this group. "They knew each other well," he wrote,
and most were members of the same Boston social club. "Many a night
after a Symphony concert" they "gathered about the same table" in the
Tavern Club, bantering in friendly exchange, "rejoicing in each other's
successes, and working for them too." Chadwick portrays a community
of equals who had fashioned a working environment of "mutual respect
and honest criticism."

Beginning in 1892, the circle also included Theodore Thomas, who,
traveling between Chicago and his summer home in New Hampshire, often stopped in Boston to enjoy the company of the "boys," as he called
them. Chadwick recalled an evening when Thomas "sat with them until
two in the morning, with the score of Beethoven's ninth symphony in
front of him, pointing out with reverent care the details of orchestral nuance as he had worked them out, his eyes flashing with enthusiasm as he
lived the music over in his mind." The fraternal bonding pictured here
excluded Amy Beach, for social custom would not have encouraged the
wife of a local physician to spend her Saturday nights with male colleagues at the Tavern Club. Yet those colleagues respected her work. In

1896, after a Boston Symphony Orchestra performance of Beach's *Gaelic* Symphony, Chadwick pronounced the composition fine enough to make her "one of the boys."

Several of the Boston composers were skilled performers as well, chiefly pianists or organists. And their compositions—operas, oratorios, symphonies and other works for orchestra, chamber music, sacred and secular choral music, solo songs, organ works, and piano music—were heard regularly in Boston, on the programs of such local ensembles as the Boston Symphony Orchestra, the Kneisel Quartet, and the Handel and Haydn Society.

Chapter 15's account of Theodore Thomas stressed his allegiance to the classics. But as an American conductor, Thomas also programmed American works, including music by the New Englanders. One reason he, along with the Boston Symphony's conductors, *and* the city's main chamber musicians, felt at home with this music was that it was composed in an idiom whose roots lay in Germany. Thomas could sit half the night with composer friends talking about Beethoven's Ninth because they shared musical ideals based on the style and sound of Beethoven.

During the "golden" years of the 1890s, Paine was professor of music at Harvard, Chadwick a faculty member at the New England Conservatory of Music (he became its director in 1897), Parker organist and choirmaster at Boston's Trinity Church (from 1893; in 1894, he was named professor of music at Yale but kept his church job until 1902), MacDowell a piano soloist and private teacher (Columbia University named him its professor of music in 1896), and Foote organist at the First Unitarian Church and also a piano teacher. Beach's husband supported her musical career until his death in 1910. Lacking any possibility of earning a living through composition, members of the Boston group composed as an avocation, supporting themselves chiefly through teaching and church work.

In 1904, two years before John Knowles Paine died, a historian of American music called him "the Nestor [a wise old king in ancient Greece] of the American composers in the great classical forms": the elder who blazed a trail followed by others. Born in 1839 in Portland, Maine, he was taught there by a German musician who had come to America with a traveling orchestra and stayed in Portland after the group broke up. Paine was already a good organist when he went to Berlin in 1858 for two years of study. Returning to the United States, he settled in Boston as organist of a local church. In 1862, he was named instructor of music at Harvard. In the years that followed, Paine composed steadily, lectured at Harvard on music, and organized a well-received Berlin performance of his own Mass in D. In 1875, Harvard established a professorship in music and hired Paine to fill it. There, while continuing to compose, he set up a music curriculum that emphasized intellectual training. In a city that by tradition looked to Harvard for leadership, Paine and his students made the university a force in American music as the century neared its end.

A century after the Boston group's heyday, three of its members stand out: George W. Chadwick, for his contribution to American orchestra music; Amy Beach, the nation's first full-fledged female composer; and Edward MacDowell, whose fame eclipsed that of any American contemporary.

CHADWICK: YANKEE COMPOSER

During 1980s and 90s, as Chadwick's music has enjoyed a modest revival, the earlier image of a proper Bostonian with a German bias has given way to that of a "Yankee composer." Born in 1854 in Lowell, Massachusetts, Chadwick grew up in circumstances that were far from prosperous. He left high school short of graduation to work for his father, a businessman who opposed his son's musical ambitions. While still working, Chadwick in 1872 managed a part-time enrollment at the New England Conservatory, where he studied organ, piano, and harmony. In 1876–77, he taught at a college in Michigan. And with money he saved, Chadwick sailed in 1877 to Germany, where he studied privately and at the Leipzig Conservatory. After a summer of travel (1879), Chadwick spent a year in Munich studying with Josef Rheinberger. In 1880, he returned to Boston, took a job as a church organist, and then joined the faculty of the New England Conservatory, an association that lasted from 1882 until just before his death in 1931.

Chadwick's teachers at the Leipzig Conservatory pegged him from the start as an extraordinary student. In June 1879, his *Rip Van Winkle* Overture for orchestra, performed on a graduation concert, was reviewed by a Leipzig critic as "uncontestably . . . the best of this year's compositions." His professors in Leipzig signed a report that reads in part: "Herr Chadwick possesses a completely exceptional talent for composition." Chadwick seems to have known from the start how to communicate in a concert hall, a talent that helped make him a leader in Boston's musical life.

In Chadwick's case, "Yankee composer" means a musician at home in European genres but approaching them through an American sensibility. Traits of his style include a fondness for pentatonic and gapped scales, distinctive rhythms from Anglo-American psalmody, African-Caribbean dance syncopations, parallel voice leading, and virtuoso or-

The orchestra of the New England Conservatory in 1915, with its conductor George W. Chadwick pictured as an inset.

chestration; all except the last separate Chadwick's music from German
prototypes. And so does his sensitivity, when setting words to music, to
characteristic English rhythms. From these traits, Chadwick evolved a
personal approach that allowed him to write cosmopolitan music with an
American flavor.

Recently Chadwick has been credited with creating an American symphonic style. We can test this claim by looking at the first movement of
the *Symphonic Sketches* (1904).

LISTENING GUIDE 22

Symphonic Sketches, First Movement (Chadwick)

Symphonic Sketches follows a standard four-movement plan (fast-
slow-fast-fast) but gives programmatic titles to each of the movements. Here, rather than offering abstract symphonic development, Chadwick translates specific images into music. An
eight-line verse linking sound, color, and mood serves as a prologue to "Jubilee," the first movement:

No cool gray tones for me!
  Give me the warmest red and green,
    A cornet and a tambourine,
  To paint MY jubilee!

For when pale flutes and oboes play,
To sadness I become a prey;
Give me the violets and the May,
But no gray skies for me!

Critic Henry Taylor Parker, who reviewed a performance in
1908, heard in "Jubilee" echoes of "Negro tunes," and he fancied
that the work was set in an American farmhouse. He also delighted in the music's "high and volatile spirits . . . the sheer
rough and tumble of it," concluding: "The music shouts because
it cannot help it, and sings because it cannot help it, and each as
only Americans would shout and sing."

"Jubilee" alternates a boisterous allegro with more pensive
music in a seven-part design (**ababab**). It is an American trait,
Parker wrote, "to turn suddenly serious, and deeply and unaf-
fectedly so, in the midst of its fooling to run away into sober

fancies and moods, and then as quickly turn 'jolly' again." The slower section shows Chadwick's New World sensibility in full bloom. Taking Foster's *Camptown Races* as a starting point, Chadwick employs three New World elements: habanera rhythm (2/4 at a moderate-to-slow tempo—a familiar accompaniment figure in Cuban song and dance), syncopation (the short-long rhythm [♪♩] in the melody's second measure, drawn from the rhythm of such English words as "river" or "money"), and a melody built from a four-note scale (1-3-5-6 of the major scale) in which skips outweigh stepwise motion. This brief passage is followed by a singing theme in the violins that, in combination with an Afro-Caribbean dance figure, brings to twentieth-century minds images of the empty plain and prairies of the Old West, familiar from movie Westerns.

But to say that Chadwick created an American symphonic style implies that other concert-hall composers followed his lead, which none actually did. The faith in edification that ruled the concert hall, together with the notion that artistically serious music ought to be grave and dignified, did not, in the long run, welcome Chadwick's personal approach. Could the standard Old World forms accommodate a more playful American mode of orchestral expression? Or did such music risk trivializing Americans' quest to find an honored place among the world's musical nations? In Chadwick's case, the answers were no and yes.

Yet although the concert hall found no lasting place for his works, the world of popular entertainment would eventually welcome a style of orchestral writing like his. A photograph taken in Springfield, Massachusetts, in 1890 of Chadwick and another man wearing each other's hats seems to comment on where he belonged in American music (see illustration below). Chadwick, staring glumly to his right, looks engulfed by the top hat he wears, while the large, handsome figure facing him dwarfs the homburg perched on his own head. The second man is Victor Herbert, Irish-born composer, conductor, and cellist, who came to New York City in 1886 and would become a dominating figure. Having arrived in this country as an orchestra player and composer for the concert hall, he soon found that arena too narrow for his talents, connecting with a much larger American public through the concerts he conducted—he took over Gilmore's Band when Patrick S. Gilmore died in 1892—and the operettas he began composing in 1894.

Chadwick (left) exchanges hats with composer Victor
Herbert in this 1890 photograph taken in Springfield,
Massachusetts.

The two men caught here in a moment of comic role playing occupied common musical ground but served institutions with different goals.
Chadwick's concert hall, centered on works, was devoted chiefly to an elevated art of music; Herbert's musical theater, centered on occasions, was
intent on bringing pleasure to its audiences. And it was through composers like Herbert that the American style Chadwick helped to invent
found its niche. That niche grew with the changing times. The leaders of
the Hollywood film industry probably had no idea who George W. Chadwick was when sound films began in the late 1920s to be accompanied
by orchestras. But they chose a musical style close to that of Chadwick's

Second Symphony and the *Symphonic Sketches*: rooted in German Romanticism, tuneful in his Yankee manner, colorfully written for the instruments, and easily accessible to a general audience.

AMY BEACH AND AMERICAN MUSICAL DEMOCRACY

Amy Marcy Cheney was born in 1867 in West Henniker, New Hampshire. It did not take her mother, an accomplished pianist herself, long to discover Amy's talent for music. Before she was two, the child was improvising harmony to Mrs. Cheney's lullaby. Beach's mother obviously had a prodigy on her hands. But she was determined not to push her daughter into music nor to exploit the child's talent in public. When she finally began giving Amy piano lessons at six, progress was swift, and before long the young girl was studying with a respected piano teacher in Boston. At sixteen, she made her public debut, playing a concerto with an orchestra in Boston in 1883. Two years later, she married Dr. Henry H. A. Beach, a forty-two-year-old widower, physician, and amateur musician. And for the next twenty-five years, she lived an active, well-rounded musical life centered in Boston.

Beach had been writing music since she was four, and in her early teens she had taken a year's worth of lessons in harmony and counterpoint from a local teacher. As a woman, she found avenues for more formal study closed to her, so she acquired scores and books and taught herself to compose. After her marriage, she concentrated more on composition, though she still sometimes played in public. (In later life, even after a long performing career, she is said to have thought of herself as a composer who played mostly her own music rather than a concert pianist.) Beach composed until well into her seventies, writing many songs and keyboard works, choral pieces, some chamber music, a piano concerto, a symphony, and even an opera. In 1895, her mother, always Beach's main musical adviser, moved in with the childless couple after Amy's father died, taking over household chores and leaving Beach free to compose.

Beach's settled life in Boston ended when her husband died in 1910, followed by her mother early the next year. In the fall of 1911, at age forty-four, she seized an independence she had never enjoyed before: she sailed for Europe, hired a manager, and began to play more often in public. After World War I forced her return to the United States, she established a new home base in Hillsborough, New Hampshire. A close friend of the widow of Edward MacDowell, who had died in 1908, Beach from 1921 on spent time each summer at the MacDowell Colony in Peterborough, New Hampshire. Beginning in 1930, she made New York City her winter home. When Beach died in New York in 1944, she left behind more than three hundred compositions and a record of pioneering achievements, as both a performer and a composer: she was the first American-trained concert pianist, part of the first generation of professional American female instrumentalists, and the first woman to compose large-scale works for the concert hall. She was also one of the first to use folk melodies to help create a distinctively American style.

Although women had taken an active part in America's music making during the eighteenth and early nineteenth centuries, except for a few families of professional musicians, they led their musical lives within severe limits. If Beach's generation was the first to produce professional women instrumentalists, that was because singers had previously been the only women encouraged to develop their skill. If Beach was the first American-trained concert pianist, that was because the parents of talented males like Gottschalk sent their sons to Europe for their musical training, whereas Beach lived until middle age under the protective wing of others, with no thought of following a professional career. And if she was the first American woman to compose successfully in large-scale forms, that was because the men who controlled such opportunities had resisted the idea that a female composer could meet the demands of the symphony, concerto, oratorio, or opera.

"Can a woman become a great composer?" asked Louis Elson, Boston critic and member of the New England Conservatory's faculty, in his *History of American Music* (1904). "Will there ever be a female Beethoven or a Mozart?" In Europe, Elson reported, these questions had been answered "quickly and in the negative." Yet he doubted that men's capacities in music were superior to women's. "We venture to believe," he wrote, "that it has been insufficient musical education and male prejudice that have prevented female composers from competing with their male brethren in art." His evidence was the career of Amy Beach, which he had followed firsthand. As a child with extraordinary talent, she had shown the energy, confidence, and character to acquire professional skills that made her a peer of male colleagues. Thus, Beach served in her own day as a symbol of what a woman musician could do if given the chance. Well-known and tireless as both a composer and a performer, she set an example that must have inspired other American women to take their talent seriously.

In later years, Beach wrote music chiefly for the kinds of programs in which she herself performed. Yet large-scale works first distinguished her from female predecessors, who by the 1890s had already composed

This program of the Handel and Haydn Society of Boston
places Amy Beach, composer of a new Mass in E-flat
(1892), in the company of the European masters.

many songs and piano pieces. Most of these works, including the Mass
in E-flat (1892), the *Gaelic* Symphony (1896), and the Piano Concerto
(1900), were written before Beach was thirty-five, a period coinciding with
the Boston group's heyday. The Handel and Haydn Society premiered
the Mass, and the Boston Symphony Orchestra introduced the symphony
and the concerto.

LISTENING GUIDE 23

Gaelic Symphony, Second Movement (Beach)

Looking back in 1917 on an orchestra work she had written more than two decades earlier, Beach explained in a program note that the melodies of her *Gaelic* Symphony "sprang from the common joys, sorrows, adventures and struggles of a primitive people. Their simple, rugged and unpretentious beauty led me to 'take my pen in hand' and try to develop their ideas in symphonic form." These comments point to a fact unknown when the symphony was premiered. Inspired by the Bohemian composer Antonin Dvořák, who during a three-year stay in the United States counseled American composers to tap the resources of folk music (see Chapter 19), Beach borrowed most of the melodies in this work from elsewhere.

The symphony's second movement unfolds in three-part form (**ABA**; slow-fast-slow), with a slow introduction and a brief concluding tag. Easy to listen to the first time as well as the twenty-first, the movement boasts a unity of theme that compensates for the sharp change of mood and tempo that the middle section introduces. The melody of the **A** section, played by the oboe, is foursquare in phrase structure and predictable in form: statement, restatement, contrast, return (**aaba**), with the second half repeated. Extended a bit, it conveys the feel of a lyric slow movement. But out of this reflective beginning grows a new, faster section in the character of a scherzo (an up-tempo instrumental movement of light character). The **B** melody, made up of sixteenth notes, is heard immediately as a varied form of the **A** melody. Broken into fragments, reharmonized, and repeated in different instrumental colors, this melody moves through many keys in a whirl of musical development. Longer lines appear against it, but the sixteenth-note motion keeps buzzing until interrupted by a silencing gesture. And now the lyric melody from the opening returns (**A**), with new harmonic shadings and fresh instrumental sounds for listeners to savor. The tag, introducing sixteenth-note motion again, brings the movement to a quick, whisper-like close.

Beach based this movement on *Goirtin Ornadh* (The Little Field of Barley), a traditional Irish melody.

Although Beach taught herself to compose in large forms, it was on a composer-pianist's smaller scale that she did most of her work. During many years before the public, she played occasional solo recitals; but more commonly she was joined by other musicians (singers or violinists), often appearing as an assisting artist on their programs. As a practiced collaborator, Beach was accustomed to fitting her style to the genre and the occasion. In an 1892 choral concert by Boston's Cecilia Society, for example, she premiered *Fireflies* (Op. 15, No. 4), a short piano piece that calls for a delicate touch and the ability to play streams of thirds smoothly in the right hand. The flashing pianistic colors and quick movement of *Fireflies*, contrasting sharply with the Cecilians' choral fare, brought variety to the evening's program.

Despite the prejudice she faced as a woman, compared with most other American musicians (male *or* female), Beach lived a privileged life. Her mother nurtured her talent from the start, and she was given the leisure and opportunity to develop her creative powers on her own. Once she married, a secure social position allowed her to play and to present her music in prestigious situations. Free from the need to make a living or to run a household, she was one of very few Americans able to devote herself to writing and performing music at a professional level without having to depend on the economic outcome. Her music found an audience, too, as is shown by the substantial royalty checks she received in later years.

Until 1911, when she made her first trip to Europe, Beach's musical

Amy Beach (1867–1944).

career was that of an extraordinary amateur, performing for select audiences, including many friends and acquaintances. When she returned to America in 1914, however, the niche she had once filled in Boston no longer existed. Therefore, becoming in effect her own manager, she began to fashion a career that involved more playing in public, for the local musical organizations that grew up in the late 1800s and early 1900s.

Musical energy abounded in these days, and groups were formed to tap this energy, from choral societies to teachers' associations and organists' guilds. Beethoven clubs, MacDowell clubs, even Beach clubs sponsored meetings and concerts. Beach herself was active in the Music Teachers' National Association (MTNA), which promoted the cause of American composers by sponsoring performances, and the National Federation of Music Clubs, which awarded prizes for new compositions. She was also among the first members of the New Hampshire Music Teachers' Association, dedicated to performing music by native and contemporary composers. In that environment, demand for traveling artists, especially pianists, ran high, though fees were modest. Beach intended much of the music she wrote either for such groups as these or for church use. Her first concert after returning from Europe in 1914 took place at Boston's MacDowell Club, where she presented two groups of songs composed overseas. "An audience of some 700 people rose *en masse* as she stepped upon the platform," a press account read, "and after an address, Mrs. Beach was showered with flowers."

As we can see from this announcement, the composer was still being called "Mrs. Beach" in her native city. Although Beach signed all her music "Mrs. H. H. A. Beach," she called herself "Amy Beach" when she was in Europe from 1911 to 1914, but then decided to revert to her married name when she returned to the United States. When asked about her choice of name, she replied that it was only "proper" for married Bostonian women to be known as "Mrs. so-and-so."

As a woman who declined the label of professional musician, Beach had no need of a separate professional name. "Mrs. Beach" defined herself socially first and artistically second: a proper married Bostonian woman who also happened to be one of the nation's leading composers. The name she chose was as unique as the role she embraced: that of a social aristocrat—at least insofar as an American could be one—with the skills of a professional musician and the artistic attitude of an enlightened amateur. "Mrs. H. H. A. Beach" may seem today an odd, quaint, or perhaps even disrespectful way of referring to Amy Beach. Yet by keeping her distance from a professional world in which she was superbly qualified to excel, Beach reminds the present-day observer that the social and artistic priorities of one era are not necessarily those of another.

19

Edward MacDowell
and Musical Nationalism

BORN IN NEW YORK IN 1860, TRAINED IN EUROPE, AND ASSOCIATED with Boston only from 1888 until 1896, when he lived there, Edward Mac-Dowell won a reputation that made him more a national than a local figure. Yet George W. Chadwick included him in his list of the "boys," even though MacDowell's musical orientation ran against the classic strain of nineteenth-century German Romanticism—from Beethoven and Schubert through Mendelssohn, Schumann, and Brahms—that inspired most of the Bostonians. Rather than being drawn to symphonies and string quartets, MacDowell identified with the "New German School" of Franz Liszt and Richard Wagner, which emphasized programmatic suggestions and musical narrative over sonata forms.

As a boy, MacDowell was an avid reader whose parents encouraged his artistic flair. In 1876, his mother took her musically gifted son to Europe for more specialized training. He was accepted at the Paris Conservatory but disliked French instruction and moved to Germany two years later. Studying piano in Wiesbaden and then in Frankfurt, he also took composition lessons. After winning a post as piano teacher at the Darmstadt Conservatory, where he taught from 1881 to 1882, MacDowell had an experience that changed the way he thought of himself as a musician. In July 1882, when he played his First Piano Concerto at a concert in Zurich that the eminent composer Franz Liszt attended, the strong response surpassed anything MacDowell had imagined. Until then, he later recalled, the idea that anybody might take his compositions seriously had never occurred to him.

Now MacDowell gave more and more attention to composing. By 1884, German publishers had issued some of his works, and other pianists had started playing them. In the same year, he married Marian Nevins, an American and a former piano student, and the couple settled in 1885 in Wiesbaden, where MacDowell taught piano and composed. Three years later, having lived nearly half his life in Europe, the twenty-seven-year-old MacDowell and his wife moved to Boston, where he launched an American career centered on composing but funded chiefly by piano teaching and playing.

In the spring of 1889, MacDowell premiered his Piano Concerto No. 2 in D minor with the Theodore Thomas Orchestra in New York, followed a month later by a performance with the Boston Symphony. In July, he presented the work again at the Paris Exposition Universelle in a concert of American music. When a respected New York critic wrote that the concerto deserved placement "at the head of all works of its kind produced by either a native or adopted citizen of America," some observers began to perceive the young composer as American music's Man of Destiny. In 1894, he played his Second Piano Concerto with the New York Philharmonic Society; the conductor, confirmed Wagnerite Anton Seidl, declared MacDowell superior to Johannes Brahms as a composer. And two years later, he played his First Piano Concerto in New York with the Boston Symphony Orchestra on a program that also introduced his Second (*Indian*) Suite to great critical acclaim.

This concert proved a turning point in MacDowell's life. Now reckoned one of the country's leading musicians, he was offered the first professorship of music at Columbia University in New York City. In the fall of 1896, he plunged wholeheartedly into teaching, but the job proved so demanding that he found little time for composition. Though he continued to write piano music, songs, and choruses, no more orchestra works appeared. MacDowell took his first sabbatical leave in 1902–3, touring the United States and Canada as a pianist. Returning to his post in the fall of 1903, he found himself in conflict with Columbia's new president over the music department's place in the university. When no resolution could be found, MacDowell resigned in 1904 amid a commotion publicized in the New York press. Emotionally drained, and perhaps still feeling the effects of a traffic accident earlier in the year, he suffered a crisis in health. By December 1904, he was showing signs of serious mental illness, which gradually worsened into a state of near-complete physical and mental helplessness. He died early in 1908 at the age of forty-seven, and was buried near his summer home in Peterborough, New Hampshire, which, through Marian MacDowell's dedicated efforts, was made into an art colony in his memory.

While MacDowell's musical talents were uncommon, it is also true that he arrived on the scene at an opportune moment. For around the time that he moved to Boston from Germany, there was a growing appetite for classical music and the building of an infrastructure to support

MacDowell and his wife, the American pianist Marian Nevins Mac-
Dowell (1857–1956), who after his death established their summer
home in Peterborough, New Hampshire, as the MacDowell Colony, a
working retreat for composers, writers, and artists.

it: ensembles, conservatories, concert halls, and opera troupes. The only
missing element was a composer to signal the nation's musical maturity.
Enter the young, handsome, charismatic—and modest—Edward Mac-
Dowell, seemingly born to the role: impeccably schooled, with European
training and reputation; an excellent pianist who performed his own music in public; an artist of broad range who also wrote poetry and showed
a knack for drawing. And his music had a sound of its own.

MacDowell obviously profited from the favored role that was thrust
upon him, but eminence brought pressures too, and they seemed to increase with the years. From a distance, MacDowell's acceptance of the
Columbia post looks like a catch-22—a reward for creative artistry carrying duties that swamped his creative vocation. After 1902, the composer
began several new works but finished none of them. His illness was partly
to blame, but MacDowell was also profoundly self-critical, with a mania
for revising compositions. Especially in later life, he seems to have lacked
the self-assurance expected of a great composer. Perhaps a few more Saturday evenings at the Tavern Club in Boston would have eased the bur-
dens of his New York years.

MACDOWELL AND
MUSICAL NATIONALISM

Not long after his return from Germany, MacDowell found himself involved in a debate about the future direction of American music. When the debate began, MacDowell did not think much of the idea of musical nationalism; he saw art as a realm separate from politics. In 1891, he announced his opposition to concerts devoted to American music (even though he had played in one in Paris two years earlier): "Whenever an exclusively American concert is given," he explained, "the players, public and press seem to feel obliged to adopt an entirely different standard of criticism. . . . Some people would run down an American concert *before* hearing the music—and others would praise it (also *before* hearing it)." In other words, all-American concerts were political events. In the long run, composers were better off having to *earn* performances purely on the basis of their work's quality.

Beyond musical politics, however, lay musical style. And here MacDowell aspired to the universality that European classics had achieved. In nineteenth-century Europe, nationalism and universality were closely connected. Music in the classical sphere was given a nationalist slant by borrowing from folk music, especially in newly emerging nations such as Poland, Bohemia, and Russia—in the same way that each nation had its own language, folklore, music, flag, and institutions, while remaining part of cosmopolitan Europe. Indeed, it was their nationalistic traits that brought composers like Frédéric Chopin, Modeste Musorgsky, and Antonín Dvořák international recognition.

MacDowell sought to achieve a similar universality by "working toward a music which should be American," as he told writer Hamlin Garland in 1896. "Our music thus far is mainly a scholarly restatement of Old-World themes; in other words it is derived from Germany—as all my earlier pieces were." And so MacDowell resolved to be an American composer in the way that Musorgsky was a Russian composer and Dvořák a Bohemian one: by treating his own country as the equivalent of a peripheral European nation, and bringing the American landscape and indigenous American materials into his own European-based style. He perceived, in other words, that the road to universality led through nationalism.

MacDowell's *Woodland Sketches* (Op. 51, 1896) reveal one way in which he claimed an American composer's identity. The work consists of ten short piano pieces whose titles refer to the American landscape and connect with the composer's personal experience. With such titles as *To a Wild Rose, By a Meadow Brook,* and *A Deserted Farm,* the individual pieces of the *Woodland Sketches* register MacDowell's impressions of the New England countryside—perhaps moments experienced on a hike. Listeners thus have good reason to accept their inspiration as American and to think of the music as a response to the challenge of nationalism.

LISTENING GUIDE 24

To a Wild Rose (MacDowell)

To a Wild Rose, the collection's first piece and MacDowell's best-known composition, is in a simple three-part (**aba**) form: statement, contrast, and return. The beginning gives the piece its character: an eight-bar melodic curve built from a motive of two eighth notes and a quarter, and avoiding both stepwise motion and the tonic pitch A until its last note.

MacDowell usually favored thick chords, enriched with sevenths, ninths, and nonharmonic tones. But here he keeps the texture transparent, never piling more than five notes in any chord. He also supports the melody's gentle movement with a simple harmonic progression. Yet dissonance becomes a factor as early as measure 2, where the right hand moves to the dominant, while the left hand remains on the tonic, adding a D as if from a voice that was not there in measure 1. This mild harmonic clash asserts a freedom that MacDowell uses only sparingly; it also prepares the ear for more dissonant moments. The more complicated harmony of the middle section moves away from the manicured neatness of the opening statement before returning to it.

In *To a Wild Rose*, dissonances bring to MacDowell's sound image of a woodland flower just enough tonal ambiguity to cast an aura of mystery around it. It is not crucial for us to picture an actual flower; rather, the music portrays the *composer's personal response to the idea* of coming upon a wild rose in its natural surroundings. MacDowell took a commonplace experience, rendered in music a personal impression of that experience, and invited others to share it through music.

If we held a real wild rose up against MacDowell's musical image, correspondences would be easy to find. The dainty one-measure melodic motive matches the idea that a flower is formed from many petals; and the symmetry of a three-part musical design fits with a rose's circular shape. Furthermore, flashes of dissonance undercut the serene atmosphere often enough to remind listeners that roses have thorns, and that a rose's perfection will be short-lived. *To a Wild Rose* fuses beauty (the tuneful surface) and truth (the dissonant undercurrent) in a musical image that celebrates the life and mourns the impending decay of a woodland flower.

The musical style of *To a Wild Rose* is rooted in European practice and no American melodies are quoted, yet the native lineage of this work is also clear. For all the years he spent in Europe, MacDowell was a born-and-bred American, and the New England countryside inspired the *Woodland Sketches* shortly after he told Garland that he was "working toward a music which should be American." What, then, constitutes American music? Is it a matter of style? nationality? subject? indigenous quotation? the composer's intent? some combination of these factors and others?

The question has long sparked interest and controversy, as noted in Chapter 16. So many different criteria have been used to measure musical Americanism that there seems little hope of finding a definition satisfactory to all. From one perspective, MacDowell's career and music show composers' dependence on Europe; from another, the American identity of a piece like *To a Wild Rose* seems indisputable; and from still another, both MacDowell and this piano piece reflect an interweaving of European and American traits that contradicts either label. Such conundrums have led one music historian to propose a "parallax" perspective, which recognizes that because each vantage point yields its own insight, different answers to the same question are not only inevitable but can be highly informative. Applying that perspective allows us to keep the question of Americanism in music open in a way that encourages reflection and comparison where partisanship and dispute have often prevailed.

NATIONALISM AND
THE *INDIAN* SUITE

Several years before the *Woodland Sketches*, in an effort to compose music that did *not* sound German-inspired, MacDowell wrote an orchestra piece based on Native American melodies. The notion of writing an Indian work dated back to his time in Germany, where in 1887 he had considered an orchestral tone poem about Hiawatha, the mythical Indian hero. Although he abandoned that project, the idea remained with him in 1891, when he told Henry F. B. Gilbert, one of his composition students in Boston, that he was "curious to see some real Indian music." Gilbert brought him a copy of Theodore Baker's *Über die Musik der nordamerikanischen Wilden* (On the Music of the North American Indians, 1882), a doctoral dissertation with a number of transcribed Native melodies. There MacDowell found the themes he used in composing his Second (*Indian*) Suite. After finishing the work, MacDowell believed that no one would hear it as European music and delayed the first performance for several years, for fear that "this rough, savage music" would not "appeal to our concert audiences."

MacDowell's suite contains five movements—*Legend, Love Song, In War-time, Dirge,* and *Village Festival*—each based on a theme he found in Baker. He once told an interviewer that of all his music, the *Dirge* in the *Indian* Suite pleased him most. MacDowell was not alone in judging this movement a success. Calling the *Dirge* "overwhelmingly poignant," his biographer, a prominent New York music critic, ranked it "the most profoundly affecting threnody in music since the 'Götterdämmerung' *Trauermarsch*" by Wagner; and composer Arthur Farwell, who worked extensively with Native American melodies himself, praised its "sheer imaginative beauty." MacDowell's *Dirge* is for an "absent" son who has died. Since the preceding movement is about war, listeners are invited to think that he has been slain in battle.

By the time MacDowell's *Indian* Suite was premiered in 1896, the American visit of a famous European musician had brought the issue of nationalism into the public arena. The visitor was Bohemian composer Antonín Dvořák, who arrived in the United States in 1892 as director of the National Conservatory of Music in New York and remained until 1895. Dvořák had been invited by Jeannette Thurber, a patron who, in setting up the National Conservatory, hoped to encourage the growth of national musical culture—if possible, with funding from the U.S. government.

Dvořák became a public advocate for musical nationalism in America. He showed particular interest in melodies native to the United States—especially plantation melodies of African Americans and Indian tunes. In the spring of 1893, he told the *New York Herald* that, after eight months in America, he was "now satisfied . . . that the future music of this country must be founded upon what are called negro melodies. . . . There is nothing in the whole range of composition that cannot be supplied with themes from this source." Then, as if to show how composers on this side of the Atlantic might proceed, Dvořák wrote his Symphony No. 9 (*From the New World*), inspired in part by African-American melody.

MacDowell, who had finished his own *Indian* Suite more than a year before the well-publicized premiere of the *New World* Symphony in December 1893, took a dim view of the attention that Dvořák's ideas received. "Purely national music," he wrote, "has no place in art, for its characteristics may be duplicated by anyone who takes the fancy to do so. . . . We have here in America been offered a pattern for an 'American' national musical costume by the Bohemian Dvořák, though what the Negro melodies have to do with Americanism in art still remains a mystery." MacDowell objected to Dvořák's meddling, and considered his prescription for national music shallow. "Music that can be made by 'recipe,'" he wrote, "is not music, but 'tailoring.'" Moreover, music based on tunes by slaves and former slaves might exude Americanism, but what would it say about the nation's character? On the other hand, the music of Indians pointed toward a heroic past, an unspoiled continental landscape, and an American people of independent spirit.

To MacDowell, the goal of musical nationalism should be elevating: to echo the "genius" of the nation. And that could only be achieved by composers "who, being part of the people, love the country for itself" and who "put into their music what the nation has put into its life." Furthermore, both composers and the public needed to seize "freedom from the restraint that an almost unlimited deference to European thought and prejudice has imposed upon us. Masquerading in the so-called nationalism of Negro clothes cut in Bohemia will not help us. What we must arrive at is the youthful optimistic vitality and the undaunted tenacity of spirit that characterizes the American man. This is what I hope to see echoed in American music."

About the *Indian* Suite's *Dirge* movement, MacDowell wrote that the Indian woman's lament over the loss of her son "seems to tell of a world sorrow." National elements thus provided a means of finding his own expression of a universal state of mind—in this case, the emotion of grief. What gave that expression force, he believed, was that it came from a sensibility reflecting the country's "undaunted tenacity of spirit." A true national art was one that framed American virtues in a way that any music lover, American or European, could understand.

The *Indian* Suite, MacDowell once told an interviewer, was "the result of my studies of the Indians, their dances, and their songs," adding that he had used and developed "themes which came to me from these people." There is no evidence that MacDowell had any direct contact with Native Americans. Rather, his "study" seems to have consisted of reading and consulting his own imagination, which pictured the heroic Indian in a setting long gone from the earth. This image had been widely circulated by Henry Wadsworth Longfellow's popular epic poem *The Song of Hiawatha* (1855). Nevertheless, MacDowell had access to Native melodies because the people themselves had kept them alive. Dispossessed of most of their territory, depleted in numbers, and more and more segregated on reservations by government policy, they still maintained many of the traditions that their ancestors had practiced before them. It is to these traditions that we now turn.

20

"Travel in the Winds"

NATIVE AMERICAN MUSIC FROM 1820

A NOVEL BY BLACKFOOT INDIAN AUTHOR JAMES WELCH, SET IN THE Montana Territory in 1870, traces the coming of white settlers to the region and their impact on the Native peoples who live there. Toward the end of the book, Fool's Crow, the main character, is summoned in a dream to take a religious journey. After days of travel and fasting, he is shown a vision of his people's future. First they are decimated by smallpox. Then a band of whites appears, riding north to occupy the land where he and his people now live. In the next episode, he is shown that land, his eyes filling "with wonder at the grand sweep of prairie, the ground-of-many-gifts that had favored his people." But then he notices that the blackhorns, the big-horned sheep on which he and his people depend for food, are missing.

As the vision continues, he sees "something that seemed not to fit in the landscape": a square dwelling built by whites. Outside that square a few tipis are pitched, with people "standing around the tipis and the buildings . . . huddled in worn blankets," in pitiful shape. Fool's Crow interprets his vision as proof that, for some unexplained reason, he and his people are being punished. He decides that it is his duty to prepare them for the future, knowing that "if they make peace within themselves," they will still be able to "live a good life in the Sand Hills," where the virtuous go after their life in this world is over. The vision reveals that his people will not vanish but survive. And although the generations to come will not live the life of their ancestors, they can still "know the way it was" through stories handed down to them, understanding "that their people were proud and lived in accordance with the Below Ones, the Underwater People—and the Above Ones."

Fool's Crow's vision touches on many elements of American Indian life during the last two centuries: the spread of Euroamerican civilization; the disruption of Native ways; survival in an alien society; and struggles

236

to adjust to minority status. So harsh was the Indians' lot that as the Civil War ended, most whites assumed that Indians were headed for extinction. Yet more than 300,000 were still alive in 1865. In some regions, Apaches, Nez Percé, Sioux, Cheyenne, Modocs, and Kickapoos hunted, traveled, threatened settlers, and stole livestock. These tribes were subject to military action, unlike the Seminoles in Florida or groups of Cherokees in North Carolina, who lived in isolation and were generally left alone. Other Indian populations survived in federal reservations and in small, out-of-the-way enclaves.

As Euroamericans extended their settlements, most found Indians to be primitive and savage and believed that they had to be either incorporated into society or separated entirely from it. Those in the first camp included missionaries who considered savagery a stage of development that education and the Christian religion could overcome. From this perspective, culture, not race, was the barrier. The second camp consisted chiefly of people who were battling Indians for land and resources. As they saw it, their rivals should be quarantined: removed from their homelands and settled on reservations that would keep them permanently apart from whites.

Yet even as Indian life was being destroyed, Euroamericans were discovering that the beliefs, tales, songs, dances, and material arts of these ancient civilizations were worth preserving. The preservation effort, carried on chiefly by non-Indians, offers twentieth-century observers their best window on earlier Indian music making. But we must also recognize, first, the incompleteness of the data that have survived; second, the difference between oral expression in its natural habitat and outside it; and third, the contrast between Native and non-Native perceptions of Indian ways.

When Europeans started settling in North America, between one and two million Indians lived in the territory that is now the United States. Aboriginal peoples were also much more diverse before the forced migrations and wars of the 1800s. At one time or another, North America has been home to as many as a thousand tribal units, most of them with their own language, and roughly sixty different language families. Yet in only about 10 percent of those units is enough known about the culture to allow any reliable description of its music.

The second issue has to do with the different forms of Indian music. Among Native peoples themselves, the music circulated orally. But the preservation effort created transcriptions (sung texts written in words or syllables and musical notation) and recordings, beginning in 1890, when cylinder machines were first used. Writing and recording allow music that exists only in Indian performance to be heard in other contexts, repeated as desired, and studied. We know that Indian forebears sang, chanted, prayed, told stories, and took part in rituals that determined *in the moment* the forms their expression took. But once a song is fixed in writing or on record, it takes on a permanent identity that it may never have enjoyed in performance.

The third issue, the gap between Indian and white attitudes, is related to the second. Until late in the 1800s, almost all knowledge about Indian music was filtered through the observations of people for whom it was a foreign mode of expression.

In 1822, Lewis Cass, governor of the Michigan Territory, quoted a Miami Indian song in an article on Native customs: "I will go and get my friends—I will go and get my friends—I am anxious to see my enemies. A clear sky is my friend, and it is him I am seeking." Aware that these words bore little resemblance to any song his readers would know, Cass explained how they were sung. His account squares with what we now know to be common Indian practices. The song has a specific purpose: to recruit volunteers for a mission of war. The text's brevity does not mean that the performance was short; Indians were known to repeat bits of text and music incessantly. Vocables (nonsemantic syllables, such as "Yeh") were also common, as was the song's use of a natural image—the sky, personified as a friend—rather than a narrative or literal description. Finally, Cass was struck by the unusual sound of the singing.

Lewis Cass describes a Miami Indian Song, 1822

There is a strong expiration of the breath at the commencement of each sentence, and a sudden elevation of the voice at the termination. The Chief, as he passes, looks every person sternly in the face. Those who are disposed to join the expedition exclaim *Yeh, Yeh, Yeh,* with a powerful tone of voice; and this exclamation is continually repeated during the whole ceremony. It is, if I may so speak, the evidence of their enlistment. Those who are silent decline the invitation.

One observer who achieved close, sustained contact with Indian peoples was Henry Rowe Schoolcraft, who in 1823 married Jane Johnston, a half-blood Native and the granddaughter of an Ojibwa chief. By 1845, Schoolcraft's contact with Indians led to a combination memoir and ethno-

Old Bear, a Medicine Man, by George Catlin (1832), oil on canvas.

graphic study, *Onéota, or Characteristics of the Red Race of America*, which included an item called *Death Song*, collected from Ojibwa sources. The song is a vivid statement in eighteen lines: the words of a brave lying wounded after a battle, gazing at the sky, where he sees "warlike birds" who may represent his fellow warriors as they enter the territory of their foes, the Dacotahs or Sioux. The text concludes: "Full happy—I / To lie on the battlefield / Over the enemy's line." The neatly constructed poem, however, turns out to be a compilation. Knowing that readers found images of Indian stoicism poetic, Schoolcraft combined several sung moments into one song: evidence that the wish to document Native life lagged behind the urge to arrange it for public consumption.

In 1847, George Copway, an Ojibwa born in Ontario whose parents were converted to Methodism by missionaries and who himself became a preacher in Illinois, published a memoir that included the five-line *George Copway's Dream Song*:

> It is I who travel in the winds,
> It is I who whisper in the breeze,
>   I shake the trees,
>   I shake the earth,
> I trouble the waters on every land.

According to Copway, he received this song at age twelve from the god of the winds himself, who appeared in a dream and explained to him the song and its power. The notion of songs as personal possessions has not been rare among Indian peoples. Also typical are the supernatural framework and the belief that songs are carriers of prophecy.

Whites' views of Indians entered a new phase after 1855, which saw the publication of Longfellow's *The Song of Hiawatha*, based on Henry Schoolcraft's researches. Selling thirty thousand copies during its first six months in print, *Hiawatha* became the most popular long poem ever written by an American. At a time when white settlement had largely wiped

George Copway.

out traditional Indian ways of life east of the Mississippi, the poem introduced dramatic, elevated images of that life as it had existed earlier. Longfellow ascribed to Indians virtues admired by Victorian-age Americans, including manliness, courage, and integrity. Having prepared the way for white settlers, Native peoples had fulfilled their destiny and would now disappear, lingering only in memories built around myth. Recent opinion has judged Longfellow's images of Hiawatha and his people to be no truer than the older stereotype of Indians as savages. Nevertheless, the poem's popularity and staying power make it the central source for understanding how Americans in the eastern half of North America viewed Indians from the mid-nineteenth century on. Just as movies and television shows today can leave lasting impressions of unfamiliar subjects in the minds of viewers, so *Hiawatha* had a powerful impact on people's opinion of Indian culture.

The latter 1800s witnessed two new attitudes. One, connected to show business and popular entertainment, trivialized Indianness. The other was a scientific interest in Native life, rooted in idealistic curiosity and requiring trained workers and institutional funding.

Show-business Indians, based on familiar images, grew more widespread as contact between Indians and white Americans decreased. Parodies of *Hiawatha* were standard fare. Another popular form was the "Wild West" show staged by William "Buffalo Bill" Cody, a plains hunter turned showman. In Cody's shows, which began in 1882 and included real Indians, whites were the good guys and Indians the enemy, a conflict carried over into other popular forms, including pulp fiction, dime novels, and, later, western movies. As in minstrel shows and other entertainments featuring ethnic characters (non-Anglo-Americans), this strain of representation emphasized Indian stereotypes.

The second response, which rejected stereotypes, took place chiefly at the U.S. government's initiative. Congress directed in 1879 that the Bureau of American Ethnology be created at the Smithsonian Institution in Washington, to find out more about the peoples with whom the army was still at war. During the 1880s and 90s, field workers were dispatched from the nation's capital to document life in tribal settings. The drive to study Indians boosted the study of Native music.

In 1882, Theodore Baker, an American music historian, published *Über die Musik der nordamerikanischen Wilden* (On the Music of the North American Indians), his doctoral dissertation at Leipzig University (used by Edward MacDowell to compose his *Indian* Suite, as we saw in Chapter 19). Baker's work, hailed as the first scholarly treatment of American Indian music, contained transcriptions of songs he had heard on visits to a Seneca reservation in New York and the Carlisle Indian School in Penn-

An Indian singer records Native vocal music on a cylinder machine.

sylvania. More than a decade passed, however, before a steady flow of Native musical studies began. A leader in that effort was Alice C. Fletcher, whose 1893 report on the music of the Omaha tribe was the first of her many scholarly contributions. Emphasizing the subject's scientific interest, Fletcher and others gathered accurate data about the music. By the early twentieth century, reports and monographs on American tribal music were appearing regularly.

The study of Indian music making was transformed after researchers started recording the music on Thomas A. Edison's cylinder phonographic machine. The recordings begun around 1890 and continuing through the next century are the basis of a major collection at the Smithsonian. The effort to preserve what remained of North America's oldest musical traditions seems all the more noteworthy when we consider the sheer foreignness of Indian music to people outside Native cultures and the delicate, highly demanding human endeavor musical fieldwork proved to be. In overcoming these two obstacles, scholars of Indian music helped to establish fieldwork as the basis of a new discipline that emphasized ethnography, recording, transcription, and cultural and musical analysis. They stand among the key founding figures of ethnomusicology, a field that only in the 1950s would gain a foothold in academia.

Following the lead of anthropologists, scholars have sometimes divided Indian peoples into six culture areas: the Plains, the Plateau (northern Rocky Mountains), the East (subdivided into Northeast and Southeast, roughly by the Mason-Dixon line), the Southwest (including California), the Great Basin (centered in Nevada), and the Northwest Coast. Though each region has its own musical traits, we can make certain generalizations about traditional Indian music style.

Traits of Traditional Indian Music

1. *Vocal texture.* Indian music is monophonic: sung by one voice or a number of voices in unison, except for drones.
2. *Musical instruments.* Indian music is vocal. Voices are accompanied by instruments, classified as idiophones (rattles and sticks), membranophones (drums with skin heads), and aerophones (whistles and flutes).
3. *Musical forms.* Indian music, relying on brief melodic fragments or constantly repeated phrases, is highly repetitive, its form shaped by the ceremony or activity of which it is part.
4. *Scale systems.* Scales of three, four, five, or six notes are common.
5. *Sung texts.* While words in everyday language are sometimes sung, many songs feature syllables that seem to have no meaning (vocables) or words taken from other Indian languages.

We can get some idea of the process of collecting Indian music by looking at an Omaha song notated in 1884 by Alice Fletcher.

Born in 1838, Fletcher studied in Cambridge, Massachusetts, and in 1881 traveled to Nebraska for her first fieldwork with the Omaha people. The experience gave her a firsthand look at the sorry conditions in which many Indians lived, making her a strong advocate for reform and education. Fletcher's outlook was also influenced by her affiliation with the Bureau of American Ethnology (BAE) in Washington, through which she administered grants of land to tribes in the western states. Fletcher did not at first think of her research as primarily musical. But she soon recognized the key role of music in Indian rituals and began collecting melodies, which she wrote down from Indian singers.

Fletcher's work owed much to her collaboration with Francis La Flesche, a man of mixed Omaha, Ponca, and French ancestry who grew up on an Omaha reservation. First meeting in 1881, the two combined forces to document Omaha traditions. Their monograph *The Omaha Tribe*

Alice Cunningham Fletcher (1838–1923), pioneer collector of music of
Plains Indian nations, confers with Chief Joseph of the Nez Percé tribe.

(1911) has been praised as the first truly ethnomusicological work, integrating Omaha music and Omaha culture. The figure below, labeled *Ritual. Song of Approach*, dates from an early stage of the collaboration. The musical source for this melody was La Flesche himself, who had learned the song in his youth. Now he sang it for Fletcher's transcribing hand, which carefully notated not only pitches, rhythms, and syllables but also the singer's phrasing and accents.

Fletcher's interest in the melodies she collected grew over time, and she became intrigued by the question of where Native music belonged in the full range of human music making. In 1888, she wrote that "the Indian scale" could not be illustrated on the piano, and "there is no notation in common use that would make it feasible to describe it." Experience as a transcriber had taught her that rather than singing out of tune, Indians sang and heard music according to a logic that had so far eluded non-Indians.

In the same year, Fletcher established contact with John Comfort Fillmore, a classical musician and teacher who believed that all music, Western and non-Western, written and nonwritten, shared a common harmonic basis. To Fillmore, Indians' departures from major and minor scales

Alice Fletcher's transcription of this traditional Omaha song was taken from a performance by her assistant, Francis La Flesche, in 1884.

reflected "an underdeveloped sense of pitch discrimination" that was likely to mature in the future. Moreover, Fillmore heard harmonic implications in monophonic Indian melodies. When he first tried to harmonize Omaha melodies that Alice Fletcher had collected, he found that "no satisfactory scheme of chords could be made without employing the missing scale tones." The experiment convinced him that though Indian melodies seldom used all notes in a standard major or minor scale, they were grounded in incomplete forms of these scales.

Alice Fletcher agreed with Fillmore's evolutionary hypothesis, at least at this point in her career. When her *Study of Omaha Indian Music* was published in 1893, only four of the collection's ninety-three melodies were left without accompaniment. The rest appeared with Fillmore's harmonizations, chiefly in major mode.

 EPILOGUE

This chapter began with a vision of Indians and their culture being overrun by whites. Perhaps Alice Fletcher's 1893 volume seems a crowning symbol of that very process, if an unintended one: a collection of Indian melodies arranged for pianists. It is true that later collections by Fletcher, Frances Densmore, and other scholars in the field discarded the idea of harmonized melodies in favor of unaccompanied ones. But in 1893, the idea of music as a branch of scientific study was just coming into existence. Music was a performing art; amateur players and singers were enjoying a booming musical culture rooted in participation. When Fletcher referred to the piano when writing about "the Indian scale," she was assuming a common framework with her readers. Indeed, it is probably more accurate to see her harmonized Omaha melodies of 1893 as evidence of respect and practicality than a mark of cultural condescension. Having uncovered a previously unknown stock of American music, she published it in a form that amateur musicians could enjoy.

As composers grew more interested in the possibilities of Indian music—especially Amy Beach, who based concert works on Indian melodies during the 1890s and after, and Arthur Farwell, who in 1901 founded the Wa-Wan Press in Massachusetts and began to publish compositions based on Native melodies—scholars de-emphasized participation in favor of preservation. Natalie Curtis, a collector writing in 1907, went so far as to say that the preservation effort had been launched on behalf of the Indians themselves: "The older days were gone; the buffalo had vanished from the plains; even so would there soon be lost forever the songs and stories of the Indian. But there was a way to save them to the life and memory of their children, and that was to write them even as the white man writes. The white friend had come to be the pencil in the hand of the Indian." How Indians were supposed to respond to white friends who offered written copies of songs and stories as a substitute for the life that had sustained them is not known. But the idea of loss behind Curtis's comment is also a theme of this chapter.

As the twenty-first century dawns, the "vanishing Americans" have reestablished a presence on the American scene. Native peoples, once members of independent, isolated cultural units, have formed themselves into a minority within a large, culturally unrelated population. And as Indians have managed to reconstruct a sense of peoplehood, even while the life that once supported it was being destroyed, music has helped to provide continuity.

The vision with which this chapter began predicted that future generations of Native peoples would still "know the way it was" through stories handed down to them. We end the chapter with a description by Tara Browner, a music scholar of Choctaw background, of the unique blend of tradition and modernity that may be found in present-day Indian music making. Song types, for example—ceremonial and ritual songs for worship and healing, social and war dances, animal songs, work songs, songs to proclaim social status, and lullabies—are "rarely 'composed' in the Western sense," but "most often came to life through a dream or vision, with the singer serving as a musical conduit and caretaker." Songs "are then learned and preserved by individuals via oral tradition, or through the medium of cassette tapes. With the exception of ethnological transcriptions, Indian music has bypassed the stage of printed notation, moving directly from oral tradition to dissemination by modern recording technology."

A Native Perspective on the Present-Day Indian Pow-wow (1999)

Many traditional dances are still preserved and performed regularly in seasonal ceremonies according to a calendric cycle. At the same time, the contemporary Pan-Indian pow-wow has become a major force for music and dance innovation among today's Indian populations, especially those with far-flung tribal memberships. Pow-wows provide a gathering place for Indian people to celebrate their culture through music and dance, and fertile ground for change, as members of diverse tribal groups interact and share music, dance styles, and dance regalia. Cassette and video tapes are sold featuring the newest songs and dance footwork, resulting in stylistic mixtures impossible only a few decades ago. Consequently, a new Pan-Indian culture, with regional music and dance layered upon [a] Plains Indian framework, is shaping an overarching "Indian" identity. Pow-wow dance styles in urban areas and outside of the Plains regions tend toward the generic, with personal interpretation of the various categories (Traditional, Fancy, Grass, and Jingle). The spread of competition pow-wows offering large prize moneys, where "different" is frequently equated with "better," escalates the rate of change in dance and regalia styles at urban events. Reservation elders, however, continue to ensure the preservation of older forms for the younger generations, continually revitalizing the pow-wow with tradition.

This photograph was taken at a modern Indian pow-wow.

Joy Harjo, a contemporary poet of Creek ancestry, has written that the urgent message she and other Native writers must continue to deliver is "the fantastic and terrible story of all our survival, / those who were never meant / to survive." At the same time, the Indian musical scene is flourishing today around the intertribal pow-wow, an amalgam of diverse elements that feels to participants like a cultural whole. Poetry and pow-wows both belong to contemporary Indian life. The obligation to keep outraged memory alive while adjusting and coming together in a celebratory way with other Indians has marked the consciousness of modern Native Americans with a profound tension, fueled by loyalty to older ways that the society in which they live has dismissed.

LISTENING GUIDE 25

War Dance Song from Southern Plains Indians

The following recording was made in August 1975 by Charlotte Heth, a scholar who is also a member of the Cherokee Nation of Oklahoma, at the sixth annual Kihekah Steh Powwow in Skiatook, Oklahoma. The thirteen male singers who joined in this intertribal performance represent a variety of Indian nations now living in Oklahoma, including the Pawnee, Ponca, Sac and Fox, Quapaw, Osage, and Kiowa. Only the last three, however, are native to the southern plains or prairie region. The others lived originally in the northern plains but were moved during the 1800s to Oklahoma, which was then Indian Territory.

The music recorded here is a southern plains war dance song, part of the Flag Parade that brought the 1975 powwow to a close. The song is accompanied by drum and sung in unison, at full volume and with the high degree of vocal tension characteristic of much Indian music. In the performance, which is repeated three times, a group of women join in briefly with a wailing sound on the second repetition, adding a new layer to the vocal texture and pushing the pitch to a higher level. Heth writes: "The solemn tone befits the ending of this important annual event."

21

"Make a Noise!"

SLAVE SONGS AND OTHER BLACK MUSIC TO THE 1880s

SLAVES WERE "GENERALLY EXPECTED TO SING AS WELL AS TO WORK," recalled Frederick Douglass, born a slave in Maryland around 1818. "A silent slave is not liked by masters or overseers," he explained: " *'Make a noise,' 'make a noise,'* and *'bear a hand,'* are the words usually addressed to the slaves when there is silence amongst them. This may account for the almost constant singing heard in the southern states." Douglass's statement points to the unique conditions in which blacks made music in nineteenth-century America. Aware that slaves' bodies were easier to control than their minds, masters could command singing to track their workers' whereabouts and monitor their mood. When slaves sang of brutality, injustice, or liberation within white hearing, they often disguised their meanings; it has long been understood that what slaves sang about was not always obvious from the words of their songs. To a slave, Douglass wrote, songs "represent the sorrows, rather than the joys of his heart; and he is relieved by them, only as an aching heart is relieved by its tears."

In 1850, almost one out of every six Americans was of African descent. The mid-century national census identified 3.6 million people—just over 15 percent of the population—as black, with 434,000 free and the rest slaves. Concentrated in the South, most heavily on cotton and rice plantations, blacks were nevertheless present throughout the country. Yet white Americans everywhere basically agreed that blacks were inherently inferior. Even among slavery's opponents, few whites endorsed the notion of black-white equality. This attitude must be kept in mind in any discussion of black music making during the 1800s. Black Americans preserved African cultural practices not only out of preference but because whites discouraged their participation in Euroamerican life. With chances for interaction limited, they relied on interactions with each other, and a strong African heritage was thus maintained.

TRADITIONAL BLACK MUSIC MAKING

Between 1800 and the Civil War, most African-American music was made by slaves. And our knowledge of it, as with early American Indian music, depends on accounts written by whites. For example, working in Georgia during the summer of 1841, New Englander Lewis Paine visited a local plantation on a holiday and saw slaves dancing to a unique kind of accompaniment. The custom was called "patting juba": placing one foot "a little in advance of the other, raising the ball of the foot from the ground, and striking it in regular time, while, in connection, the hands are struck slightly together, and then upon the thighs." Patting juba could substitute not only for fiddling but drumming, which was banned in many slave states. An 1845 Georgia law also kept loud instruments of any kind out of slaves' hands for fear they would be used to call together conspirators. Slaves got around that prohibition by dancing to the accompaniment of sticks, bones, tambourines, and hand clapping.

Travelers in the South were also struck by the way slaves sang while they worked. Communal work songs help workers fulfill their tasks by pacing their activity, coordinating their movements, and rallying their spirits. All these situations were noted by observers of African Americans

In 1853, Lewis Miller sketched this Negro dance in Virginia, picturing stately-looking movements accompanied by fiddle, banjo, and bones.

in the nineteenth century. Often they described responsorial singing (traceable to Africa), with strict rhythm and short phrases, the leader improvising calls and the group responding.

Anonymous Portrayal of Stevedores in Mobile, Alabama, Singing As They Unload a Steamboat, 1857

The men keep the most perfect time by means of their songs. These ditties, nearly meaningless, have much music in them, and as all join in the perpetually recurring chorus, a rough harmony is produced, by no means unpleasing. I think the leader improvises the words . . . he singing one line alone, and the whole then giving the chorus, which is repeated without change at every line, till the general chorus concludes the stanza.

White observers came to recognize blacks' talent for making songs out of their life experiences. But even when they sang Euroamerican melodies, African Americans had their own way of performing them. William Mason, Lowell Mason's concert-pianist son, heard an example sung by a group of black laborers shortly after the Civil War. As Mason told the story to a colleague, he was "sitting upon a hotel piazza watching some negro roustabouts unload the cargo of a steamer. As they worked they whistled or sang one melody, which seemed to him exactly like Verdi's anvil chorus [from *Il Trovatore*], until a certain point was reached." But then,

they uniformly turned aside and ended Verdi's melody improperly. Hearing this for an hour or more finally awakened a missionary spirit in the conscientious musician, and he strolled down to the wharf to give the dusky singers a lesson, and secure artistic justice to Verdi's music. But when he began to teach them the correct interpretation, he seemed to them to be spoiling their melody, which upon farther investigation proved to be Geo. F. Root's *"Tramp, Tramp, Tramp, the Boys Come Marching."*

Observers in different places often cited the same performing customs. A man who had lived in Jamaica in the late 1700s described a responsorial approach in the singing there, noting the rhythmic precision. A Russian visitor to a black Methodist church in Philadelphia around 1812 confirmed that the worshipers' singing was apt to go on for a long time.

In every psalm, this observer wrote, "the entire congregation, men and women alike, sang verses in a loud, shrill monotone. This lasted about half an hour. . . . Afterwards . . . all rose and began chanting psalms in chorus, the men and women alternating, a procedure which lasted some twenty minutes." Comments like these point to the source of blacks' music making: the cultural heritage of Africa.

Of all the different kinds of black music that emerged in the nineteenth century, none matched the impact of the "spiritual" songs. The circulation of spirituals after the Civil War gave many white Americans their first hint that if the United States was a nation with its own distinctive music, the ex-slave population was in large part responsible.

SONG OF THE "CONTRABANDS"

Shortly after hostilities between North and South broke out in April 1861, refugee slaves began seeking protection at Fortress Monroe, Virginia. Their masters demanded the slaves' return, but the fort's commander refused, calling them "contraband of war," or captured property. The now-freed blacks were put to work in the fort, but the military could not provide them enough shelter or clothing. So in August, the American Missionary Association proposed a campaign of contraband relief, and soon the Reverend Lewis C. Lockwood arrived at Fortress Monroe as missionary to the ex-slaves. Lockwood's first encounter with Southern black singing left a deep impression. "They have a prime deliverance melody, that runs in this style," he wrote in his first report. " 'Go down to Egypt— Tell Pharaoh / Thus saith my servant, Moses— / Let my people go.' Accent on the last syllable, with repetition of the chorus, that seems every hour to ring like a warning note in the ear of despotism."

Lockwood's report was published in October in a Northern abolitionist newspaper. In December, the same paper printed a twenty-stanza transcription of *Let My People Go. A Song of the "Contrabands"* in regularized English. "The following curious hymn," the notice reported, came from Lockwood, who had taken down the text "verbatim" from contraband dictation. Soon the melody was also available to the public, for a sheet-music version of *Go Down, Moses* was advertised for sale before the year was out.

The printed circulation of the spirituals had begun. During the war and for some time after, it depended on white advocates like Lockwood, who were eager to document the spirituality and creativity in the black soul. Therefore, the story of how slave songs moved beyond slave communities is revealed chiefly in the black singers' interaction with northern white clergymen and teachers.

An 1872 Arrangement of "Go Down, Moses"

First published in 1872, Theodore F. Seward's arrangement of *Go Down, Moses* manages to resemble white hymnody while holding on to traits that listeners had found impressive when the contrabands sang the song.

Using a Bible story to comment on their own lives, the slaves fashioned a spiritual song with dignity and moral force. Just as God delivered Israel from bondage, so, predicted the song, would blacks be delivered. While Seward's version begins like a ballad, the voice shifts: from the narrator (in verses 1, 4–7, 9–11, and 16) to Moses (2–3), to God (8, 12–15), to the words of a slave (17–24). The form is familiar from white revival hymnody: strophic with a refrain. Within each verse, the singing is respon-

sorial, a leader alternating with a chorus. *Go Down, Moses* takes its force
from this repeated response and chorus, embodying the voice of God. And
the message, sung six dozen times in harmony during a complete performance, is a flat command: "Let my people go." The slaves' confidence that,
as God's people, they would soon be free links this solemn litany to their
joyous "jubilee songs" (spirituals that rejoice in the expectation of better
things to come), despite its different mood.

1. When Israel was in Egypt's
   Land,
   Let my people go.
   Oppressed so hard they could
   not stand,
   Let my people go.
   　Go down, Moses, way down
   　in Egypt land,
   　Tell ole Pharaoh, Let my peo-
   　ple go.

2. Thus saith the Lord, bold
   Moses said,
   Let my people go.
   If not I'll smite your first-born
   dead,
   Let my people go.
   　Go down, Moses, etc.

3. No more shall they in bondage
   toil,
   Let my people go.
   Let them come out with
   Egypt's spoil,
   Let my people go.
   　Go down, Moses, etc.

4. When Israel out of Egypt came,
   Let my people go.
   And left the proud oppressive
   land,
   Let my people go.
   　Go down, Moses, etc.

5. O, 'twas a dark and dismal
   night,
   Let my people go.

When Moses led the Israelites,
Let my people go.

6. 'Twas good old Moses and
   Aaron, too,
   Let my people go.
   'Twas they that led the armies
   through,
   Let my people go.

7. The Lord told Moses what to
   do,
   Let my people go.
   To lead the children of Israel
   through,
   Let my people go.

8. O come along Moses, you'll
   not get lost,
   Let my people go.
   Stretch out your rod and
   come across,
   Let my people go.

9. As Israel stood by the water
   side,
   Let my people go.
   At the command of God it
   did divide,
   Let my people go.

10. When they had reached the
    other shore,
    Let my people go.
    They sang a song of triumph
    o'er,
    Let my people go.

11. Pharaoh said he would go
across,
Let my people go.
But Pharaoh and his host
were lost,
Let my people go.

12. O Moses the cloud shall
cleave the way,
Let my people go.
A fire by night, a shade by day,
Let my people go.

13. You'll not get lost in the
wilderness,
Let my people go.
With a lighted candle in your
breast,
Let my people go.

14. Jordan shall stand up like a
wall,
Let my people go.
And the walls of Jericho shall
fall
Let my people go.

15. Your foes shall not before you
stand,
Let my people go.
And you'll possess fair
Canaan's land,
Let my people go.

16. 'Twas just about in harvest
time,
Let my people go.
When Joshua led his host di-
vine,
Let my people go.

17. O let us all from bondage flee,
Let my people go.
And let us all in Christ be free,
Let my people go.

18. We need not always weep and
moan,
Let my people go.
And wear these slavery chains
forlorn,
Let my people go.

19. This world's a wilderness of
woe,
Let my people go.
O, let us on to Canaan go,
Let my people go.

20. What a beautiful morning
that will be,
Let my people go.
When time breaks up in eter-
nity,
Let my people go.

21. The Devil he thought he had
me fast,
Let my people go.
But I thought I'd break his
chains at last,
Let my people go.

22. O take yer shoes from off yer
feet,
Let my people go.
And walk into the golden
street,
Let my people go.

23. I'll tell you what I likes de
best,
Let my people go.
It is the shouting Methodist,
Let my people go.

24. I do believe without a doubt,
Let my people go.
That a Christian has the right
to shout,
Let my people go.

White foes of slavery took the spirituals as evidence of the slaves' human capacity and their fitness to live as free Americans. In the struggle against slavery and its aftermath, *Go Down, Moses* and other spirituals signaled the involvement of Southern black people in what was to be a long campaign for equality.

BLACK SPIRITUAL SONGS

Slave Songs of the United States (New York, 1867), collected and published by William Francis Allen, Charles Pickard Ware, and Lucy McKim Garrison, is the first of many anthologies in which black spirituals are preserved. It was the work of three Northern antislavery activists who worked during the Civil War to educate freedmen on the Sea Islands near Port Royal, South Carolina. Compiled before folklore and ethnomusicology were academic disciplines in the United States, the collection shows respect for the songs' unlettered, untrained creators. And the compilers made a good team. Before arriving at Port Royal, Massachusetts natives Allen and Ware knew little of black Americans or their music, but their duties gave them contact with both. Allen taught in a freedmen's school for more than eight months (1863–64), and Ware, his cousin, worked as a plantation superintendent on St. Helena Island (1862–65). Garrison was the most accomplished musician of the three. Born in Philadelphia, she was a pianist and violinist who by age fifteen was giving piano lessons. The scholarly expertise behind *Slave Songs* was chiefly Allen's; Ware supplied the largest number of transcriptions, while Garrison—with help from her husband, the literary editor of *The Nation*—collected and edited transcriptions and saw the work through the press.

Slave Songs contains 136 melodies with texts, arranged geographically. The introduction admits that the published melodies "convey but a faint shadow of the original," for the singers' inflections "cannot be reproduced on paper." Encountering a culture profoundly different from their own, the compilers still recognized it *as* a culture, and worked to set down this repertory of "old songs . . . before it is too late," knowing that associations with slavery were making the freedmen reluctant to sing them. The uniqueness of the spirituals lay chiefly in their differences from white hymnody, especially the precedence given to rhythm. "The negroes keep exquisite time in singing," Allen wrote, "and do not suffer themselves to be daunted by any obstacle in the words." This comment is an early example of cultural relativism, which refuses to make cultural difference a measure of quality in either direction.

Among the varieties of spiritual song the compilers encountered, the "shout"—a hymn of exalted spirits with a strong rhythmic drive—proved most foreign to white customs of worship. Shouts, which could last for hours, followed regular religious meetings. Benches were rearranged, pushed back to the wall, and the singers formed a ring, around which they shuffled. Allen was surely on the mark when he concluded: "This remarkable religious ceremony is a relic of some native African dance."

A Southern Ring-Shout Described in a Newspaper Report, 1867

The foot is hardly taken from the floor, and the progression is mainly due to a jerking, hitching motion, which agitates the entire shouter, and soon brings out streams of perspiration. Sometimes they dance silently, sometimes as they shuffle they sing the chorus of the spiritual, and sometimes the song itself is also sung by the dancers. But more frequently a band, composed of some of the best singers and of tired shouters, stand at the side of the room to "base" the others, singing the body of the song and clapping their hands together or on the knees. Song and dance are alike extremely energetic, and often, when the shout lasts into the middle of the night, the monotonous thud, thud of the feet prevents sleep within half a mile of the praise-house.

Ring dancing was and is found in many parts of Africa. Indeed, during the time of slavery, the ring shout was a way to bring transplanted Africans together. The ring allowed a synthesis of all the elements of African-American music, including calls and hollers; call and response; additive rhythms and polyrhythms; heterophony, blue notes, bent notes, and elisions; hums, moans, and vocables; off-beat melodic phrasings and parallel intervals and chords; constant repetition of rhythmic figures and melodic phrases; game rivalry; hand clapping, foot patting; and a rock-steady pulse. Spirituals now a century and a half old were thus conceived within the same African-based performance tradition as blues, jazz, soul, and hip-hop. Apart from the astonishing continuity that this notion reflects, it is hard to think of another body of performing techniques so readily updated and refreshed, from generation to generation, without growing dated or stale.

In slave culture, spirituals were created and maintained by singers steeped in these elements, many of which cannot be written down. But whereas Allen, Ware, and Garrison compiled *Slave Songs* to document a disappearing oral practice, an effort began in the early 1870s to turn black spirituals into a written repertory accessible to all. The 1872 publication of *Go Down, Moses* is one example of the result.

THE SPIRITUAL TRANSFORMED

After the war, Fisk University in Nashville, founded in 1865 with a white faculty, was one of the schools organized by Northern missionary societies to educate the Southern freedmen. Dependent on donations from the North, the school struggled to find income in its early years. Then in 1870, the choir formed at Fisk under the direction of Northern-born faculty member George L. White performed at a national teachers' convention in Nashville, to such enthusiasm that White began to imagine a fund-raising tour of the North by a select group of singers, emphasizing spirituals. In the fall of 1871, the Fisk Jubilee Singers set out on their bold venture. After performing in Oberlin, Ohio, for a convention of Congregational ministers who were deeply touched by the singing, and receiving further endorsement from New York's leading clergymen, the Jubilee

The Jubilee Singers of Fisk University, Nashville, Tennessee, photographed around 1880.

Singers became a sensation in the Northeast. Having far surpassed the college's financial expectations, they continued to tour for the next seven years (1871–78), including journeys to the British Isles and the European continent. Their performances during those years enriched Fisk University by $150,000.

The civilized image the Jubilee Singers presented with their neat dress and concert demeanor helped them bring the past of Southern slaves to the notice of Northern Protestants. And Theodore F. Seward's arrangements, published in book form and sold at the concerts, could be sung by anyone. One chronicler writes: "Hills and valleys, parlors and halls, wherever they went, were vocal with Jubilee melodies"—melodies tailored to please many who would have found their original form incomprehensible.

CD 1
26

LISTENING GUIDE 26

Deep River (Traditional)

Spirituals come in a variety of moods and styles. The gentle rhythmic propulsion built in to the familiar *Swing Low, Sweet Chariot*, for example, breathes confidence that life's journey is almost over and heaven within easy reach. *Deep River*, however, beginning with a brief melisma (three notes on one syllable) that can make the beat ambiguous, invites freer rhythm. The text views the Jordan River as a boundary between a life of toil and an afterlife of rest in heaven's "campground." The drawn-out descent of the first syllable and the energy required by the octave leap on "over" suggest a tough journey ahead, for the river is an abyss and the way home strenuous. The arrangement sung here, for four-voice mixed choir, emphasizes choral sound and rich harmony over rhythm. First hummed quietly, the eight-bar melody is then sung to the words and repeated, more forcefully and with added voice parts. A vigorous contrasting section follows—"Oh, don't you want to go to that gospel feast?"—before the hushed, reverent-sounding opening mood returns to end the performance.

The recording was made in the 1950s by the Tuskegee Institute Choir under the direction of William Dawson. Dawson's arrangement carries on the Fisk tradition of black college choirs performing this African-American repertory on the concert stage.

As pictured in the spirituals, the slave's place in the world overlaps with that of the Christian sinner. Both view life as a hard journey, and both seek eternal peace when death brings release from this "vale of tears." A key difference is that while Christian sinners are weighed down by a sense of their own wrongdoing, slaves suffered more acutely from the wrongs of others. Nevertheless, white sinner and black slave held in common a sense of standing alone in a hostile world, and black spirituals appealed across cultural barriers by communicating how it felt to live in that state.

"Home" is a key notion in many spirituals. The slaves, though, sang not about the domestic institution that songs like *Home, Sweet Home* celebrate but rather an *idea* of home. Home might be eternal, as in *Deep River* and *Swing Low, Sweet Chariot*; or it might be in the world, as in *Got a Home in That Rock* or even *Steal Away* ("Steal away home"), where it refers to freedom; or it might be either one, as in *Sometimes I Feel Like a Motherless Child*.

A spiritual about the sufferings of Jesus invites listeners to imagine his torment. *He Never Said a Mumblin' Word* reviews the events of the Passion, including Christ's judgment before Pontius Pilate, the crown of thorns, the whipping, the nails, and two stanzas' worth of flowing blood. While we can picture onlookers cringing at all this brutality, the victim silently accepts his fate:

> O they took my blessed Lawd,
> Blessed Lawd, Blessed Lawd,
> O they took my blessed Lawd,
> An' he never said a mumblin' word,
> Not a word, not a word, not a word.

In this spiritual, words seem to fail the singers. Faced with a crime so appalling, they can only register numbed amazement by repeating the same words over and over again.

Spanning emotions from abject woe to joyful hope, the black spiritual stands as a remarkable legacy from one of American history's most degraded chapters. Writing on the spiritual in 1878, the first historian of black American music reflected: "The history of the colored race in this country" proved that "no system of cruelty, however great or long inflicted, can destroy that sympathy with musical sounds that is born within the soul."

BLACK PROFESSIONAL MUSICIANS

The end of the Civil War brought freedom to Southern slaves and a widening range of professional opportunities, including musical ones. Free blacks in the North, however, had been finding niches in the American music business for decades.

Born in Philadelphia in 1792, Francis "Frank" Johnson, a violin and keyed-bugle player and prolific composer, seems to have been largely self-taught. Johnson worked in an urban scene of military bands, dance orchestras, and concert ensembles where success hinged on pleasing more than one audience. An account from 1819 calls him the "leader of the band at all balls," the "sole director of all serenades," and the "inventor-general of cotillions."

From the 1820s into the 1840s, the keyed bugle was the band's virtuoso instrument. Johnson mastered it so well that during a trip to London in 1837–38, he received from Queen Victoria a silver bugle in appreciation. On this London trip, Johnson attended promenade concerts—a format, first introduced in Paris by Philippe Musard (1833), then popularized in London by Louis Jullien, that mixed an informal atmosphere, refreshments, and plenty of dance music. After returning home, he be-

Francis Johnson (1792–1844), composer, bandleader, and bugler of Philadelphia.

came the first to stage promenade concerts in the United States, attracting crowds in the thousands.

According to one Philadelphia observer, Johnson added to his other talents "a remarkable taste in distorting a sentimental, simple, and beautiful song, into a reel, jig, or country-dance." This statement may mean only that Johnson was good at adapting song melodies to dance forms. But it might also mean that he and his musicians enlivened the music with rhythmic complexities as a way of exercising their African heritage. In other words, they treated notation not as composers' music but as performers' music.

It is not easy to imagine experienced dance musicians—especially African Americans who are heir to a rich tradition of oral performance—playing the same strains over and over again from written music, without embellishment. Johnson's musicians were accomplished professionals: they read music, played both wind and string instruments, and were able to perform in a variety of styles. A member of the abolitionist Hutchinson family singing group commented in 1842, after meeting "the old Fellow" Johnson and his men in a Massachusetts railroad station: "They are a *Rough* sett of Negroes." While this says nothing about their playing, it suggests that musical freedoms relating to ring-shout techniques were also part of their performing vocabulary.

Another niche where a few black entertainers found work was the musical stage, on which William Henry "Juba" Lane became a full-fledged star. Born around 1825, possibly in New York, Lane won fame as a teenager when English novelist Charles Dickens saw him perform during his American tour of 1842 and called him "the greatest dancer known." Lane became the first black member of a white troupe when he joined Charley White's minstrels in 1846 as a tambourine player and a jig dancer. In 1849, he went to England, where his performances wowed English critics. One of them, admitting that he could not have imagined what dance steps such as the "Virginny Breakdown" or the "Louisiana Toe-and-Heel" might look like, wondered how Juba could "tie his legs into such knots, and fling them about so recklessly, or make his feet twinkle until you lose sight of them altogether in his energy?" Another critic noted the "marvelous harmonies" Lane seemed to coax from the tambourine, which he played so well, this writer claimed, that he would not have been surprised to hear Juba play a fugue on it.

During these years, a few African-American musicians also began to appear on the concert stage, most notably Elizabeth Taylor Greenfield, also known as "the Black Swan." Born a slave in Natchez, Mississippi, around 1824, she was taken as a young child to Philadelphia, where she

Elizabeth Taylor Greenfield (1824?–1876), ex-slave and concert singer, on the eve of her departure for Europe.

grew up free in a Quaker household. She received singing lessons as a girl and learned to play harp, piano, and guitar on her own. But it was her voice that caught listeners' attention: an instrument of wide range and unusual sound. In 1851, she settled in Buffalo, New York, where she made her concert debut. After touring in the northern United States and Canada, she traveled to England in the spring of 1853 for further vocal study. Harriet Beecher Stowe, who was visiting at the time to promote antislavery sentiment, helped introduce Greenfield to socially prominent patrons there, and in 1854, she sang for Queen Victoria. Returning to America, Greenfield continued a musical career that included concertizing, teaching in Philadelphia, and staging programs in the 1860s with an opera troupe. As the first black American concert singer to win acclaim on both sides of the Atlantic, Greenfield was able to parlay her English training and public experience into something of an American career as a vocal star.

Harriet Beecher Stowe Describes a Salon Performance by "the Black Swan," 1853

Miss Greenfield's turn for singing now came, and there was profound attention. Her voice, with its keen, searching fire, its penetrating, vibrant quality, its *timbre* as the French have it, cut its way like a Damascus blade to the heart. She sang the ballad, "Old Folks at Home," giving one verse in the soprano, and another in the tenor voice. As she stood partially concealed by the piano, Chevalier Brunsen thought that the tenor part was performed by one of the gentlemen. He was perfectly astonished when he discovered that it was by her. This was rapturously encored.

Songs of the Later
Nineteenth Century

BY 1850, THE EUROAMERICAN SETTLEMENT OF WESTERN NORTH America was well under way. With some 10 million Americans, or 44 percent of the population, taking part in this westward expansion, tales were told and written, pictures painted, and songs composed to relate their experiences on the land.

Sweet Betsey from Pike, one offbeat response to this epic migration, was first published by John A. Stone in 1858 in a San Francisco songster (a collection of song lyrics without music). *Sweet Betsey* relied from the start on oral tradition, for it was sung to *Villikins and His Dinah*, a familiar four-line waltz tune with a refrain made out of vocables. In eleven stanzas, the song offers glimpses of a couple's trip across the continent, starting with their traveling party.

Betsey's character locates her outside the world of sheet music, where heroines tend to embody Victorian virtue. On the Overland Trail, only her determination, physical toughness, and self-reliant spirit let her survive. Sexual repression is absent from this song. As an unmarried couple traveling for months across the country, Betsey and Ike seem to face no barriers to lovemaking. Further, Betsey mocks Victorian norms by falling out of love with Ike, running away from Brigham Young, and responding to a California miner with an earthy outburst. Betsey's confession that she's "chock full" of a desert laxative is not what one expects to hear from the belle of the ball.

To sing *Sweet Betsey*, a person needed only to know the tune *Villikins and His Dinah*, whose many repeated notes fit the delivery of a comic text, and whose refrain placed nonsense vocables where a moral message might have been expected. Appearing in *Put's Golden Songster*, a collection of song lyrics that most likely sold for less than a single piece of sheet music, *Sweet Betsey* flouted the very idea of elevation.

Sweet Betsey from Pike

Sweet Betsey's emphasis on story recalls the traditional ballad, but love and journeying are treated unconventionally. By stanza 2, Betsey's feet hurt, and more troubles are on the way. When the couple enter Utah territory, they encounter Mormons, whose leader, Brigham Young, was famous for polygamy. He ogles Betsey, who flees to avoid becoming another of his wives. West of the Great Salt Lake, Betsey is hit by a spell of craziness and rolls in the sand, but she and Ike continue their trek through mountains and finally reach the mining town of Placerville, California, in the High Sierras. They celebrate their arrival by stepping out in society. Betsey accepts a local miner's request for a dance—with a warning that no fair damsel from traditional balladry or "lady" in a Victorian song would ever have uttered: "Don't dance me hard; do you want to know why? / Dog on you! I'm chock full of strong alkali!" Betsey and Ike become husband and wife, but their marriage fails, presumably because Betsey is beautiful, women are scarce in Placerville, and female nature is inconstant, or so the thinking went.

The territorial expansion of the mid-1800s took place not only through St. Louis and Utah, but also through port cities like New York, Philadelphia, and Baltimore. Another song in *Put's Golden Songster*, set to the tune of *Pop Goes the Weasel*, confirms that fact, and not in an idealized way:

> You go aboard of a leaky boat,
> And sail for San Francisco;
> You've got to pump to keep her afloat,
> You have *that*, by jingo.
> The engine soon begins to squeak,
> But nary thing to oil her;
> Impossible to stop the leak
> *Rip* goes the boiler.

Later stanzas complain about the food, drunken crew members, and unhealthy conditions aboard ship.

On land, meanwhile, miners, loggers, homesteaders, Mormons, farmers, soldiers, and cowboys joined with Chinese train workers to complete the transcontinental railroad in 1869; all contributed to the large body of song that took shape during the process.

Some cowboy songs struck a realistic tone. For example, *The Captain of the Cowboys*, written in 1873 to *Captain Jinks*, a well-known English tune, delivers a stern warning to inexperienced cowpokes:

> If a visit to Blackjack Ranch you pay,
> By way of advice, just let me say,
> You'd better not come on branding day,
> If beauty is your portion;
> For what with dust and what with blows
> what with blows, what with blows,
> A dirty face and a broken nose
> Will likely change your notion.

A cowboy song by Daniel E. Kelley, however, paints a picture far removed from dust and broken noses. Idealizing the out-of-doors, it has come to be the best-known of all Western songs. The words and music were first published together in 1905.

LISTENING GUIDE 28

Home on the Range (Kelley)

Oh, give me a home where the buffalo roam,
Where the deer and the antelope play;
Where seldom is heard a discouraging word
And the skies are not cloudy all day.
 Home, home on the range,
 Where the deer and the antelope play;
 Where seldom is heard a discouraging word,
 And the skies are not cloudy all day.

Later stanzas follow in the same vein, to an attractive **aaba** waltz
tune. Nature's unspoiled beauties are celebrated: clear air, balmy
breezes, glittering stars. Indians have been removed ("The red
man was pressed from this part of the West"). The landscape is
the stuff of legend.

 This song's appeal clearly owes much to the idea of home.
The key word is emphasized—sung at the melodic peak of the
first stanza's first phrase and again on the refrain's first two
downbeats and highest note. "Home" reverberates through the
song as it does through Bishop and Payne's *Home, Sweet Home*,
to which it surely owes a debt. Few would take literally the
song's image of wild deer and antelope cavorting under cloud-
less skies, watched by ranch hands who are incurable optimists.
Yet the connection of life on the range to a vision of home ele-
vates the cowboy into a mythic figure, and the song offers a
peek into his dreams. To the superior male beings who live
there, the song suggests, home is not just a domestic arrangement but a state of mind: a reward for mastering a perilous
environment.

  The songs that Westerners actually sang were more likely to dwell
on loneliness and misery than on lone rangers forging heroic lives. In fact,
only when settlers organized themselves into groups—the Mormons or
the grangers (the Grange was an organization created in 1867 to further
the interests of farmers)—did they succeed in bettering their lot.

SPANISH SONGS OF THE SOUTHWEST

Long before westward expansion began, parts of the Southwest and southern California had been settled by people moving north from Mexico. And there, Spanish-language singing traditions flourished, separate from the English-language ones we have been discussing. Mexican-American song of the late 1800s can be glimpsed through the work of Charles F. Lummis, a Massachusetts native who crossed the country on

Writer and folk song collector Charles F. Lummis (1859–1928), photographed in Los Angeles with his daughter Turbesè and son Jordan (1903).

Composer Arthur Farwell (1872–1952), photographed in the early 1900s by Charles Lummis when Farwell was transcribing songs that Lummis had collected.

foot in the mid-1880s and fell in love with the culture he found in the West. Lummis came to believe that life in California "before the gringo" arrived had been "the most beautiful life that Caucasians have ever lived anywhere under the sun." And he showed his love for the singing he heard there by collecting Hispanic folk songs.

A journalist by trade, Lummis started transcribing songs in Spanish soon after he arrived in Los Angeles in 1885. In the early 1900s, he obtained a wax cylinder machine and hired trained musicians to notate the recordings he made. One who joined the project was American composer Arthur Farwell. Visiting Los Angeles on a 1904 lecture tour, Farwell was invited to Lummis's house, and there he encountered "a little world of Spanish-Californians and Indians." Farwell was enchanted by their songs. "I swam in the musical atmosphere of them—the suave or vivacious songs of the Spanish settlers and the weird, somber, and mysterious songs of the dwellers of the desert." Farwell spent the summers of 1904 and 1905 in Los Angeles transcribing hundreds of the melodies Lummis had recorded. Almost two decades passed before any were published, but *Spanish Songs of Old California* (1923), though containing only fourteen songs, was a noteworthy collection.

In the manner of folklorists, Lummis named the singers he had recorded. At the same time, although recorded with guitar, the songs were published with piano accompaniments—proof that Lummis and Farwell were more interested in having them sung than in preserving them for study. Indeed, by the early 1920s, Farwell was involved in a movement to encourage community singing by amateurs. "In community song movements under my direction," he wrote, the Spanish California songs "have been sung, and are being sung, by large numbers of people year after year with increasing enthusiasm and delight." In Farwell's day, musical scholarship was still considered an accessory of performance. Preserving a song was first and foremost a step toward singing it.

The Mexican-American songs collected by Lummis and arranged by Farwell offer glimpses of a sensibility different from anything found in nineteenth-century American sheet music. In *La hámaca* (The Hammock), the singer lies in a hammock, musing about how sweet life can be when one is in love. And *El capotín* (The Rain Song) is as much about romantic disappointment as the weather. (Fearing that his passion is not returned, the singer pleads for an end to his misery while the music continues its sprightly raindrop imitation.) These songs were also musically distinctive, with flexible rhythm, melody, and form. Lummis and Farwell believed that they could enrich the experience of English-speaking Americans, for the songs conjured up "a world of romantic adventure" far removed from the Victorian values that dominated English-language song of the post–Civil War years, and treating love as one of life's great mysteries.

SHEET MUSIC AND ITS OFFSPRING

After the Civil War, the sheet-music trade showed little interest in the central issues of the day. The hardships of war widows and ex-slaves and the bitterness of Southern whites may have been acute social realities, but they were not the stuff from which song hits were fashioned. Songwriters returned to subjects and sentiments popular in the 1820s and 30s: brief, nostalgic or cautionary dramas or vignettes.

Moreover, the verse-and-chorus form of Stephen Foster and contemporaries remained as prominent after the war as it had been before. The key to popular-song composition still lay in inventing a brief, catchy musical statement, usually four bars long, and then repeating it: the main statement was heard in the introduction, the verse (usually more than once), the chorus, and the piano tag, if there was one. Thus, formal ingenuity counted for little; redundancy was welcomed and embraced.

LISTENING GUIDE 29

Silver Threads among the Gold (Danks)

Silver Threads among the Gold (1873), with words by Eben Rex-ford and music by Hart P. Danks, is a good example of the stan-dard recipe for post–Civil War popular songs. The piano intro-duction previews the main melody: a pair of two-bar phrases, the first starting high and moving downward, and the second reversing direction. Both emphasize leaps of a sixth—wide for a signature interval, but written to sound more graceful than strenuous.

Shine / With up - on / the my / ros - es brow / of to - / the day; / May;

Life / I is / will fad - ing / kiss your fast / lips a - / and way; / say—

Sung *legato* (smoothly) and at a moderate tempo, the gently flowing melody fits the subject: the ripeness of married love. The beginning "Darling, I am growing old," a flat, truthful declaration, is immediately softened by the poetic title line. To a person viewing life from this song's perspective, the passing of time brings a deepening of affection. Musical form contributes to the comfortable atmosphere. The four-bar main statement supplies the **a** section of the verse, which unfolds in an **aaba** structure; the chorus repeats the verse's second half (**ba**) in four-part harmony; and the piano introduction and tag present the main idea as well, for an overall form of **aaababaa**. The words of the chorus also repeat the four lines that begin the first stanza. All this repetition makes for a structure in which love is a force of stability: a haven shielding partners from the ravages of time.

In 1904, more than thirty years after this song was published, British-born Richard Jose, a minstrel tenor known for his high notes, made a hit record of it for Victor. That version is heard here.

INDUSTRIALIZATION AND THE RISE OF GOSPEL MUSIC

In the years between the Civil War and World War I, the United States became the world's foremost industrial nation. And as industry advanced, agriculture declined. By 1910, when manufacturing jobs were on the rise, farm workers made up only 31 percent of the labor force, compared with 53 percent in 1870. Changes in the nation's economic and social structure touched all aspects of American life, music included. Industrialization brought more people into cities, where industries were concentrated. As that trend continued, the popular-song trade came more and more to be ruled by the tastes of city dwellers.

Industrialization did more than shift workers from the countryside to the city; it changed the nature of work and, in the process, alienated many workers. A machinist testified in 1883: "The different branches of the trade are divided and subdivided so that one man may make just a particular part of a machine and may not know anything whatever about another part of the same machine." Wages for such workers were low and job security nonexistent. Thus, while industrialization brought great wealth to a few and raised the country's standard of living, it also made the lives of many workers more uncertain. Such working conditions form the background for a key religious development of the postwar years: the Protestant urban revival movement, which also borrowed from the popular-song and sheet-music trade.

Revivals aimed at bringing the gospel—the glad tidings of Jesus and the kingdom of God—to unchurched Americans of all social and economic classes. One of the movement's leaders was Dwight L. Moody. Born in 1837 in Massachusetts, Moody moved to Chicago in the mid-1850s, where he prospered in the shoe business. He began Christian work with the YMCA (Young Men's Christian Association) and in 1864 founded a nondenominational church. Moody's preaching emphasized God's love, soft-pedaled His wrath, and cultivated sentiment over theology. He also favored simple, popular hymns like William Bradbury's *Jesus Loves Me*.

In the early 1870s, Moody held evangelical meetings in Great Britain, accompanied by his musical director, Ira Sankey, who led group singing and sang solos while playing the reed organ. The impact of these meetings was enormous. Kindling a national revival in Scotland, they made Moody and Sankey famous, and soon they were making evangelical tours of the United States. Singing played a key role in the work of changing sinners into Christians. Moody and Sankey and other traveling evangelists found in "gospel" hymns—sacred songs in popular musical dress—

Singer, compiler, and gospel hymn writer Ira Sankey (1840–1908), at the reed organ, is pictured with Fanny Crosby (1820–1915), who wrote the words for more than nine thousand hymns, including many gospel favorites.

a way to give their audiences easy access to Christianity's spiritual truths. Gospel hymns fed a desire to connect with God in an attitude of praise, with little concern for edification.

By 1875, evangelical revivalism was not only a religious force to be reckoned with but a successful business in the United States. Huge crowds flocked to Moody's meetings, where they heard massed choirs trained by Ira Sankey. And the next year, Sankey gathered the hymns he had used in Britain, added some by like-minded colleagues, and brought out *Gospel Hymns* (1876), a collection that was to be a best-selling hymnal until well into the twentieth century. With copies being sold at Moody's meetings, royalties of some $360,000 were paid during the book's first ten years in print. To deflect any hint that they might be mercenary, Moody and Sankey channeled proceeds from the hymnal into church work.

Beautiful River, a hymn from the collection, reflects the gospel approach that Moody and Sankey promoted. Baptist clergyman Robert Lowry wrote the words and music, inspired by a scene from the Book of Revelation. Sounding like a march, *Beautiful River* exudes comradeship:

Shall we gather at the river,
Where bright angel feet have trod
With its crystal tide forever
Flowing by the throne of God?
    Yes, we'll gather at the river,
    The beautiful, the beautiful river
    Gather with the saints at the river,
    That flows by the throne of God.

Beautiful River also lends itself well to the subject of baptism. No anxiety about Judgment Day clouds the sunny picture offered by this hymn.

Another of the book's selections, *Sweet By and By*, is a daydream of heaven by a composer outside the revivalist circle. New Hampshire native Joseph P. Webster studied music with Lowell Mason in Boston in the early 1840s and eventually settled in Elkhorn, Wisconsin. He published some four hundred songs and hymns during his lifetime, including *Lorena* (1857), a Civil War favorite.

LISTENING GUIDE 30

Sweet By and By (Webster)

Sweet By and By was composed in 1867 to words by Elkhorn resident (and pharmacist) S. Fillmore Bennett. The music sustains the reverie of Bennett's text, avoiding complication: only three chords are used (tonic, dominant, subdominant), and not a single accidental sharp or flat. At the same time, unbroken rhythmic flow is equally important. Webster instructs performers: "With much feeling and in perfect time." This is an unusual direction, for slowing the tempo is a standard way to emphasize feeling in a sung text. And with regular eighth notes in the piano and dactylic rhythm (♩ ♪♪) in the vocal parts, *Sweet By and By* joins strict tempo with smooth declamation—again an unusual pairing. Only the dotted rhythm in the chorus (and beginning each phrase of the verse) enlivens the song's tranquil surface.

Sweet By and By follows a familiar form: piano introduction, unison verse, harmonized chorus. But unlike most secular songs of the day, its main interest lies in the chorus, which introduces the title phrase and main message, and whose length is doubled by a repeat. An echo effect between male and female voices invites singers and listeners to savor a rosy view of eternity: believers will meet on a "beautiful shore" when their days on earth are over. The air of serene confidence radiating from this hymn must have disarmed the doubts and fears of many.

In the repeat, diminuendo gradually to the end.

LABOR SONGS

During the late 1800s, labor unions began to play a role in the struggle to control a changing workplace. Joining forces to seek better pay and working conditions, workers found that the threat of striking could be an effective bargaining tool. Given the unequal balance of power, it is no surprise that they explored many ways of boosting morale and confirming solidarity. Singing was one. And labor songs, written for jobs ranging from mining to farming, are another musical legacy of the post–Civil War years.

Leopold Vincent's *Alliance and Labor Songster* (1891) was compiled for use at meetings of the Farmers Alliance, which by 1890 claimed more than three million members. One example from that collection, *The Right Will Prevail*, sung to the tune of *Sweet By and By*, illustrates the uncompromising tone that labor songs usually took:

> When the Workingmen's cause shall prevail
> Then the class-rule of rich men shall cease,
> And the true friends of Labor will hail
> With a shout the glad era of peace.
>   Right will reign by-and-by,
>   When the Workingmen come into power;
>   Right will reign, by-and-by,
>   Then the gold thieves shall rule men no more.

Readers will recognize an impulse for parody harking back to the broadside ballads of the 1700s. Here, the author transformed a gentle affirmation of heavenly peace into an attack on capitalists. We can only speculate about the full range of meanings this song carried in 1891. For some, the use of *Sweet By and By* must have signified confidence: just as believers would go to heaven, workers would prevail over bosses. On the other hand, if triumph was to be postponed into some vague "by and by," perhaps others took this version more pessimistically, as in a later parody that promises: "There'll be pie in the sky when you die."

Since labor songs were militant, they were often sung to melodies whose original texts drew clear lines between right and wrong. Civil War songs were favorites. (Many labor songs were based on the *Battle-Hymn of the Republic* and on Root's *Battle Cry of Freedom* and *Tramp, Tramp, Tramp*.) So were other patriotic songs, including *God Save the Queen*, sung in the United States to "My country, 'tis of thee." As part of a campaign to shorten working hours, the following lyric was published for that melody in 1865:

GEORGE-McGLYNN, ANTI-POVERTY

LAND AND LABOR SONGS,

A Choice Collection of One Hundred and Thirty Popular, New and Original
Compositions, with Radical Words, to Favorite Old Familiar Tunes,
also about Eighty New Pieces of Music, arranged for

Quartets and Solos, with Ringing Choruses,

ALL DESIGNED FOR

Land and Labor Lectures, Anti-Poverty Societies, George-McGlynn New Cross
Crusade Meetings, Knights of Labor Assemblies, Trade Union Associations,
and all Orders or Lodges intended to improve the

Physical, Moral, Social and Spiritual Condition of Mankind,

ESPECIALLY PREPARED FOR

THE UNITED LABOR PARTY CAMPAIGNS,

Also for Amusements, the Home Circle, and to Cheer and Encourage Every Friend of

JUSTICE, PEACE AND PROGRESS.

By B. M. LAWRENCE, M. D.,

AUTHOR OF CELESTIAL SONNETS, THE NATIONAL LABOR SONGSTER, TEMPERANCE
AND PROGRESSIVE SONGS, ETC., ETC.

COPYRIGHTED BY B. M. LAWRENCE, M. D.
1887.

Songsters like this one, published in 1887, circulated pro-labor messages cheaply, relying on familiar music for much of their impact.

Ye noble sons of toil,
Who ne'er from work recoil,
  Take up the lay;
Loud let the anthem's roar
Resume from shore to shore,
Till Time shall be no more.
  Eight hours a day.

Finally, management was not the only target of the nineteenth-century labor press. In 1893, a Philadelphia journal parodied a famous hymn, Arthur Sullivan's *Onward, Christian Soldiers*, to attack Christian outreach. Here is the first stanza of *Modern Missionary Zeal*, which reads like something out of the tumultuous 1960s:

Onward! Christian soldiers;
　On to heathen lands!
Prayer book in your pockets,
　Rifles in your hands.
Take the happy tidings
　Where trade can be done;
Spread the peaceful gospel
　With a Gatling gun.

Thoughts like these proceeded not from the music business, still a bastion of Victorian values, but from what amounted to an underground press, which attacked establishment beliefs. Labor songs thus reveal another face of American musical democracy: one that, rather than affirming the established social order, gives it a critical look and invites citizens to imagine that it could be otherwise.

23

Stars, Stripes, and Cylinders

SOUSA AND THE PHONOGRAPH

IN AUGUST 1898, A NEWSPAPER IN WAYNE COUNTY, PENNSYLVANIA, carried a poem that declared the Keystone Band of Lake Como, in the state's northeast corner, one of the town's chief assets.

> The grand old town of Como lies resting 'neath the hills,
> While its waters run on daily, in quiet rippling rills;
> And its sights and scenes are glorious—in fact, are simply grand,
> But there's one thing does excel all else—it's the music of its band.

Local pride stands behind this glimpse of an amateur group that played for summer picnics, winter entertainments, and civic occasions as they arose. People outside Lake Como may not have thought much of the Keystone Band, but the group was valued at home because the isolation of rural towns encouraged self-sufficiency. Local bands affirmed local self-respect. In newspapers of the time, there are next to no critical reviews of any band performance.

The Keystone Band stands in a line that began in the 1700s with local militia bands, blossomed during the Civil War into a national patriotic movement, and continued as an amateur pastime even after elite professional wind bands came into prominence. The professional band, led in the postwar years by Patrick S. Gilmore and John Philip Sousa, brought polished musical performances to the ears of more Americans than any other ensemble. But behind bands like Sousa's lay a vast network of amateur groups that, like church choirs, were part of many people's musical experience as performers and listeners.

Between the Civil War and World War I, the wind band flourished, for it was well matched to the character of town and city life. As technological progress gave people more leisure time, civic functions multiplied:

Photographed around 1887, this band from Baraboo, Wisconsin, seems to have used a camping trip as an occasion to play.

parades, picnics, dedications, store openings, as well as concerts, dances, and other social functions. By playing music that the public enjoyed, at a volume that could be heard outdoors, a band enlivened these occasions. In cities, the performers might be professionals who played in theater orchestras during the winter season and added more outdoor work in the

Lookout Mountain, Tennessee, is the site of this 1864 photograph of a Civil War brass band's performance.

summers. In villages and towns, players of all ages were recruited to form amateur bands. Band instruments were inexpensive, and the music required only modest technique. The playing of amateur bands reverberated across the land in these years: bearers of a tradition of democratic music making that has continued through the twentieth century.

SOUSA, AMERICAN BANDS, AND THE MARCH

Band concerts were not new in the late 1800s, but earning a living by playing in them was. Patrick S. Gilmore led one of the first such outfits until he died in 1892. And in that year, John Philip Sousa formed the band that set the professional standard from that time forward. Sousa is a key figure in American music history. As a prolific composer for the stage and concert hall, he put his stamp on a well-known popular form: the march. As a conductor, he thrilled audiences with a blend of showmanship and polished performance. When Sousa came on the scene, the wind band was already a leading provider of music to the public, but by the time his performing career ended in 1931, the professional band was a thing of the past, and an amateur reincarnation, the school band, had begun to flourish.

Born in 1854 in Washington, D.C., the son of a U.S. Marine Band member, Sousa began playing violin as a boy. He studied in a local conservatory of music and at age fourteen entered the Marine Band's apprenticeship program. Discharged from the Marine Corps in 1875, he settled in Philadelphia, played in theater orchestras, developed his conducting skills, and returned to Washington in 1880, at the age of twenty-five, as leader of the Marine Band. During his dozen years in that post, Sousa also composed vigorously, especially marches and operettas. In 1892, he moved to New York and formed his own band, which at first contained forty-six members, including some who left Gilmore's band when the leader died. By the 1920s, Sousa's band numbered about seventy.

Sousa and his men proved a popular draw at fairs and expositions, settling in for weeks at a time. The band also spent half the year or more touring North America by rail. European trips were organized in the early 1900s, and a world tour in 1910–11. With concerts seven days a week and usually twice a day, Sousa's tours were not for the faint of lip. During a week-long swing through southern Michigan in 1913, for example, the band played fourteen concerts in twelve cities, performing in theaters that housed operettas, musical comedies, and the variety shows known as vaudeville.

Boasting shiny instruments and dressed in military-style uniforms, Sousa's men affected an impressive spit-and-polish demeanor and played as if they were a single, well-tuned instrument. In concerts, Sousa liked to begin with a classical work such as an overture. When the number ended and applause began, rather than leaving the stage, he would turn back to the musicians, call out the name of the first encore—perhaps a popular song arrangement or a Sousa march—and give the downbeat before applause had died away. That encore might be followed by another; or Sousa might move on to the next number printed in the program. Not knowing what music to expect, the audience was kept in a state of anticipation. And so were the players.

The second scheduled number typically featured an instrumental soloist. Next came another ensemble piece, such as a suite by Sousa. A vocal selection usually followed, sung by the band's soprano soloist; and a rousing instrumental number completed the first half. Except for the last, all these selections were encored. And the second half continued in a similar vein. From a variety of music—classical and popular, vocal and instrumental, loud and soft, solo and ensemble—Sousa the conductor wove collages of sound on the spot, responding to the occasion and the atmosphere in the hall.

Sousa had begun tailoring encores to audience taste even before he formed his own band. In 1889, the Marine Band was in Fayetteville, North Carolina, to commemorate the hundredth anniversary of the state's ratifying of the U.S. Constitution. There the crowd, prepared to listen politely but coolly to this government ensemble, was instead whipped into an emotional and enthusiastic frenzy as the band launched into *Dixie*. The spontaneous outburst brought tears to the conductor's eyes. Sousa even used encores to comment on audience behavior. At one matinee concert, he muttered to the band: "If they're going to act like children, we'll give them children's music!" And he ordered up the *Mother Goose* march, a medley of nursery-rhyme tunes. From that time on, the story goes, a restless audience might lead some bandsman to remark: "The Old Man's about ready to give 'em 'Mother Goose'!"

Spontaneity and showmanship aside, Sousa's band had the skill to play classical works originally written for orchestra. Sousa liked to say that as well as entertaining audiences, he hoped to educate them too. Wagner, whom Sousa once called "the Shakespeare of music," was a particular favorite; the band also played Sousa's arrangements of Grieg and Richard Strauss, not to mention older works like Bach's Toccata and Fugue in D minor.

Although Sousa made no attempt to hide his distaste for syncopated dance music (including ragtime) in its native setting, he was willing to mix it into concerts. Audiences seemed to love ragtime, and Sousa be-

This cartoon from 1907 depicts Sousa's "characteristic poses" on the podium.

lieved that his band's performances raised the music above its origins. The concept of "high" and "low" musical values was assumed by many musicians and critics of that day, including Sousa. In 1899, he likened a syncopated tune to a low-born woman made respectable by the band's attentions. "I have washed its face, put a clean dress on it, put a frill around its neck," Sousa wrote. "It is now an attractive thing, entirely different from the frowzly-headed thing of the gutter."

Sousa's best-known compositions are his marches. As a dance-based form, the march features a steady beat, regular phrase structure, and repeated sections. For Sousa, however, the beat of his marches was not just steady; it was "military." Growing up in the nation's capital, Sousa was seven years old when the Civil War began and twelve when it ended. He spent his youth and young manhood connected with the Marine Band, which his father served and he himself would conduct. Sousa felt deeply the military cost of the freedom that Americans enjoyed, and that knowledge inspired his marches. His capturing of a martial tone in marches like *The Gladiator* and *The Gallant Seventh* summoned others to celebrate America's fighting spirit, through which democracy had been won and would be preserved. Patriotism was Sousa's great subject. For him, the most potent patriotic symbol of all was the American flag. *The Stars and Stripes Forever*, Sousa's best-known march, glorifies the flag, and its words deliver a warning to potential enemies:

Let despots remember the day
When our fathers with mighty endeavor
Proclaimed as they marched to the fray
That by their might and by their right it waves forever.

In all, Sousa composed 136 marches, three-quarters of which follow a standard musical form that he adopted around 1880, though he did not invent it: a brief introduction followed by three or four repeated strains (often sixteen bars), with the most memorable melody in the third strain, or "trio," which is in a new key and provides the musical climax. Starting simply and often softly, a typical Sousa trio increases in volume and complexity, blossoming into the sound of the full band. (Sometimes a contrasting "break strain" is sandwiched between repeats of the trio.) Throughout, his marches feature plenty of counterpoint between instruments.

The Sousa band consisted of three instrumental sections—trumpets, trombones and euphoniums, and clarinets—that might carry a melody, with the rest (saxophones, French horns, tuba, and percussion) filling in the texture. In peak moments of a Sousa march, the main tune was often doubled in two octaves or even three, while other voices presented one or more countermelodies. The musical space, chopped into units of predictable length, brims with melody and counterpoint—a prime reason Sousa's marches are still relished today.

Catchy tunes are another key feature; some were written by Sousa himself, but more than a quarter of his marches quote melodies that were already well-known or composed for another purpose. The *Revival March* of 1876, for example, is built around the gospel hymn *Sweet By and By*, and *Ancient and Honorable Artillery Company* (1924) features *Auld Lang Syne*. In several other marches, Sousa recycled melodies composed for his operettas—for example, the *El Capitan* march (1896), which borrows melodies from *El Capitan* the operetta, written the previous year. By far Sousa's most successful stage work, *El Capitan* toured North America for four years and played another six months in England. As with other popular music of the day, Sousa and his publishers milked the marches for commercial gain by arranging them for an astonishing variety of combinations. Published in both band and orchestra arrangements, the *El Capitan* march was also available for piano (two, four, or six hands); banjo; guitar; guitar duet; mandolin; mandolin and piano; mandolin, piano, and guitar; mandolin and guitar; two mandolins and piano; two mandolins and guitar; zither; and two zithers. Sousa copyrighted each of these versions separately; most were aimed at the vast market of amateur performers.

LISTENING GUIDE 31

The Stars and Stripes Forever (Sousa)

In *The Stars and Strips Forever* (1897), Sousa composed an American classic by inventing for the trio a memorable, songlike melody and then playing it off against interludes of a different character. Cast in two halves in A-flat, the trio's melody fills thirty-two bars. It relies on a four-note motive that moves mostly stepwise and lends itself to circular melodic shapes.

The melody (**abac**) traces its own climactic curve through four eight-bar sections. Not until bar 27 do we hear an A-flat as the root, or main note, of a tonic triad. And, having long avoided the tonic, Sousa finds two ways to emphasize it. First he sets A-flat at the top of an octave leap, sustaining it as the melody's highest note. Then he invents a new motive centered on the tonic and moving in quarter notes, bringing the tune to a resolute close in a rush of activity.

Sousa follows the trio with a break strain that is virtuosic for the lower brass, unusually active in rhythm and harmony, and without a hint of tunefulness—intended apparently to wipe out the trio's lyric mood so that its return will sound fresh. The device works, partly on the strength of the new strain's disruptive, slashing character, and partly because the piccolo section adds a countermelody to the trio's repeat. After the break strain is heard again, the trio tune returns once more, this time with percussion in full cry and a low-register countermelody to balance the piccolos on top. *The Stars and Stripes Forever* goes out with the band's full artillery blazing: a deft blend of lyric melody, historical reference (the piccolo sound recalls fifes), and military clamor.

As well as military and concert bands, professional groups included circus bands and even family bands that toured on entertainment circuits; in amateur ranks, lodge bands, industrial bands, ethnic bands (German, Italian, African-American, even Native American), children's bands, and institutional bands (including prison groups) also flourished. (Around 1913, trumpeter and singer Louis Armstrong was playing cornet in a reform-school band in New Orleans.) New Hampshire–born Helen May

John Philip Sousa in his uniform as leader of the U.S. Marine band.

Butler, a violinist and cornetist, organized and led a professional Ladies Military Band during the century's early years. A tally of the band's concert performances between 1900 and 1913 yields 203 appearances in Boston, 110 in Buffalo, 126 in St. Louis, and 130 in Charleston. Presenting "music for the American people, by American composers, played by American girls," Butler and her musicians bucked stereotypes of the time by showing that women could endure the hardships of touring life and please enough paying customers to survive in the music business.

SOUSA AND RECORDED MUSIC

Thomas A. Edison invented the phonograph in 1877. By 1890, bands were beginning to make recordings, and Sousa, as the leader of two famous bands, took part. Before mid-1892, he conducted the U.S. Marine Band in more than two hundred recordings, and the Sousa band made more than four times that many between 1897 and the early 1920s. Yet Sousa disliked the phonograph and conducted very few of his own band's recordings. As an artist-businessman, he faced a choice: should he block the band from recording altogether, or should he use the medium to keep the band's name before the public? In choosing the second course, Sousa recognized the power of recordings to attract audiences to his concerts. He quelled his own doubts by turning the band's recording sessions over to other conductors, chiefly band members.

What were Sousa's qualms about recordings? For one thing, recording technique around 1890, when Sousa was first involved, was so primitive that little thought could be given to artistry. A photo of the Marine Band making cylinder recordings shows ten Graphophone machines arranged in front of the band. After the title of the selection was announced, the band would perform the work in an arrangement that lasted less than two minutes; new wax cylinders were then placed on the machines, and the process was repeated. In this way, ten recordings of a march could be made every few minutes.

Sousa mistrusted an enterprise that placed music in the service of technology. He also deplored the record companies' refusal in those early days to pay composers for the use of their works. But more than that, Sousa considered recordings an assault on the ecology of musical life. He testified at a congressional hearing in 1906 that the phonograph was discouraging many Americans from singing and playing themselves, a trend that could "ruin the artistic development of music in this country." Sousa remembered growing up in Washington at a time when, "in front of every

Published in 1891, this photograph shows the U.S. Marine Band recording in the Washington studio of the Columbia Phonograph Company.

house in the summer evenings you would find young people together singing the songs of the day or the old songs." But now, he complained, "you hear these infernal machines going night and day." In Sousa's view, the change was bad for the art of music, which ought to develop "from the people." "If you do not make the people executants," he told the congressmen, "you make them depend on the machines."

A generation later, Sousa could look back on a time of robust growth for amateur performance in America. Music teaching was widespread, and a vast range of music and musical information was published. The instrument business, from pianos to winds and strings, was booming. Choral societies existed in virtually every sizable city. Glee clubs, choruses, and banjo and mandolin clubs flourished on college campuses. The piano was the parlor instrument par excellence, and many could play it. And amateur bands flourished. The growing appetite for music was being fed chiefly by amateur singers and players for their own delight and edification. But Sousa worried that the phonograph's encouragement of consumption without participation threatened the base of amateur performers whose love for music sustained the work of professionals.

By the time the United States entered World War I, tours by Sousa, other professional outfits, and circus bands, plus the growing circulation of phonograph records, brought the sound of polished wind ensemble playing to more and more listeners. And bands were only part of the tide of professional music making that swept across the nation in the twentieth century's early years. Theaters were built where audiences could gather to watch and listen. Railroads now linked communities large and small, creating a national market for consumer goods. And entrepreneurs, centered increasingly in New York City, used the transportation network to bring musical entertainment to more and more customers. By the early 1900s, popular entertainment was well on its way to becoming modern "show business." And the workings of this new entertainment industry depended on a new approach to creating and marketing popular song.

24

"After the Ball"

THE RISE OF TIN PAN ALLEY

ONE MAN WHO LEFT A VIVID ACCOUNT OF OLDER WAYS YIELDING to new in the entertainment world was song publisher Edward B. Marks. In 1934, drawing on forty years' experience, Marks published a memoir that describes fundamental changes around 1890, when New York publishers were transforming the popular-song trade, and 1900, when theatrical consolidation was nationalizing show business.

In the late 1800s, New York City became the capital of popular-song publishing. "Tin Pan Alley," the nickname given the publishing district that took shape in New York around 1890, is also an apt metaphor for an approach new to the trade: populist in tone, noisy with the sound of song pluggers, and shameless in the pursuit of commercial advantage. Tin Pan Alley's economics, like its atmosphere, differed from that of older publishing firms. The nineteenth century's flagship music publisher was Oliver Ditson & Co. of Boston. From its founding in the 1830s, Ditson's business grew spectacularly, and by 1890 the company had bought the catalogues of more than fifty other publishers and set up new firms in Philadelphia, New York, Chicago, and Cincinnati. Ditson published many popular songs, but they made up only a fraction of the firm's comprehensive catalogue. As the century's end approached, the company had grown into a colossus that took pride not only in financial strength but in service to the edifying art of music. Ditson would eventually collapse under the weight of its lofty goals and huge inventory.

In contrast, M. Witmark & Sons of New York City, founded in 1884, traveled light. Undistracted by thoughts of duty, the Witmark firm originated in a hunger for profit and a personal snub. In the mid-1880s, a traveling minstrel troupe hired a fifteen-year-old boy soprano named Julius Witmark. The youth struck a deal with New York publisher Willis Woodward that, for a share of the proceeds, he would sing a particular song in

Woodward's catalogue as often as possible during the troupe's upcoming national tour. Witmark made good on his part of the bargain, and the song enjoyed strong sheet-music sales. But all he got from Woodward in return was $20 and a dismissive pat on the shoulder. Julius and his brothers retaliated by opening M. Witmark & Sons, using their father's name because they were all under legal age.

Catching the flavor of Tin Pan Alley's commercial origins, this story also illustrates how its location in New York City allowed songs to be promoted. First, a theatrical troupe is in New York recruiting personnel, looking for new material, and planning its next tour. Second, a music publisher enlists a troupe member to plug one of his songs. Third, that song becomes a hit, thanks in part to the singer's efforts. And fourth, the publisher reaps the rewards from sales of the sheet music, for he has copies on hand wherever the troupe plays. In contrast to Ditson, Tin Pan Alley firms published *only* popular songs, pouring much of their energy and money into promotion.

Publisher Edward B. Marks saw the songwriters of early Tin Pan Alley as a seedy, decadent breed. Most were careless businessmen who, instead of retaining rights to their songs and collecting royalties, often sold them to a publisher for ready cash, which they then squandered. Songwriters wrote "according to the market," Marks charged, and yet at the same time believed themselves superior to the public "to whom they pander." Publishers were also a mixed lot. In pre–Tin Pan Alley years, Marks recalled, the leading figures had been old-school gentlemen. But to survive in the "particularly insane business" of the 1890s and later, it helped

The T.B. Harms firm, whose 1891 Broadway location is pictured at the right, became the leading publisher of stage music after the turn of the century.

to be "more of a Bohemian." A salesman at heart, Marks himself relished life in the trade: the personal associations, rivalries, adventures, and risks that fueled a high-energy enterprise, where the possibilities of financial bonanza or ruin were always present. To get performers to keep plugging the songs in his catalogue, Marks visited an average of "sixty joints a week," while Joe Stern, his partner in the firm of Joseph W. Stern & Co., dropped in at some forty more.

As Marks and his competitors scrambled to sell their songs in Tin Pan Alley's marketplace, the amusement world was changing in ways that deeply affected the popular-song trade. Aware that vast audiences could now be reached outside New York, theatrical producers began sending more of their shows on regional and national tours. In August of each year, theater owners from around the country went to New York and competed to lure "direct from Broadway" companies to their towns. As the number of shows on the road increased, booking agents emerged as middlemen to coordinate their touring. In 1896, six of these agents joined together to form the Syndicate, a group that controlled most major theaters in New York and many outside. By 1906, the Syndicate boasted a network of some seven hundred theaters nationwide, and touring on its circuit was coming to be an orderly process, directed from New York. As well as scheduling shows, the Syndicate controlled their content down to such details as the removal or addition of songs.

Consolidation also took place in variety entertainment, known after the turn of the century as vaudeville. Its roots lay in New York's music halls, concert saloons, beer gardens, and variety houses where Marks plugged his songs. And vaudeville also owed much to the large numbers of immigrants who had arrived by boat from Europe. In the form that crystallized around 1900, vaudeville combined a wide range of performers—comedians, jugglers, acrobats, actors, animal trainers, singers, and instrumentalists, of every nationality—into an evening's entertainment at cheap prices. A standard vaudeville format called for nine acts, each running about fifteen minutes. Shows often began with a "dumb act" while latecomers straggled in and from there built to a climactic eighth act that featured the star. A particular group of acts might play a given theater for one night or several weeks, depending on the community's size and the main star's drawing power.

As the Syndicate had done for musical theater, the Keith-Albee organization brought order to vaudeville when in 1906 it formed the United Booking Office of America, connecting thousands of performers and theater managers. In 1927, Keith-Albee combined with the Orpheum circuit, which played a similar role in the West. A smaller circuit in the South, the Theater Owners Booking Association (TOBA), brought black talent to black theaters and audiences, a market that Keith-Albee and Orpheum never tried to serve. Vaudeville czars held such power over performers who played their circuits that performer Harpo Marx considered the head of the Keith-Albee empire "more powerful than the president of the United States."

In what was fast becoming national show business, stage performers were considered the most effective boosters of sheet-music sales, and song publishers competed fiercely for their attention in New York City. For by 1900, Tin Pan Alley publishers knew well the riches that one best-selling song could bring.

In 1892, banjo player and songwriter Charles K. Harris, living in Milwaukee, wrote a ballad that became the hit of the decade. Harris recalled later that the song took shape from an idea that had popped into his mind: "Many a heart is aching after the ball." With that line as a starting point, he fashioned a story in three long verses, each followed by a thirty-two-bar chorus. Then, since his own grasp of musical notation was shaky, he solicited the help of a local arranger to provide a score and a piano accompaniment. Disenchanted by earlier experience with New York pub-

In the early 1900s, venues across the country, such as the Grand Theater in Buffalo, New York, offered variety entertainment for low prices.

The powerful manager B. F. Keith opened the Gaiety, his first major vaudeville theater, in Boston in 1894.

lishers, whose royalty payments he had found too small, Harris decided
to publish the song himself. His strategy for plugging *After the Ball* proved
excellent. A road company was playing a Broadway show in Milwaukee,
and Harris arranged a meeting with the cast's leading baritone. The singer
agreed to sing the new song in the show, and his first performance drew
a five-minute standing ovation, with six encores of the chorus. Harris

Once Charles K. Harris's *After the Ball* (1892) became a hit, Harris
brought out an edition with an illustrated cover suggesting the perils
of romance on public display.

promised the singer $500 and a share of the income from sales, and from then on his song was sung in every performance.

More than any American popular song before it, *After the Ball* triggered an economic bonanza. Orders for the song poured in as the road company moved toward New York. Oliver Ditson ordered 75,000 copies, and John Philip Sousa programmed an arrangement of the song for his band at the Chicago World's Columbian Exposition (1893). Before long, Harris was earning $25,000 a month from sales, and on the strength of his success decided to open a popular-song publishing business in New York, where he moved permanently in 1903.

CD 2
3

LISTENING GUIDE 32

After the Ball (Harris)

In *After the Ball*, an old man recalls the evening "long years ago" that doomed him to a life of loneliness. He and his sweetheart were attending a dance. When she grew thirsty, he went to get her a drink. Returning with a glass of water, he found her kissing a stranger. And in the shock of that moment, he dropped the glass, which shattered irreparably. So did his heart. Only years later did he learn that the stranger was his sweetheart's brother— a fact she had tried to explain but that he had refused to hear.

The song's cover pictures a dance floor filled with men and women dressed in formal finery. Some couples whirl vigorously, others are locked in close embraces, and others seem occupied with gossip and flirtation. The picture suggests the display of personal charms in a competitive public arena, an image that separates *After the Ball* from earlier songs of courtship and love. Moreover, it is a waltz, and a century ago the waltz, a dance that called for partners to embrace, could carry erotic overtones. Harris's song dramatizes that risk.

After the Ball struck a responsive chord in its time. Perhaps audience members and amateur performers found appeal in the story or the proverb-like moral delivered by the chorus. But it is the music that brings emotion to a tale that might otherwise be taken as a sermonette. While the serene, lilting ball music maintains the illusion of calm control, the words portray feelings as fragile as the glass dropped by the song's disappointed lover.

The long melody of the verse is held together by a four-bar rhythmic cell that goes on through its entire sixty-four bars:

♩. | ♩ ♩ | ♩. | ♩. or ♩. | ♩ ♩ | ♩. | ♩. . The chorus shifts to a more con-
centrated, catchy tune (**aa¹a²b**), based on a new four-bar rhythmic motive whose arrival is a welcome contrast. Until its last
phrase, the chorus dwells on this figure as single-mindedly as
does the verse on its rhythmic cell. But then Harris drops the
chorus figure and, returning to that of the verse, brings the
song's two sections together on the title line.

The recording we are hearing, made in the late 1920s by
Bradley Kincaid, the first big country radio star, shows that this
sentimental ballad stayed alive in rural America long after its
days as a hit song had passed.

As the opera and minstrel stage had done in an earlier day, musical
comedy and vaudeville now provided the sheet-music business's main
marketing arm. But for all the changes in songwriting that took place—
new subjects, fresh cover designs, more stars' endorsements, a growing
emphasis on female glamour—Tin Pan Alley's ultimate goal remained
the same as that of publishers and songwriters in the day of Stephen Foster and George F. Root: to sell sheet music to home performers in quan-
tities as large as possible.

The variety of song types sung on American stages around the turn
of the century was enormous: airs from opera and operetta, Victorian parlor songs, Tin Pan Alley numbers of every description, songs in foreign
languages, songs from blackface entertainment, even religious songs.

Each carried its own style of singing. Moreover, performers had their own techniques and mannerisms, and many stars owed their fame to a personal way of approaching songs. As in earlier days, popular songs were performers' music: outlines to be filled in according to each performer's personality and skill.

Below is a chronological list of sixteen popular songs that can be seen as a microcosm of early Tin Pan Alley's offerings. Each won great commercial success, selling a million or more copies of sheet music. All are in major keys and share a familiar musical form: a brief piano introduction, followed by a verse and a chorus. All but three are waltzes, all but two were published in New York, and all but one (*Daisy Bell*, by an English songwriter) are American in origin. While they carry the antique aura of a bygone age, many Americans can still sing or whistle at least the title lines.

A Selection of Hit Songs, 1892–1905

The Bowery (1892)	Charles H. Hoyt and Percy Gaunt
After the Ball (1892)	Charles K. Harris
Daisy Bell (1892)	Harry Dacre
The Sidewalks of New York (1894)	Charles B. Lawlor and James W. Blake
The Band Played On (1895)	John E. Palmer and Charles B. Ward
Sweet Rosie O'Grady (1896)	Maud Nugent
When You Were Sweet Sixteen (1898)	James Thornton
My Wild Irish Rose (1899)	Chauncey Olcott
You Tell Me Your Dream (1899)	Seymour Rice and Albert H. Brown
A Bird in a Gilded Cage (1900)	Arthur J. Lamb and Harry Von Tilzer
In the Good Old Summer Time (1902)	Ren Shields and George Evans
Sweet Adeline (1903)	Richard H. Gerard and Harry Armstrong
Meet Me in St. Louis, Louis (1904)	Andrew B. Sterling and Kerry Mills
My Gal Sal (1905)	Paul Dresser
Wait 'till the Sun Shines, Nellie (1905)	Andrew B. Sterling and Harry Von Tilzer
In the Shade of the Old Apple Tree (1905)	Harry H. Williams and Egbert Van Alstyne

The songs on the list explore a wider range of moods than the era's popular nickname, the Gay Nineties, might imply. *After the Ball's* cautionary theme is echoed more lightheartedly in *The Bowery*, which warns of the dangers lurking in a notorious New York district where "they say such things, and they do strange things." This song, *The Sidewalks of New York*, and *Meet Me in St. Louis, Louis* (which refers to the international fair of 1904) are the only numbers that are geographically located. But three others, like *Sidewalks*, also reveal glimpses of life in Irish neighborhoods: *The Band Played On*, *Sweet Rosie O'Grady*, and *My Wild Irish Rose*. Edward Marks called the years between the Civil War and the early 1890s "the heyday of the Irish-American in the theater," and a time when Irish ethnic conventions established themselves in song. All four Irish songs look on life's brighter side. Optimism also pervades *Daisy Bell*, *In the Good Old Summer Time*, and *Wait 'till the Sun Shines, Nellie*.

Five songs besides *After the Ball* deal with the separation of sweethearts. *When You Were Sweet Sixteen* and *Sweet Adeline* tell of lovers parted by some unnamed cause; in both, the singer hopes for reunion. In *You Tell Me Your Dream* and *In the Shade of the Old Apple Tree*, one of the partners has died. But the most unusual parted-lovers song is Paul Dresser's *My Gal Sal*, in which death cuts short an unusual friendship.

As described by "Jim," Sal was a person of mature years and plenty of experience.

> They called her frivolous Sal,
> A peculiar sort of a gal,
> With a heart that was mellow,
> An all 'round good fellow,
> Was my old pal;
> Your troubles, sorrows, and care,
> She was always willing to share,
> A wild sort of devil,
> But dead on the level,
> Was my gal Sal.

The kind of woman a man would describe in the language of male comradeship is rare in Tin Pan Alley song. But then, *My Gal Sal* rejects the romantic conventions that ruled the day's songs about women. We never learn why some called her frivolous, or why Jim hails her as wild, though excessive drinking and extramarital sex are implied. By Tin Pan Alley's code of conduct, these are signs of depraved character in a woman. But this song treats "old pal" Sal's behavior as if it were that of a man, who might not be condemned for such appetites.

The earthiness of *My Gal Sal*, published in 1905, would have been unlikely in a Tin Pan Alley song a decade earlier. It was not that songs had previously ignored the possibility of sex outside marriage; rather, songs touching the subject treated their female characters as fatally stained. Between the Civil War and 1890, Edward Marks observed, "sniffly songs for the strayed sister, whom her virtuous co-females delighted to pity," were popular. In these numbers, "dishonor was always presented as the equivalent of death, which usually accompanied it in some form about the fifth verse." Though no songs on the list of sixteen fit this category, *A Bird in a Gilded Cage* comes close. The female subject of this song dishonors the institution of matrimony by marrying "for wealth, not for love," and in the second and last verse, she dies. The narrator pictures a cemetery, then muses on the "tall marble monument" marking the unfortunate woman's grave:

> And I thought she is happier here at rest,
> Than to have people say when seen:
> [Chorus:] She's only a bird in a gilded cage,
> A beautiful sight to see . . .

Songs from another ethnic group that overturned some of the trade's inhibitions may have paved the way for *My Gal Sal*. The group, a new generation of African Americans, brought fresh energy to the music of Tin Pan Alley. As the century drew to a close, minstrelsy featured black troupes as well as white, but the minstrel tradition put the crop of young black performers and songwriters who appeared on the New York scene in a bind. Its character types were too rigid to accommodate their talents yet too widely accepted for black entertainers to ignore. Moreover, during the 1880s, a new kind of black character had appeared: the "coon," a shiftless black male who could also be dangerous.

The lyrics of "coon" songs feature references to watermelon, chicken, alcohol, gambling, and other demeaning stereotypes of African-American life. Having caught on with white audiences, coon songs were part of the legacy that younger black artists inherited when they entered show business. The Gay Nineties were also a time when racial segregation was established as law in the South and lynching was on the increase. As author and lyricist James Weldon Johnson saw it, "the status of the Negro as a citizen had been steadily declining for twenty-five years; and at the opening of the twentieth century his civil state was, in some respects, worse than at the close of the Civil War."

Any African American who worked in show business was faced with the conflict between pleasing an audience and knowing that many standard crowd-pleasing devices openly ridiculed black people's capacities and character. Entertainers dealt differently with the conflict. According to Marks, leading figures like Bert Williams and George Walker were

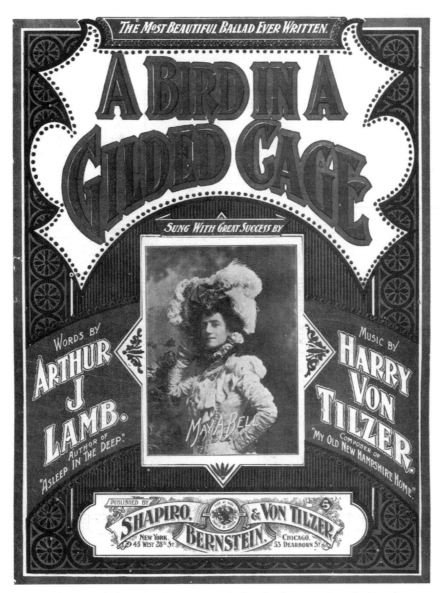

As the cost of photographic images declined, pictures of professional singers such as May Bell were used more and more to plug sheet-music editions of songs such as this well-known hit.

"outwardly resigned to all sorts of discrimination. They would sing 'coon,' they would joke about 'niggers,' they accepted their success with wide-mouthed grins as the gift of the gods." But the brothers James Weldon and J. Rosamond Johnson were different: "emphatically new Negro," as Marks saw it, and eager to change the caricature. "Their father was a minister—and they combined a clerical dignity, university culture, and an enormous amount of talent." The Johnson brothers "wrote songs sometimes romantic, sometimes whimsical, but they eschewed the squalor and the squabbles, the razors, wenches, and chickens. . . . The word 'coon' they banished from their rhyming dictionary, despite its tempting affinity with moon."

Together with racist conventions, however, the new generation of entertainers also inherited the cakewalk. Rooted in African tradition, this new way of moving onstage originated in a contest held during slavery times in which couples competed to show the fanciest strutting, and the winners received a cake or some other prize. Long parodied in minstrel shows, the cakewalk was now being performed to music with an electrifying, driving rhythm that made syncopation the norm rather than the exception. During the 1890s, the musical style that accompanied cakewalking earned the label of "ragtime" (though the style did not originate in Tin Pan Alley). And ragtime proved widely appealing, a strong presence in turn-of-the-century popular music.

On our list of sixteen, the number most influenced by ragtime is *Wait 'til the Sun Shines, Nellie* (1905). Nellie, the girlfriend of Joe, is worried because she's bought a new gown to wear to a picnic, which is threatened by rain. Joe reassures her with the song's title line. Composer Harry Von Tilzer's verse relies on a rag-derived syncopated motive, with offbeat accents restricted to the measures' first two beats. The rhythm lends a slightly tentative quality to the verse, underscoring Nellie's fretfulness, which is shouldered aside by the chorus's confident arrival in striding, foursquare march time.

Another leading black showman of the time was Ernest Hogan, whose most famous song, *All Coons Look Alike to Me*, is both demeaning to its black characters and unquenchable in musical liveliness. The subject is courtship. In the verse, the male protagonist tells ruefully how Lucy Janey Stubbles has dumped him for a "coon barber from Virginia." But her sneering dismissal in the chorus mocks the very idea of love, except perhaps as a ploy to corral a partner for display in public and sex in private.

The song's cover shows a slim, pert Ms. Stubbles appraising several black men who, apart from their grotesquely distended lips, look entirely different from each other. The picture makes it clear that she is not really saying she can't tell her suitors apart. Rather, the difference that really matters—a willingness to spend money according to *her* wishes—cannot be seen by the naked eye. In an era when songs often idealized romance, an outlook like this, no matter how thickly layered with irony, took sheet-music buyers into a realm of male-female relations beyond Tin Pan Alley limits.

Choice Chorus, with Negro "Rag," Accompaniment, Arr. by MAX HOFFMANN.

All coons look a - like to me, I've got an-oth-er beau, you see,

The piano accompaniment to the final "choice" chorus of Ernest
Hogan's *All Coons Look Alike To Me* (1896) is a fully realized rag, in
contrast to earlier choruses, where the piano plays only chords in
quarter-note rhythm.

The chorus made this song famous, for Hogan's title line, detached
from the song, could be turned into a racial slur, dismissing a whole people in one jeering slogan. And the strong, memorable tune was durable
enough to stand up to instrumental performance. In January 1900, New
York's Tammany Hall played host to piano players from across the country, gathered for the Ragtime Championship of the World Competition.
The three who reached the finals were required to demonstrate their skill
by "ragging" *All Coons Look Alike to Me* for two minutes in front of the
judges.

Hogan's music makes an especially strong impact in the second, or
"choice," chorus printed in the sheet music, where the accompaniment
approaches the style that would soon emerge in piano ragtime. But more
than that, its vitality and strut, in the end, seems to outweigh the force of
the racist words. Tapping into a vein of high-spirited energy, whatever
the emotional cost, the music resists self-pity and the notion that even
rampant racial prejudice and political oppression could defeat the spirit
of people capable of inventing music this joyful, appealing, and complex.
As the new century began, white Americans were finding themselves be-
holden to blacks for music that seemed, more than any other, to catch the
modern spirit.

PART THREE

The Twentieth Century

"To Stretch Our Ears"

THE MUSIC OF CHARLES IVES

PROLOGUE

IN THE LATTER 1800s, AS THE HISTORY OF MUSIC IN AMERICA WAS starting to be written, historians took classical, popular, and folk music to be a hierarchy, with classical music on top, popular on the bottom, and folk music somewhere in between. These historians viewed the United States as too young to have achieved much in the art of music, which meant the classical sphere. Taking Europe as the standard, they pointed out that only since the Civil War had Americans begun to build a proper foundation: a concert life in the Old World mode, with masters like Beethoven and Wagner at its center. That foundation had been laid in some cities, and a few home-grown composers were writing works for the concert hall. But only when concert halls and opera houses began programming American works would the United States earn full membership in the family of Western musical nations.

As some writers of the time saw it, American composers were handicapped by the lack of a traditional base in folk music. While American Indian music and "Negro" slave songs were distinctive, neither could represent the whole United States, as did unwritten songs and dance music in many European countries. The musical life of Old World nations seemed an organic whole, rooted in common people's song and bearing fruit in classical compositions. American musical life seemed fragmented by comparison. Amateur performance flourished but, centered in the popular sphere and seemingly led by commercial interests, it was thought to carry little artistic value.

A glimpse at turn-of-the-century musical life suggests the respect in which classical music was held. With subsidies won by appeals to civic pride and the ideal of transcendence, symphony orchestras were formed in a number of major American cities. New York's Carnegie Hall, designed for classical performance, was built in 1891, Boston's Symphony Hall in 1900, and Chicago's Orchestra Hall in 1904. In New York, resident companies performed whole seasons of grand opera, and the Metropolitan Opera Company toured other cities as well. Traveling singers, pianists, and violinists brought their art to communities large and small; performers who specialized in European classical music were among the day's top celebrities. Metropolitan daily newspapers employed well-informed critics who discussed serious musical issues at a sophisticated level.

In an age when almost all musical performances were heard live, the charisma of virtuoso performers added to the aura of transcendence that surrounded the concert hall and opera house. Through much of the nineteenth century, Americans believed that the training needed for such performances could be gained only in Europe. But by the latter 1800s, these skills were being taught in the United States. Conservatories of music, founded chiefly to teach beginners, added more European-trained musicians to their staffs. Other teachers set up private studios. And the growing ranks of amateur performers included singers and players of classical as well as popular works.

Colleges, universities, and conservatories provided posts for many of the nation's leading composers of the day: Paine at Harvard, Chadwick at the New England Conservatory, Parker at Yale, and MacDowell at Columbia, all appointed between 1875 and 1896. When they joined the teaching profession, they struck a bargain in which they traded freedom for economic security and took on pedagogical tasks they may not have relished. They and their generation set a precedent that many later musicians have followed. The United States can boast neither a long tradition of aristocratic patronage nor a horde of citizens with an appetite for classical music. But since the 1700s, Americans *have* believed deeply in the practical and edifying power of education. And so it was more in education's name than in the name of art that classical music won a beachhead in the academy, which has served ever since as an unofficial but powerful patron.

CHARLES E. IVES, AMERICAN COMPOSER

Charles Edward Ives was born in 1874 in Danbury, Connecticut. George Ives, Charles's father, had studied music in New York City, led a Danbury band during the Civil War, then returned to his hometown to work as a performer and teacher of music. Charlie Ives, as family members knew him, showed uncommon talent on the keyboard, began composing at eleven, played snare drum in his father's band, and took his first post as a paid church organist at fourteen. In 1894, the year Charlie enrolled at Yale College, his father died, a loss that he mourned for the rest of his

Charles Ives (1874–1954) attended the Hopkins Grammar School in New Haven, Connecticut, where he pitched for the school baseball team. He is pictured here with battery-mate Franklin Miles (1894).

life. After an academically ordinary career at Yale, which included composition study with Horatio Parker, Ives graduated in 1898, moved to New York City, and began a career in business that led him into life insurance and estate planning.

Unconnected with New York's public musical life, Ives composed prolifically in private, at least until 1917, when an illness brought both his business and musical lives to a temporary halt. Three years later, he printed, at his own expense, the large-scale Piano Sonata No. 2 (*Concord*), and *Essays Before a Sonata*, a prose companion piece. In 1922, his self-published *114 Songs* appeared in print. Neither of these works drew much notice from critics, performers, or the public. Yet they were part of a large body of music unlike that of any other composer, living or dead, much of it radically forward-looking in style yet rooted in American musical traditions and history. In the 1930s, younger American composers began to discover Ives, delighted to find an older figure whose music spoke with a voice so original. As musicians gradually woke up to Ives's music—the *Concord* Sonata was premiered in 1939, and in 1947 he won a Pulitzer Prize for his Symphony No. 3 (composed some forty years earlier)—they encountered a figure whose background was as unusual as his musical approach.

Ives credited his father with shaping his musical outlook. George Ives had considered music a spiritually precious thing and conveyed his love for it to his son. And he was something of a visionary when it came to acoustics. Charles remembered an experiment of George's in which violin strings were "stretched over a clothes press and let down with weights," intended to produce quarter-tone subdivisions of the scale. George's teaching methods could also be unconventional. On the one hand, "Father knew (and filled me up with) Bach and the best of the classical music, and the study of harmony and counterpoint etc., and music history." On the other,

> he would occasionally have us sing, for instance, a tune like *The Swanee River* [Foster's *Old Folks at Home*] in the key of E♭, but play the accompaniment in the key of C. This was to stretch our ears and strengthen our musical minds, so that they could learn to use and translate things that might be used and translated (in the art of music) more than they had been.

Such ear-stretching schemes taught Ives that euphony was not the only kind of harmony worth hearing; that two key levels sounding at the same time offered wide possibilities for focusing one's ear; and that even the most familiar Stephen Foster song could be defamiliarized.

George E. Ives (1845–1894), father of
Charles Ives, was a town musician and
bandmaster in Danbury, Connecticut.

 IVES'S SONGS

114 Songs is a collection of songs written throughout Ives's life as a composer; as Ives declared in a "Postface" to the work, he had "merely cleaned house" to produce it. The variety of musical styles is enormous. A consideration of three songs, written between 1897 and 1921, will suggest something of their diversity and their connectedness.

Although the three exhibit great differences in sound, each is unmistakably Ivesian. Indeed, according to Ives's musical philosophy, sound could never reflect more than part of a composition's essence. "My God! What has sound got to do with music!" he bursts out in *Essays Before a Sonata*. This paradoxical blast was Ives's response to the attitude that composers should tailor their music to performers. "It will fit the hand better this way—it will sound better," a violinist is supposed to have told Ives, provoking these often-quoted words. A bit later in the same paragraph he writes: "That music must be heard is not essential—what it *sounds* like may not be what it *is*." With statements like these in mind, it is clear that any discussion of the music must be on the lookout for Ivesian traits that reach beyond the realm of sound.

LISTENING GUIDE 33

The Circus Band (Ives)

The Circus Band sets a text by Ives himself that views a slice of life through a boy's eyes. A circus has come to town, and the company parades down Main Street to the strains of a band. So the vocal line is laid over a march in the piano. Ives shows here that he can write a three-strain march (see Chapter 23), but this is not exactly a conventional march. For example, the introduction to the trio starts with a thumping sound made by densely packed chords in no particular key: Ives called this sound piano drumming, an effect he worked out as a boy while practicing drum parts on the piano. The sixteen-bar break strain jumps to a new key, then clouds it with chromatic streams of chords. These moments are unexpected in a street march, just as march form challenges the norms of the art song.

The heart of *The Circus Band* lies in the way voice and accompaniment are connected. The band (i.e., piano) makes the music, carrying the parade past a thrilled singer who responds to the spectacle. In the first strain, the vocal line moves up from midrange to an outburst on "Ain't it a grand and glorious noise!" In the second, the boy gets so excited that he falls behind the accompaniment and is left scrambling to make up beats. And at the start of the last trio, Ives turns the pianist briefly into another parade watcher. As a countermelody in octaves starts in the left hand, the accompanist is supposed to shout: "Hear the trombones!"

Our recorded performance is not of Ives's voice-and-piano original but an arrangement for unison chorus and orchestra by George Roberts, who knew Ives personally and is said to have made the orchestration in line with the composer's wishes. (No shout encouraging the trombones is heard here.)

An 1873 issue of *Harper's* magazine carried this etching of the circus coming to town, suggesting the excitement captured in Ives's song *The Circus Band* (1897).

LISTENING GUIDE 34

Serenity (Ives)

In *Serenity*, Ives created a modern musical frame for a well-known nineteenth-century hymn. When sung to a conventional hymn tune, the verses of Quaker poet John Greenleaf Whittier seem homey and comforting. But the calm of Ives's setting is far from homey. Calling *Serenity* "a unison chant," Ives gives the voice an incantation: narrow in range and to be sung "very slowly, quietly and sustained, with little or no change in tempo or volume throughout." Except for one measure at the end of each stanza where hymnbook harmony appears, the accompaniment consists of two dissonant chords (B-F-A-C and C♯-G-B-E) not related by any standard tonal scheme. They are simply repeated until a listener accepts their connection.

The stillness that Ives conjures up with this combination of words and music is no more stable than the mysterious tonality and wisps of quoted material that echo in the song. Just as nature can be quiet and unthreatening, the human soul can be relieved of "strain and stress." But the music suggests that both are temporary. The best that humans can manage are moments of hushed contemplation, tuned to glimpsing a "beauty of [God's] peace" that cannot be sustained.

Ives left a description of the experience that inspired *The Housatonic at Stockbridge*, a song that

> was suggested by a Sunday morning walk that Mrs. Ives and I took near Stockbridge, the summer after we were married. We walked in the meadows along the river, and heard the distant singing from the church across the river. The mist had not entirely left the river bed, and the colors, the running water, the banks and elm trees were something that one would always remember.

Ives sketched the first part of a composition for strings, flute, and organ shortly after that walk in 1908. He completed it some years later, and then in 1921 fashioned it into a song for voice and piano, using a poem by Robert Underwood Johnson. Another comment by Ives reveals that the hymn tune being sung that morning was Dorrnance by Isaac Woodbury, a younger contemporary of Lowell Mason. "Housatonic Church across River sound like Dorrnance," he jotted in a note to himself, adding: "River Mists, leaves in slight breeze river bed—all notes & phrases in upper accompaniment . . . should interweave in uneven way, riversides colors, leaves & sounds—*not* come down on main beat."

The Housatonic at Stockbridge shows Ives working to unite a place, a visual image, a memory, and a poem. One striking feature of the song is its textural layering. Just as we can see a river's banks through morning mist, so an added layer of sound blurs the song's outlines without hiding them. The piano introduction creates the effect of foreground and background. While the left hand is solidly anchored in C-sharp major, the right—printed mostly in notes smaller than normal—plays a stream of very quiet, disjunct eighth notes in no particular key. Ives's score says that the small right-hand notes "may be omitted, but if played should be scarcely audible." Ives also directs that the right-hand layer "be listened to separately or sub-consciously as a kind of distant background of mists seen through the trees or over a river valley, their parts bearing little or no relation to the tonality, etc. of the tune."

Another trait is unity through the repetition of a motive (a short repeated musical figure). The vocal line is built around a motive of four (sometimes three) repeated notes followed by a descending major third. To suggest how it pervades the melody, here is the text, with italics showing words and syllables sung to that figure:

Contented river! in thy dreamy realm
The cloudy willow and the plumy elm:
Thou beautiful! *From ev'ry dreamy* hill
What eye but wanders with thee at thy will,
Contented river! And yet overshy
To mask thy beauty from the eager eye;
Hast thou a thought to hide from field and town?
In some deep current of the sunlit brown.
Ah! There's a restive ripple, and the swift
Red leaves September's firstlings faster drift;
Woulds't thou away, dear stream? *Come whisper near!*
I also of much resting have a fear:
Let me tomorrow thy companion be,
By fall and shallow to the adventurous sea!

Quotation—the borrowing of a preexistent melody—also plays a key role in *The Housatonic at Stockbridge*. From DORRNANCE Ives took the first eight bars:

and made them the basis for his vocal line. Because DORRNANCE was part of the experience that inspired this song, his quotation of it is understandable. But the example points to a larger question: Why did Ives, composing in the classical sphere, repeatedly quote melodies from the popular and traditional spheres?

Ives quoted to infuse his compositions with spiritual power. Believing that the purest-hearted performers were plain folks, singing and playing in the course of their everyday lives, he often quoted melodies that they loved and sang in their own way—including hymn tunes that most trained musicians scorned. As a boy, he had heard these melodies in their natural habitat, and under his father's leadership, at outdoor camp meetings:

> The farmers, their families and field hands, for miles around, would come afoot or in their farm wagons. I remember how the great waves of sound used to come through the trees—when things like *Beulah Land . . . Nearer My God to Thee . . . In the Sweet Bye and Bye*, and the like were sung by thousands of "let out" souls. . . . Father, who led the singing, sometimes with his cornet or his voice, sometimes with both voice and arms, and sometimes in the quieter hymns with a French horn or violin, would always encourage the people to sing their own way.

The gap Ives cites between written and sung hymns relates to his distinction between music and sound. It is clear that sung versions inspired his melodic quotations. He found in the spontaneity and freedom of the singing the spiritual power he came to call "substance." Ives explained:

> It wasn't the music that did it, and it wasn't the words that did it, and it wasn't the sounds (whatever they were—transcendent, peculiar, bad, some beautifully unmusical)—but they were sung "like the rocks were grown." The singers weren't singers, but they knew what they were doing—it all came from something felt, way down and way up.

While he never defined substance in so many words, Ives did offer many examples of "manner," the label under which he grouped technical skill, standard musical customs and forms, academic knowledge, and even sound itself. One of Ives's best-known stories reveals his distinction between substance and manner. A "young man" is questioning George Ives (see box).

Charles Ives on Music versus Sound

"How can you stand it to hear old John Bell (the best stone-mason in town) sing?" Father said, "He is a supreme musician." The young man (nice and educated) was horrified—"Why he sings off the key, the wrong notes and everything—and that horrible, raucous voice—and he bellows out and hits notes no one else does—it's awful!" Father said, "Watch him closely and reverently, look into his face and hear the music of the ages. Don't pay too much attention to the sounds—for if you do, you may miss the music."

For Ives, the difference between music and sound, substance and manner, lay in attitude. Substance was a matter of putting your whole soul into the making of music, regardless of talent or skill. To say that hymns were sung "like the rocks were grown" was to suggest that the singers' feelings were so deeply grounded in belief and nature that they approached the geological. Hymns tapping such emotional depth could hardly be trivial, no matter what the professors said.

Ives quoted melodies to suggest what might have given performances substance in the first place. Following the camp-meeting singers' lead in *The Housatonic at Stockbridge*, Ives decorates and embellishes DORRNANCE rather than quoting it literally. The voice begins by following the tune's melodic outline, then gradually dissolves into a paraphrase.

LISTENING GUIDE 35

The Housatonic at Stockbridge (Ives)

In *The Housatonic at Stockbridge*, Ives uses musical complexity to evoke substance. Convinced that "man as a rule didn't use the faculties that the Creator had given him hard enough," he places tough demands on listeners, as if coaxing them to feel that their effort would bring its own rewards. In his setting of lines 5 through 8 of Robert Underwood Johnson's poem, the following things are happening simultaneously:

1. The left hand establishes the key of C-sharp major, in 4/4 time, with pitches outside the key also played against it.

2. The right hand, written in small notes, creates a hushed layer of aural mist with a three-beat unit centered on B, and interweaves with the left hand in an "uneven way" by "*not coming down on the main beat.*"

3. The vocal melody, over a C-sharp in the bass, gravitates toward E major and is coordinated with the left hand.

4. The hymn tune DORRNANCE, neither quoted literally nor imitating an actual congregation, is paraphrased with more and more freedom as the song continues.

5. The vocal line is unified motivically, first by four (or three) repeated notes followed by a descending third, then by the five-note figures from the second and third measures of DORRNANCE.

These musical traits are joined to poetic lines that call the river's appearance a "mask" for its true nature, proof of Ives's belief that a "transcendental" reality lies behind what the senses can perceive. By carrying listeners along on a tide of sometimes complementary, sometimes contradictory sounds, images, ideas, and words, Ives aims to bring them into proximity with the spiritual current he calls substance.

The *Housatonic at Stockbridge,* with its musical layering and hymn-tune quotation, is a song with more than one voice. When Ives recommends that the piano's right hand be listened to separately, as background, it is as if he is thinking of his composition as a convergence of musical impulses from different sources and directions. Listeners may identify Dorrnance, or they may hear the unifying motive, reminiscent of Beethoven's Fifth Symphony, a work Ives admired and quoted in several compositions. More than one voice can also be heard in *The Circus Band* and *Serenity*. In *The Circus Band*, Ives gives different voices to the vocalist (the bystander) and the pianist (the band), then varies the pianist's with drumming and one joyous shout. And the separate musical and textual quotations in *Serenity* call on listeners to shift their aural point of view as the song unfolds. To Ives, these changes of voice help carry listeners beyond the experience of manner and into the deeper spiritual region of substance. Each new layer or voice offers an aural glimpse of what lies on the other side of the sound.

IVES'S INSTRUMENTAL MUSIC

Ives's instrumental compositions reveal many of the same traits as his vocal works. Quotations, layering, and changes of voice abound. The composer's impatience with hierarchy can lead to jarring contrasts—quotations from Beethoven symphonies, for example, next to fiddle tunes and gospel hymns—and dense overlappings. In *Putnam's Camp*, for orchestra, Ives creates the illusion of two bands, each playing a different piece, marching toward each other. In *The Unanswered Question*, a single trumpet intones the same angular figure over a string ensemble's consonant, organ-like chords while four flutes respond with growing agitation to the trumpet's calls. Harmonic dissonance in *Putnam's Camp* comes to a head in a roar of cacophony, while in *The Unanswered Question* clashes between layers come and go, each time yielding to the serene euphony of the string background. In creating sounds that stretch the ears and minds of listeners, Ives was following the lead of his intellectual heroes, Ralph Waldo Emerson and Henry David Thoreau, who probed hidden unities and mysteries of human existence.

The Piano Sonata No. 2 (*Concord*), printed in 1920 with the *Essays Before a Sonata* but composed between 1909 and 1915, is the ultimate Ivesian synthesis. As Ives wrote, it "is an attempt to present (one person's) impression of the spirit of transcendentalism that is associated in the minds of many with Concord, Mass., of over a half century ago. This is undertaken in impressionistic pictures of Emerson and Thoreau, a sketch of the Alcotts, and a scherzo supposed to reflect a lighter quality which is often found in the fantastic side of Hawthorne." By honoring a group of New Englanders in an esteemed European form, Ives declared the universality of both. By commemorating literary Americans linked to transcendental philosophy, he suggested their impact on his own outlook. By combining sonata-style thematic development with quotation and layering, he proclaimed their compatibility and his own command of the composer's craft. By accompanying his sonata with a book-length introduction, he admitted that a composer of music like this had some explaining to do. And by having these items printed rather than adding them to his stock of unpublished manuscripts, he made a bid for public recognition as a composer.

For all its American subject matter, there is no denying the influence of the European musical past in the *Concord* Sonata. *Emerson*, reflecting Ives's admiration for the eminent philosopher, essayist, lecturer, and poet, is a long, imposing, and varied first movement, drafted as part of a piano concerto that Ives never finished. The second movement, named after novelist and short-story writer Nathaniel Hawthorne, is a racing, fantasy-like scherzo that pulls some startling musical jokes. *The Alcotts* is shorter and simpler, somewhat reminiscent of the parlor and inspired by the family of Bronson Alcott, philosopher and organizer of a Utopian community (and father of Louisa May Alcott, author of *Little Women*).

Only with the fourth movement, *Thoreau*, does Ives break with the usual character of the European sonata. Instead of taking the decisive tone of a typical finale, the movement begins softly, mixes dreamy reflection with livelier moments, and fades away at the end. Yet rather than seeming anticlimactic, the quiet last movement brings the sonata to a satisfying close. In its final measures, the sound of Thoreau's flute across Walden Pond echoes a theme that listeners have already heard in *Emerson*, *Hawthorne*, and *The Alcotts*. Ives took from European Romanticism this "cyclic" way of unifying a large work by presenting the same theme in more than one movement. Yet he uses the principle in a new way. Rather than presenting the complete theme early in the work, as was customary, he offers bits and pieces of it in the first two movements; then he brings the third (*The Alcotts*) to a triumphant close by presenting the theme *for the first time* in its definitive and fully harmonized form; and finally, he returns to it—now a gentle lyric line over a quiet dissonant background—as the *Thoreau* movement nears its conclusion. Ives also does not follow several other key traits of the Romantic-era sonata: standard key structures, for example (much of the sonata is atonal or polytonal); patterns of repetition (Ives repeats few phrases and no sections literally); and standard formal outlines (such as **ABA**, theme and variations, rondo, and sonata-allegro).

The end of the *Concord* Sonata suggests a prophecy Ives made a few years later in the "Postface" to *114 Songs*. The art of music, he wrote, was progressing, not declining, and its progress would be understood best by people singing, playing, and composing in the course of their daily lives.

Charles Ives on the Future of Music (1922)

The instinctive and progressive interest of every man in art will go on and on, ever fulfilling hopes, ever building new ones, ever opening new horizons, until the day will come when every man while digging his potatoes will breathe his own epics, his own symphonies (operas, if he likes it); and as he sits of an evening in his backyard and shirt sleeves smoking his pipe and watching his brave children in *their* fun of building *their* themes for *their* sonatas of their *life*, he will look up over the mountains and see his visions in their reality, will hear the transcendental strains of the day's symphony resounding in their many choirs, and in all their perfection, through the west wind and the tree tops!

Ives knew from experience the resistance his music would meet. But in visionary moments like this one, he could imagine a future in which his works could help people attune themselves to the spiritual dimension of human life in an interconnected universe.

Because Ives's music came to public knowledge long after it was written, the story of its discovery and performance belongs to a later time. From the 1930s on, Ives's profile was recast more than once, as "new" works were discovered and views of them and him adjusted to fit the perspectives of composers, critics, and historians at that particular time. His contributions include a substantial body of music, some of it radically individual in style; an original aesthetic philosophy; and a symbolic presence that has served as a barometer of attitudes toward American composition during the last two-thirds of the twentieth century.

Ives was photographed by W. Eugene Smith around 1947, when he was in his early seventies.

26

"Come On and Hear"

THE EARLY TWENTIETH CENTURY

IN 1903, BROADWAY SONG-AND-DANCE MAN GEORGE M. COHAN wrote a patriotic number, *I Want to Hear a Yankee Doodle Tune*, that included the following lines:

> Oh, Sousa, won't you play another march?
> Yours is just the melody divine.
> Now you can take your *William Tell*,
> Your *Faust* and *Lohengrin* as well,
> But I'll take a Yankee Doodle tune for mine.

Cohan could be sure that his audience would recognize *William Tell*, *Faust*, and *Lohengrin* as the names of famous operas. For while opera in the early 1900s was the most glamorous of musical genres, it was also part of the common culture.

In New York City, the Metropolitan Opera opened its doors in 1883. Backed by wealthy patrons, the new enterprise won a firm financial footing in the later 1880s by specializing in German opera, especially the music dramas of Richard Wagner. From the start, the Metropolitan company toured after its New York season. In 1890, with a few Italian operas added to its repertory, the company traveled as far as San Francisco and Mexico. Ten years later, in a tour of twenty-three cities, the Metropolitan spent five months on the road. In 1906, the company was caught in the San Francisco earthquake, bringing an abrupt end to its April tour when sets, costumes, and most of the orchestra's instruments were lost.

Through much of the twentieth century, the opera repertory in the United States has resembled the symphony orchestra's, emphasizing classic works rather than new ones. Yet during the 1910s especially, the Metropolitan encouraged creative attempts. In 1911, the company presented Victor Herbert's *Natoma* and held a competition for an American opera,

Stranded in San Francisco by the 1906 earthquake, some members of New York's Metropolitan Opera Company try on California hats for size.

won by Horatio Parker's *Mona*, which was produced in 1912. In 1918, Charles W. Cadman's *Shanewis*, featuring Native American melodies and based on a story involving Indian cultural conflict, was successfully produced on the Met stage. None of these works, however, won an enduring place in the repertory.

As the Metropolitan was staging the classical sphere's most enduring musical dramas, a more accessible kind of show came into its own on Broadway. *The Merry Widow*, a Viennese import by Franz Lehár, made its New York debut in 1907. And suddenly, operetta (comic opera) became a major force on the popular musical stage. Featuring singers trained for opera, elaborate musical numbers, and plots carried by spoken dialogue, operetta was a European form that settled easily into formula. Rudolf Friml, another leading operetta composer, once said that the formula depended on "old things: a full-blooded libretto with luscious melody, rousing choruses, and romantic passions." *The Merry Widow* had these ingredients, and American audiences took it to their hearts. Within a few months of its New York opening, several road companies were playing Lehár's work on theatrical circuits, and its songs sold widely, both in recorded form—on cylinders, phonograph records, piano rolls—and as sheet music.

Composer and cellist Victor Herbert was one of the Americans who competed successfully with the Hungarian-born, Vienna-based Lehár and the English team of W. S. Gilbert and Arthur Sullivan, whose operettas had long been favorites on the American stage. The Irish-born Herbert, who was trained in Germany, played cello in orchestras through his early years, composed classical works, and earned the respect of his colleagues. He took over Patrick S. Gilmore's band when the leader died in 1892, and later conducted the Pittsburgh Symphony Orchestra. Herbert helped bring about changes in the music business by working for the passage of the 1909 copyright law that secured composers' royalties on the sale of recorded cylinders, discs, and piano rolls. In 1914, he helped to found the American Society of Composers, Authors, and Publishers (ASCAP), an organization that to this day ensures that composers are paid for performances of their music. And between 1894 and his death in 1924, he composed forty operettas.

If operas belong to the classical sphere and musical shows and revues to the popular, operetta lands somewhere in between. Like musical shows, operettas depend on speaking to carry the plot—usually involving highborn characters who search for true love and find it. Yet operetta takes its emotional tone and vocalism from opera. The characters reveal that they are living in an exalted state by singing songs, duets, and choruses built around ringing high notes: proof of their ardent passion. Victor Herbert could write an operetta in 1910 (*Naughty Marietta*) and an opera in 1911 (*Natoma*) without making any radical change in his musical style.

Naughty Marietta fits Friml's list of ingredients perfectly: old things (it is set in 1780s New Orleans), a full-blooded libretto (Marietta, a disguised noblewoman, finds her lover through music), luscious melody (*I'm Falling in Love with Someone, Ah! Sweet Mystery of Life*), rousing choruses (*Tramp, Tramp, Tramp, The Italian Street Song*), and romantic passions (a jilted mulatto beauty's plight exposes Louisiana's racial caste system).

Naughty Marietta opens at dawn on the central square of New Orleans. To hear the city wake up in Herbert's orchestration is to realize that he was a master of orchestral effect. Moreover, one vocal number in particular points up his ability to bring musical richness into comic opera without sacrificing immediate appeal.

LISTENING GUIDE 36

CD 2
7

I'm Falling in Love with Someone (Herbert)

The verse to *I'm Falling in Love with Someone* could almost be that of a popular song. But the chorus moves quickly into deeper waters. Instead of sailing straight into the tune, Herbert writes an expressive effect into the score: a hushed tone (*pp*) and a free tempo through the first two bars, as the title line is sung in a mood of wonder. Regular waltz time sets in only in bar 3. And a melodic leap of a ninth ends the first eight bars with a vocal intensity unexpected in a popular song.

In the second half of the chorus (**aba'b'**), impassioned vocalism goes even further, as the leap of a ninth is topped by a final cadence high in the tenor's range. The message of this theatrical love song may be intimate, but it is also written to be heard in the farthest reaches of the hall. And the journey from a quiet, mid-range *pianissimo* to this ringing climax takes place in just thirty-two bars. (The vocalist is John McCormack, who first sang this number onstage.)

AFRICAN-AMERICAN TRADITIONS AND POPULAR MUSIC

Most black American musicians grew up in communities that maintained the musical practices of the ring shout, where "signifying" made each performance seem spontaneous. To signify, singers and players might use syncopation against a strict beat, bend certain pitches (especially a major scale's third and seventh degrees), explore varied instrumental and vocal sounds, or vary material rather than strictly repeat it. These devices form a common folk heritage for many black musicians, who can also

Will Marion Cook (1869–1944), brought the skills of a classically trained musician to an African-American musical theater that boomed in New York from the mid-1890s until the early 1910s.

draw on European traditions if they choose. And as a set of traits that can be borrowed, written down, and published, they are freely accessible to anyone.

One composer who successfully drew on both traditions was Will Marion Cook, born in 1869 in Washington, D.C. Though he attended the Oberlin Conservatory in Ohio and studied violin in Berlin, Cook found the classical sphere closed to him because of his race. Forced into show business, Cook lavished his skills on New York shows with black casts that, though now forgotten, contain music still worth hearing. *In Dahomey* (1903), the first black-produced show to run at a regular Broadway theater, made an international impact. After a warm reception in New York, it played for seven months in London, then toured England and Scotland before returning to the United States for more performances. According to his contemporary James Weldon Johnson, who was also black, Cook "believed that the Negro in music and on the stage ought to be a Negro, a genuine Negro." And in that spirit, *Swing Along*, a number from *In Dahomey* whose text Cook also wrote, uses syncopation and dialect to celebrate black folk culture.

LISTENING GUIDE 37

Swing Along (Cook)

Swing Along, based on the syncopated rhythms of the cakewalk and of ragtime, celebrates African-American body movement. The number opens with a four-bar intro and a catchy, loose-jointed melody. A brief instrumental transition leads to the next vocal section, but not in strict tempo. The second strain continues the mood of the first:

We'll a swing along, yes a swing along
An' a lif' a' yo' heads up high,
Wif pride an' gladness
Beamin' from yo' eye.
We'll a swing along, yes a swing along,
From a early morn till night.
Lif' yo' head an' yo' heels mighty high
An' a swing both lef' an' right.

Like the first, this strain presents a sixteen-bar tune, but one
with more variety (**abac**). Cook brings back the first strain with a
more syncopated accompaniment. And from there on, he develops his material, with forward momentum yielding to the dramatic gestures and production-number tone of Broadway, as the
voice rises to a high-note climax. *Swing Along* proves that a musician as talented as Will Marion Cook could fit together folk-
style speech, syncopated dance music, sophisticated harmony,
and dramatic singing.

We'll - a   swing a - long,____   yes - a,   swing   a - long,____   an' - a

(slurring the voice)

lif' - a   yo' heads____   up   high,_____

Our recording features baritone Donnie Ray Albert and The
Black Repertory Ensemble of Chicago in an arrangement by Hale
Smith.

A tale that demonstrates the power of black folk music was told by
W. C. Handy, an Alabama-born musician who came to be called "the Father of the Blues." Not long after the turn of the century, he and his band
were playing a dance in Cleveland, Mississippi, when "an odd request"
reached the bandstand: "Would we object if a local colored band played
a few dances?" Happy to be offered a paid break, Handy agreed, and
three young instrumentalists, with "a battered guitar, a mandolin and a
worn-out bass," took the stage. "They struck up one of those over-and-
over strains that seem to have no very clear beginning and certainly no
ending at all. The strumming attained a disturbing monotony, but on and

Alabama-born W. C. Handy as a youth of
nineteen (1892), when he played with a
cornet band in Evansville, Indiana.

on it went, a kind of stuff that has long been associated with cane rows
and levee camps."

Handy could not imagine that anyone would find this music appealing, but he was wrong:

> A rain of silver dollars began to fall around the outlandish, stomping feet.
> The dancers went wild. . . . There before the boys lay more money than my
> nine musicians were being paid for the entire engagement. Then I saw the
> beauty of primitive music. They had the stuff the people wanted. It
> touched the spot. Their music wanted polishing, but it contained the
> essence. Folks would pay money for it. . . . That night a composer was
> born, an *American* composer.

After witnessing the impact of local tunes, Handy listened to them more
closely, wrote some down, and arranged them for his band. In 1912, he
published the *Memphis Blues*, the first blues song in sheet-music form.
Handy's story offers one version of how the marketplace discovered the
blues.

SCOTT JOPLIN AND THE RISE OF RAGTIME

One reason W. C. Handy could bring music from the black folk tradition into the popular sphere was that Scott Joplin had already paved the way. Joplin, born in 1868, must have absorbed the traditional elements in his music as he grew up, the son of an ex-slave and his free-born wife, near the Texas-Arkansas border. But he also took piano lessons from a local German-born music teacher that made him appreciate music as an art

Scott Joplin (1868–1917), the King of Ragtime.

form. Joplin traveled in his early years as a minstrel troupe member, and in 1893 spent time in Chicago during the World's Columbian Exposition. Though evidence is sketchy, this gala celebration has often been cited as crucial in introducing the music soon to be called ragtime to a large audience. When the fair ended, Joplin traveled to St. Louis and from there to Sedalia, a central Missouri town where he lived from 1894 to 1901.

Sedalia was a railroad hub with a thriving community at the center of the region's commerce and transportation. Sedalia was also full of travelers in search of entertainment, and the city boasted two theaters as well as saloons and dance halls. During his late twenties and early thirties, Joplin enrolled in music courses at a local black college, played for dances, and worked for a time as a pianist in two of Sedalia's brothels. He also belonged to one of the city's two black social clubs, the Maple Leaf Club, to which he dedicated the *Maple Leaf Rag*, his most famous composition.

When in 1896 the first syncopated songs were published under the "ragtime" label, the style was already familiar to those who knew black folk tradition; but for those who did not, ragtime brought the novelty of a fad. Once ragtime numbers appeared in print, their impact was quickly felt. Popular songs grew more likely to offer saucy, unsentimental glimpses of love as well as simple syncopation. By 1898, ragtime songs were appearing on the musical stage. In the meantime, instrumental ragtime began to circulate in cylinder recordings and piano rolls as well as sheet music, and in arrangements for ensembles like Sousa's band.

Ragtime is thought to have been named for the "ragged rhythm" whose accents cut across the meter's alternating strong and weak beats. But a more recent theory holds that it was named, by its black practitioners, for the hoisting of handkerchiefs (rags) to signal a dance. The term seemed demeaning even to Scott Joplin, the declared "King of Ragtime." In 1908, for example, he wrote: "What is scurrilously called ragtime is an invention that is here to stay." Joplin made this comment in the *School of Ragtime: 6 Exercises for Piano*, which opened the music's "weird and intoxicating effect" to anyone who mastered its notation. *School of Ragtime* explains syncopation as unusual groupings of sixteenth notes against a strict beat, demanding that every note "be played as it is written." In publishing his piano rags, Joplin was pursuing three related goals: to give the music a salable form, to expand its range of customers, and to raise its status. For as long as piano ragtime stayed in the oral tradition, those who mastered it had only their skill as performers to sell.

Joplin's *Maple Leaf Rag* was published in Sedalia in 1899. It won great commercial success, reportedly selling more than a million sheet-music copies, and it has endured in the piano repertory. Like other instrumental rags, the piece evolved from the connection of syncopated rhythms to the form of the march.

LISTENING GUIDE 38

Maple Leaf Rag (Joplin)

Maple Leaf Rag contains four strains, each sixteen bars long, each repeated at least once, and with the left hand providing a steady pulse for the right hand's rhythmic trickiness. The strict beat never flags, nor does the regular procession of squarecut phrases. But the melodies, harmonies, and sounds offer variety and surprise. Marches and rags usually ease into the melody through an introduction, but the *Maple Leaf Rag* plunges right into the first strain. Likewise, piano ragtime is normally propelled by a left hand that alternates an octave on the beat and a chord after it; but here, Joplin delays that loping figure until the second strain. Also unusual in the first strain is the dynamic plan: a loud beginning, a drop of volume, and a *crescendo* back to the level of the start. The last six bars play on the lowered and raised third—C-flat and C-natural in the key of A-flat—

in blues-like fashion, in an age before the blues took formal shape.

Like many marches, the *Maple Leaf Rag* is a four-strain piece with a trio in D-flat, the subdominant of A-flat. Unlike marches, however, the first strain, not the trio, carries the main melody, which returns after the second, creating a form of **AABBACCDD**. The fourth strain's move back to A-flat reconfirms the opening as the heart of the composition.

Joplin left Sedalia in 1901 and traveled through the Midwest for several years. In 1907, he settled in New York City, where he worked as a composer, arranger, and teacher until his death in 1917. *Treemonisha,* an opera written to his own libretto, occupied much of Joplin's energy in those years. Set in the Southwest countryside, the story seems laced with elements of autobiography. It centers on Treemonisha, a girl of eighteen who hopes to lead her community out of ignorance and superstition by teaching them the value of education. Joplin called his work a grand opera. "I am a composer of ragtime music," he explained, "but I want it thoroughly understood that my opera 'Treemonisha' is not ragtime." Joplin announced plans for a 1913 performance by forty singers and an orchestra of twenty-five, but it never happened.

Joplin used to tell friends and rivals that he would be dead for twenty-five years before people appreciated his accomplishments. But this recognition did not arrive until after 1970, when a ragtime revival took place with Joplin as its central figure. New recordings of his music were made; his rags were republished; *Treemonisha* was performed and recorded; ragtime orchestras were formed; an Academy Award–winning film, *The Sting,* was released (1973), with a score made up of Joplin's compositions. Although Joplin in his own lifetime never won the niche he sought for himself outside the popular sphere, his music has now earned its own kind of classic status.

IRVING BERLIN AND
JAMES REESE EUROPE

Scott Joplin's years in New York overlapped with the start of the longest songwriting career in American history: that of Irving Berlin. Joplin may have been the King of Ragtime, but it was Berlin who had the reputation during the 1910s as America's chief ragtime composer. This was because the big ragtime successes were songs, not piano music, and Irving Berlin won his reputation by writing such hits as *Alexander's Ragtime Band*.

In 1916, an observer wrote that in the years after ragtime was first introduced, "only songs having to do with the negro" were perceived as ragtime songs. The same was also true of Berlin's early songwriting years, up to and including *Alexander's Ragtime Band* (March 1911). But the summer of 1911 marked a turning point. For in *That Mysterious Rag*, published in August, no black protagonist is implied, nor do black characters appear in any of Berlin's later ragtime songs. Moreover, from this time on, Berlin used the word "syncopated" instead of "ragtime" to describe his own songs in that vein. Syncopated songs soon came to symbolize the spirit of liberation that appeared in New York society and quickly spread elsewhere. And one mark of that new spirit was the craze for dancing.

Since the mid-1800s, dancing had not enjoyed much social prominence in the United States, being reserved chiefly for private functions such as formal balls or banished to dives that encouraged illicit behavior. But starting in 1912, public dance halls opened in large numbers, and so did hotel ballrooms and dance floors in cafés, restaurants, and cabarets. A flood of new dances fueled the explosion. While dancing had formerly been an activity of learned steps and motions of the feet, the new dances—many of them infused with syncopation and bearing such names as the fox-trot, turkey trot, Texas tommy, and bunny hug—encouraged more spontaneous movement. Women and men now began to move their whole bodies to the beat. And many new songs emphasized rhythm over melody. Popular music was now an extension of dancing as well as singing, playing, and listening.

Irving Berlin played a key role in this transformation. A force in the profession for almost half a century, he became a trendsetter in the 1910s, when he mastered the carefree new sensibility. Having emigrated with his family from Russia to New York City at the age of five (1893), he grew up in a Jewish neighborhood on the Lower East Side without much formal education. While still a teenager, Berlin published songs for which he wrote words, music, or both. Having a sharp business sense as well as talent and tenaciousness, he won such success that after a dozen years

Irving Berlin (1888–1989), photographed between 1913 and 1919, when
he and Ted Snyder were partners in the firm of Berlin and Snyder,
music publishers on Tin Pan Alley.

in the trade he established his own publishing firm, Irving Berlin Music,
Inc. (1919). Describing his working method, Berlin once explained: "I get
an idea, either a title or a phrase or a melody, and hum it out to something definite." But if "humming out" sounds like a casual process,
Berlin's perfectionist streak made it anything but that. A friend recalled
having more than once sat "beside Irving at his tiny piano" and listened

while he composed. "He would go over and over a lyric until it sounded perfect to my ears. Then he'd scrap the whole thing and begin over again. When I asked Irving what was wrong, he invariably said, 'It isn't *simple* enough.' "

To highlight the variety of Tin Pan Alley genres, an edition of the songs Berlin wrote between 1907 and 1914 divides them into groups: (1) ballads, (2) novelty songs, (3) ragtime and other dance songs, and (4) show songs. Ballads stood the closest in style and mood to the older Victorian songs; a novelty song sketched a brief, comic story; ragtime numbers include all songs with that word in their titles or that mention ragtime in their texts; and show songs were performed in a stage production in Berlin's own day.

The years 1912–17 have been described as both the end of Victorian calm and the beginning of a cultural revolution. And Berlin's early work embodies both, mixing old-fashioned waltz songs and ballads with such novelties as *My Wife's Gone to the Country (Hurrah! Hurrah!)* and *If You Don't Want My Peaches (You'd Better Stop Shaking My Tree)*. Ethnicity was a key subject in these years, for immigrants poured into New York's melting pot until 1914, when war broke out in Europe. The popular theater maintained black stereotypes from the minstrel show and added other groups, each with its own built-in story. Thus, as well as coon songs with black characters, Berlin's early work includes songs with Italian, German, and Jewish protagonists, and even a few "rube" songs involving gullible country folk.

Three 1911 songs show Berlin celebrating the spirit of those eager to end American Victorianism once and for all. *Alexander's Ragtime Band* responds to the charisma of black musicians and the excitement of their playing. *That Mysterious Rag* recognizes the style's haunting, distracting traits and removes it from a racial setting. And in *Everybody's Doing It Now*, not included in the songs on our CD set, ragtime is an infectious dance music—a fad uniting younger Americans in a spirit of uninhibited fun.

LISTENING GUIDE 39

Alexander's Ragtime Band (Berlin)

Alexander's Ragtime Band may seem free of black references, but the name Alexander itself was associated with black minstrel-show characters. Although the song lacks ragtime syncopation, it begins in C and includes a chorus in F, just as the trio strain of a typical instrumental rag moves into the subdominant key. The urging of the text—"Come on and hear / Come on and hear / Alexander's Ragtime Band"—conveys the buzzing excitement that black influence brought to popular song. Most of all, Berlin's song registers the impact of black musical performance. This band can take a conventional bugle call, or the first phrase of Stephen Foster's *Old Folks at Home*, and make it sound "like you've never heard before."

Just thinking about Alexander and his bandsmen is enough to make the singer bubble with high spirits. Had Americans ever before looked forward so eagerly to listening to music?

And if you   care to hear the   Swa - nee Riv - er   played   in

rag - time,—— Come on and   hear,—— Come on and hear—— Al - ex -

an - der's rag - time   band.——

LISTENING GUIDE 40

CD 2
11

That Mysterious Rag (Berlin)

That Mysterious Rag, written a few months after *Alexander*, confirms the impact of ragtime but treats it as a kind of music that is more to be feared than relished. The text tells of a melody so disturbingly unforgettable that even sleepers are not immune. "If you ever wake up from your dreaming," warns the verse, "A-scheming, eyes gleaming, / Then if suddenly you take a screaming fit, / That's it!" Once planted in the brain, the music takes over, as if the victim were bewitched, invaded by a parasite, or besotted with a drug. The chorus, cast in an unusual twenty-four-bar form, lays out symptoms:

> That mysterious rag.
> While awake or while you're a-slumbering,
> You're saying,
> Keep playing
> That mysterious drag,
> Are you listenin'?
> Are you listenin'?
> Look! Look! You're whistlin'
> That mysterious rag.
> Sneaky, freaky, ever melodious
> Mysterious rag.

It would be hard to find another Berlin song that delivers its title phrase so awkwardly. Perhaps, by making "that" the first word of the chorus, then extending the three-letter word "rag" over eight beats, he was suggesting the demented state into which an obsessed listener could slip.

Although *Everybody's Doing It Now* contains relatively little syncopation, this song also emphasizes rhythm. The title, a pun daringly racy for that day, refers to ragtime dancing. The verse notes the music's energizing effect: "Ain't the funny strain / Goin' to your brain? / Like a bottle of wine, / Fine." And the chorus tells us that this electric new musical style—"Hear that trombone bustin' apart?"—was driving dancers to throw restraint to the winds:

> See that ragtime couple over there,
> Watch them throw their shoulders in the air,
> Snap their fingers, Honey, I declare,
> It's a bear, it's a bear, it's a bear,
> There!

At the same time Irving Berlin was offering ragtime as an emblem of current fashion, a black musician working in New York was reminding the public of the music's African-American roots. Born in 1880 in Mobile, Alabama, and raised in Washington, D.C., James Reese Europe played piano and violin but hoped most of all to be a conductor. Around 1903, he moved to New York and was soon conducting shows there. In 1910, Eu-

James Reese Europe (1881–1919) poses as a conductor with members of New York City's Clef Club (1914).

rope joined with others to create the Clef Club, a booking agency for African-American musicians and ensembles: the first real effort to harness the city's black musical talent. The club's roster of players in its peak years numbered more than two hundred, ready to form a dance orchestra at a moment's notice.

Europe's protégé, bandleader and singer Noble Sissle, remembered that before his mentor came into prominence, the New York social elite had favored Viennese waltzes, rendered by gypsy bands playing stringed instruments. But after members of white society heard Europe's syncopated music, they began hiring the Clef Club. Europe and his men were hired because they were the best performers of the music their rich customers wanted to hear. "The wealthy people," Sissle explained, "would not take a substitute when they could buy the original."

Noble Sissle on James Reese Europe's Clef Club

Whatever was the last waltz the gypsy band played, the Clef Club would start off by playing it in ragtime. All of a sudden, people commenced getting up and trying to dance it. And this was the beginning of the Negro taking over New York music and establishing our rhythms. . . . We played in parlors, drawing rooms, yachts, private railroad cars, exclusive millionaires' clubs, swanky hotels, and fashionable resorts. I think we boys who came to New York and were in the music profession at that time lived through the happiest and most interesting time in the development of American music.

When the United States entered World War I in 1917, Europe was asked to organize a band for the Fifteenth Infantry. Nicknamed "the Hellfighters," the ensemble was sent to France to bring troops a taste of home. The band was a huge success (with the French people as well as the American soldiers), mixing syncopated numbers into their performances. After the war, Europe and the Hellfighters left the army and toured the United States, billed as "65 Musician Veterans of the Champagne and Argonne." In March and early May of 1919, part of the band recorded some two dozen sides in New York under Europe's direction, playing mostly popular songs. But the Hellfighters' saga ended abruptly in Boston on May 9, when a crazed band member stabbed Europe before a performance. He died later that day. The loss of this eminent musician was not taken lightly: Europe was the first African American to be honored by the city of New York with a public funeral.

 EPILOGUE

On April 8, 1920, Charles Tomlinson Griffes, the thirty-five-year-old director of music at the Hackley School for Boys, north of New York City, died of an abscessed lung. Though not widely known, several compositions by Griffes had been performed in New York in recent years: in 1917, *Sho-Jo* (a stage pantomime) and *Five Poems of Ancient China and Japan* for voice and piano, and the following year a new piano sonata. *The Pleasure-Dome of Kubla Khan* was played in 1919 by the Boston Symphony Orchestra, and so was the *Notturno für Orchester*, by Leopold Stokowski and the Philadelphia Orchestra. As these titles suggest, Griffes's imagination was far from provincial. If his older contemporary Charles Ives drew on the experience of a New England boyhood, Griffes's outlook was more cosmopolitan. He left a substantial body of work at his death, including many art songs, a smaller number of piano pieces, and works for chamber ensemble, ballet, and orchestra. His career is evidence that, for all the ferment that surrounded social dancing, ragtime, and the music of Tin Pan Alley and Broadway in the 1910s, an environment also existed for composers in the classical sphere who were interested neither in writing operas nor in grounding their work in folk and popular music.

27

Blues, Jazz, and a Rhapsody

THE JAZZ AGE DAWNS

THE HARDSCRABBLE CONDITIONS IN WHICH THE BLUES BEGAN HAVE been traced to the Deep South, to small towns and rural regions, Mississippi Delta plantations, and industries that demanded heavy manual labor. Lacking education, property, and political power in a segregated society, the creators of the blues led lives of hardship in rural isolation. Yet the songs they wrote take a unique attitude toward separation and loss. Where sentimental songs express passive emotional longing, the blues' focus on real suffering in people's lives might even include laughter. The blues tradition is one of confrontation and improvisation.

Like ragtime, the blues took shape in oral tradition. The work song may be an ancestor, and "field hollers," sung by solitary workers, were also an influence. Apparently developing during the 1890s, early blues was accompanied by instruments, especially guitar, which provided a foundation of harmony and rhythm. Several performing techniques rooted in folk culture came to be earmarks of blues performance. One had to do with pitch: the so-called blue third and seventh scale degrees in major mode, shaded or flattened for expression. A second blues trait was a rasping singing style. A third technique was a call and response between voice and instrument(s).

To write down a blues song goes against the idea that blues is a spontaneous kind of music. Yet during the 1910s, sheet music was still the main way popular music was marketed. W. C. Handy introduced the blues song into print in 1912, and a new popular genre was born. Published blues songs showed certain distinctive traits. One was a three-line poetic stanza, with the first two lines the same and the third rhyming: statement, restatement, response. Another was strophic form: each stanza was sung to the same music, twelve bars (three four-bar phrases) of a standard harmonic progression. By the latter 1910s, blues conventions included not only a mood and certain performing customs but also a poetic shape and style, a musical form, and a characteristic pattern of harmony.

LISTENING GUIDE 41

St. Louis Blues (Handy)

Handy's *St. Louis Blues* (Memphis, 1914), which he called "the wail of a lovesick woman for her lost man," has won a place in twentieth-century song akin to that of *Home, Sweet Home* in the nineteenth. The harmonic progression is the now-familiar twelve-bar blues. The first four-bar phrase revolves around a tonic chord; the second is divided into two bars of subdominant (mm. 5–6) and two of tonic (mm. 7–8); and the third begins with two bars of dominant (mm. 9–10), returning to tonic in measure 11 and preparing to begin the same cycle again. Performers since Handy's time have embellished this scheme with substitute chords while maintaining its pillars: tonic harmony in measures 1, 7, and 11; subdominant in measure 5; and dominant in measure 9.

Since the tango was in 1914 a popular new dance in Memphis, Handy added for contrast a second section (eight bars) with a tango beat. And he ended with a third section (twelve bars), labeled "chorus" and based on the *Jogo Blues*, a number he had published separately a year earlier. The result, with repetitions, was a song that fit none of the day's standard forms: a sixty-four-bar equivalent to a three-strain rag (**AABBCC**).

Our recorded performance from 1925, sung by Bessie Smith with Louis Armstrong (cornet) and Fred Longshaw (harmonium), shows two masters of the blues idiom engaged in call-and-response interchange. Smith's lament over lost love is complemented, line by line (and in **AABBC** form), by Armstrong's cornet responses. Although the reed-organ accompaniment offers no rhythmic drive, its presence in a role usually filled by the piano puts this eloquent musical dialogue in a sound world all its own.

In the eleven years between the publication of Handy's *St. Louis Blues* and its recording by Smith-Armstrong, the blues developed on three dif-

Measure no.:	1	2	3	4
Harmony:	I (Tonic)			
Text:	Got de St. Louis blues jes	blue as ah can	be. _____.	

	5	6	7	8
	IV (Subdominant)		I (Tonic)	
	Dat man got a heart lak a	rock cast in the	sea. _____.	

	9	10	11	12
	V (Dominant)		I (Tonic)	
	Or else he wouldn't	gone so far from	me. _____.	

This diagram summarizes the twelve-bar blues harmonic progression, which underlies the first and third strains of Handy's *St. Louis Blues*.

ferent levels. The "down-home" Southern folk blues, rooted in regional customs and the main source of all blues performance, continued in oral tradition. In the meantime, blues songs also found their way into the entertainment business. In 1920, Mamie Smith, a theater and cabaret singer, made history with her recording of *Crazy Blues*, accompanied by a small ensemble she called her Jazz Hounds. The success of this recording, the first by a black singer of a blues song, surprised its producers: 75,000

Gertrude "Ma" Rainey (1886–1939) was a Georgia native and one of the first "classic" blues singers. The Georgia Jazz Band, with which she is pictured here, includes pianist Thomas A. Dorsey, later a leader in the field of gospel music.

copies were sold in a few months' time, chiefly in black neighborhoods. "Classic blues" singers such as Gertrude "Ma" Rainey and Bessie Smith carried on this tradition as professional entertainers, working the black stage circuit. Their recordings, first marketed as "race" records, meaning black musicians performing black music for black listeners, must have appealed to audiences across racial lines. Bessie Smith's first recording, *Down Hearted Blues* (1923), sold 780,000 copies within six months.

A third branch of blues song emerged from Tin Pan Alley shortly before 1920, and these songs became a popular music fad in the early 1920s. Some blues numbers were syncopated fox-trots, for dancing. Others were simply pop songs. And still others were "real blues": songs with twelve-bar choruses and three-line stanzas, set to blues harmonies, and steeped in melancholy. Tin Pan Alley disconnected the idea of the blues from its racial origins, sometimes using the word simply as a trendy way to talk about gloom.

THE RISE OF JAZZ

The origins of the syncopated dance music called jazz remain a matter for speculation. But virtually all authorities agree that the city of New Orleans played a key role and that its African-American citizens took the lead.

Among the traits that made New Orleans musically unique were its mixed French and Spanish heritage, a long-standing devotion to opera, the presence of many free blacks in pre–Civil War years, and their freedom to assemble for various festivities. Education and musical training were also available to some blacks. Yet it would be wrong to imagine that blacks and whites mingled freely in the post–Civil War years. A caste system based on color and language split New Orleans's black citizens into French-speaking, lighter-skinned Creoles who lived downtown and darker-skinned English speakers, many of them migrants who had moved from the country into uptown New Orleans neighborhoods.

In the early 1900s, then, three distinct groups of New Orleans musicians—one white and two black—were playing the ensemble dance music from which jazz evolved. While they shared instrumentation, repertory, and some audience members, contact among them was limited.

It seems likely that jazz grew out of ragtime dance music as musicians in the city began playing it early in this century. Dances imported from Paris in the 1840s such as the polka, the schottische, and the quadrille, had long dominated the New Orleans scene. In the 1890s, however, new dances began replacing them, especially the two-step, a simple walking and sliding movement well suited to ragtime. Later, between 1911 and 1914, the two-step was complemented by sexier new dances such as the turkey trot, which featured flapping arm movements and enough contact between partners' bodies to warrant criticism from the Vatican, and which called for a new, earthier accompaniment.

Another trait should also be considered: the remarkable expressiveness with which black New Orleans musicians played dance music. Even before 1900, visitors to the city mentioned local musicians' aptitude for melodic playing. Perhaps some players' melodic inventions, together with new rhythmic emphasis, brought a different character to their performance of ragtime. Yet pinpointing when, where, and how jazz first diverged from ragtime, and from blues as well, is difficult if not impossible, for even in these early years "jazz" refers to a way of performing that was improvised, not written down.

A typical turn-of-the-century New Orleans dance ensemble was led by a violinist, joined by several wind instruments, plus a rhythm section

The Piron and Williams Orchestra of New Orleans, around 1915. Members include (standing) Jimmie Noone, clarinet; William Ridgley, trombone; Oscar Celestin, cornet; John Lindsay, bass; (seated) Ernest Trepagnier, drums; A.J. Piron, violin; Tom Benton, mandolin-banjo; John A. St. Cyr, banjo; and (in front) Clarence Williams, piano.

of drums, guitar, and double bass, the last usually bowed rather than plucked. Then, following the national trend of replacing guitar and double bass with the banjo and tuba, New Orleans bands also dropped the violin and adopted the saxophone family. As the 1920s dawned, melody was generally assigned to the cornet player, who was often the band's leader.

By that time, the New Orleans jazz ensemble's three melodic voices—cornet, clarinet, and trombone—had assumed different roles and performing styles. Joe (King) Oliver and other cornetists born in the city before 1895 played the lead melody without much variation. Against the cornet lead, the clarinetist wove a countermelody, often in eighth notes and over a wide range of the instrument. Clarinets were sometimes missing from pre-1920 New Orleans ensembles, but never trombones, which played in what was called the "tailgate style," with frequent smears (slurs through several pitches) and a mixture of countermelody in the tenor range and doubling of the bass line. The players' drive for expressiveness may be heard in the earliest recordings made by Oliver, Sidney Bechet, and others, which incorporate blue notes and portamento—purposeful sliding from one note to the next—into an expressive melodic style.

Well before these black New Orleaneans began recording, however, the American public had discovered jazz as a riotous new form of popular entertainment. In late 1916, the Original Dixieland Jazz Band was hired for an engagement in New York. Made up of five white New Orleans players (cornet, clarinet, trombone, drums, and piano), the group caused a great stir and was the first jazz group to make recordings, in 1917 (Victor). *Livery Stable Blues* featured rooster sounds from the clarinet, cow moos from the trombone, and horse neighing from the cornet. In the hands of the ODJB, jazz was thus introduced as a nose-thumbing parody of standard music making, and the public found the result hilarious.

In the years after World War I, jazz was seen in some circles as a symptom of civilization's decline. Many community leaders had opposed ragtime, and now they made jazz a target. One complaint linked jazz with the illegal liquor trade that sprang up after Prohibition became law in 1920. With its eccentric sounds, earthy rhythms, and the encouragement of brazen dance styles, jazz came to be linked with the moral drift that educators and the clergy had been deploring since the war's end.

In wartime, Americans had united against the common German foe. But peace brought new complexity and social unrest. As African Americans migrated in large numbers from the Southern countryside into the cities of the North in search of better jobs, they changed the culture of the areas where they settled. And they met resistance from whites. The Ku Klux Klan, whose constitution pledged "to unite white male persons, native-born Gentile citizens of the United States of America," was reorganized in 1915, and by 1924 its membership reached 4.5 million. It was hardly a coincidence that in 1924, the year of the Klan's greatest popularity, criticism of jazz also reached its peak.

MUSICAL MODERNISM IN NEW YORK

As blues and jazz were making their way into public consciousness, a movement to introduce modern music into the concert hall was also taking shape. In the years before World War I, several modern European composers—the Austrian Arnold Schoenberg, the Russian Igor Stravinsky, the Hungarian Béla Bartók, and the Frenchman Erik Satie, among others—had rejected key aspects of the Romantic tradition that had long dominated Western concert halls and opera houses. The new works of these composers, tending to favor shorter themes, dissonant harmonies, and discontinuous rhythms, were not written with Romantic notions of aesthetic beauty in mind, nor did most performers or audiences welcome them warmly.

Among the leaders in modern music were composers from Europe who moved to the United States and promoted the cause of new music on these shores (chiefly from New York City). The most prominent was Edgard Varèse, who arrived in New York from Paris in 1915. In 1921, Varèse founded the International Composers' Guild, to serve "composers who represent the true spirit of our times," as he announced in a manifesto. He criticized performers for often being more interested in judging new music than understanding it. "Not finding in it any trace of the conventions to which [they are] accustomed," he wrote, they denounce new music as "incoherent and unintelligible." Two years later, a group of American composers, finding Varèse's idea of the time's "true spirit" too exclusive, left the Guild and formed the League of Composers. Their stated goal was "to bring the entire range of modern tendencies before the public." The creation of these two organizations signaled that composers in America were now banding together, regardless of nationality, in the name of modernism.

In his 1941 book *Our New Music*, the composer Aaron Copland called the "violent upheaval" in twentieth-century music proof of revolutionary change. He listed almost three dozen composers who were active in New York in the 1920s, developing their own kind of music. But one famous name is missing: that of George Gershwin. Its absence seems especially curious because Gershwin's *Rhapsody in Blue* (1924), introduced at a concert organized to show the many faces of the music called jazz, struck many as *the* embodiment of the true spirit of their time in a modern musical idiom.

GERSHWIN AND THE *RHAPSODY IN BLUE*

George Gershwin was born in Brooklyn in 1898 to parents who had immigrated from Russia. His boyhood was marked by an interest in athletics and an indifference to school. Music was seldom heard in the Gershwin household until 1910, when the family bought its first piano so that older brother Ira could learn to play it. But George soon took over the instrument. He progressed quickly and about 1912 began lessons with a teacher who recognized his talent and introduced him to the world of classical music. In 1914, however, Gershwin dropped out of high school and went to work for a Tin Pan Alley publishing firm. Hired as a song plugger, he spent endless hours at the keyboard, which improved his playing, though he no longer took lessons. In 1917, Gershwin left that job and found work as a rehearsal pianist on Broadway, where his flair for songwriting was noticed. The following year, a prestigious publisher offered him a weekly salary for the right to publish songs he might com-

George Gershwin (1898–1937), pianist, songwriter, and composer.

pose in the future. And within a few years, Gershwin established himself as a writer of hit songs and Broadway scores, while continuing on the side to develop his craft through private study in composition.

In November 1923, Canadian mezzo-soprano Eva Gauthier presented in New York a "Recital of Ancient and Modern Music for Voice." Her modern selections included songs by Bartók and Schoenberg, and half a dozen songs billed as jazz, including Irving Berlin's *Alexander's Ragtime Band* and two numbers by George Gershwin, who accompanied that part of the program. The American songs delighted Gauthier's audience, and so did Gershwin's performance. Playing from sheet music, the young pianist took off from what was written on the page in a way that sounded spontaneous. Gershwin's freewheeling approach to performance—he played *in the style of* an improvisation, though most details were planned—owed much to jazz, and it brought the recital a sense of fun not often heard in the concert hall.

On February 12, 1924, at a concert in New York's Aeolian Hall by Paul Whiteman's Palais Royal Orchestra, Gershwin played the featured piano part in the premiere of his *Rhapsody in Blue*, a "jazz concerto" commissioned for the occasion. Billing his concert "An Experiment in Modern Music," Whiteman caught the attention of New York's leading music critics. With discussions of jazz very much in the air, it is no surprise that the unveiling of a new jazz concerto by an up-and-coming young songwriter attracted public notice. What *is* surprising, however, is that Gershwin's piece lived up to the ballyhoo of preconcert publicity. Bringing together three separate strands of musical development—the rise of blues as a popular song form, the spread of jazz as an instrumental music, and the push for modernism in the classical sphere—the *Rhapsody in Blue* has since come to be reckoned both an American classic and a piece emblematic of its time.

The Rhapsody in Blue

Gershwin's *Rhapsody in Blue* plays upon the widely accepted boundaries separating the classical, popular, and traditional spheres. From the opening clarinet smear through the blues-tinged themes to the syncopation that enlivens tunes and transitions, the work claims African-American folk music as part of its pedigree. Gershwin's experience as a popular-song writer also leaves its mark on the work's harmony and melody, with phrases and periods cast in the four-, eight-, and sixteen-bar units of popular song. Finally, the *Rhapsody*'s title and its length, as well as virtuoso passages, sections of near-symphonic development, and the soaring character of the last theme, show the influence of the European piano concerto. They also reflect Gershwin's early classical training on piano and his private study of classical composition during the second half of his life. Gershwin's references are not borrowed tune quotations but evocations of different musical styles; this is the work of a composer who understood and believed in the artistic worth of all three spheres of American music.

LISTENING GUIDE 42

Rhapsody in Blue (Gershwin)

The start of *Rhapsody in Blue* establishes a blues connection through a clarinet melody (the main theme) whose expression owes much to blue notes, both the natural (raised) and flat (lowered) third and seventh degrees. After an upward sweep to B-flat by way of A-natural, measures 2 and 4 emphasize A-flat, the blue seventh; and in measure 3, the playing on both D-natural and D-flat creates a blue third.

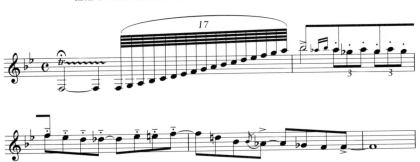

The opening lacks a solid beat, but triplets in measure 2 and off-beat accents in measure 3 promise rhythmic energy. In its next appearance, the main theme is treated as a three-bar statement, answered by a two-bar blue-note figure—a stylized call-and-response surely inspired by the blues.

This section's closing theme also emphasizes the blue third and seventh in E-flat.

In addition to the blues scale, the freedom of sound, pitch, and rhythmic inflection that Whiteman's soloists show on the recording give the work's opening measures the character of the day's most prominent African-American folk style.

The *Rhapsody*'s harmonic idiom is that of the Broadway stage song and overture: based on the major-minor tonal system, with many triads enriched by sevenths, ninths, elevenths, or other nonharmonic tones. And its melodies share with popular songs a trait that helps to imprint them firmly on the listener's memory: they restate their first phrase before moving on to a contrasting phrase. For example, when the first theme's five-bar opening phrase moves from orchestra to piano, Gershwin states *and* restates it, then moves on to a contrasting four-bar phrase and a return. The result is a melody in a standard form (**aaba**) that makes a songlike impression on the ear, though slightly off-center because it fills eighteen bars instead of the usual sixteen. From here on, listeners are more likely to hear the **a** phrase as the start of a full-blown theme than a separate five-bar statement, for the rest of the melody is now expected. And something similar happens to the closing theme, which Gershwin makes the start of a sixteen-bar **aaba** pattern. As melodies like these two well up from within the musical flow, the *Rhapsody in Blue* takes on the character of a medley or a Broadway overture.

Like earlier ones, the last theme of *Rhapsody in Blue* follows the statement-restatement pattern. Yet two traits mark it as more symphonic (and classical) than songlike (and popular). The first is its start-and-stop rhythm. A melody in a popular vein would be unlikely to follow a quarter-note beginning with tones sustained as long as these. The second is that the phrase starting in the melody's seventeenth bar is a development of the theme's opening gesture, not the contrast one expects in a song. Rather than being rounded off with a return, this theme has no real destination. Its last four bars are a turnaround leading back to the start of another twenty-four-bar statement.

Andantino moderato con espressione

In addition to combining elements from the different spheres—blues-drenched melodies cast in popular-song forms, symphonic themes harmonized as if they were numbers out of a

Broadway orchestra pit—Gershwin also sets styles against each other. For example, the opening is jazz in the Original Dixieland Jazz Band vein, with the clarinet, then the muted trumpet giving out the melody, in sounds that seem to mock the standard approach to playing these instruments. But the piano brings virtuosity and the more serious tone one expects from a soloist in a tuxedo. Here, rather than exploring organic formal links, Gershwin behaves more like a film director cutting from one scene to another. Recognizable, satisfying melodies give *Rhapsody in Blue* continuity; at the same time, Gershwin's wide range of sources and near-cinematic approach give the work a slightly disjointed feel.

Introduced with fanfare and performed often, *Rhapsody in Blue* played a role in defining American musical modernism in the mid-1920s. To several New York critics, Gershwin emerged from the work's premiere as the American composer who most closely resembled Stravinsky. A group of older composers and critics also applauded Gershwin's home-grown approach. Younger composers who had to compete with Gershwin, such as Virgil Thomson and George Antheil, took a dimmer view of the *Rhapsody*. But the work met its toughest opposition from critics who wrote for journals with an intellectual mission—especially Paul Rosenfeld, music critic of *The Dial*. Rosenfeld placed the classical sphere securely above the popular, and he branded Gershwin with the popular label. In an effort to define American modernism, Rosenfeld rejected Gershwin in favor of Aaron Copland, also Brooklyn-born and of Russian-Jewish heritage, just two years younger than Gershwin, and in the mid-1920s the composer of works inspired by jazz. While Gershwin was honing his professional skills in front of mass audiences, Copland had been studying in France (1921–24) under the tutelage of harmony teacher Nadia Boulanger, an experience that also introduced him to the modern music scene in Paris.

Copland's jazz-inflected Piano Concerto, premiered in 1927, allowed Rosenfeld to compare what he claimed to be Copland's elevation of jazz into art with Gershwin's refusal (or inability) to do more than leave it at the level of popular entertainment. For Rosenfeld, true modernism was to be found only in high art. Thanks in part to such modernist views, committed to maintaining a gap between art and entertainment, it is only recently that Gershwin's work is beginning to be understood not only as a hugely popular composition but a challenge to the hierarchy of American music that has proved deeply influential in this century.

28

"The Birthright of All of Us"

CLASSICAL MUSIC, THE MASS MEDIA, AND THE DEPRESSION

IN THE LATTER 1800s, THEODORE THOMAS AND OTHER CONDUCTORS established the American symphony orchestra as an ensemble grounded in European classics. They emphasized works written by German-speaking composers because they judged them to be the best music. By the turn of the century, audiences were also hearing works by Tchaikovsky, Dvořák, Rimsky-Korsakov, Debussy, Sibelius, and others, with their fresh approaches to melody and form. Like Thomas, some conductors were friendly to the cause of American composers, but American music remained marginal on concert programs.

The years 1890 to 1930 saw a major change in American society from a Victorian culture based on thrift to one more ready to spend. Musical life benefited from that shift, with growing investment in musical instruction, growing opportunity for amateur performance, and the establishment of permanent orchestras in such cities as San Francisco (1911), Los Angeles (1919), Seattle (1926), and Kansas City (1934). Symphony orchestras were supported by a combination of box-office receipts and private gifts. The role of wealthy citizens was crucial, yet orchestras survived because members of the general public also supported them. And as orchestras thrived, conductors emerged as star performers.

Like other performers, symphony conductors were publicly defined as charismatic artists. Yet conductors also had to face tough issues, intellectual and aesthetic. Was music really in a state of crisis? Were modernist composers the legitimate heirs of Beethoven and Wagner? And should their "revolutionary" new works be programmed, putting public support at risk? Should the U.S. concert hall continue to identify with Germanic classics? Did American composers deserve a larger place on concert programs? Was jazz a healthy source of inspiration for new American music? Questions like these, debated by musicians and critics, were far from academic ones for conductors, who based their programming on the answers.

The careers of three illustrious conductors—Arturo Toscanini, Serge Koussevitzky, and Leopold Stokowski—who led major orchestras during the first half of the century show that these questions could be answered in different ways. The Italian-born Toscanini first came to the United States in 1908 as principal conductor at the Metropolitan Opera, a post he held until 1915, when he returned to Italy. He served as artistic director at the La Scala opera house in Milan from 1921 until 1929, when a Fascist takeover of the Italian government caused him to quit. Returning to New York, he conducted the New York Philharmonic Society orchestra until 1936. In 1937, the National Broadcasting Company created an orchestra expressly for Toscanini, now seventy years old. And from then until he retired in 1954, he conducted the NBC Symphony in concerts, radio and television broadcasts, and on recordings.

Toscanini's reputation outstripped that of any other classical musician. He was sometimes proclaimed the "greatest conductor of all time," and the promotional forces behind the NBC Symphony helped spread this message. In performance, Toscanini was noted for his energy, the command he brought to the podium, his demands for perfection, and his musical memory. Adding to the legend were his abiding hatred for political fascism and his towering rages when rehearsals went badly.

Serge Koussevitsky (1874–1951), conductor of the Boston Symphony Orchestra from 1924 to 1949, in action.

Toscanini conducted the music of virtually every major Classical and Romantic composer as well as works by such modern masters as Richard Strauss, Debussy, Ravel, and Prokofiev.

Serge Koussevitzky, a native of Russia, began conducting in his early thirties, giving concerts that emphasized works by Russian composers. He left Russia after World War I and settled in Paris, forming an orchestra that included in its programs new scores by French and Russian composers, including Prokofiev and Stravinsky. In 1924, at the age of fifty, he was named conductor of the Boston Symphony Orchestra, a post he held until 1949. Aaron Copland, whose music he championed, later wrote that Koussevitzky combined skill on the podium with "his passion for encouraging whatever he felt to be new and vital in contemporary music." That included works by living American composers such as Roy Harris, Walter Piston, Samuel Barber, and William Schuman, not to mention commissions of works by Stravinsky and other leading Europeans. In the summer of 1940, the Berkshire Music Center opened at Tanglewood, a Massachusetts estate, with Koussevitzky as director and Copland as assistant director. And in later years, contemporary composers including Paul Hindemith and Olivier Messiaen taught there as guests. Koussevitzky has been praised for the emotional power he brought to performances, especially of Russian music and such French composers as Debussy.

The London-born Leopold Stokowski came to the United States in his early twenties (1905) and in 1909 was named music director of the Cincinnati Symphony Orchestra. Three years later, Stokowski began a twenty-five-year stint as conductor of the Philadelphia Orchestra. If Toscanini was known as a servant of the composer's score, Stokowski was known for showmanship. Tall and striking, he made his Philadelphia string sec-

This photograph of conductor Leopold Stokowski (1882–1977) was taken in Hollywood in 1937.

tion famous for their singing sound. In 1940, he appeared onscreen in Walt Disney's *Fantasia*, with animated characters including Mickey Mouse—the first conductor to achieve the status of entertainment star. A champion of twentieth-century music, Stokowski conducted over two thousand first performances—most by American composers. Among the premieres were works by Varèse, Ives, Copland, Henry Cowell, and Griffes, as well as the American premieres of Stravinsky's *The Rite of Spring*, Mahler's Eighth Symphony, Berg's *Wozzeck*, and Schoenberg's *Guerrelieder.*

These sketches portray three very different figures. Toscanini was a passionate champion of the classics. Koussevitzky was drawn less by classic scores than new musical experiences, and he cultivated friendships with composers. Stokowski came to hold an aggressively democratic philosophy, which he linked to technological progress. Believing that most adults had "difficulty in absorbing ideas and impressions," Stokowski did much of his crusading for new music at concerts aimed at young listeners.

Leopold Stokowski on Music's Universal Appeal (1943)

Music is a universal language—it speaks to everyone—is the birthright of all of us. Formerly music was chiefly confined to privileged classes in cultural centers, but today, through radio and records, music has come directly into our homes no matter how far we may live from cultural centers. This is as it should be, because music speaks to every man, woman, and child—high or low, rich or poor, happy or despairing—who is sensitive to its deep and powerful message.

The contrasting careers of these three conductors show the symphony orchestra between the wars as an arena with established norms that was also open to fresh approaches. They also are a reminder that the most prominent names in the American classical sphere were performers, including violinists Fritz Kreisler and Jascha Heifetz, pianists Artur Rubinstein and Vladimir Horowitz, and singers Amelita Galli-Curci, Ezio Pinza, and Kirsten Flagstad, for example. Most were foreign-born; all made their reputations presenting European masterworks to audiences in Europe and the United States. Live performance remained the public's chief point of contact with classical music, though after electrical recording replaced the acoustic process in 1925, listeners could experience something closer to concert-hall sound at home.

The new medium of radio broadcast a wide variety of music, most of it popular but certainly not all. In 1926, NBC presented Koussevitzky and the Boston Symphony in the first live network concert, attracting a million listeners. Five years later, NBC paid $100,000 for the right to broadcast grand opera live from the Metropolitan in New York; soon those broadcasts were the second-most popular on daytime radio. In the 1800s, arrangements, excerpts, and simplifications had made operas and symphonies into fare for the general public. By the 1930s, thanks to new kinds of musical transmission, such works were being widely listened to in their original versions—as composers' music.

COMPOSERS, THE GOVERNMENT, AND THE MARKETPLACE DURING THE DEPRESSION

On August 17, 1937, Mexican composer Carlos Chávez conducted the Orquesta Sinfónica de México in the first performance of Aaron Copland's *El salón México*, which was inspired by a 1932 visit to a Mexico City dance hall. Copland, knowing that he lacked the experience to plumb the depths of the Mexican character, tried instead to catch "the spirit of the place."

> In some inexplicable way, while milling about in those crowded halls, I had felt a live contact with the Mexican "people"—that electric sense one gets sometimes in far-off places, of suddenly knowing the essence of a people—their humanity, their shyness, their dignity and unique charm. . . . It was at such a moment I conceived the idea of composing a piece about Mexico and naming it *El Salón México*.

Copland traveled to Mexico City for his work's premiere, "nervous about what the Mexicans might think of a 'gringo' meddling with their native melodies." But he was gratified by the warm response of orchestra players, audiences, and critics, who "seemed to agree that *El Salón México* might well be taken for Mexican music." In the summer of 1938, the work was played in London, leading to publication by the English firm Boosey and Hawkes. A few months later, Koussevitzky and the Boston Symphony Orchestra gave the work its first American performance. What happened next was a surprise. Copland recalled in the 1970s that Boosey's American agent

Composer Aaron Copland (1900–1990) in the 1930s.

called my piece an "American Bolero" and proceeded to fill orders for scores and rental parts that soon came in from all over. One year after publication in 1938, Boosey put together a list of orchestras that had played *El salón México*: fourteen American orchestras ranging from the BSO to the Women's Symphony in Chicago; two radio orchestras; and five foreign ensembles. Never in my wildest dreams did I expect this kind of acceptance for the piece.

Yet Copland had tried from the start to make *El salón México* audience-friendly. Using local melodies for themes, he kept them recognizable, and he stayed within the major-minor tonal system.

Aaron Copland on Music Listeners (1941)

The old "special" public of the modern-music concerts (of the 1920s) had fallen away, and the conventional concert public continued apathetic or indifferent to anything but the established classics. It seemed to me that we composers were in danger of working in a vacuum. Moreover, an entirely new public for music had grown up around the radio and phonograph. It made no sense to ignore them and to continue writing as if they did not exist. I felt that it was worth the effort to see if I couldn't say what I had to say in the simplest possible terms.

LISTENING GUIDE 43

El salón México, excerpt (Copland)

El salón México shows Copland's blend of old and new ingredients to forge a style that concert audiences found appealing. Instruments are used in a modern way. The prominent percussion, solo trumpet, and statement of a key melody by the bassoon are three of the many touches reflecting the work's twentieth-century pedigree. The rhythm, based on asymmetrical groupings and syncopation, is also modern; Copland seldom allows listeners to settle into a comfortable expectation of the beat. But if rhythm and sound are fresh, harmony and melody are more traditional. The harmony may not move as expected, but consonance is emphasized over dissonance. And rather than inventing "Mexican" tunes, Copland borrowed his from folk-song books. Full of innovative details, *El salón México* still carries a familiar ring.

Our excerpt contains the work's first half, which contrasts two kinds of music. The first is fast, intense, syncopated, and based on short melodic fragments (motives). The second is slow and broadly tuneful. Yet even in the latter, the tunes are not simply arranged and presented. Rather, they are recomposed and stylized, in the manner of twentieth-century composition. After a bright, fanfare-like opening (**A**), the tempo slackens, and the trumpet plays a pair of melodic phrases that, having set a new tone, give way to the real tune (**B**). This tune is played first by the bassoon over a bass-and-timpani vamp, then repeated glowingly by the strings. Now the fast opening music (**A**) returns. Repeating fragments in ever-changing keys and rhythmic patterns, Copland develops his material symphonically, at one point bringing back the **B** material and juxtaposing it with **A**. Lurching syncopations lead to the return of the opening fanfare, answered by percussion, and the first half of the piece ends with a dramatic silence.

El salón México was composed during the deepest economic depression in U.S. history. The country had emerged from World War I as a creditor nation—one that took in more money from overseas than it spent. And the economy boomed during the 1920s, which saw a 50 percent increase in manufacturing output. By 1929, the United States was producing major shares of the world's coal (40 percent), petroleum (70 percent), hydroelectric power (30 percent), steel (50 percent), and natural gas (more than 90 percent). In October 1929, however, the stock market collapsed. And when many banks failed during the next couple of years, production, consumption, and investment declined, unemployment rose sharply, and confidence in the economic future crumbled. Farming, heavy industry, and the blue-collar workforce in general bore the brunt of the hardship.

The Depression made a deep impact on musical life. Some larger institutions like symphony orchestras and the Metropolitan Opera survived on patronage and a bigger pool of listeners, reached through radio broadcasts and recordings. New-music activities, however, struggled to attract financial backing. With less money in the hands of audience members (who could listen to broadcasts for free), work for performers evaporated. Meanwhile, the invention of sound film in 1927 removed the need for the players who had previously accompanied silent films in orchestra pits.

Between 1929 and 1934, about 70 percent of all musicians in the United States were unemployed, a trend the American Federation of Musicians, the national musicians' union, was powerless to buck. In 1935, as part of a massive relief effort labeled Federal Project Number One, the national government took action, setting up the Federal Music Project as a way of supporting the out-of-work. At its peak, the program employed sixteen thousand musicians and funded twenty-eight symphony orchestras, as well as many dance bands and folk-music groups. More than a million music classes were given to 14 million students. Created with public money to keep artists from starving, Federal Project One exposed some parts of the country to original artworks, live theater, and symphony orchestras for the first time. As a silver lining to economic distress, the Depression years brought more abundant access to classical music than Americans had ever enjoyed before.

Adversity also led composers to write in more conservative styles and focus on regional and national subjects. Virgil Thomson, a Kansas City native who studied at Harvard and then in Paris under Nadia Boulanger, displayed his own brand of modernism in the *Sonata da Chiesa*, a dissonant chamber work of 1926. But a decade later, scores for two government-sponsored films, *The Plow That Broke the Plains* (1936) and *The River* (1937), confirmed his credentials as a composer who could write American-sounding music. His most notorious work was the opera *Four Saints in Three Acts* (1934), to a libretto by American expatriate writer Gertrude Stein, whom he met in Paris. Set in sixteenth-century Spain, the libretto celebrates the lives of St. Theresa, St. Ignatius, St. Settlement, and

St. Chavez while following no perceptible plot. Thomson declared his opera's style "simple, melodic, and harmonious . . . after twenty years of everybody's trying to make music just a little bit louder and more unmitigated and more complex than anybody else's." In one unforgettable moment, a soloist and male chorus alternate in singing "Pigeons on the grass, alas," words whose incongruity seems calculated to baffle and delight at the same time. Thomson's Midwestern roots and Harvard education were mixed with strong Gallic sympathies; he particularly admired French composer Erik Satie, noted for satire and musical simplicity.

During the 1930s, a sense of cultural unity grew among Americans. Economic hardship had something to do with this trend, and so did reduced immigration. President Franklin D. Roosevelt was elected in 1932 by a coalition that crossed ethnic and class lines, including blacks as well as whites and many working people. Federal One programs found artistic worth where it had been overlooked in the past, in folk culture and local life. Murals in post offices featured American themes. Painters and photographers such as Thomas Hart Benton and Dorothea Lang took ordinary people in American settings as their subjects. While artistic works such as these portrayed the United States as an array of local settings, each with its own character, citizens were encouraged to think of such localities as examples of a larger *American* consciousness.

Such was the background for the nationalism of Roy Harris—born in Oklahoma, raised in California, trained in Paris—who aspired to compose on behalf of all Americans. An essay he wrote in 1933 claims that "wonderful, young, sinewy, timorous, browbeaten, eager, gullible" American society was in the process of finding a common racial identity that would override local differences. In Harris's view, rhythm was the key that separated Americans from Europeans—especially the "asymmetrical balancing of rhythmic phrases." Moreover, he wrote, pointing to aspects of his own works, American music showed a fondness for modal harmony and a tendency to avoid definite cadences.

Musically, Harris, Thomson, and Copland in these years all belong in the camp of stylistic conservatism. Yet each had his own sound and approach. Copland put a New World stamp on four large-scale works of the period by borrowing American folk and popular melodies. In two ballets about the West, *Billy the Kid* (1938) and *Rodeo* (1942), cowboy and Western tunes appear. *A Lincoln Portrait* (1942) for orchestra, featuring a narrator who speaks words of Abraham Lincoln, quotes Stephen Foster's *Camptown Races* and a New England folk song, *Springfield Mountain*. *Appalachian Spring* (1944), a ballet set in rural Pennsylvania during the last century, contains a set of variations on the Shaker tune *Simple Gifts*.

Famed teacher Nadia Boulanger and students—Walter Piston, John Alden Carpenter, Boulanger, Roy Harris, conductor Serge Koussevitzky, violin soloist Zlatko Baloković, Mabel Daniels, Jean Françaix, and Edward Burlingame Hill—at the premiere of Piston's Violin Concerto No. 2, Symphony Hall, Boston, 1939.

While the idea of writing accessible music attracted many composers of the 1930s, however, others scorned that notion. Roger Sessions, for example, upheld European modernism, warning against a retreat from "universal principle" into "the accident of locality." Sessions's dissonant, chromatic idiom testified to his belief in continuous stylistic evolution as one universal principle. Indeed, the presence in the United States during the 1930s and 40s of such eminent composers as Schoenberg, Stravinsky, Bartók, and Hindemith—driven here by the rise of fascism in Europe— did much to maintain European authority over American classical composition.

But for Henry Cowell, an American with a different take on modernism, exploration was always a key part of composing. Born in California in 1897, Cowell spent much of his early life in poverty and had little formal schooling. Yet by 1914, his unusual talent and intellect were recognized, and he began studying music with Charles Seeger, a composer and faculty member at the University of California at Berkeley, who encouraged Cowell's fondness for experimenting. At an early age, Cowell later explained, he had decided to use "a different kind of musical material for each different idea that I have." The result was that, "even from the very start, I was sometimes extremely modernistic and sometimes quite old-fashioned, and very often in-between."

Cowell won a reputation first as a composer-performer who treated the piano like no one before him. *The Tides of Manaunaun* (c. 1917) features tone clusters made by pressing down adjacent keys in blocks of sound spanning more than an octave. *Dynamic Motion* (c. 1916), representing the New York subway, calls for the player to hammer out clusters with fists, forearms, and elbows in the manner of a virtuoso. *Aeolian Harp* (c. 1923) and *The Banshee* (1925), on the other hand, use the piano more like a harp than a percussion instrument, calling for the performer to play on the strings as well as the keyboard. Between 1916 and 1919, Cowell also worked on a treatise exploring fresh acoustical possibilities in the overtone series, published in 1930 as *New Musical Resources*.

LISTENING GUIDE 44

The Banshee (Cowell)

The Banshee, Cowell's most famous piece, written in 1925, is played on the strings of the piano. Suggesting the wails of a spirit he called "an Irish family ghost, a woman of the inner world" who arrives to claim the soul of someone who has just died, he composed a score that calls for the player to stand in the crook of a grand piano while an assistant sits at the keyboard and holds down the damper pedal. Lasting slightly less than two and a half minutes, the music begins softly, builds up to high intensity, then fades away. Rather than inviting the player to massage the open string bed freely, Cowell specifies tempo, volume level, pitch, and touch in precise detail. His instructions call for sweeping the strings with the flesh of the finger, or with the nail. Sometimes the hand moves across many strings, in one direction or back and forth. Sometimes one string (or more) is swept lengthwise, or plucked. Melodic fragments and even chords also float to the surface of this sonic exploration.

By the late 1920s, Cowell was drawing on folk and non-Western music, including Chinese, Japanese, African, South Indian, and Javanese as well as Irish. The *United Quartet* (1936) makes use of ostinatos, drones, and stratified textures in ways that help to explain his claim that the work "should be understood equally well by Americans, Europeans, Orientals, [and] higher primitives." Cowell spent the years 1936–40 in San Quentin prison after being convicted on a morals charge for which he was later pardoned. He remained active there as a musician and composer. In 1939, he wrote several works for percussion ensemble at the request of composer John Cage, who was then musical director for a dance company in Seattle.

Once released from prison, Cowell married the ethnomusicologist Sidney Robertson, who introduced him to the music of William Walker's *Southern Harmony* (1835), a shape-note tunebook. Between 1944 and 1964, Cowell wrote, for various instrumental combinations, eighteen *Hymns and Fuguing Tunes*, inspired by early American hymnody, as well as eighteen of his twenty symphonies. And he and his wife traveled widely, in 1956 surveying the music of Ireland, Germany, Greece, Turkey, India, Pakistan, Iran, and Japan with the support of a foundation grant, and in 1961 representing the United States at international conferences on music in Teheran and Tokyo. These travels led to such works as *Ongaku* (1957), in which Western instruments imitate Japanese ones, and *Persian Set* (1957) for a chamber orchestra that includes the tar, a Persian string instrument.

While seeking to live "in the whole world of music," as he once put it, Cowell was also a tireless advocate for his fellow American composers. As editor of *New Music* from 1927 to 1936, he published the scores of many, including Ruth Crawford, Carl Ruggles, and Charles Ives, whose biography he and his wife brought out in 1955. Cowell also promoted new music concerts through composers' societies. He wrote hundreds of articles, gave countless interviews on behalf of new music, and served as an overseas ambassador for the work of his American colleagues. And he taught composition, both privately and through institutions, counting among his pupils Burt Bacharach, John Cage, George Gershwin, and Lou Harrison.

Henry Cowell's career was living proof that neither European-based modernism nor American nationalism was broad enough to encompass the creative imagination of American composers between the two world wars. Further proof came from the young California-born John Cage, who predicted in a 1937 talk that the use of noise to make music would "continue and increase until we reach a music produced through the aid of electrical instruments." Cage's *Imaginary Landscape No. 1*, premiered in 1939, was scored for muted piano, a suspended cymbal, and two phonograph turntables—a hint that his imagination was taking a path that in the future would be linked with Ives, Cowell, and others whose experimental bent would come to be seen as another kind of American tradition.

"All That Is Native and Fine"

AMERICAN FOLK SONG AND ITS COLLECTORS

BY THE MID-1800s, GERMAN SCHOLARS UNDERSTOOD FOLK SONG AS an expression of peasant life, composed not by one person but by a whole community. Later students of folklore, granting that collective transmission changed the songs, believed they had been composed by individuals, who were not necessarily peasants. How did creation and transmission really work in folk traditions? And what did it mean that people low in the social order had preserved such artful songs?

If folk songs were to be studied, they first had to be collected, as in the five volumes of Francis James Child's *The English and Scottish Popular Ballads* (1883–98). This monumental work contains texts and commentary on 305 ballads and their variants, a repertory known as the Child ballads. For Child, a ballad was a literary creation, and he did his work in libraries. Searching through printed sources and manuscripts, he published the texts (not the tunes) of what he considered the oldest English-language ballads. One, *The Gypsy Laddie* (Child number 200), tells of a band of gypsies stopping by the dwelling of an absent nobleman and singing so sweetly that his wife falls in love with one of them, runs off with him, and is then pursued by her husband. Child prints eleven versions and comments on their differences. The husband is called Lord Cassilis in three versions; Cassle, Castle, Corsefield, and Cashan in others; and in one collected in America, Garrick. The laddie is variously known as Johnie, Jockie, Faa (a last name), Gipsy Davy, and Gypsie Geordie. In some versions, the husband finds his lady, then hangs gypsies—fifteen of them, or sixteen, or seven. In some, the lady regrets her change in status. In another, the gypsy denies any interest in sex.

The dignity of the ballads, together with their ancient lineage and the scholarship of Child and others, gave them academic prestige. And the disagreement over origins sparked intellectual debate. American versions of approximately one-third of Child's ballads were located, leading many to think of the ballad as the most important Anglo-American folk form.

Folk-song study entered a new stage in the twentieth century, when scholars realized that the ballad belonged to a living tradition. The new collectors turned to the folk themselves for material, in an attitude of respect for oral tradition and the people who still carried it on. A key figure among them was Cecil Sharp, whose career began in England under the aegis of the Folk-Song Society, formed in 1898 to collect and publish folk songs. Its founders were musicians determined, in the words of composer Sir Hubert Parry, to "save something primitive and genuine from extinction" and "put on record what loveable qualities there are in unsophisticated humanity." Parry called traditional folk music one of "the purest products of the human mind," though now in danger of being driven out by "the common popular songs of the day." Parry's themes—the age and authenticity of folk song, fear for its survival, the virtues of the folk, and nostalgia for a precommercial era—were sounded often by collectors in Britain and the United States.

In the early 1900s, Sharp began to study the oral tradition that still existed in England and Scotland. His way of collecting a song was standard for his time: singers were asked to repeat what they had sung until Sharp had transcribed the melody accurately and written down a complete version of the text. In 1907, he published *English Folk-Song: Some Conclusions*, based on his own collection and analysis of some 1,500 examples. Sharp's study concludes that folk melody is based on modal rather than major or minor scales and that folk songs were composed by individuals, then transmitted by a communal process.

In 1915, Sharp learned from Olive Dame Campbell, a Massachusetts native living in Appalachia, that a community maintaining an ancient folk-song tradition existed in the mountains of North Carolina. The following year, he launched a collecting expedition in the western part of the state. The fruits of Sharp's trip appeared in *Folk Songs of the Southern Appalachians* (1917), a joint publication with Olive Campbell and the first major collection of the mountain people's music.

Counting both England and America, Sharp collected no fewer than twenty-eight versions of *The Gypsy Laddie*. On September 1, 1916, in Flag Pond, Tennessee, he notated a version in seven stanzas with an added refrain. Here the emphasis is on the conversation between husband and wife when he catches up with her. No revenge is taken; no gypsies are hung. The wife refuses to return home and then, in the last two stanzas, regrets her decision. The next day in nearby Rocky Fork, Tennessee, Sharp heard a five-stanza version whose melody is quite different, drawing out

English folk song collector Cecil Sharp (1859–1924) paid several visits to America, transcribing songs from residents of Appalachia. Here, Sharp and his assistant Maud Karpeles (at right) collect from Mrs. Doc Pratt of Knott County, Kentucky, in 1917.

the first and third lines, and repeating the fourth line of each stanza. The wife has left behind a child as well as home and husband. And he returns home alone, after repossessing her expensive shoes.

As we observed in Chapter 4, ballads favor event over explanation. In no version of *The Gypsy Laddie* are listeners told why the lady might want to leave, nor does either of these examples describe her departure. Instead, husband and wife are plunged immediately into the consequences of her leaving. Characters speak in plain, formulaic language, with standard epithets, such as the "milk-white" horse the squire rides in both versions and the lady's "lily-white hand" in the second.

In 1916, Cecil Sharp found the English ballad tradition flourishing in the southern Appalachians. Having encountered ballads in England scattered among a few older singers, he had now discovered a place where these songs were "interwoven with the ordinary avocation of everyday life." Olive Campbell's collecting turned up some of the same ballads but was not restricted to them. Campbell collected all the music she encountered, including religious songs and hymns, popular music, and instrumental tunes.

Campbell shared Sharp's belief that some of the songs in oral tradition were aesthetically better than others. She even imagined a social role that the better songs might play. In 1916, she wrote that the folk movement in the mountains "seeks the recognition and preservation of all that is native and fine." "We would like to have the people recognize the worth and beauty of their songs," she explained. By encouraging the singing of them in mountain schools, "we would like to have them displace the inferior music that is now being sung there." The so-called inferior music was part of a larger change that industrialization was bringing to Appalachia, as a way of life rooted in subsistence farming was being transformed into one dominated by coal mining.

Even before Cecil Sharp ever set foot in America, Massachusetts-born scholar Phillips Barry had developed a more inclusive philosophy of ballad collecting. His work showed that whatever its origin, a song went through a process of communal re-creation when it entered oral tradition. By working to document that process, Barry refocused the issue of repertory. He and other collectors, taking the singers' own preferences as their starting place, recovered from oral tradition not only old ballads of English origin, but also ballads composed in America.

The late 1800s saw a rising interest in indigenous American traditions. In 1888, the American Folklore Society was founded, with the intent of gathering and publishing songs and stories from English, African-American, Indian, Mexican, and French-Canadian cultures. After 1900, many state folklore societies were established, dedicated in large part to collecting and preserving folk song from the Old World, especially Child ballads. In the meantime (1914), the U.S. Department of Education itself declared a "rescue mission" for folk songs and ballads, in the belief that they were an endangered species. Some twenty regional collections had resulted from this effort by mid-century.

THE ARCHIVE OF AMERICAN FOLK SONG AND THE RISE OF "URBAN FOLK" MUSICIANS

By the latter 1920s, it was clear to anyone paying heed that the United States was home to a rich, diverse assortment of music in the traditional sphere. One symbol of that recognition was the founding in 1928 of the Archive of American Folk Song at the Library of Congress in Washington, D.C. The idea seems to have come from Robert Winslow Gordon, a scholar and collector who was named the library's first sound archivist.

Gordon, who had an academic background, had for years been collecting folk songs and writing about them in *Adventure*, a popular magazine focused on the out-of-doors.

Well before interest in the study of folk music surfaced at the Library of Congress, however, the music business had discovered its commercial possibilities. For the genre now known as country music claims roots in Anglo-American traditions found in the South. The core of Southern culture was British, but the fiddlers, balladeers, and gospel singers who carried on its musical side borrowed freely from nineteenth-century popular songs and dances and the music of black entertainers. In the years before 1920, local events such as fiddle contests and medicine shows allowed talented white Southern performers to earn money for singing and playing.

The evolution of country music into an industry began between 1920 and 1925, when show business first recognized its possibilities. In 1922, radio stations in Atlanta and Fort Worth started broadcasting local singers and players. By 1925, so-called barn-dance programs were established on the radio, with the WSM Barn Dance from Nashville, later the Grand Ole Opry, the most famous. In the meantime, Ralph Peer, who in 1920 had supervised Mamie Smith's *Crazy Blues*, traveled south in 1923, and in Atlanta recorded "Fiddlin' " John Carson. When Peer heard Carson's voice, he was unimpressed and decided to stick to fiddle tunes. But a local distributor, recognizing that Georgia farmers and mill workers would like Carson's singing as well as his playing, talked Peer into letting the fiddler sing. Sales proved the local man right.

In 1927, Peer went to Virginia to record the Carter Family—A. P. Carter, his wife, Sara, and their sister-in-law, Maybelle Glenn—who accompanied their singing with autoharp and guitar. Peer suggested that the Carters record old songs, which they performed in the same informal style favored at family gatherings, as well as songs by A. P. Carter himself.

LISTENING GUIDE 45

Can the Circle Be Unbroken (A. P. Carter)

A. P. Carter's *Can the Circle Be Unbroken*, recorded in New York in 1935, is a response to the death of a mother. As in ballad singing, the story speaks for itself, with no show of emotion. The refrain declares faith in the blessings of eternal life ("There's a better home a-waiting, / In the sky, Lord, in the sky"). But the

The Carter family, including A. P. Carter, his sister-in-law Maybelle (left), and wife Sara (right, who usually played autoharp). Residents of the Clinch Mountains of Virginia, the family won fame in the South after they began to record their music making in 1927.

stanzas offer grim details: the arrival of the hearse; a plea to the undertaker ("That body you are hauling, / Lord, I hate to see her go"); and after the burial, a house full of tearful brothers and sisters. Accompanied by Maybelle's guitar and Sara's autoharp, Carter sings the verses, and the women join him on the chorus. This number thrives on repetition, as do parlor and gospel songs of the 1800s. In fact, verse and chorus are sung to the same music: **aa'** for both. The procession of square-cut phrases, however, is subverted by the three-beat second bar of **a'** in the verse, and of both chorus phrases, pushing the musical structure out of phase with the expected delivery of the words, which becomes: "May the circle be unbroken by and / By, Lord, by and by."

By the latter 1920s, then, Appalachian music was being circulated not only orally but by radio, on record, and even in print. As profits grew, questions of ownership cropped up. Claims for the purity of even the oldest songs could no longer be maintained, for recordings and radio broadcasts were now part of the transmission and selection process.

Robert Winslow Gordon left his post at the Archive of American Folk Song in 1933. His replacement, John A. Lomax, turned the archive into a real force on the music scene. Born in 1867, Lomax grew up in Texas with a deep interest in black music. Graduating from the University of Texas in 1887, he worked in that school's administration for some years. He also taught English at a Texas college, with time off (1906–7) for M.A. study at Harvard. Lomax's interest in cowboy songs led to a published collection of them in 1910. After his book appeared, he was elected president of the American Folklore Society and traveled and lectured widely, helping to boost the visibility of folklore studies. By the early 1920s, Lomax had left the academic world for banking, though he continued to collect songs and ballads. In 1932, out of a job at sixty-five, he convinced a New York publisher to sign him up for a comprehensive collection to be called *American Ballads and Folk Songs*. He then approached Carl Engel, chief of the Library of Congress music division, who agreed to furnish him with equipment if Lomax would deposit his recordings at the library. In July 1933, Lomax was named honorary consultant to the Archive of American Folk Song for a stipend of $1 per year.

Knowing that black folk songs were poorly represented in American collections, Lomax made them the focus of a four-month-long collecting trip that he and his son Alan, eighteen years old and a college student,

After accompanying his father, John Lomax, on a long folk-song-collecting trip in 1933, Alan Lomax (b. 1915) devoted himself to traditional music, including a 1948 radio program, "Your Ballad Man."

began in the summer of 1933. In their search for African-American musicians insulated from white traditions, they visited Southern peniten-
tiaries and prison camps. In one Louisiana prison, the Lomaxes found the
remarkable singer and guitarist Leadbelly [Huddie Ledbetter]. John Lomax arranged for his parole, and between 1935 and 1948 Leadbelly
recorded many songs for the Library of Congress archive.

In 1937, the Archive of American Folk Song, supported since 1928 by
donations and outside monies, began receiving a stipend from Congress.
Alan Lomax was hired as a staff member. In a collection compiled by him
and his father, Lomax set down his belief in folk song as a living force.

Alan Lomax on What Folklorists Offer Their Audiences

He goes where book-learning is not. He lives with the under-
privileged. He brings back the proof in their songs and stories
and dances that these folks are expressive and concerned about
the beautiful and the good. In doing so, he continually denies
the validity of caste lines and caste barriers. . . . The folklorist
has the duty to speak as the advocate of the common man.

Rather than an observer, then, a collector of folk song was an agent with
a political goal.

Alan Lomax became a folk-song collector during troubled times. He
reached maturity during the Depression and, just as the economy was re-
covering, saw war break out in Europe. Lomax came to perceive folk music as the distilled political expression of working people, hence a means
to rally popular sentiment against evil. Convinced that he was working
on behalf of true American patriotism, Lomax treated folk song as an ideological equivalent of the broadside ballads and abolition songs of earlier days.

In March 1940, a landmark concert was held at New York's Forrest
Theater for the benefit of migrant farm workers. Billed as a "Grapes of
Wrath" evening, after John Steinbeck's 1939 novel, the concert was historic because the featured artists were folk musicians. Festivals during the
1930s had placed folk singers and players in front of paying audiences.
And some had sung on the radio, at union events and political rallies,
and even in clubs. Nevertheless, to present them in an evening concert
setting, on a New York theater stage, and in support of a political cause

Oklahoma-born Woody Guthrie (1912–1967) parlayed
genuine folk roots and political radicalism into a prominent place in the folk revival movement that began in the
latter 1930s.

was a novel idea. Among the singers who appeared that night, Woody
Guthrie, newly arrived in the city, seems to have left the strongest impression.

Born in 1912 in Oklahoma, Guthrie was a talented, prolific writer who
also sang and played guitar and managed to avoid formal schooling in
any of these pursuits. From his teenage years, he lived a wandering life,
including stints as a laborer, street singer, and hobo. In the course of his
life, Guthrie wrote or adapted more than a thousand songs, reflecting his
travels and emphasizing the Depression, the dust bowl drought of 1935,
New Deal politics, and union organization. Scornful of music with no
message, Guthrie sang his politically inspired songs on picket lines,
marches, and protest meetings. Alan Lomax, who heard Guthrie for the
first time at the "Grapes of Wrath" concert, found him "miraculously"
untouched by popular singing styles, a genuine political radical, and a
gifted entertainer.

Lomax's respect increased even more as he experienced Guthrie's talent as a songwriter. During a cross-country trip to New York City in early

1940, Guthrie had come to hate a popular hit that seemed to be everywhere that winter, Irving Berlin's *God Bless America*. As Guthrie saw it, Berlin's song, whose text invoked the timeless phrase "home, sweet home," glossed over social inequality as if it were God's will. In February, shortly after reaching New York, Guthrie wrote a song in six stanzas that answered the falsely inspirational quality of Berlin's hit. The fourth stanza reveals a hard edge of disenchantment:

> Was a big high wall there that tried to stop me
> A sign was painted said: Private Property.
> But on the back side, it didn't say nothing—
> God Blessed America for me.

And the sixth challenges Berlin's song directly:

> One bright sunny morning in the shadow of the steeple
> By the relief office I saw my people—
> As they stood there hungry,
> I stood there wondering if
> God Blessed America for me.

A few years later, and with changes, Guthrie's number became *This Land Is Your Land*, a song hardly less affirmative than Berlin's.

After the "Grapes of Wrath" concert, Lomax invited Guthrie to Washington to record for the Archive of American Folk Song. He soon discovered that the singer had a huge repertory (including *Gypsy Davy*, Child Ballad No. 200, which Guthrie sang to his own guitar accompaniment). And he learned too that Guthrie used the phonograph to expand his repertory and refine his style. Alan's sister Bess Lomax, who shared a house with Guthrie in 1941, recalled that countless repetitions of blues recordings by Blind Lemon Jefferson and T-Bone Slim helped him work on vocal delivery.

LISTENING GUIDE 46

So Long, It's Been Good to Know You (Guthrie)

Guthrie recorded his own song, "So Long, It's Been Good to Know You," at the Library of Congress in March 1940, accompanying himself on guitar. In waltz time and strophic verse-and-chorus form, this ballad takes an unsentimental look at the impact of Depression-era droughts and dust storms on the people of the west Texas plains. Partway through a series of choruses and interludes, Guthrie breaks into story-telling mode over a guitar background. Using the chorus as an ironic punch line, he tells of a preacher who, facing the same hardship his worshipers were going through, decided to "cut price on salvation and sin." Calling his flock together for a message of consolation, he prepared to read his sermon. But, finding the meeting house too dusty, "he folded his specs and took up collection" before heading out of town, singing "So long, it's been good to know you."

The artless quality of Guthrie's voice and delivery, and the rolling rhythm that carries him over the rough edges in his singing and playing, set a standard that many folk-revival musicians took as a model of authenticity.

It was also during this stay in Washington that Guthrie became the musical mentor of Pete Seeger, a young musician who, like Alan Lomax, came to folk music through inclination rather than birthright, and was also working at the Archive of American Folk Song. Born to a concert-violinist mother and a father (Charles) who was a modernist composer, teacher, and musicologist, Pete Seeger was introduced to folk music in the mid-1930s by his father and stepmother, the composer Ruth Crawford Seeger, who lived in Washington. Ruth Seeger balanced motherhood and household duties with transcribing melodies that the Lomaxes had

Ethnomusicologist Charles Seeger, his wife, the composer Ruth Crawford Seeger, and their children Michael and Peggy, pictured in Washington around 1937.

recorded for the archive. Pete, who had imbibed radical politics in his own family circle, dropped out of college after two years, learned the five-string banjo, and moved to Washington. He arrived there at a time when a young man with his background, talent, work habits, and politics could make an impact as a folk musician, a career that until then had not existed.

The New York "Grapes of Wrath" evening in 1940 gave Pete Seeger his first chance to see Woody Guthrie in action and to experience the power of political folk music in a concert setting. Alan Lomax later said that from that night forward, "Pete knew it was his kind of music, and he began working to make it everybody's kind of music." To Seeger, folk styles were perfectly suited to the political messages that he, Guthrie, and Lomax wanted to convey, the opposite of Tin Pan Alley and Broadway offerings. Yet how were these "urban folk" musicians to make a living selling their noncommercial songs?

Early in 1941, Seeger joined with Lee Hays, Millard Lampell, and Guthrie to form the Almanac Singers. Singing about peace, war, and politics, the group set up Almanac House, a cooperative in New York City's Greenwich Village, where they lived and held weekly musical gatherings. They sang at union and political rallies, and occasionally on the radio. They also made recordings. The Almanacs have been called the first urban folk-singing group, pursuing a goal stated by Lampell: "We are trying to give back to the people the songs of the workers." Guthrie sum-

The Almanac Singers, including (left to right) Woody Guthrie, Millard Lampell, Bess Lomax, Pete Seeger, Arthur Stern, and Sis Cunningham, around 1941.

marized the group's activist philosophy: "The biggest parts of our song collection are aimed at restoring the right amount of people to the right amount of land and the right amount of houses and the right amount of groceries to the right amount of working folks."

Yet, though they rejected the label, the Almanac Singers possessed the talent and charisma of successful entertainers. And as they sang for a widening range of audiences, their music struck a responsive chord, even with listeners who did not share their political outlook. After the United States entered the war, the Almanacs added anti-Nazi songs to their repertory. They even auditioned successfully at the Rainbow Room, a swanky nightclub atop a Rockefeller Center skyscraper, singing these words to the Appalachian tune *Old Joe Clark*:

> Round and round Hitler's grave
> Round and round we go,
> We're going to lay that poor boy down
> He won't get up no more.

> I wish I had a bushel
> I wish I had a peck
> I wish I had old Hitler
> With a rope around his neck.

Cecil Sharp and Robert Winslow Gordon thought of folk music as coming from the past. In contrast, Pete Seeger, the Lomaxes, and the Almanac Singers approached it as a living force in the present. To Woody Guthrie, performing in something close to his native vernacular, such categories as folklore and folk music hardly existed. To urban folk musicians, on the other hand, the labels marked an identity that they had imagined into being. If the idea of folklore is understood as a conscious construction, then it is clear that the figures this chapter has shown in action—Sharp, Olive Dame Campbell, Gordon, and the circle of Lomax and Seeger—belong in the same company.

30

From New Orleans to Chicago

JAZZ GOES NATIONAL

TWO KEY JAZZ MUSICIANS EMERGED IN THE 1920s: FERD "JELLY Roll" Morton and Louis Armstrong, both New Orleans natives steeped in the city's musical traditions. Born in 1890 of Creole parents, Morton began playing piano at ten and received his first professional experience as a pianist in New Orleans, some of it perhaps in Storyville, the city's red-light district. New Orleans may have been the cradle of Morton's art, but its nursery was black vaudeville and cabaret entertainment, in which he worked from 1907 to 1923, visiting many parts of the country.

Morton was employed for a time in Chicago during World War I. He returned there in the spring of 1923, making his first recordings and beginning to publish his compositions through a Chicago firm. In 1926, he organized the Red Hot Peppers for an epic set of Victor recordings. Record sessions could be haphazard affairs in those days, but not when Morton was the leader. Baby Dodds, the group's drummer, recalled that Morton worked "on each and every number" in rehearsal until he was satisfied. "You did what Jelly Roll wanted you to do, no more and no less."

Morton moved to New York in 1928. But in an environment dominated by large dance orchestras, his emphasis on New Orleans styles was considered old-fashioned. Work opportunities gradually dried up, and Morton fell into obscurity, convinced that he was the victim of a voodoo curse. He resurfaced in 1938, opening a small jazz club in Washington, D.C. Morton also presented himself at the Library of Congress, anxious that his role in the history of jazz—he claimed to have invented it—be documented. In a landmark encounter, he was interviewed at length by Alan Lomax, illustrating his recollections at the piano. After a trip to California in 1940, he became ill and never recovered. His death in Los Angeles in July 1941 was marked by only a part of the jazz community.

Ferd "Jelly Roll" Morton and the Red Hot Peppers, who recorded New Orleans–style jazz in Chicago in 1926–27.

Louis Armstrong was born in poverty in New Orleans (1901), the son of a laborer who deserted the family and a mother who worked as a domestic and perhaps a prostitute. While Armstrong grabbed some schooling as a boy, he claimed as his real diploma the common sense and consideration he learned from his mother. Armstrong went to work at the age of seven. He also formed a vocal quartet with friends, who sang on street corners for tips. In 1913, the twelve-year-old boy was declared delinquent and sent to the Colored Waif's Home, a local reform school, where he received his first instruction in music. He left the home two years later as a cornet player determined to make a career as a musician. By 1918, when cornetist King Oliver left New Orleans for Chicago, Armstrong took his place in a band led by trombonist Edmund "Kid" Ory.

In 1922, Oliver, who was leading his Creole Jazz Band in a Chicago cabaret, invited Armstrong to join his group as second cornetist. Oliver's band impressed musicians who heard them play, and Armstrong's reputation began to grow, especially after the band began recording in 1923. The next year, Armstrong left Oliver for the Fletcher Henderson Orchestra in New York. But late in 1925, he returned to Chicago and for the next several years performed in clubs and theaters while also leading record dates with small groups. The sixty-five recordings that Armstrong and his Hot Five and Hot Seven groups made in 1925–28 are now recognized as a body of musical classics.

In 1929, Armstrong moved to New York and soon appeared in *Hot Chocolates,* a Broadway revue. Then he embarked on a career as a solo entertainer: a jazz trumpeter who also sang, led a big band, hosted his own radio show, and appeared in films, all by virtue of supreme musicianship and a personality that seemed to welcome and embrace everyone. He also toured the world for the U.S. State Department in the 1950s. A heart attack in 1959 slowed his pace somewhat, but he kept performing until a few weeks before his death. When Armstrong died in 1971, he could claim an audience as large and varied as that of any musician in the world.

Except for their hometown, Morton and Armstrong held little in common. They were men of different generations and temperament. They took different musical approaches, their career paths differed sharply, and there is no record of the two working together. Yet both of these New Orleans natives reached artistic fulfillment in Chicago: a Northern city whose environment allowed jazz, both commercially and artistically, to flourish.

Chicago's jazz scene was rooted in the African-American population on the city's South Side. In 1910, approximately 44,000 black residents lived there. Between 1916 and 1919, the great migration from Southern states added thousands more, so that by 1920 the count stood at almost 110,000. This demographic shift, besides strengthening black political influence in the city, also ushered in the city's jazz age. Cabarets, vaudeville and movie theaters, and dance halls were opened to serve the growing market for black musical entertainment. And by the later 1910s, some of these establishments were featuring the energetic, syncopated, often raucous-sounding dance music that, under the name of jazz, was gaining national attention.

The cabarets in which Chicago's jazz scene flourished were South Side "black-and-tans," where black and white customers mingled. Some clergymen condemned the cabarets as dens of iniquity, yet they brought jobs and paying customers to the South Side. And they supplied residents with professional entertainment, cast in familiar idioms of speech, humor, dancing, and music. The undisputed leaders of the Chicago jazz scene, however, were black musicians, and they deeply impressed young white jazz musicians, including banjoist and guitarist Eddie Condon. Condon's description of King Oliver's band playing at the Lincoln Gardens in 1922 has often been quoted: "It was hypnosis at first hearing. Everyone was playing what he wanted to play and it was all mixed together as if someone had planned it with a set of micrometer calipers." Before long, listeners elsewhere had a chance to hear Oliver's group. For on an April day in 1923, he and his musicians traveled to the Gennett Studio in Richmond, Indiana, and made their first recordings.

Joe "King" Oliver and the Creole Jazz Band, including Louis Armstrong (holding trombone in foreground) and Lilian Hardin (piano),
who recorded in Richmond, Indiana, in 1923.

Oliver's Gennett sides are a landmark in the history of jazz. Not only
do they represent the first major set of recordings by black jazz musicians,
but they seem to have broken the color barrier. From 1923 on, the music
of black jazz performers as well as white was preserved and circulated
on record. The Oliver band's remarkable blend of freedom and discipline
has been taken as another kind of landmark: an exemplar of classic New
Orleans jazz.

LISTENING GUIDE 47

Dippermouth Blues (Oliver)

Dippermouth Blues, recorded in April 1923, is attributed to Oliver.
The form is simple: a four-bar introduction, nine choruses based
on the twelve-bar blues harmonic progression, and a two-bar final tag. (In jazz parlance, a chorus is the theme, including both
melody and harmonic structure, that is stated and then varied,
as in classical theme-and-variations form. The twelve-bar blues
cycle in *Dippermouth Blues* is heard nine times; each cycle is
called a chorus.) The first two choruses, plus the fifth and ninth,
are played by the full ensemble. (This is the texture sometimes

called "collective improvisation" and identified with New Orleans jazz.) The other five choruses are devoted to solos: by clarinetist Johnny Dodds (numbers three and four) and by Oliver (numbers six, seven, and eight), whose last chorus ends with a two-bar "break" (a brief span of time during which the beat, while still present, is not played) and bass player Bill Johnson's shout: "Oh, play that thing!"

The most celebrated part of *Dippermouth Blues* is Oliver's cornet solo. For one thing, it is played with a variety of muted effects, an Oliver trademark. For another, it is accompanied by melody instruments as well as the rhythm section, so that Oliver's line is part of a web of counterpoint. Finally, it is a "set" solo: a melody in the style of an improvisation that Oliver worked out and repeated when his group performed this piece. Here, transcribed from the recording, are the first eight bars. (The piano, bass, and drum parts are not notated, being largely inaudible on the recording.)

Honore Dutrey's trombone melody shares nothing with Oliver's cornet. From the upbeat smear that kicks off the solo to the offbeat accents in bars 3 and 4, to the vigorous pickup gesture in bar 8, the trombone's function is to keep momentum going at the ends of phrases. Concentrating on what would otherwise be dead spots between melodic statements, this is a good example of the "tailgate" trombone style. Meanwhile, Dodds and Oliver carry on another kind of dialogue. Dodds's melody could just as well be an independent solo, but with Oliver as the featured player, he leaves windows through which the leader can be heard against the trombone and rhythm section. Because this was a set solo in which Dodds knew what to expect, he could plan phrases that dovetailed with Oliver's, in the manner of a call and response.

Oliver's playing relied on sound variety, which is hard to notate, for its impact. Other typical traits may also be heard: a fondness for the middle register, a tendency to embellish a melody rather than inventing a fresh one (mm. 1–4), and a strong rhythmic thrust.

While only a brief sample, this eight-bar transcription shows the balanced relationship among melodic voices that is typical of New Orleans jazz.

To listen to Armstrong as the leader of the Hot Five and Hot Seven groups is to understand why he became one of the most influential of all

American musicians. In 1927, for example, Armstrong recorded *Struttin'
with Some Barbecue* with four other players. The piece begins and ends
with ensemble choruses in the New Orleans mode, full of call-and-
response interchange. In between, the trombonist and clarinetist each play
a solo half a chorus long, and Armstrong plays a complete solo chorus.
His role in *Struttin'* is far more prominent than was Oliver's in *Dippermouth Blues*: his lead cornet in the ensemble sections takes center stage by
virtue of powerful sound and rhythmic energy, and his solo's inventiveness outshines that of his fellow players.

Armstrong's impact could be magnetic. Trumpeter Max Kaminsky,
after hearing him live for the first time in 1929, recalled having felt "as if
I had stared into the sun's eye." And he added, "no one knew what swing
was till Louis came along." Examples of Armstrong's solo artistry in these
years are legion. Another can be heard on *West End Blues*, a tune by Oliver
that Armstrong recorded in 1928 with pianist Earl Hines and three other
musicians.

Louis Armstrong and his Hot Five, including Lil Hardin (piano), Edmund "Kid" Ory (trombone), Johnny Dodds (clarinet), and Johnny St.
Cyr, banjo.

LISTENING GUIDE 48

West End Blues, performed by Armstrong With the Hot Five (Oliver)

After an opening fanfare, the first chorus of *West End Blues* begins gently, with Armstrong delivering Oliver's melody straight. His line through the entire chorus, however, shows restlessness creeping in. After a plain rendition of the first four-bar phrase, he turns the second into an unadorned call (mm. 5–6) and a florid response (mm. 7–8). And in the third phrase, the serene melody is dissolved by Armstrong's decorations. Later choruses include a solo by the trombonist, a delicate call-and-response duet between the clarinetist and Armstrong (who sings his responses), and a rippling solo chorus by Hines on piano. The last chorus, played by everyone, starts with another surprise: Armstrong begins the melody an octave higher than before, sustaining a high B-flat for almost four bars. Then the tension is released in an improvised burst, based on a repetitive phrase that seems to break loose from rhythmic restriction, floating freely above the accompaniment. Armstrong's climactic conclusion manages to sound both spontaneous and structurally inevitable.

The musical synthesis that Armstrong achieved in the latter 1920s drew on three sources that were already present in the music of Chicago's South Side. The first was the African-American oral tradition, with its practice of "signifying," that is, taking a preexisting melody, harmony, rhythm, or form and commenting on it, as a gesture of respect or even fun. Armstrong was also gifted with an awareness of the moment that enabled him to make inspired musical choices. The second influence came from the cabarets, where he learned how to be an effective entertainer. Those who worked in Chicago's competitive show business needed to be able to make artistic statements that would impress club managers, contractors, and bandleaders. Jazz musicians there learned to work out solo statements that would instantly grab the spotlight.

The third influence was the demand for instrumental virtuosity. According to songwriter Hoagy Carmichael, Armstrong owed much of his technical command to the prodding of conservatory-trained Lil Hardin, the jazz pianist to whom he was married from 1924 until the 1930s. "Lil worked the fat off Louis," Carmichael wrote. "She got a book of the standard cornet solos and drilled him. He really worked, even taking lessons from a German down at Kimball Hall, who showed Louis all the European cornet clutches." Although the claim of the classical teacher has not been verified, Carmichael's comments reveal Armstrong as a performer who was eager to learn all the tools of the musician's trade.

It has sometimes been assumed that the black oral tradition, the demands of audience taste, and formal musical training are incompatible. Indeed, each influence has been described here as if it belongs to a separate musical domain: the traditional, popular, and classical spheres. Yet even within these spheres, the values that infuse them—continuity, accessibility, and transcendence—are capable of being combined. In Louis Armstrong's musical consciousness, these values were uniquely blended, each playing a role in the work of one of the century's most remarkable artists.

Armstrong's playing in the latter 1920s coalesced out of the energies of Chicago's nightlife. But the music of Ferd "Jelly Roll" Morton drew its strength from elsewhere. At a time when Armstrong's example was making solo *improvisation* increasingly important in jazz, Morton maintained *composition* as its vital force. "My theory," Morton once said, "is to never discard the melody." Thus his improvising concentrated on varying the melody, and his organizing principle was the varied *repetition* of whole sections. By around 1930, more and more jazz musicians, like Armstrong, were basing their improvisations chiefly on harmony, so that after an opening melodic statement only the piece's harmonic pattern mattered. Perhaps Morton's preference for melodic variation reflected his rootedness in ragtime, whose rhythm, melody, and multistrain forms he absorbed growing up.

BIX BEIDERBECKE: AMERICA'S FIRST JAZZ LEGEND

The Chicago jazz scene also gave birth to the career of Leon "Bix" Beiderbecke, a white jazz cornetist of whom Louis Armstrong once wrote: "The first time I heard Bix, I said these words to myself: There's a man as serious about his music as I am." Born in 1903 into a prosperous Iowa family, Beiderbecke began piano lessons at the age of five, but, finding his teachers' approaches to classical music unappealing, he lost interest and in fact never learned to read music fluently until late in life. As a teenager, recordings by Nick LaRocca and the Original Dixieland Jazz Band caught his ear, and he taught himself cornet by playing along with them. His parents, unhappy with their son's musical taste and academic performance, sent him to Lake Forest Academy, north of Chicago. Here he discovered the city's jazz scene; he also confirmed his resistance to school and fondness for alcohol. After being expelled from the academy in 1922, Beiderbecke stayed in the Midwest, living wherever he could find work playing jazz. Catching on with other young white musicians who emulated black players, he began recording in 1924 with the Wolverines Orchestra. Over the next several years, he won admiration from musicians and knowledgeable fans for his warm sound and melodic originality.

In 1927, Paul Whiteman hired Beiderbecke, along with a few other jazz improvisers, to enliven his dance orchestra's performances. With Whiteman, and with various groups in New York between 1927 and 1929, he made many influential recordings. By the time he left Whiteman in 1929, however, heavy drinking had taken its toll, and Beiderbecke was able to work only sporadically from then until he died in the summer of 1931.

Although Beiderbecke was little known by the public while he was alive, his memory took on a mythic aura. Starting among musicians, the legend spread to the general public after the appearance of Dorothy Baker's novel *Young Man with a Horn* (Boston, 1938), based loosely on Beiderbecke's life and later made into a movie. Certain facts about Beiderbecke—his intuition, talent, alcoholic consumption, short life, and almost mystical devotion to music—helped to create the myth that would make him a symbol of the Roaring Twenties. But race was also a factor.

It was no accident that the first legendary jazz musician was white. In the 1930s, the general public would hardly have looked on a black figure as a positive symbol of anything. Moreover, the legend surely reflected the way white jazz musicians saw their own place in society.

Leon "Bix" Beiderbecke (1903–1931), legendary jazz cornetist from Iowa.

Armstrong, Morton, and Oliver could claim by birthright the African-American folk traditions whose reservoir of melody and rhythm nourished their performances. But for whites, the process of becoming a jazz musician required a more self-conscious break with their social and musical background; they had to construct their own artistic base. Moreover, as economic depression and the rise of radio and the movies changed the shape of popular entertainment in the 1930s, the marketplace for jazz changed with it.

By the late 1930s, when the Swing Era had pulled big-band jazz into the forefront of popular music, work for white jazz musicians was plentiful. But big-band work, based on written arrangements, lacked the spontaneity of the small New Orleans and Chicago jazz ensembles. Hence, a notion about jazz musicians took shape that had hardly existed during Beiderbecke's lifetime: jazz musicians who improvised well and resisted popular formulas could be more than entertainers, they could be artists. As the audience for swing-band music grew, so—among a few aficionados—did the belief that it was artistically inferior to earlier jazz. And Bix Beiderbecke became a symbol of one who had taken the artist's path, in spite of limited technique and a disorderly personal life.

The Beiderbecke legend has continued to evolve. One view has the cornetist actually refusing a musical education and aspiring to a kind of downward mobility, while another finds him more a victim of isolation than one who chose it, unable to connect with any tradition that spoke to his own sensibilities. Both views assume that Beiderbecke thought of jazz in modern terms—as primarily a solo improviser's art—and that he never doubted the artistic worth of his own skills. While his recordings might seem to support these assumptions, there is also reason to question them. Against the claim of refusing education, for example, Beiderbecke is also known to have been full of pride after he flawlessly played the written trumpet solo on Whiteman's recording of Gershwin's *Concerto in F*. Perhaps the conflict that haunted Beiderbecke lay in a lack of confidence that his chosen calling, an improvising jazz musician, was a worthy one. Perhaps, though he rebelled against his upbringing, he never transcended its values.

There is no denying the power of Beiderbecke as a symbol of bohemian artistry crushed by the music business's commercial demands, even though, on closer inspection, he looks more like a remarkable intuitive artist who lost faith in the instinct that first sustained him. Yet whatever the truth of the Bix legend, its existence suggests that by the latter 1930s, some white jazz musicians were finding it useful in helping them shape their own artistic identities, and fans of jazz were taking the music seriously.

31

"Crescendo in Blue"

ELLINGTON, BASIE, AND THE SWING BAND

ALTHOUGH PAUL WHITEMAN WAS THE MOST PROMINENT BAND-leader in New York City during the 1920s and after, a substantial number of black musicians also launched successful careers there. The craze for blues singing set off by Mamie Smith's *Crazy Blues* recording (1920) encouraged other female singers to follow suit—including Bessie Smith, whose classic version of Handy's *St. Louis Blues* with Louis Armstrong was recorded in 1925. (See Chapter 27, LG41.) The "Harlem stride" school of piano playing also blossomed. Taking up where ragtime performers left off, James P. Johnson, Willie "The Lion" Smith, and Thomas "Fats" Waller, among others, honed their styles around multistrain pieces, fast tempos, and trademark flourishes of technique.

In Prohibition-era New York, however, dance orchestras seized artistic leadership in jazz. The Fletcher Henderson Orchestra in 1924 began a long-term engagement at the Roseland Ballroom in midtown Manhattan: a black band playing for largely white audiences. Thanks to arrangements by Don Redman and soloists like Armstrong and tenor saxophonist Coleman Hawkins, Henderson could include hot jazz numbers in a menu of waltzes, popular songs, and more conventional dance music. Henderson's is considered the first dance orchestra that, while playing written arrangements, achieved the rhythmic lilt called swing. But by the end of the decade, another New York jazz orchestra had gained even more prominence. Led by Duke Ellington, this group was to be a presence on the music scene from the 1920s into the 1970s.

Edward Kennedy Ellington, born in Washington, D.C., in 1899, once wrote: "When I was a child, my mother told me I was blessed, and I have always taken her word for it." He started piano lessons at seven, studied commercial art in high school, and began playing piano professionally

The Fletcher Henderson Orchestra, New York, 1924–25. The trumpet player in the middle of the back row is Louis Armstrong.

with Washington-area dance orchestras at seventeen. He seems always to have had a talent for leadership.

In 1923, Ellington moved to New York. For the next several years, he led groups in midtown clubs. He also began to record. Late in 1926, Ellington hired as his manager Irving Mills, who belonged to a white music-publishing family. Personal connections with bootleggers enabled Mills to book Ellington and his musicians into the Cotton Club in Harlem, where the band entertained white audiences, playing for floor shows and dancing over the next three years (1927–30). It was here that Ellington hit his stride as a composer. Working with such distinctive-sounding musicians as saxophonists Harry Carney and Johnny Hodges, clarinetist Barney Bigard, trumpeter Bubber Miley (replaced in 1929 by Cootie Williams), and trombonist Joe Nanton, he fashioned an ensemble that, while playing a varied repertory, specialized in his own original music. Between 1932 and 1942, Ellington traveled the United States, made two successful European tours, and recorded extensively with a fourteen-piece orchestra: six brass (three trumpets, three trombones), four reeds (two alto saxophones plus a tenor and a baritone, all doubling on clarinet), and a rhythm section of four (his own piano, plus double bass, guitar, and drums). Through these years, he produced larger works to complement his popular songs (*Mood Indigo*, *Sophisticated Lady*, and *Take the A Train*, the latter actually composed by Billy Strayhorn, who joined the band as a composer and arranger in 1939) and short instrumental pieces. In 1943, Ellington began a series of annual Carnegie Hall concerts with *Black, Brown, and Beige*, a fifty-minute suite in five large sections, commemorating the history of African people in the New World.

After World War II, Ellington enlarged his band, even as economic conditions forced most big bands out of business. Touring both at home and abroad, playing dances, concerts, and festivals, the band maintained a core of older favorites in its repertory. Meanwhile, Ellington continued to write new compositions, including the score to Otto Preminger's film *Anatomy of a Murder* (1959). In the 1960s, Ellington began to be noticed in the halls of official American culture. He was awarded the Presidential Medal of Honor (1969), won honorary doctorates from universities, and was elected to the National Institute of Arts and Letters. In the years since his death in 1974, he has been more and more widely recognized, not only as a jazz musician but as an important twentieth-century composer.

Billy Strayhorn, Ellington's close collaborator, observed that "Ellington plays the piano, but his real instrument is his band." Indeed, Ellington sought tonal "charisma" from his players, and he worked to discover timbres that would seize listeners' attention. Experience taught him that some musicians revealed their inner selves most deeply in their sound,

Edward Kennedy "Duke" Ellington (1899–1974), composer and bandleader, in a publicity photo taken in 1934.

and that audiences knew it. Audience response to the first note of a solo by alto saxophonist Johnny Hodges, for example, "was as big and deep as most applause for musicians at the end of their complete performance."

Ellington appreciated the collaborative role of his audiences. "I travel from place to place by car, bus, train, plane," he writes, "taking rhythm to the dancers, harmony to the romantic, melody to the nostalgic, gratitude to the listener." And he knew how rhythm can bring musicians and audience members into sync: "When your pulse and my pulse are together, we are swinging, with ears, eyes, and every member of the body tuned into driving a wave emotionally, compellingly, to and from the subconscious." In Ellington's view, musicians performed their best for knowledgeable listeners—especially on those rare occasions when "audience and performers are determined not to be outdone by the other, and when both have appreciation and taste to match."

But again, sound—sometimes called "the Ellington effect"—was Ellington's trump card, making his band instantly recognizable and emotionally potent. The chief architect of the Ellington effect as it emerged in

On the road with Ellington. Card players in this candid railroad car shot include singer Ivie Anderson, drummer Sonny Greer, and Ellington himself.

East St. Louis Toodle-Oo, a composition of the latter 1920s, was trumpeter Bubber Miley. Miley had discovered that by blowing, gargling, and humming at the same time and shaping the sound with a plunger mute, he could "growl" through his trumpet. Ellington loved this sound and maintained it in his arsenal of effects after Miley left the band.

The trumpet growl was sometimes used in the "jungle music" the band played to accompany the Cotton Club's exotic floor shows. In *Concerto for Cootie* (1940), though, written to show off the talents of trumpeter Cootie Williams, the trumpet growl is liberated from the jungle and used as one of many sound qualities at Williams's command. *Ko-Ko*, from the same year, opens with a menacing sound built on the foundation of Harry Carney's room-filling baritone sax. Another kind of Ellington sound is heard in a family of pieces slow in tempo, rich in harmony, delicately blended in timbre, and meditative in atmosphere, of which *Mood Indigo* is the most famous.

LISTENING GUIDE 49

Old Man Blues (Ellington)

Ellington's *Old Man Blues* (1930) shows that he could be as playful in his use of musical form as he was inventive in his use of sound. For in this piece, which bears no connection to the twelve-bar blues, Ellington spars with listeners' expectations through extensions, omissions, and the introduction of new melodic strains. *Old Man Blues* also illustrates the quality of wordless singing that the plunger-mute technique can produce. And this imitation of the voice, bordering on the comic, leads us to hear many Ellington passages as conversations among instruments, often in the form of the call-and-response pattern.

After its introduction, *Old Man Blues* presents a conversation of sorts between trombonist Nanton and clarinetist Bigard. Only in the next chorus, however, after a suprising key change, is the main melody (**A**) introduced. The piece teems with more unexpected details. The second strain (**B**), for example, appears twice, and each time two bars early. The trumpet solo in the fourth **A** section evokes a standard piece of stage business by beginning hopelessly behind the action and then catching up. And the brass section's break just before the last **A** is twice as long as expected. The quality of playing is sharp, disciplined, and crackling with excitement.

The following table outlines the work.

Formal function*	Featured instrument(s)	Key
I^8	soprano saxophone	E♭
A^{30} (aaba')	trombone and clarinet	
B^{20} (vcd)	♩ 𝄾 ♩ 𝄾 | (4)	
	saxophone section (8)	
	trumpet section (8)	
A^{32}	brass tune (16)	F
	trombone (8)	
	brass tune (8)	
A^{32}	baritone saxophone and piano	
	brass backing on bridge	
A^{30}	soprano saxophone backed by	
	brass (16)	
	trumpet (14)	
B^{10} (c'x)	saxophone section (6)	
	brass (4) 𝄾 ♪ ♩ ♩ ♩ | ♪ ♩ ♪ ♩	
A^{32}	brass tune with clarinet swoops (16)	
	trombone and clarinet (8)	
	brass tune (8)	

*I stands for intro; **A**, **B** for full thematic statements; a, b, c, d for parts of thematic statements; v for vamp; x for extension; and superscript numbers for the number of bars.

Diminuendo and Crescendo in Blue (1937) shows Ellington working on a larger scale—too large to fit the three-minute limit imposed by the ten-inch 78-rpm recording. In fact, this work was written to fill an entire record, with the *Diminuendo in Blue* on one side and the *Crescendo in Blue* on the other. The title also refers to the twelve-bar blues, the jazz tradition's most familiar form, with its three four-bar phrases, its characteristic harmonic progression, and the implied call-and-response built into each phrase. Ellington uses this form, on which many players in the band were capable of improvising at length, as the basis for an ingeniously shaped piece in which improvisation plays only a small role.

LISTENING GUIDE 50

Diminuendo and Crescendo in Blue (Ellington)

Barney Bigard once said of Ellington: "At first, just after I joined Duke . . . I used to think everything was wrong, because he wrote so weird." The opening of *Diminuendo and Crescendo in Blue* illustrates that side of Ellington. On the one hand, the first four choruses function together as an adventurous introduction. On the other, they comment on the twelve-bar blues as an instrumental form. In each chorus, we hear the ingredients of standard blues form. Yet by changing some element in each—by delaying a harmonic arrival point, by switching the expected ordering of melodic statements or the character of calls and responses, or by adding measures—Ellington sows seeds of doubt in his listeners. Are we hearing blues choruses, or not? We cannot be sure, until Chorus 5 arrives.

Thus, *Diminuendo in Blue* moves from dissonance to consonance, from loud to soft, from density to spareness, from rhythmic disruption to smoothness, and from formal ambiguity to formal clarity. Once Chorus 5 establishes the structure clearly, the ear is free to shift focus from form to the flow of events—changes in texture, sound, time intervals between calls and responses, melodic invention. Beginning on a note of manic disconnection, the piece settles into a groove, hits a point of calm, and then reverses the process in the *Crescendo* section. And it is unified not only by the harmonic progression that underlies all twenty-two of its choruses but by the melodic motive that begins the *Diminuendo*, that returns in the seventh chorus in the saxes as the start of a longer melody,

that begins the *Crescendo* and is heard through its first three choruses, and that reappears at the beginning of both Chorus 8 and Chorus 11 of that section.

Diminuendo and Crescendo in Blue and Old Man Blues are only two works among more than 1,100 that Ellington composed and copyrighted in the course of his career. In about 20 percent of these works, he shared authorship with musicians who played with him, and he collaborated with others in the rest. Even when Ellington was the sole composer of record, collaboration lay at the heart of his music making. For as well as imagining fresh tone combinations, Ellington composed by working with his musicians so that their tonal personalities—their particular sound, way of playing, and inventiveness—actually helped to create the music. When trumpeter Fred Stone spent a few months with Ellington in 1970, he reflected that the band was the only outfit he knew "where you are not required to match the sound of the previous member. You must function as an individual."

BASIE AND KANSAS CITY

In a region that might seem an unlikely place for jazz to have flourished, Kansas City, Missouri, boasted a wide-open nightlife. For Americans who lived in the area bounded on the south by Houston, on the west by Albuquerque, and on the northwest and north by Cheyenne, Wyoming, and Sioux Falls, South Dakota, Kansas City was the center of commerce and gateway to the markets of the East. Many Westerners went there in search of entertainment, which was plentiful because local officials wanted it to be, and the city was controlled by a political faction that protected gambling, prostitution, and, during Prohibition, the selling of liquor. With its variety of good-time venues, Kansas City was a place where jobs for jazz musicians were plentiful, if low-paying.

By 1930, a distinctive style of orchestral jazz was developing in Kansas City, especially in a band led by local native Bennie Moten. Based on a rhythm section that played a driving four beats to the bar, Moten's music relied heavily on the twelve-bar blues and on riff-based arrangements. The arrangements, written chiefly by Eddie Durham of the trombone section and William "Count" Basie, the pianist, led to performances that blended solo and ensemble passages effectively. Moten's band recorded for Victor in 1932, but in the Depression-plagued United States, they never found much work outside Kansas City. In the spring of 1935, Bennie Moten died unexpectedly. And in August of that year, big-band jazz entered the public consciousness with a bang when a jazz-oriented white dance band led by clarinetist Benny Goodman opened at the Palomar Ballroom in Los Angeles.

Born in Chicago in 1909, Goodman was a virtuoso jazz improviser who worked in New York from 1928 until 1934, when he formed his own dance orchestra. The new Goodman band played in a New York theater, recorded, and began appearing regularly on "Let's Dance," an NBC radio series. Goodman's exacting standards as a leader made his band a model of ensemble discipline and polish, playing a mixture of jazz tunes and popular songs of the day. In May 1935, the band began a cross-country tour with only mixed success. But a Los Angeles performance on August 21, broadcast nationwide to great acclaim, touched off a wave of enthusiasm and publicity so strong that it has been credited with launching the Swing Era, a new age of popular music. The jazz-oriented dance band was now the preferred popular-music medium and would remain so for the next decade. Shortly after Goodman's success in Los Angeles, Count Basie formed a nine-piece group in Kansas City, hiring many of the Moten band's players and beginning an engagement at the Reno Club. Before long, broadcasts on the club's radio hookup drew outside attention to the band. And by 1936, Basie's Midwest group, managed by a prominent white booking firm, was coming into its own as a swing band with a national following.

Basie was born in 1904 in Red Bank, New Jersey. Indifferent to school, he was drawn from an early age to music. Although piano lessons taught him little about reading music, he learned quickly by ear. Basie quit school before finishing junior high to pursue a career in show business—not to get rich but because "I liked playing music, and I liked the life." He showed an instinct for getting ahead, first in New Jersey and then in Harlem, where he landed a job as pianist with a traveling theater company. When that tour ended, he returned to Harlem and worked in clubs there, meeting such local pianists as Fats Waller and Willie "The Lion" Smith.

In 1926, Basie toured with another vaudeville act. When engagements ran out in Kansas City in 1927, he was hired at a theater there to accompany silent movies. By 1929, Basie had joined Moten's band. And there he gained the experience that made it possible after Moten died to recruit local players for his own group at the Reno Club. Almost everybody in that band was a good soloist, he remembered, and the group worked mostly off "head arrangements"—arrangements that, rather than being written down, were assembled from the ideas (out of the heads) of band members.

Basie's big break came when John Hammond, a producer for Columbia records working in Chicago, heard the band on the radio. Support from Hammond and Willard Alexander of the MCA booking agency helped to transform Basie's local group into a polished, nationally known ensemble. Musicians were added. Female singer Billie Holiday was hired to join male singer Jimmy Rushing. New arrangements were commissioned. And the band polished its image to please audiences outside the rough-and-ready confines of the Reno Club. Yet the musical approach that Basie had worked out in Kansas City, and that had caught John Hammond's ear in the first place, remained intact. If Ellington sought players with a unique sound, Basie "knew how I wanted each section to sound" and therefore how each section member should sound. Basie kept the blues prominent in the band's repertory. Soloists also played a key role. "I have my own little ideas about how to get certain guys into certain numbers and how to get them out. I had my own way of opening the door for them to let them come in and sit around awhile. Then I would exit them. And that has really been the formula of the band all down through the years," he said late in life.

These comments tell us that Basie's musicians were steered by the leader's will and taste, but leave out an essential collaborative part of the band's sound: the rhythm section, especially after guitarist Freddie Green joined Basie in 1937. Walter Page's resonant walking bass kept the beat, which was given a top as well as a bottom by Green's even, on-the-beat guitar chords. The precision and firmness of Page and Green left drummer Jo Jones free to use the bass drum for accents instead of pulse marking. By moving his own timekeeping to the double "high-hat" cymbal, Jones lightened the rhythm section's sound without sacrificing intensity. Basie himself had arrived in Kansas City as an experienced stride player who used his left hand as a rhythmic engine. But by the time he and the band headed east in 1936, he had worked out a new, stripped-down style that would remain his signature for the rest of his career.

Basie's rhythm section was a four-man accompanying unit, and within it he played his part as a group member to perfection. In opening the door for his soloists, inviting them in to hang around for a while, and then showing them the way out, Basie was acting as accompanist-in-charge, a role that suited his temperament, character, and personal style. Described as one of the great "comp artists" of all time—the jazz term means to play chords as a *comp*lementary *accomp*anist to a featured soloist—Basie deftly blended artistic control with self-effacement, leading as well as following.

The chief soloist during the band's early years was tenor saxophonist Lester Young, a Mississippi native who played with Basie from 1936 until 1940. Young has been called the most original jazz improviser between Louis Armstrong and Charlie Parker: a musician of striking individuality. Playing with little vibrato, Young managed a sound both light

In 1939, the Basie band played an engagement at the Apollo Theater in Harlem. Members pictured here include Lester Young (tenor sax, far right), Walter Page (bass), Freddie Green (guitar), Jo Jones (drums), and Basie (piano).

and intense, and capable of carrying highly compelling ideas. He proved that swing did not require high volume and that understatement could be commanding. Young might improvise *against* a tune's phrase structure as well as with it, stay silent on beats where accents were expected, signify on musical clichés, and use strikingly original melodic intervals.

LISTENING GUIDE 51

Lester Leaps In (Young)

Young's solo on *Lester Leaps In* (1939) is supported by Basie and the rhythm section. The tune is based on the harmonies of Gershwin's popular song *I Got Rhythm*, following a standard thirty-two-bar form: statement, restatement, contrast, and return (**aaba**). The solo has been transcribed and analyzed by more than one scholar, and each has found something different to praise. One has called attention to the melodic formulas that connect this solo to other parts of the piece. Another takes the solo as evidence of Young's fondness for asymmetry: breaking down binary units of two, four, and eight bars with three- and five-bar phrases. The transcription printed here is by Gunther Schuller.

While most of Young's melodic material sounds newly invented, elements of the original also return as reference points. Except for the dissonant C at the start of the last section, he follows the original harmonic structure, but he both follows and moves away from Gershwin's phrase structure. For all of Young's asymmetrical whimsy, however, his signifying never loses its secure rhythmic groundedness. His own gift for swinging is partly responsible, but so is the rhythm section of Page, Green, and Jones playing behind him. And Basie's punctuating dialogue with Young's solo line adds both to the swing and the asymmetry.

In an interview long after Young's death, Basie mentioned him as a player who could be counted on to swing. The rhythmic energy of the Basie band freed Young to explore asymmetry as a solo improviser. Or perhaps one could say that the rhythmic security provided by Basie allowed Young to signify on a more sophisticated, even structural level than would otherwise have been possible. Young was a gifted improviser because he possessed a sovereign command of both vocabulary (melodic inventiveness) and syntax (the adroit placement of notes and phrases in the musical structure). With another supreme master of syntax behind him, he ventured as a soloist into terrain that no jazz soloist before him had visited.

EPILOGUE: THE SWING ERA AND THE HARLEM RENAISSANCE

When the United States entered World War II in 1941, swing bands were dominating the nation's popular-music scene. And many of the most successful ones were white. Broadcasting and recording, featuring both vocalists and instrumentalists, performing popular songs as well as jazz numbers, playing in hotels and ballrooms, and touring to play dances and in theaters, these ensembles were loved by a wide range of Americans, especially younger ones. Between 1939 and 1942, a band led by trombonist Glenn Miller reached a level of popular success unmatched by any other group of the time.

Swing triumphed for two main reasons. First, it captured jazz's improvisatory spirit in written arrangements for large dance bands. By the latter 1930s, whole bands were playing in the style of an improvisation, and audiences loved it, especially when they knew the original tunes. And second, jazz-based styles circulated widely through radio, recording, and film. As the 1930s came to an end, the popular music that most Americans were dancing to, singing, and adopting as their own vernacular expression bore an African-American pedigree.

Our study of African-American music so far has emphasized the folk and popular spheres. But in the years after World War I, black musicians also worked to establish a beachhead in the concert hall. The cultural movement known as the Harlem Renaissance, under way by around 1920 and led by black intellectuals, including philosopher Alain Locke, social scientist W. E. B. DuBois, and poet and author James Weldon Johnson, focused primarily on the arts. Cultural achievement, the leaders hoped, would crack the seemingly impregnable wall of racism, for once black writers, painters, and composers showed their mastery of classical techniques, whites would be forced to give up their stereotype of black inferiority. The Harlem Renaissance ideal prescribed work that reflected the artists' black heritage, but in culturally prestigious (European) form.

CD 3

LISTENING GUIDE 52

Water Boy (sung by Robeson)

Musical arrangements linking the African-American folk heritage to the concert stage met the Harlem Renaissance goal of elevation. They did so by applying the resources of classical technique and expression to materials considered raw in their original state. *Water Boy*, for example, combines a pair of prison work songs to create a showcase for baritone Paul Robeson: actor, concert singer, and political activist. In the minor-mode title song that frames this **ABA** structure, a thirsty worker calls out for a drink of water. And the major-mode *Hammer Song*—the two-stanza **B** section—boasts of the prisoner's strength as a worker and laments his losses at cards. Sung in Robeson's commanding, cultivated voice, accompanied by Lawrence Brown at the piano in this 1926 recording, *Water Boy* brings poetic dignity to the character of a robust, sensitive, uneducated, and oppressed male prisoner.

The generation's most versatile black composer was William Grant Still. Born in 1895 in Mississippi, Still grew up in Little Rock, Arkansas. He attended Wilberforce College in Ohio and the Oberlin Conservatory. Later formal study included lessons with George W. Chadwick and Edgard Varèse. Still earned his living in popular music, however, beginning in 1914 as a dance orchestra performer. In 1916, he worked as an arranger for W. C. Handy's music-publishing company in Memphis, producing the first band version of *St. Louis Blues*. In 1919, Still accompanied Handy to New York, where he continued in the publishing business and played in Handy's bands. He joined a black-owned recording firm in New York in 1921 as manager and arranger, and from 1921 to 1923 he played oboe in the pit orchestra of Noble Sissle and Eubie Blake's *Shuffle Along*, the decade's most successful black Broadway show. A polished professional arranger and composer, Still also continued to compose classical works, including ballets, operas, symphonies, chamber music, and vocal pieces. His *Afro-American Symphony*, premiered in 1931 by the Rochester Philharmonic Orchestra with Howard Hanson conducting, marked the first time in history that a major orchestra had performed a black composer's symphony.

The performance of Still's symphony was a landmark for the aspirations of the Harlem Renaissance, creating a precedent for others to follow. Yet something was happening in the popular sphere during the 1930s that also testified to black achievement: there was a growing recognition of the artistic potential of jazz, which would alter the whole shape of musical life—especially the relations among the popular, classical, and folk spheres—as the century continued. The consequences of that development, both for African-American musicians and American music in general, are hard to overestimate.

32

The Golden Age of the American Musical

ON THE FIRST TWO EVENINGS OF DECEMBER 1924, A PAIR OF SHOWS opened on Broadway that dramatize a split between the up-to-date and the old-fashioned. *Lady Be Good!*, with music and lyrics by George and Ira Gershwin—the brothers' first Broadway collaboration—was performed on December 1 at the Liberty Theater; the lighthearted tale about a stage brother and sister featured dancer Fred Astaire and his real-life sister Adele. And the next evening, *The Student Prince*, with music by Sigmund Romberg and lyrics by Dorothy Donnelly, received its New York premiere. Set in nineteenth-century Germany, this show tells the story of a crown prince who is sent to the university at Heidelberg to sample the life of a student. The Hungarian-born Romberg, who immigrated to the United States in 1909, composed *The Student Prince* in the tradition of the Viennese operetta, with soaring melodies and rousing choruses. In contrast, the score of *Lady Be Good* took a modern tack. Earlier that year, George Gershwin had been proclaimed a musical innovator with his jazz concerto, the *Rhapsody in Blue*, and now he and Ira were trying their hand at a Broadway show. The result was groundbreaking. George's command of a jazz-flavored musical style was matched by Ira's skill at setting vernacular speech to his brother's music. The American musical theater had found a fresh native idiom.

Before the decade was out, the gulf between *Lady Be Good!* and *The Student Prince* was bridged by another composer-author team in a work blending new elements effectively with old ones. *Show Boat*, with a book and lyrics by Oscar Hammerstein II and music by Jerome Kern, received its New York premiere in 1927. Based on a novel by Edna Ferber, *Show Boat* is set in the Midwest, spanning an era from around 1890 to the 1920s. The show is a bittersweet romance between Gaylord Ravenal, a river gambler, and Magnolia, the daughter of a showboat captain. Early in Act I,

As with shows in the past, songs from Kern and Hammerstein's *Show Boat* (1927), including *Can't Help Lovin' Dat Man*, were sold as sheet music for amateur performers.

after Magnolia has fallen in love, she asks a black stevedore named Joe about Ravenal. Joe tells her to ask the river "what *he* thinks." And then he sings *Old Man River*. As personified by Joe, the river is a mighty force, indifferent to human struggles. The sober melody and the philosophical text lend authority to Joe and support his view of the characters' trials and tribulations.

LISTENING GUIDE 53

Can't Help Lovin' Dat Man (Kern and Hammerstein)

If Kern's melody for *Ol' Man River* manages to be folklike and dramatic at the same time, *Can't Help Lovin' Dat Man* borrows directly from the blues. Julie LaVerne, the show boat's sultry songstress, sings this number, whose verse is labeled "Tempo di Blues" and is set in twelve-bar blues form. These words are sung over Tin Pan Alley's standard blues accompaniment of repeated quarter notes. And the chorus that follows, in thirty-two-bar **aaba** form, continues in a style spiced with blue notes. Julie's number becomes a marker of racial identity. A black character named Queenie marvels that she has never heard "anybody but colored folks" sing that song. And soon, unmasked as a woman with African-American blood who has been passing for white, Julie is forced to leave the show boat.

The recording—featuring Helen Morgan, the show's first Julie LaVerne, and made in 1928—departs from the song's onstage performance. It starts with the opening section of *Mis'ry's Comin' Round*, a song cut from *Show Boat* during its pre-Broadway try-outs. Then Morgan, backed only by a rhythm section, sings the first two sections of the chorus (**aa**), which segues immediately into an orchestra version of the verse. At this point, Morgan returns with Kern's verse and chorus. And from here on, the performance is given an unusual color by the use of a bassoon to fill in the ends of phrases and add a countermelody to the song's last eight bars.

Ol' Man River and *Can't Help Lovin' Dat Man* were conceived for particular characters and moments in *Show Boat*. Yet for all their differences in style, their form is the same: a verse followed by a thirty-two-bar chorus. For in fact, Kern wrote the songs of this tightly woven theatrical work so that they could circulate independently, in sheet-music form, as theater songs had been doing in the United States since the 1790s, and in recordings.

From 1924, when they wrote *The Man I Love*, to George's death in 1937, the Gershwin brothers collaborated on songs for musicals, movies, and the opera *Porgy and Bess*.

Most show songs that won popularity in the years between the wars were songs about romantic love. Courtship and love, treated almost as rituals in many earlier songs, now emerged as absorbing, sometimes mysterious personal adventures. Since the plots of virtually all shows of the day involved characters seeking someone to love, the demand for love songs on Broadway was great. As one New York tunesmith put it, the songwriter's craft lay chiefly in saying "I love you" in thirty-two bars.

Two different states of the amorous mind are caught in a pair of songs by top teams of the day: Richard Rodgers and Lorenz Hart's *My Heart Stood Still* (1927), and *The Man I Love* by George and Ira Gershwin (1924). Both songs illustrate how masters of the genre could seize upon a detail—a fantasy or a fleeting moment—and make it a meditation on the workings of the human heart. *My Heart Stood Still* reflects on love at first sight; *The Man I Love* is pure anticipation, as a woman reveals her romantic dream of a future love. Both songs admit dependence on time-worn clichés, but these clichés are transcended by the songs' expression, which is graceful and self-aware.

LISTENING GUIDE 54

My Heart Stood Still (Rodgers and Hart)

Rodgers and Hart's *My Heart Stood Still* dwells on an instant by suspending time—freezing the frame, in effect—and exploring the experience of love at first sight. Reliving the moment, the character remembers a feeling of physical shock: Hart's lyrics, comprised of one-syllable words, suggest that the impact lingers on, and Rodgers's melody confirms that suggestion. Each of the first two lines breaks off with a hint of breathlessness, the last word falling on a short, unaccented quarter note. And the third line's melody mirrors the meaning, as downward quarter-note motion leads to three strokes (half note, half note, whole note) on the three final words. Just as the heart skips a beat, the melody "stands still" in this vivid moment of remembering.

I took one look at you, That's all I meant to do;

And then my heart stood still!

The chorus of *My Heart Stood Still* uses the thirty-two-bar **aaba** form also employed in *The Man I Love*, and three of its four sections also end with the title line. In the release, or **b** section, the focus shifts to the beloved's response, which is similar. From this telepathic flash we return to the singer, who claims to have missed true happiness before the "thrill" (highest note of the song) of that "moment" (the first two-syllable word in any **a** section) "when my heart stood still."

The new emphasis on this kind of romantic love accompanies the rise of individualism. Before around 1880, most Americans had little reason to doubt that the ties linking people to their family, community, church, and occupation formed the main social reality of their lives. Between 1880 and 1900, however, these connections began to loosen, and from the 1920s on, Americans were more likely than before to downplay traditional social ties and define themselves in personal terms.

By the end of World War I, songwriters were absorbing this spirit of individualism. The portrait of love that came to dominate the Broadway stage and Tin Pan Alley concentrated on lovers who were infatuated and preoccupied with each other beyond anything else, who dwelled in a "world" of two, sometimes only one if the love affair had ended—or, as in *The Man I Love*, had yet to begin. Family, friends, society, and community barely existed in this world.

It is striking that so many songs took this approach in the years after World War I and so few before it. And the new subject matter called for new musical expression, especially in the realm of harmony, where an enriched vocabulary that Edward MacDowell had called a "shadow language" appeared. Using chords with sevenths, ninths, and added or altered tones almost anywhere in a song, Kern, Gershwin, and other songwriters tapped into harmony's power of suggestion in a way that intensified emotions, especially that of yearning.

The enriched harmony of Golden Age popular song came primarily from the songwriters' contact with the European classical sphere. Kern, Gershwin, Rodgers, and Cole Porter all received classical training, and German and Russian compositions of the later nineteenth century and early modern French works were part of their musical experience. Composers such as Liszt, Tchaikovsky, and Ravel had enlarged the harmonic vocabulary of Western music in general, and popular songwriters borrowed from their palette. The general kinship between European Romanticism and the idiom of American popular song is reflected in the way songwriters use chromaticism to intensify harmonic progressions that lead the listener, in a regular pattern of tension and release, from one phrase to the next.

LISTENING GUIDE 55

The Man I Love (Gershwin)

For all the merit of Ira Gershwin's lyrics in *The Man I Love*, George's music gives the song its substance. By emphasizing the lowered seventh scale degree, a note dissonant with the tonic harmony, the melody conveys restlessness. The fantasy is described in three eight-bar sections of an **aaba** form. Each begins by hovering around the seventh, then gradually works its way downward, from restlessness toward calm. And each describes a different stage of the imagined romance. The first section vows confidence that Prince Charming will show up; the second section choreographs the meeting ("He'll take my hand," but "I know we both won't say a word"). Then, after an eight-bar speculation—in a new key and to a different tune—about when the meeting will happen, the last section imagines an idyllic future. In each **a** section, the same melodic figure is heard six times, and the parallel statements suggest the singer's growing certainty.

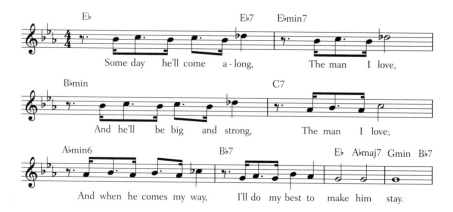

The character who sings *The Man I Love* knows that listeners will find her fantasy a long shot. Yet by dwelling on one melodic figure ("the man I love"), she seems determined to stay the course. Unified but not overwhelmed by that repeated figure, the melody symbolizes confidence "that he'll appear," and listeners are invited to believe as well. (To demonstrate that a rich harmonic idiom accompanies—perhaps even casts a shadow of doubt on—the singer's vision, the music example retains chord indications that appear in the sheet music.)

The songs of Broadway and Tin Pan Alley's Golden Age celebrated individuals who loved with a passion strong enough to overshadow other social connections. And the music suggested that love with such high expectations had to be more dynamic than stable. Whatever the lyrics might say, the harmonic richness that bathed them reminded listeners that romance between "free" modern individuals could be perilous. Just as the simple diatonic idiom of an earlier age's parlor songs pointed outward to the network of home, family, and religious relations, the restless harmonies of Broadway and Tin Pan Alley, joined to sophisticated lyrics, seem to point inward.

THE MUSICAL STAGE AND SCREEN

Generally speaking, songs from Golden Age Broadway musicals have proved more enduring than the shows in which they appeared. Yet it is worthwhile to look at two classic stage works and a new genre—Gershwin's *Porgy and Bess* (1935), Rodgers and Hammerstein's *Oklahoma!* (1943), and the Hollywood film musical—as a reminder of how show music could function in a dramatic context.

George Gershwin called *Porgy and Bess* a "folk opera." His belief that a label was needed is understandable, for the work's precise nature was contested from the start. Gershwin's Broadway background raised doubts about whether he was up to a full-fledged operatic challenge. The score called for opera singers, but the show played nightly in a Broadway theater. Knowledge that massive cuts took place before the New York premiere has also fed the view that the work is more a succession of musical numbers than an operatic whole, as has the popularity of some individual numbers. Moreover, commercial success for *Porgy and Bess* first came in 1941 when, stripped of its recitative, it was played as a Broadway musical: a drama of separate musical numbers linked with spoken dialogue.

Porgy and Bess features songs of remarkable variety. The memorable melodies of the best known have made them enduringly popular. These songs include *Summertime*, a lullaby that invokes the spirituals of slavery times; *My Man's Gone Now*, sung by the widow of a man killed in an onstage brawl; Porgy's banjo song *I Got Plenty o' Nuttin'*, in **aaba** form; and the love duet *Bess, You Is My Woman Now*. The principals of the opera are also members of a larger community, virtually always onstage, whose character Gershwin portrays in communal songs. Instead of borrowing traditional spirituals, Gershwin wrote new ones, ranging in mood and technique from songful exaltation (*Leavin' for the Promise' Lan'*) and consolation (*Clara, Clara*) to stark desolation (*Gone, Gone, Gone*) and even simultaneously chanted prayers (*Oh, Doctor Jesus*), inspired by Gershwin's visits to black South Carolina churches while he was composing the work. There is also a picnic episode where the amoral Sportin' Life gets the community, softened up by a day of carousing, to join him in a mockery of biblical teaching, sung in call-and-response dialogue full of blue notes (*It Ain't Necessarily So*).

The choral numbers in *Porgy and Bess* firmly embed its tale of romantic love in a distinctive social setting. Much the same may be said of Rodgers and Hammerstein's *Oklahoma!* Based on a Broadway play from the 1930s, this show brought together a composer and a lyricist-librettist who had earlier worked successfully with other collaborators. The reception of *Oklahoma!* (1943), which ran on Broadway for 2,248 performances, surpassed that of any earlier Broadway musical. Set on a farm in the wide-open spaces of Indian territory just after 1900, *Oklahoma!* explores the old-fashioned virtues of country folk, with melodramatic touches added. Curly, a cowboy, is in love with Laurey, a virtuous young woman. Wanting to make Curly jealous, Laurey attends a box-lunch social with Jud, a brooding ranch hand. But Curly bids everything he owns in an auction for Laurey's picnic basket, and she marries him. Picking a fight with Curly, Jud is killed by accident; and the bride and groom ride off to begin their life together.

Why *Oklahoma!* won such extraordinary success has been the subject of much speculation. But for Rodgers himself, the key was that "everything in the production was made to conform to the simple open-air spirit of the story." By working forward from the setting and story rather than backward from standard musical-comedy ingredients, Rodgers, Hammerstein, and Company played with convention in a way that gave *Oklahoma!* an atmosphere all its own.

Oklahoma! (1943) marked the start of a collaboration between composer Richard Rodgers (left) and lyricist-librettist Oscar Hammerstein II that continued until Hammerstein died in 1960.

The show was also a response to the United States' involvement in World War II, which dominated the national consciousness in 1943. While it may be exaggerating to call *Oklahoma!* a patriotic musical, Rodgers later commented that the show, featuring country folk from the past with an uncomplicated view of life, aimed to give wartime audiences both pleasure and optimism. These Oklahomans, the show implied, embodied the spirit that would carry the nation through bad times. Thus, at a historical moment when the world seemed mad with aggression and brutality, *Oklahoma!* struck a responsive chord by offering audiences a vision of Americans as good-hearted people in a land filled with promise for the future.

A new context for popular songs emerged at the end of the 1920s: the movie musical. During the 1930s and 40s, the eight leading Hollywood studios made several hundred movies per year. Among the musicals produced were some whose use of music broke new ground: the animated cartoon, the story musical based on fantasy, and the dance musical.

In 1928, Walt Disney produced a short film picturing a cartoon character called Mickey Mouse as captain—with Minnie Mouse as crew—of a boat transporting a collection of animals down a river. At a time when the industry was changing from silent film to sound, the animation of *Steamboat Willie* was made to a metronome's beat, and rhythmic energy pulses through the assortment of whistles, cowbells, and tin pans featured in the sound track. The characters find musical instruments in unlikely places: Minnie Mouse cranks a donkey's tail to make the animal sing, while Mickey plays on a bull's teeth as though on a xylophone. Within a decade, Disney began to make feature-length animated films, still relying on music to carry the action, as in *Snow White and the Seven Dwarfs* (1937).

Among movie musicals based on fantasy, perhaps the era's greatest achievement was MGM's *The Wizard of Oz* (1939), which dramatized the children's tale by L. Frank Baum and featured a score by Harold Arlen and E. Y. Harburg. The film, made for more than $2.5 million at a time when a loaf of bread and a gallon of gasoline cost six cents each, relied heavily on special effects. In the familiar story, twelve-year-old Dorothy is lifted up by a cyclone from the plains of Kansas and whirled into the magic land of Oz. There she meets several strange companions who join her in a visit to the Wizard, who helps her return home. The Kansas sequences are filmed in sepia-toned black and white, but Dorothy's adventures in Oz, where she encounters a yellow brick road and an Emerald City, appear in color.

Over the Rainbow, the film's most famous song, has a clear function in the story: it shows the strength of Dorothy's imagination as she pictures a place more interesting to live than the Kansas flatland. Convinced

This image from *The Wizard of Oz* (1939) shows Judy Garland as Dorothy and Billie Burke as the Good Witch.

that the film needed a melody here with breadth and sweep, Arlen filled the bill with a ballad based on bold upward leaps. Sung by the sixteen-year-old Judy Garland playing a preadolescent, the song could not revel in the kind of romantic love that dominated the day's popular music. But with Harburg's words sketching a vivid fantasy supported by Arlen's expansive music, the number takes on a grandeur of its own.

By the late 1930s, the Hollywood musical had settled on a more-or-less standard framework: a modern-day romantic comedy that featured four or five songs and a dance or two. The key figure in the so-called dance musical was Fred Astaire, a veteran of vaudeville and Broadway, whose talents included a feeling for light comedy, reliability as a singer, and utter perfection as a dancer, though not the handsomeness of a romantic screen idol.

In 1933, Astaire signed a contract with RKO studios, and before long he was paired with actress-dancer Ginger Rogers in a collaboration, now recognized as one of the miracles of Hollywood's studio era, that by 1939 had produced nine films and established the dance musical as a genre.

In this scene from the 1935 film *Top Hat*, Ginger Rogers and Fred Astaire are dancing to Irving Berlin's *Isn't This a Lovely Day?*

Films starring Astaire and Rogers were sparked not by *more* dancing but by the use of dance to further narration and establish character. Astaire, who as a star won the right to choreograph these dances and even to help edit them, brought to his work the care of a perfectionist who might spend weeks on a three-minute dance routine. He also brought an unparalleled dramatic flair. And the drama is contained within the dancing, the only really serious element in the Astaire-Rogers films. Only rarely do the characters they play show much distinctiveness; the interest and the fun lie in how the couple overcome misunderstandings and other obstacles to a romantic happy ending through singing and dancing.

The years after World War II saw the studios' decline and a crisis for the Hollywood film industry. Many factors contributed, but none more directly than the rise of television, as radio had challenged phonograph recordings in the 1920s. When studio leaders realized that they could not compete with television, they joined forces with the new medium. Studios began producing TV series as well as, even instead of, movies. Moreover, they sold off their backlist of old movies for broadcast on the air, making television, in effect, a museum of film. The form in which these films appeared—reduced to tiny size and regularly interrupted by commercials—was far from the originals, and songs and dances in musicals, considered extraneous to the plot, were sometimes cut. Nevertheless, a new generation of Americans was able to grow acquainted with movies of an earlier day that, like some of their featured songs, occasionally approached elegance.

33

Classical Music in
the Postwar Years

AFTER WORLD WAR I, A GAP HAD OPENED BETWEEN THE CONCERT
hall and composers who were exploring the contemporary world through
music. By the 1940s, a Euro-American modernist tradition had existed for
several decades, and the end of World War II opened the door to a fresh
infusion of new music and ideas. The supply of music in the classical
sphere was growing much faster than the concert hall's demand. The concert hall's ruling formula combined edification (through the classics) with
virtuoso performance, and the notion that art could be glamorous as well
as dignified. To change that formula would risk alienating an audience
whose members found those ingredients appealing. Was it still reasonable to expect the concert hall to do justice to the classical sphere as it
now existed in the United States? And if not, what alternatives might be
found?

These were some of the questions classical musicians in America
grappled with after the war.

THE UNITED STATES
AFTER WORLD WAR II

The United States in 1946 was the world's chief military power. And as
manufacturers turned from weapons to new cars and new houses, the domestic economy boomed. The postwar era brought a new level of prosperity. Thousands of military veterans returned to school, supported by
the GI "Bill of Rights." Perhaps the most telling social trend, however,
was the increase in marriage rates and fertility. Births rose from less than
2 million per year before the war to 3.8 million in 1947 and then edged

higher, topping 4 million in every year between 1954 and 1964. Feeling more optimistic than their parents' generation, more and more young adults married, bought houses, and started families.

But even as peace and prosperity promised a bright future, dangers clouded the postwar mood. One was the atom bomb, a symbol of American superiority in science and the perils of progress. The Soviet Union, a wartime ally, now occupied much of Eastern Europe, and governments taking orders from the Communist regime in Moscow were set up in these countries against the people's will. From 1950 until 1953, U.S. soldiers fought in Korea in a conflict that started as a civil war but soon involved troops from China, which in 1949 had also been taken over by a Communist regime. The sweetness of victory had turned sour on the international front as the United States found itself in a global cold war. Moreover, the Nazi attempt to rid Europe of Jews and other "undesirables"—the Holocaust—left faith in human nature itself badly shaken.

Peace and abundance led in postwar America to a rising standard of living, and also to social restlessness. The conflicting realities of prosperity and anxiety, of wealth and discontent, of moral purpose and corruption, led many postwar artists and intellectuals to a pessimistic outlook. On the international front, new enemies replaced old; at home, Americans grew increasingly conscious that there was no adversary more to be feared than the evil within themselves.

SCHOOLS, PATRONAGE, COMPOSERS, AND THE CONCERT HALL

With several leading European composers now living on American soil, the United States no longer seemed a provincial outpost of European music-making. Home-grown classical performers such as conductor-composer Leonard Bernstein also contributed to that impression. And a growing number of professional schools were now serving the classical sphere, from conservatories to college and university departments that expanded their programs as military veterans returned to civilian life.

Teachers also benefited from Americans' support for music instruction. Both private universities and tax-supported state institutions set up professional programs for aspiring performers, composers, teachers, and writers, with curricula focused on Western art music. By the mid-twentieth century, many musicians were finding college-level teaching a way to buy time for work of their own, as scholars, composers, and performers.

Performances are the main things musicians have to sell, and the classical sphere's primary marketplace has long been the concert hall: the infrastructure of orchestra and recital halls, opera houses, and the local, regional, and national agencies that recruit their customers. But in the postwar years, the academy, while still tied to the work of the concert hall, diversified into subdisciplines that together formed an independent force. Grounded in a changing view of music history, some branches of the academy welcomed musical repertories (pre-Bach and modern) that the concert hall had excluded. And in a nation where home-grown classical composers had never played more than a small role in the concert hall, the academy included them in its framework.

Thus new composers' music, supported by the academy, and by commissions, prizes, and fellowships, gained listeners more readily outside than inside the concert hall. This academic environment shared certain

Five of America's leading classical composers of the postwar era were photographed studiously avoiding each other's gaze: (from left) Samuel Barber, Virgil Thomson, Aaron Copland, Gian Carlo Menotti, and William Schuman.

features with scientific laboratories. In 1958, Milton Babbitt likened himself and other "specialist" composers—working outside the confines of general audience esteem, or critics' approval, or the skills of most performers—to mathematicians and physicists. Freed from the need to engage with any but a specialist audience, they could explore music in the manner of researchers. At that point, the gap between concert hall and composer widened into a true split.

The concert hall in the 1920s and 30s, the one institution where the priorities of composers, performers, critics, impresarios, and audiences all had to be considered and reconciled, remained the public embodiment of the classical sphere. The academy's emergence after World War II challenged that position. As university teachers rewrote music history, and examples of specialized new music multiplied, the concert hall looked increasingly like part of a historical age that might be winding down. The academy could ignore impresarios and the general audience—both essential to the concert hall, which relied on the public for support. To a large extent, composition in postwar America reflects the split of a single hierarchy, built around the concert hall, into complementary venues with different preferences and goals.

 POSTWAR COMPOSITION

The postwar academic environment steered some composers toward approaches that could be rationally explained. Foremost among these was the serial approach invented by Arnold Schoenberg in Vienna in the early 1920s. The first and most basic form of serialism is found in twelve-tone music, in which the composer arranges all twelve pitches of the chromatic scale into a particular sequence, or series, also called the tone row. Here, twelve-tone technique substitutes for major-minor tonality, which Schoenberg abandoned around 1910, believing that music had long been evolving toward total chromaticism. Serialism offers a way to order pitches systematically without the gravitational pull of key centers.

Composers in America approached the twelve-tone technique in a variety of ways. Roger Sessions, who taught composition at the University of California and Princeton, believed with Schoenberg that certain historical laws were inherent in the nature of music itself and had been moving since the 1930s toward a more chromatic style. In 1953, he wrote a violin sonata whose opening theme contained twelve different pitches. "I caught myself using the twelve-tone system," Sessions later reported.

Aaron Copland also explored twelve-tone technique in works of the postwar era. The most dramatic proof of serialism's postwar reach, however, came from Igor Stravinsky, long considered the polar opposite of Schoenberg. In the early 1950s, Stravinsky discovered the music of Schoenberg's pupil Anton Webern and began writing twelve-tone music himself.

No musician seized more eagerly on the constructive possibilities of twelve-tone technique than Milton Babbitt. Trained as a mathematician, and teaching at Princeton University, Babbitt found beauty in the idea of a system of rationally ordered sounds. Starting with the work of Schoenberg, Webern, and Alban Berg, he extended their innovations by serializing nonpitch elements as well: rhythm, dynamics, timbre, and register. Babbitt's extensions of the serial principle produced music whose network of internal connections and relationships was formidably complex, despite such plain titles as *Three Compositions for Piano* (1947) and *Composition for Four Instruments* (1948). And Babbitt's passion for intellectual control would lead him during the late 1950s into the realm of electroacoustics.

If a musical Rip Van Winkle had fallen asleep in 1940 and awakened twenty years later, the varieties of new music would surely have surprised him. What prewar commentators had sometimes dubbed an "atonal school" had developed by 1960 into a range of idioms—freely chromatic, twelve-tone, systematically serialized, electronic, chance-based—with only atonality in common. Schoenberg's "emancipation of the dissonance" was now fully on display in the United States, as composers made music out of previously excluded sounds. In tandem with the opening up of academic positions, this emancipation brought fresh energy and excitement to the contemporary music scene.

While composers who were exploring atonality took intellectual leadership, their music was most apt to be heard outside the traditional concert hall, especially in festivals devoted to new music. Yet new works featuring triads, tonal centers, and tuneful melodies had certainly not disappeared. The composers of such music often combined these traits with angular melodies, dissonant harmonies, irregular rhythms, and an expanded range of sound to express the temper of the times. Their place in the classical sphere is reflected in the list of Pulitzer Prize–winners in music. The first was awarded in 1943, to a cantata by William Schuman, followed by a Howard Hanson symphony (1944) and in 1945 by Aaron Copland's *Appalachian Spring*. During the two postwar decades, only one atonal work—Elliott Carter's String Quartet No. 2 (1960)—won the prize. Awards in other years went to Charles Ives's Symphony No. 3 (composed four decades earlier in a tuneful idiom); symphonies by Walter Piston;

operas by Gian Carlo Menotti, Samuel Barber, Robert Ward, and Douglas Moore; and a film score by Virgil Thomson.

Against this background of opposing outlooks and fragmented institutions, Elliott Carter emerged during the 1950s as a unique figure: a respected composer who worked his way toward a more and more complex atonal musical style while steering clear of musical systems. Born in New York in 1908, Carter attended Harvard College. In 1932, he went to Paris to continue his schooling in the liberal arts while also studying music with Nadia Boulanger. His works of the 1930s were generally considered "neoclassical," but after the war he began writing music of marked

Elliott Carter (b. 1908) in the early 1970s outside Lincoln Center in New York.

individuality: a piano sonata (1946), a sonata for cello and piano (1948), and his first string quartet (1951). From the piano sonata on, admirers saw each new work by Carter as a daring advance. And in 1962, Carter's music received a compliment that boosted his already solid reputation: Stravinsky, whose age, eminence, and barbed comments on the musical scene had made him an imposing presence, pronounced Carter's Double Concerto for piano, harpsichord, and small orchestra a masterpiece.

By the time Stravinsky's tribute was published, Carter had already won distinction beyond the Pulitzer Prize, though his recent music remained unknown to the public at large. Carter's innovative use of rhythm had drawn particular attention. But in 1959, he offered a cautionary view of composition. "One technical fad after another has swept over 20th-century music as the music of each of its leading composers has come to be intimately known," he wrote. "Each fad lasted a few years, only to be discarded by the succeeding generation of composers, then by the music profession, and finally by certain parts of the interested public." That process, Carter warned, left in its wake many "gifted composers whose music . . . is suffocated . . . by its similarity to other music of the same type." By calling recent trends fads, Carter was condemning the tendency to try out styles without committing to them. In his view, a composer's style constituted an artistic identity, beyond the reach of fashion. As for his own music, it resisted explanation by any standard theoretical system.

LISTENING GUIDE 56

String Quartet No. 1, excerpt (Carter)

Nearly half a century after it was written, Carter's String Quartet No. 1 seems on its way to a place in the standard chamber music repertory. It is also a work Carter has singled out as crucial to his own development. While preparing to compose the quartet, Carter found himself contemplating the question of "humanly experienced time" as imagined by German novelist Thomas Mann in *The Magic Mountain*. The First Quartet is a commentary on the passing of time itself, especially in the realm of dreams. But how might one compose music whose subject is time? Part of Carter's answer was to abandon a steady beat and unchanging meter, standard devices sometimes taken to represent clock time. Another part was to "personalize" the instruments in the hope that listeners might hear them as a conversation among contrasting musical voices.

The result of these imaginative leaps is music relying less on repetition than on "many-layered contrasts of character—hence of theme or motive, rhythm, and styles of playing." The recorded example, in which each instrument establishes its own character and rate of speed, shows the textural complexity that confronts the listener before the performance is even thirty bars old. In following Carter's complex musical textures, listeners may find it helpful to imagine that the composer has divided his authority among four performing rivals.

For some composers, the impulse to write music came more from science than from literature. As early as 1917, Franco-American composer Edgard Varèse had proclaimed: "I dream of instruments obedient to my thought." Two decades later, Varèse forecast a time when composers would render their scores directly "on a machine that will faithfully transmit the musical content to the listener."

Varèse was one of many composers who in the century's earlier years imagined music made or altered electrically. Progress was slow until the magnetic tape recorder was perfected in the late 1940s; from then on, electroacoustic music came into its own. An international survey published in 1974 estimated that more than 2,000 composers, working in some 500 electronic music studios, had by then produced more than 10,000 electronic compositions, not to mention their wide use in popular genres. The trends outlined here have since accelerated, especially the increasing variety of sounds and the technology's accessibility and appeal. Moreover, with one instrument able to produce the sound of many, the demand for acoustic music and its performers has dropped.

In 1952, the first American tape-music concert took place. The music was made with equipment entirely different from the standard "hardware" of a musical education: tape recorders, a generator of sound sig-

Edgard Varèse (1883–1965), French-born American composer, listening in 1959 to his *Poème électronique.*

Milton Babbitt (b. 1917) at the RCA synthesizer.

nals, devices for filtering sound, scissors, razor blade, splicing block, and magnetic tape. While Western music making had always involved some acoustical know-how, electroacoustic music posed different challenges. A new sound palette was available, but to control it required knowledge and experience that few musicians possessed.

Although Varèse was nearing seventy when the technology he had imagined came into general use, he used it in *Poème électronique* (1957–58). Collaborating with the Swiss architect Le Corbusier, Varèse composed this work for the Brussels World's Fair of 1959. Here, he realized his long-time dream of creating music to exist in space as well as time. The work was tape recorded and then played through 425 loudspeakers, arranged so that the sound could sweep across and around the curves of Le Corbusier's building. Varèse's achievement proved fleeting, however, for the pavilion was torn down after the fair closed.

Composers of electroacoustic music in the early 1950s faced huge amounts of tedious labor: recording sounds on tape, rerecording them, and then manually splicing the bits of tape together to create the music itself. In 1959, however, the Radio Corporation of America installed in the Columbia University studio the Mark II, an advanced model of an electronic sound synthesizer that became the heart of the Columbia-Princeton Electronic Music Center. The synthesizer, which constituted and shaped the sounds, did away with the need to rerecord and to splice tape. Further, an instrument able to control precisely such elements as rhythm, dynamics, and timbre as well as pitch proved well suited to Milton Babbitt's ideal of totally organized music. He used the Mark II to create his *Composition for Synthesizer* (1961) and *Ensembles for Synthesizer* (1964). He also combined live performance with synthesized sound in such works as *Vision and Prayer* (1961) and *Philomel* (1964).

LISTENING GUIDE 57

Philomel, excerpt (Babbitt)

Sung to words by poet John Hollander, *Philomel* unites virtuoso singing with electronic wizardry to create a modern version of an ancient myth. Philomela and Procne are daughters of the King of Athens. Procne, who has married King Tereus of Thrace, asks Tereus to bring her sister from Athens for a visit. On the journey, the king grows enchanted with the grace and beauty of Philomela. Overcome by lust, he rapes her, then cuts out her tongue to guarantee her silence. After imprisoning Philomela in a secluded Thracian cottage, he tells Procne that her sister has died on the voyage. Philomela, however, weaves a tapestry depicting Tereus's crime and sends it to Procne, who understands its message. Procne rescues Philomela, and the two return to Athens. The sisters than avenge the rape by inviting Tereus to a banquet and serving him the cooked flesh of his own son. When Tereus discovers what he has eaten, he pursues the sisters into the forest. The gods protect Philomela by turning her into a nightingale.

Hollander's text is sung by the character Philomela, a soprano, accompanied by the recorded voice of Bethany Beardslee (who commissioned the work and sings it here) and a "score" of synthesized sound. The recorded excerpt, from the second section, shows Philomela, now a nightingale, singing an "Echo Song." Asking a thrush, a hawk, an owl, a raven, and a gull for help in adjusting to her new form, she is refused each time by the echoing tape. (In the third section, she finds her own true voice.) Babbitt's demanding score requires the singer to negotiate a range from F-sharp below middle C to B above the staff, as well as speaking and acting the role.

Although Varèse, Babbitt, and others explored the new medium vigorously, John Cage was the first American to complete a tape composition: *Imaginary Landscape No. 5* (1952). And later that year, Cage composed a remarkable work he called *Williams Mix*.

LISTENING GUIDE 58

Williams Mix (Cage)

Cage began work on *Williams Mix* by gathering a "library" of sounds divided into six categories. The letters on the score indicate the different sound categories; the shapes show how the tape was cut and spliced. Track 1 on this page, for example, begins with a D (manually produced) sound that gives way to a bit of A (city) sound mixed with D. After a brief silence, C (electronic) sound is mixed with F (small) sound. Underlined capital letters signify sounds that are given a patterned rhythm by rerecording a loop of tape. And sound categories are further modified by the small letters "c" and "v" that follow each capital. The first means that the sound has been controlled—from the standpoint of pitch, timbre (sound quality), and loudness. The second means that the sound has not been controlled. In track 1, for example, the first instruction, "Dvvv," calls for a manually produced sound whose pitch, timbre, and loudness have not been controlled—i.e., catalogued.

Cage produced the score by a process of random ordering, involving charts, chance, and the *I-Ching* (the Chinese *Book of Changes*, which he had encountered when he began to study Zen Buddhism in the late 1940s). Sounds were chosen by consulting sixteen charts built around the six sound categories with their controlled and uncontrolled permutations. The charts were constructed out of numbers arrived at by tossing coins and keeping track of the results (heads or tails), and the numbers were interpreted and transferred to the charts by consulting the *I-Ching*. If *Williams Mix* sounds like a random collection of sounds, that is exactly what Cage intended.

Williams Mix united Cage's interest in technology with a new philosophical outlook he adopted in the early 1950s. The philosophy, religion, and art of the West assumed that humans, created in the image of God, were destined to rule over nature. From a non-Western perspective, however, human beings were simply one of many species of life, and nature itself tended more toward randomness than order. The cumbersome process of composition that lay behind *Williams Mix*—255 seconds of music that took Cage and collaborators nine months to create—was inspired by a principle found in Indian philosophy: "Art is the imitation of Nature in her manner of operation."

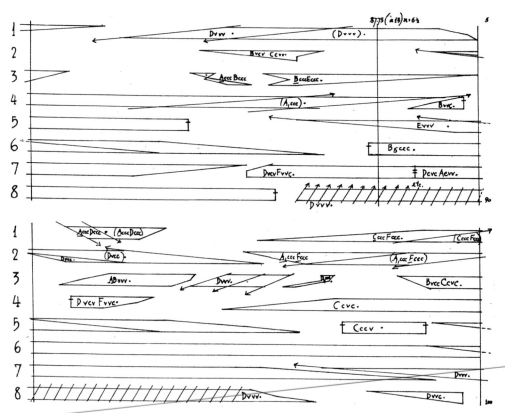

A page from the score of John Cage's *Williams Mix* (1952). The eight lines represent eight-track reel-to-reel tape that runs at fifteen inches per second.

In Cage's earlier days, he had assumed that the opposite of sound was silence, and that music was built on the duration of sounds. Then, in 1951, Cage decided that absolute silence did not exist: that sounds were always present, some intended and others not. If a composer embraced both kinds of sounds, the consequences could be profound. Once Cage dissolved the split between intention and nonintention, he avidly explored the latter. Much of his creative energy went toward setting up mechanical procedures that would bring sounds into compositions independent of his own will, hence with no deliberate link to other sounds.

4'33", Cage's most famous work, was composed the same year as *Williams Mix* but copied nature's manner of operation in an entirely different way. Conceived as a three-movement structure whose proportions—30", 2'23", and 1'40"—were determined by chance methods, *4'33"* prescribed no intentional sounds at all. Cage's "silent" piece invited listeners to pay attention to random sounds in the environment, in effect emptying themselves of expectations. Among other things, *4'33"* could be viewed as a spiritual exercise, a means of quieting the will so that an infinite realm of possibilities may be experienced.

Concert hall audiences rejected these ideas. Still, Cage had never counted on the concert hall for much support, nor did he enter academia. From early in his composing career, he managed to scrape together a living by collaborating with other artists, chiefly dancers. In the 1940s, he served as accompanist for a dance company headed by Merce Cunningham, later becoming its music director (1953). The early 1950s found him

John Cage (1912–1992), composer and explorer of unintended sounds.

collaborating with other composers, including Morton Feldman, Christian Wolff, Earle Brown, and David Tudor, all of whom assisted him in preparing materials for *Williams Mix*. Meanwhile, Cage had also become a friend and champion of the painters Robert Rauschenberg and Jasper Johns, whose rise to fame as members of the New York School of Abstract Expressionism helped indirectly to further Cage's own work.

Cage's ideas won him a reputation during the 1950s, if not as a composer then as either a satirist or a musical anarchist. These opinions persisted well into the 1960s and, in some quarters, even up to his death in 1992. Yet though often scorned and attacked, Cage also found himself in increasing demand as a lecturer and performer. In Europe, under Cage's influence, the German composer Karlheinz Stockhausen began in the mid-1950s to experiment with chance operations. Many younger Americans took Cage's example as a jumping-off point for work of their own. *Silence* (1961), the first of several compilations of Cage's lectures and writings, established him as a significant writer on music; winning a wide readership, it has remained in print to this day.

Music in the Western world has long been considered an art of expression, and Cage wrote his last "intentionally expressive" music in 1951. His composing philosophy, which replaces intellectual analysis and the pursuit of one's desires with "purposeless play," offers a radical prescription for emptying the mind, in contrast to academic instruction and the Western musical tradition itself, which both strive to fill it. On the strength of that liberating doctrine, Cage is often proclaimed a key figure in twentieth-century music.

John Cage Explains Why He Writes Music (1957)

And what is the purpose of writing music? One is, of course, not dealing with purposes but dealing with sounds. Or the answer must take the form of paradox: a purposeful purposelessness or a purposeless play. This play, however, is an affirmation of life—not an attempt to bring order out of chaos nor to suggest improvements in creation, but simply a way of waking up to the very life we're living, which is so excellent once one gets one's mind and one's desires out of its way and lets it act of its own accord.

In 1959, Igor Stravinsky (center, foreground) conducted a New York performance of his earlier work *The Wedding*, with composers (left to right) Samuel Barber, Lukas Foss, Aaron Copland, and Roger Sessions as pianists.

 EPILOGUE

On April 6, 1964, a composition for baritone voice and three clarinets was premiered in California whose symbolic importance far outweighs its length (barely ninety seconds). *Elegy for J.F.K.*, composed by the eighty-one-year-old Igor Stravinsky, mourns the assassination on November 22, 1963, of President John F. Kennedy. Stravinsky, who died in 1971, filled a unique place in American musical life: an embodiment of a musical age governed by axioms thought to be historically necessary. Stravinsky's embrace of twelve-tone technique in the 1950s had raised serialism in some circles to near-axiomatic status. And now the Russian-born master, long an American citizen, was using his rarefied art to commemorate the nation's fallen leader.

But as we mark this moment of quiet homage, we hear offstage rumblings: the start of a stylistic earthquake that would soon overwhelm the notion of historical necessity in classical composition. To be sure, atonality and serialism were well established. But so were diatonic approaches, as used by Samuel Barber, whose *Antony and Cleopatra* opened New York's new Metropolitan Opera House in 1966, and William Schuman, who continued composing after assuming the presidency in 1962 of the Lincoln Center for the Performing Arts. In April 1965, Charles Ives's Symphony No. 4, composed between 1910 and 1916, was heard in full for the first time. That event, suggesting links between Ives and other "experimental" American composers, including Henry Cowell, Harry Partch, Lou Harrison, Conlan Nancarrow, and John Cage, raised new questions about this nation's dependence on the European past. Electroacoustic possibilities were also being explored. And in 1964, Terry Riley composed *In C*, whose obsessive repetition of simple diatonic fragments outlined a style that was soon labeled "minimalist." Finally, with only Igor Stravinsky left from a past when great composers were thought to define the heart of musical endeavor, other kinds of music were also challenging the classical sphere's place atop the nation's musical hierarchy.

34

"Rock Around the Clock"

THE RISE OF ROCK AND ROLL

IN 1959, A PRESTIGIOUS UNIVERSITY PRESS PUBLISHED A BOOK OF essays called *The Art of Jazz*, a title meant to be provocative. Over the past two decades, the editor told his readers, a body of criticism had accumulated around jazz—the kind of writing "that only an art can inspire and that only an art deserves." Gathered in *The Art of Jazz*, these writings focused on the music itself, especially as preserved on record. While far from the most lucrative popular music in the postwar years, jazz was the only one then being taken seriously by critics. Popular-music stars received plenty of publicity, but it was a kind that treated them more as celebrities than as artists.

That situation changed after 1965. Today, many writers are critiquing popular music and exploring its history. This new inclination owes much to the example of jazz critics, who, by discussing jazz in a way that only an art deserves, vouched for the music's excellence. But only *by treating performances as the equivalent of compositions* were they able to claim authority for their judgments. Phonograph records made that possible by turning onetime performances into permanent works. Fashioned by singers and players in collaboration with composers, arrangers, producers, and technicians, recordings were defined not by musical notation but by their sound; they became the means through which historical trends could be traced, first in jazz, then in other kinds of popular music.

 YOUTH AND IDENTITY

No social fact about music in the years after World War II is more noteworthy than the growing influence of teenagers in the marketplace. While the rise of the youthful popular-music fan has often been linked to the advent of rock and roll in the 1950s, teenagers had actually entered the popular sphere's marketplace with a bang at least a decade earlier. In 1944, when the twenty-nine-year-old crooner Frank Sinatra played an engagement at New York's Paramount Theater, his popularity was so great that his fans—mostly females belonging to the "bobby-socks brigade," ages twelve to sixteen—packed the theater long before the show began. When he appeared onstage, they screamed in adoration. "Girls have plucked hairs from his head and, at somewhat less trouble to him, have collected clippings of his hair from the floors of barbershops," a magazine article reported. "One Sinatra fan carried around in a locket what she insists is a Sinatra hangnail."

What gave a popular singer the power to inspire such adoring reverence? To experts of the time, generational conflict seemed the best explanation. The winner of a "Why I Like Frank Sinatra" essay contest, held in 1946 in Detroit, called Sinatra "one of the greatest things that ever happened to Teen Age America," because he made up for feelings of neglect. "We were the kids that never got much attention," the author explained. "But he's made us feel like we're something. . . . He gives us sincerity in return for our faithfulness."

Frank Sinatra (1915–1999) in the early 1940s, as singer with the Tommy Dorsey Orchestra.

In the postwar era, a growing "generation gap" did much to transform the popular sphere, especially as a business enterprise. Its cause was simple: American youth in those years was searching for social identity. Novelist J. D. Salinger's *The Catcher in the Rye* (1951), written from an adolescent's perspective, seemed to speak for the whole postwar generation. Its hero, sixteen-year-old Holden Caulfield, experiences growing up as a process of disillusionment. The adult society described in the book is so corrupt—"phony" is a key word—that only through a teenager's eyes can innocence be glimpsed. Movies also took up the theme, with a young Marlon Brando and an even younger James Dean playing characters who sullenly resisted adult notions of virtue and respectability. Dean's career involved starring roles in only three films, the most famous being *Rebel Without a Cause* (1956), before he was killed in a car crash at age twenty-four. Many youngsters, like Dean's characters, felt alienated, and they found reasons to blame older generations for creating a society that evoked such feelings.

Postwar teenagers also grew up with money to spend and exposure to an array of media that now included television as well as recordings, movies, newspapers and magazines, and radio. By the 1950s, the mass media were introducing Americans to experiences far beyond their own. Within popular music, many middle-class youngsters chose the cultural alternative of downward mobility to claim turf that was supposedly more authentic than that of their elders. "If rock 'n' roll had had no other value," declared a writer who was a teenager in those years, "it would have been enough merely to dent the smug middle-class consciousness of that time."

FROM RHYTHM AND BLUES TO ROCK AND ROLL

As the decade of the 1950s dawned, rhythm and blues, the industry's label for black popular music, stood relatively low in the music-business hierarchy. The music can be traced back to styles of the Mississippi Delta as modified in Chicago and other cities, but with influence from black swing bands, such as Lionel Hampton's, and the small-band, up-tempo-blues approach of Louis Jordan, with elements of piano boogie-woogie mixed in. The ensemble makeup was far from standard. Groups might feature a lead singer or an instrumentalist or both, plus an assortment of other instruments. The rhythm section might include double bass or electric bass guitar, plus drums, guitar, and a keyboard instrument (piano or organ). The backup group might also include any combination of voices, wind instruments, guitar, or organ. The meter was always duple, with the so-called back beats—the second and fourth of a four-beat measure—often accented. Beyond these fundamentals, rhythm and blues featured lead singers (e.g., Clyde McPhatter, Sam Cooke) who might work alone or as part of a group (the Drifters, the Orioles, the Coasters). The song lyrics, mostly about love life, gravitated during the 1950s increasingly toward teenagers. Twelve-bar blues and thirty-two-bar song forms predominated.

An increase in the number of companies that produced rhythm-and-blues records points to the music's growing strength in the postwar marketplace. Famous bandleaders like Hampton and Jordan recorded on major labels. But much of the music came from new, independent firms, including Savoy (founded in 1942 in Newark, New Jersey), King (1944, Cincinnati), Modern (1945, Los Angeles), Atlantic (1947, New York), Aristocrat-Chess (1947, Chicago), Peacock (1949, Houston), and Sun (1952, Memphis). Direct, unself-conscious, celebrating bodily joys, rooted in black traditions, yet stylized for distribution in the modern marketplace, postwar "race" music was targeted for black listeners, though most company owners and producers were white.

Rhythm and blues owed much to broadcasting. During the 1930s, there had been no such thing as a radio station aimed at black listeners. As black radio began to take shape, however, the new record labels began to serve them. And after the war, across the southern United States, black radio matured, with the founding of stations centered on rhythm and blues and also, depending on their location, offering gospel, traditional blues, or jazz. The R&B artists active in recording and broadcasting were also experienced live performers who learned their trade in the theaters, dance halls, clubs, tent shows, and other black venues that comprised the "chitlin circuit." Broadcasting increased the diversity of their audience: whites could listen to black radio, and they could buy records by black artists. As one industry figure put it, "you could segregate schoolrooms and buses, but not the airwaves."

Another avenue to rhythm and blues opened up in 1951 when white Cleveland disc jockey Alan Freed learned from a local record store owner that white youngsters were buying records previously thought to be exclusively "Negro music." Freed, then working as a classical-record host, responded by starting "The Moondog Show," a youth-oriented program centered on rhythm-and-blues recordings and broadcast across the Midwest. As Moondog, Freed won immediate success, speaking the language of his mostly teenage audience. Before long, he was organizing live rhythm-and-blues shows in Cleveland that attracted racially mixed crowds.

Alan Freed, who, working in Cleveland in the early 1950s, became one of the first white disc jockeys to play rhythm-and-blues recordings for white youth.

Alan Freed would soon win national fame for introducing white teenagers to rhythm and blues. But no contribution was more lasting than the label he gave the music: "rock and roll." Although Freed borrowed the term from African-American song, where it was sometimes used to mean sexual intercourse, only insiders knew that. The general public accepted "rock and roll" as a name that was free of racial overtones and fit the style. In fact, the label has been claimed as a key to the racial crossover. For when white show-business entrepreneurs began substituting "rock and roll" for "rhythm and blues," racial identification was glossed over, and young white fans of the music were spared conflict. The new label encouraged white acceptance of the music by suppressing its black roots.

A white author who was twelve years old in 1955 explained that he and his friends found rock and roll appealing because it "provided us with a release and a justification that we had never dreamt of." The music made it easy to offend grown-ups, to mock "the sanctimoniousness of public figures," and to draw a "clear line of demarcation between *us* and *them*."

Together with excitement, the new music offered a chance to redefine "us" and "them." By casting their lot with performers like Chuck Berry, Little Richard, and Jerry Lee Lewis, white middle-class teenagers could feel as if they were taking a stand for freedom, high spirits, emotional truth, and fun, and against the confining proprieties of middle-class life. The music testified that youth now constituted a social group with its own modes of expression. Moreover, the freedom to draw lines was granted not by parents, teachers, or clergy but by the consumer marketplace. Youngsters in comfortable circumstances could now get a taste of feeling rebellious without actually having to rebel. And in the mid-1950s, no entertainer was better known for redrawing the boundary lines than Elvis Presley.

ELVIS PRESLEY IN MEMPHIS

That story begins with Presley, born in 1935 in Mississippi, as a teenager in Memphis, where he and his parents had moved in the late 1940s. Presley's mother and father had little money to spare for their son's musical education. But as a youth with an avid appetite for music, he sampled a wide variety. Elvis was a fan of local black radio, especially WDIA, where B. B. King, a singer and guitar player from the Mississippi Delta, was just starting out as a disc jockey. Memphis was also a place where white gospel quartet singing flourished. That tradition, which grew out of singing schools of the nineteenth century, had been started by publishing firms that hired male quartets to travel and perform from the company's sacred tunebooks. By the mid-twentieth century, some quartets were making records and singing on the radio. Though their repertory was all sacred, they were polished performers who bantered with their crowds and sang spiritual songs that listeners could tap their feet to. Gospel quartet music was the center of Presley's musical universe for a time.

Indeed, there seems to have been no kind of music that the young Elvis Presley did not love. He listened to Eddy Arnold, Hank Williams, and other country stars, and to such pop singers as Teresa Brewer, Bing Crosby, Eddie Fisher, and Perry Como. He attended classical orchestra concerts at an outdoor Memphis park. Dramatic tenor Mario Lanza and the Metropolitan Opera radio broadcasts were also on his menu of listening favorites. Accounts of Presley's early years leave the impression of a painfully shy loner with a rich fantasy life revolving around music. "I just loved music. Music period," he later told an interviewer. Though without formal training or experience as a performer, he nursed an obsessive wish to become a singer. And that desire led him, shortly after he graduated from high school, to the office of Sun Records, founded and run by Sam Phillips.

Phillips, a white native of Florence, Alabama, had moved to Memphis and in 1950 opened a recording studio to provide a place where black entertainers would feel free to play and record their music. By 1953, that dream had led to rhythm-and-blues hits on the Sun label by such black artists as Rufus Thomas and Junior Parker. In that year, the eighteen-year-old Elvis Presley showed up at the Sun studio and paid $3.98 plus tax for the chance to be recorded, singing to his own guitar accompaniment. Presley chose a pair of sentimental ballads for the occasion, and Phillips's assistant made a note next to the boy's name: "Good ballad singer. Hold." And that was where Presley's singing career rested for about a year.

In the summer of 1954, Scotty Moore, a guitarist who led a country music band, was looking for a singer to record with, and Sam Phillips suggested Presley. An audition was set up at the Sun studio. Toward the end of the session, "this song popped into my mind that I had heard years ago," Elvis later recalled, "and I started kidding around with it." The song was *That's All Right*, a rhythm and blues number by Arthur Crudup, a Mississippi-born bluesman.

Guitarist Scotty Moore Describes Elvis Presley's First Recording Session

All of a sudden . . . Elvis just started singing this song, jumping around and acting the fool, and then Bill [Black] picked up his bass, and he started acting the fool, too, and I started playing with them. Sam, I think, had the door to the control booth open—I don't know, he was either editing some tape, or doing something—and he stuck his head out and said, "What are you doing?" And we said, "We don't know." "Well, back up," he said, "try to find a place to start, and do it again."

Surprised that Presley even knew a song by Arthur Crudup, Sam Phillips was struck even more with the originality, freshness, and exuberance of the performance.

Artistic breakthroughs of such consequence are rare, and eyewitness accounts of them even rarer. This story pinpoints the moment when an artist who would soon number his fans in the millions first unlocked the door to a fresh realm of personal expression. But if the connection that forged the key was made by the creative mind of Elvis Presley, he stumbled onto it through musical collaboration. The creative spark lit by Presley's clowning was fanned by the musicians in the studio with him and also by Sam Phillips, who captured the moment on tape.

The musical process behind *That's All Right* contradicts the assumption that the role of creator is always filled by a composer. For what was actually composed in the Sun studio was a *record*: a recording of a performance whose elements included Arthur Crudup's song, Elvis Presley's singing, Scotty Moore and Bill Black's accompaniment, and Sam Phillips's response to the result. In fact, rock and roll itself was grounded in recording. It became popular not so much through live performances but through records played on the radio. That the makers of rock and roll embraced technology from the start is dramatized by Presley's Memphis audition; Sam Phillips was interested in how Presley sang, but also in how he sounded on tape.

Phillips knew immediately that something important had happened in Elvis's first recording session. In 1959, he told a Memphis reporter that in the early 1950s "you could sell a half million copies of a rhythm and blues record" but no more, because the appeal to white youngsters was limited. "They liked the music, but they weren't sure whether they ought to like it or not. So I got to thinking how many records you could sell if you could find white performers who could play and sing in this same exciting, alive way." In Elvis Presley, Phillips found what he had been looking for: a singer who discovered in a black performing style a catalyst for an exciting, alive style of his own.

Considering the obscurity in which his career began, Presley's rise to

Elvis Presley (1935–1977), singing in Memphis in 1956 to an audience of ecstatic young listeners.

fame took place with amazing speed. The arena open to a singer of his background was that of country music, so after his first Sun recording was released, he began touring the South with a troupe headlined by country star Hank Snow. Radio appearances on the Grand Ole Opry from Nashville and the Louisiana Hayride from Shreveport were also sandwiched in. The role of professional performer encouraged the shy young man to shed some of his natural inhibitions, unleashing a magnetic, sexually charged onstage presence that worked young audiences into a state of frenzy. But if Presley's showmanship seemed to spring from God-given talent and an innate grasp of audience psychology, he also showed an interest in self-improvement. His first manager recalled a day in 1955 when he dropped by the Presley house and found the singer "with a stack of records—Ray Charles and Big Joe Turner and Big Mama Thornton and Arthur 'Big Boy' Crudup—that he studied with all the avidity that other kids focused on their college exams." Presley soon left Sam Phillips's Sun Records for RCA Victor and found a new manager. *Billboard* magazine's comment on the move recognizes Elvis's challenge to the industry's marketing structure: "Altho Sun has sold Presley primarily as a c.&w. [country-and-western] artist, Victor plans to push his platters in all three fields—pop, r.&b., and c.&w."

Another factor in Presley's rise to fame was his presence on national television. In January 1956, he made the first of several appearances on "Stage Show," a CBS variety program featuring the swing musicians Tommy and Jimmy Dorsey and their big band. Elvis raced onto the stage and swung into a performance of Joe Turner's *Shake, Rattle, and Roll*, complete with acrobatic gyrations and bursting with the sheer joy of performing. By the time he made his last appearance on "Stage Show" in March, he was riding a wave that carried him to Hollywood for a screen test. Records, radio, television, and press coverage had made a national star of a young man who, less than two years earlier, had discovered his musical persona in a recording studio in Memphis. At twenty-one, Presley in early 1956 was the hottest act in show business, though what *kind* of an act was still open to debate.

RACE, GENRE, AND ROCK AND ROLL

Elvis Presley rode to stardom on the tide of a cultural phenomenon so strong and inevitable that the music would probably have happened without him. His main achievement was the huge audience of teenagers that he captured for rock and roll almost overnight.

Rock and roll owed much of its popularity to differences from the music of Tin Pan Alley. Musical traits included a driving 4/4 time, accenting the first beat of each bar and some backbeats; a fondness for twelve-bar blues form; the use of amplified instruments, especially electric guitar; blues-influenced singing; and alternating vocal sections with instrumental ones played by tenor sax, electric guitar, or keyboard soloists. Many early rock-and-roll hits were white performers' versions of rhythm-and-blues songs, with lyrics about love and sex. The rather grating singing style of many performers, wholly unsuited to Western art music or even Tin Pan Alley, derived from rural music, both white and black.

Thus, rock-and-roll performers drew a hard line between themselves and the Broadway–Tin Pan Alley kinship with the classical sphere. They also distanced themselves from folk and blues singers by embracing technology and avidly pursuing commercial success; from jazz musicians by emphasizing fixed versions of pieces that were easily accessible to audiences; and from gospel performers through their secular subject matter. And unlike rock and roll, rhythm and blues and country music were intended for grown-up listeners. Ray Charles, whose recordings ranked high on rhythm-and-blues popularity charts, insisted that "I never considered myself part of rock 'n' roll." Charles thought of Chuck Berry, Little Richard, and Bo Diddley as the leaders in that style, and he found "a towering difference" between their music and his own. "My stuff was more adult," he explained. "It was more difficult for teenagers to relate to . . . more serious, filled with more despair than anything you'd associate with rock 'n' roll."

Rock and roll's impact on the popular music business was revealed by its domination of *Billboard*'s popular, or "Top 100," record-sales chart. But that was only the start. Until the mid-1950s, each *Billboard* chart reflected a market with its own performers, radio stations, and retail outlets; the idea of a disc crossing over from one chart to another was unheard of. Record industry professionals were caught off guard in the summer of 1955, when *Rock Around the Clock,* by Bill Haley and the Comets, the top single on the popular (i.e., white) chart, also appeared on the rhythm-and-blues chart. Then Chuck Berry's *Maybellene,* which topped the rhythm-and-blues charts, appeared in the fall on the popular chart and remained there for fourteen weeks. And then *Heartbreak Hotel,* by Elvis Presley, topped *both* the popular and country-western lists, while also rising to No. 5 on the rhythm-and-blues chart. Rock and roll was proving to be a truly interracial expression. Barriers that had long separated country music, rhythm and blues, and pop seemed in danger of collapsing.

Bill Haley and the Comets, whose hit *Rock Around the Clock* helped to start the national craze for rock and roll in the mid-1950s

The spectacle of eroding barriers in the music business mirrored a historic change that was under way in American society. For as young white listeners reveled in a new, black-inspired popular music, black Americans had entered a new phase in their fight to secure the rights of citizenship. *Brown vs. Board of Education* (1954), the Supreme Court decision that declared school segregation illegal, touched off a period of conflict. White Southern opposition, while denying violent intent, fueled an environment that condoned violence, and politicians found ways to encourage the defiance of court orders without actually advocating it.

In the civil rights movement, black Southerners fought with dignity for civil liberties, using the weapons at their disposal, including civil disobedience and nonviolent confrontation. They also educated whites about the evils of segregation. In 1955, a boycott led by the twenty-six-year-old

Reverend Martin Luther King Jr. succeeded in desegregating public transportation in Montgomery, Alabama. And in the early 1960s, "sit-ins" and "freedom marches" came to be standard nonviolent tactics. Black citizens joined forces to secure the equality guaranteed in principle by federal court decisions, and eventually by the landmark Civil Rights Act that Congress passed in 1964, followed by the Voting Rights Act of 1965.

The mass media also helped to weaken racial barriers. In the Montgomery boycott's early days, the city's newspapers either ignored the story or attacked the nonriders for undermining the bus system. But a local TV station that covered the boycott drew attention to Montgomery when the national network began picking up its telecasts. Before long, reporters were arriving to follow what seemed to many non-Southerners a modern morality play: an example of ordinary Americans standing up for basic rights. With outside witnesses on the scene, white authorities were constrained from using physical violence. At the same time, their presence encouraged the black leadership and its followers.

Meanwhile, Southern white youngsters were beginning to cross the color line to embrace so-called race music—at least as embodied in the new style called rock and roll. And that fact makes it seem no coincidence that in 1954–55, when the laws supporting segregation in the South were being challenged, young white audiences around the country were embracing black-derived musical styles as their own. Teenagers who bought rock-and-roll records surely did so more as fans of the music than as champions of racial equality. Yet by accepting rock and roll with enthusiasm, white teenagers endorsed a sensibility shaped by black Americans. The tide that carried rock and rollers to fame was grounded in a process of social change that reached far beyond music.

35

Songs of Loneliness
and Praise

POSTWAR POPULAR TRENDS

ONCE ROCK AND ROLL'S ECONOMIC STRENGTH WAS REVEALED, AND with the advent of the 45-rpm single, the record business boomed. Revenues from record sales increased from $191 million in 1951 to $514 million in 1959; the first big leaps took place in 1955 and 1956, when teenagers entered the marketplace in droves. From 1955 on, the Top 100 *Billboard* chart measured the preferences of a younger segment of the population than ever before.

The pop single, though, was only one of many products in a market that now included the "long-playing" record (33 1/3 rpm). The Tin Pan Alley songwriting tradition remained alive and well. As we have seen, the popular sphere's main goal has always been audience accessibility; this preoccupation has also kept Broadway shows separate from opera, which aspires to transcendence in line with its classical pedigree. Yet a number of hit shows of the 1950s (and before), by Rodgers and Hammerstein, Lerner and Loewe, Bernstein and Sondheim, Frank Loesser, and others, have showed clear signs of transcendence by being revived in later years. Moreover, during "The Age of Rock," beginning around 1955, some songs—standards—written as early as the 1920s by Broadway and Tin Pan Alley tunesmiths were still being performed.

Standards were fundamental to the popular-song trade, and economics suggest why. At the end of the 1950s, Irving Berlin and Cole Porter, among others, were still making a handsome income from songs they had written in the past, and the Gershwin, Kern, and Hart estates remained lucrative. Indeed, one reason the older tradition endured was that many of its leading songwriters were still on the scene. Another was the presence of experienced singers who had learned their trade with Swing Era big bands. A third reason was the large adult audience, people who had grown up with the music and still considered it theirs. A fourth was that

448

jazz musicians had drawn many of their own standards from popular song, and listeners were used to hearing their favorite songs in multiple versions. Finally, there was the issue of quality. As early as 1925, *Variety* had recognized the uncanny match between words and music that American songwriters were achieving. As lyricist Yip Harburg put it: "Words make you think thoughts; music makes you feel a feeling; and a song makes you feel a thought."

In the postwar era, then, the classical sphere's ideal of transcendence won a beachhead in the popular sphere. And one of its champions was Frank Sinatra. Between 1953 and 1961, Sinatra recorded no fewer than sixteen "concept albums"—proof that the "single" disc was not the only way for a pop singer to reach the public on record. The twelve songs on *Frank Sinatra Sings Only the Lonely*, for example, an album of Nelson Riddle arrangements recorded in 1958, span almost three decades, starting in the early 1930s. As a group, they maintain a generally melancholy mood, with Riddle's orchestrations providing a contemporary sound. Aimed at adults, a concept album like this one connected songs that had been written separately, and testified to the excellence Sinatra found in the work of such songwriters as Harold Arlen, Johnny Mercer, Matt Dennis, Sammy Cahn, and Jimmy Van Heusen.

Meanwhile, country music in the postwar years was also flourishing. With prosperity growing in the South, the demand for amusement quickened. The Grand Ole Opry now had radio competition from other barndance programs, and jukeboxes reverberated with songs by such country entertainers as Eddy Arnold, Kitty Wells, and Hank Williams. Country

Hank Williams (1923–1953), singer, guitarist, and songwriter whose music continued to be a presence in country music long after his early death.

songs also appeared in the popular mainstream. In 1951, *Tennessee Waltz*, by the country writer and performer Pee Wee King, was turned into a national hit record by Patti Page, in a performance style essentially free of regional traits. The song's mainstream success seemed to indicate that Southern songwriters' emotional directness could jump barriers of social class and geography.

Country musicians have been praised for tackling such subjects as adultery, divorce, and drunkenness when other traditions were avoiding them. The music was chiefly a male enterprise until after the war, when female stars began to emerge. In 1952, J. D. Miller's *It Wasn't God Who Made Honky Tonk Angels*, a song sung by Kitty Wells, answered Hank Thompson's *The Wild Side of Life*, which accuses women of faithlessness in a chorus beginning: "I didn't know God made honky tonk angels."

LISTENING GUIDE 59

It Wasn't God Who Made Honky Tonk Angels (Miller, sung by Kitty Wells)

Accompanied by lead guitar, steel guitar, fiddle, and bass, Kitty Wells's performance pictures a woman sitting in a roadhouse as the jukebox plays Thompson's *The Wild Side of Life*. She rejects the idea behind Thompson's song. Her two-stanza rebuttal, granting the heartbreak of romance, puts the blame not on women but on men—especially married men who pretend to be single. The music is straightforward. Verse and chorus are sung to the same music, and the fiddle separates the two verses with an instrumental version of the whole. Rather than being "done wrong" by wild women, the song argues, men hold the upper hand. Singing without emotional display, Wells's character declares women the victims of male dishonesty.

Postwar country music was living proof of the staying power of old forms, styles, themes, and sounds, as the fiddle and steel guitar remained basic instruments. By mid-century, some 650 radio stations were broadcasting live hillbilly talent. Saturday night broadcasts on Nashville's WSM, including a half-hour segment on NBC, made the Opry the undisputed leader of barn-dance radio programs. One performer who established himself at the Opry was mandolin virtuoso Bill Monroe, born in

Bill Monroe (1911–1996), a key figure in the founding of bluegrass music, performs in the 1970s with the Blue Grass Boys, consisting of his own mandolin, plus fiddle, banjo, guitar, and double bass.

1911 in the bluegrass state of Kentucky. In the world of country music, where borrowing from mainstream pop was considered forward-looking, Monroe's string-band sound and acoustic instruments—mandolin, five-string banjo, fiddle, guitar, double bass—gave his group an old-fashioned flavor. Most of his music was vocal, but in instrumental numbers the melody instruments took solo choruses, in the manner of jazz musicians. Up-tempo numbers were very fast. And Monroe pitched his music high, with the tenor—which he sang himself—set above the lead and sometimes reaching as far up as the C above middle C.

Monroe and his musicians brought an uncommon blend of ancient and modern to country music. Audiences found the music fresh and exciting, even if the songs did look backward in time. Asked in 1977 to define his style, dubbed "bluegrass" in the latter 1950s, Monroe called it "the old southern sound, that was heard years ago, many, many years ago in the backwoods, at country dances." Elsewhere he recalled that in writing a fiddle tune called *Land of Lincoln*, he made the piece "go the way I thought Abraham Lincoln might have heard it—a tune like he might have heard when he was a boy from some old-time fiddler." Monroe meant by oldness the kind of mysterious, mythic simplicity that only folk traditions can preserve. Bluegrass was a modern *representation* of Appalachian folk music, reconstituted for the concert stage. Its vocal style was impersonal and stylized in the manner of Anglo-American folk singing, and the high range favored by many singers can be traced back to various folk practices, from black field hollers to Primitive Baptist hymnody. The piercing vocal tone is a direct legacy from Bill Monroe: the "high lonesome sound" that for many listeners has given the music's deadpan delivery an impassioned edge.

LISTENING GUIDE 60

It's Mighty Dark to Travel (Monroe)

It's Mighty Dark to Travel, a Bill Monroe song performed by Monroe and His Blue Grass Boys (1947), displays the classic style of bluegrass music during its early years. In a standard bluegrass approach that may seem contradictory, the song is about loneliness, but the music is up-tempo and in major mode. The chorus, sung five times, embodies Monroe's signature sound: a lead vocal (delivered by guitarist Lester Flatt), Monroe's own high tenor harmony, and an instrumental accompaniment featuring Monroe's mandolin, the banjo of Earl Scruggs, and Chubby Wise's fiddle, supported by string bass. The voices sing without vibrato, locking their sustained notes into the center of the pitch. Behind them, a steady stream of picked or bowed sixteenth notes pours out. In fact, that stream never runs dry, whether during the verses, which Flatt sings alone, or the fiddle's opening statement of the eight-bar chorus melody, or the "solo" chorus statements played first by the banjo, then the mandolin, and then the fiddle. Contrasts appear often: between verses and choruses, vocal and instrumental statements, and sections that feature individual instruments. But the ensemble sound and the driving rhythm provide a continuity that is equally compelling.

Beginning in the mid-1950s, the music's mix of ancient and modern traits caught the fancy of young fans who were to play a role in its development. Rather than country music lovers, they were folk performers, including Mike Seeger—son of Charles and Ruth Crawford Seeger, and Pete Seeger's half-brother—and Ralph Rinzler, who would become a major promoter of bluegrass. Perhaps no bluegrass musician impressed them more strongly than Earl Scruggs, who played five-string banjo with Monroe and the Blue Grass Boys, and then with the Foggy Mountain Boys. Scruggs was admired and copied for his three-finger "up-picking" style with metal picks, which allowed him to play a continuous stream of fast-moving notes while maintaining a loud, powerful tone. His virtuosity introduced a new era in which banjo players were virtuoso soloists.

In 1957, Mike Seeger brought out on Folkways a historic LP, *American Banjo Scruggs Style*. Seeger's recording offered an anthology of fifteen different banjo players' work. The accompanying brochure, written in part by Ralph Rinzler, told how Bill Monroe had organized a new kind of band in 1945, and then continued: "The banjo along with many of the 'old-time' songs had been revived, and numerous 'bluegrass' bands, patterned on those of Scruggs and Monroe, were soon doing performances and making recordings for well-known companies." This sentence is important both for the notion of revival and for calling the music "bluegrass." Rinzler implied that Scruggs's music was old: a *rediscovery* of something set aside. He also was the first writer to use the label that stuck to Bill Monroe's musical style and that of his followers.

Earl Scruggs in 1957 was a musician working in the country music business. And that makes *American Banjo Scruggs Style* a crossover record, taking music made in the popular sphere and relocating it in the traditional sphere's Appalachian folk genre. By 1959, the idea that bluegrass was folk, not popular, music was spreading. Alan Lomax included some in Folksong '59, a Carnegie Hall concert he staged in April. A few months later, Mike Seeger produced a second Folkways LP: *Mountain Music Bluegrass Style*, with a detailed guidebook about the music. And then an article by Lomax in *Esquire* magazine characterized bluegrass as "folk music with overdrive." "The bluegrassers," he wrote, "have developed the first true orchestral form in five hundred [i.e., three hundred plus] years of Anglo-American music, and their silvery, pinging sound provides a suitable, yet modern and 'hot,' setting for the songs of the frontier with which America has recently fallen in love."

Lomax's remarks indicate that as the 1950s drew to a close, jazz was not the only music bringing historical consciousness into the popular sphere.

THE FOLK REVIVAL AND THE POPULAR SPHERE

Our story has moved from the heart of the popular sphere to the notion of revival: the embrace of traditional music by people outside the communities in which it originated. Although centered on traditional music, the "folk revival" met the goals of all three spheres—the transcendence of the classical, the accessibility of the popular, and the continuity of the traditional. Other than live singing and playing, its chief medium was the

LP recording. Packages such as Mike Seeger's two bluegrass albums revealed transcendent value in music that had taken shape without three customary agents of transcendence: notation, formal training, and aesthetic criticism. They also confirmed that not all music made in the name of commercial accessibility was ephemeral. The folk revival put music that had stood outside history into historical perspective, making the three spheres seem less separate than they had before. Only after 1965 did the idea take hold that the classical, popular, and traditional spheres were separate branches of musical activity *and also* parts of an interdependent whole: a whole with a history.

In the early 1970s, the folk singer Pete Seeger gave five reasons why many young people were attracted to folk music:

1. a desire to learn more about their country's heritage;
2. a belief that "do-it-yourself" activities countered the passive attitude fostered by television;
3. a belief in the excellence of American folk songs;
4. an understanding that folk songs do not condescend to the social groups that were often their subjects;
5. the chance that folk songs offer performers to comment on current events.

Seeger also recognized the difference between revivalists and people making the same music by birthright. It took sophistication, he wrote, "to sing an old spiritual without wondering if someone will call you an Uncle Tom." And he added: "Maybe we had to wait a few years till we were far enough away from our past to be able to pick and choose the good from the bad." In other words, the folk revival was a modern representation of a culture less sophisticated than the revivalists' own. But some Americans, especially young ones, heard in traditional music an authenticity and directness missing from other popular music, and from modern life itself.

The folk revival included a blues revival, launched in the late 1950s. The blues' early history traces a winding path through traditional and popular music. Originating in Southern African-American oral tradition, blues by the 1910s were appearing as published popular songs. Bessie Smith and other classic female blues singers after 1920, although their roots were folk, were entertainers whose records circulated widely. Moreover, both black and white jazz musicians performed blues numbers. Meanwhile, "down-home blues" continued to flourish in the Mississippi Delta, where it had originated. Its performers were male, not female; and where classic blues artists usually performed with a piano or small jazz ensemble, these men accompanied themselves on guitar. In contrast to the theaters and clubs in which female blues artists performed, Charlie Patton and Robert Johnson worked during the 1930s in juke joints and logging camps, and on street corners for tips.

By the late 1930s, Chicago was a center for blues performance. "Big Bill" Broonzy, a black singer, guitarist, and songwriter, had come to the city from Arkansas in 1920, and in the 1930s began making records and singing in South Side nightspots for black audiences. Yet when Broonzy worked elsewhere, he was sometimes made a symbol of racial politics. In a New York concert in 1939, he heard himself introduced as "an ex-share-

Publicity shot of William Lee Conley, a.k.a. Big Bill Broonzy (1893–1958), an early representative of the blues revival that blossomed in the late 1950s.

cropper"—a surprise for one who had not farmed since 1916. Rather than trying to reconcile the expectations of his different audiences, Broonzy accommodated both. For black audiences, he sang and recorded blues numbers; for white audiences, he sang work songs and back-country blues he learned from records and books.

So began the blues revival, whose first phase peaked around 1969. Its achievements were many, including the reissue of early blues recordings; the launching of further research; the discovery of new singers in the older folk tradition; the rediscovery of older singers who had fallen into obscurity; the staging of public events featuring blues artists; and the emulation of their styles by young performers. The revival was thus a cultural intervention by white devotees. By recasting the blues tradition in their own image, revivalists turned the blues into a music chiefly for white Americans and Europeans.

It was no coincidence that the blues revival began during the civil rights struggle. Against the background of a campaign that pitted Southern black activism against Southern white resistance, the music was hard to separate from racial politics. And once traditional blues performers won appreciation as artists, the injustice of their low rank in society seemed to symbolize the plight of black Americans in general. Blues revivalists, while taking up the cause of traditional blues artists to rescue them and their art from poverty and obscurity, ended up using the blues symbolically to wage battles of their own.

GOSPEL MUSIC IN CHICAGO

Blues and black gospel music share a tonal idiom, a rhythmic approach, and a rootedness in traditional black culture, but their functions are entirely different. Blues is a secular music, tied to work and entertainment; gospel is a sacred music, performed in worship. Blues speaks for individuals, gospel for communities. Where blues states problems of human existence, gospel solves them through Christian doctrine. Blues fits in many settings; gospel belongs to the church. Not until the 1960s did gospel music circulate widely outside black communities.

Black gospel music exemplifies the attitude of praise, in contrast to edification. Praise is directed not toward worshipers but to the Almighty, whom it seeks to glorify by offering the best in human expression: the most heartfelt, ecstatic, artful, and therefore worthy. The emotionally direct yet disciplined musical stylizations of black gospel performers have proved to be among the most powerful agents of praise in the modern Christian church.

Antiblack prejudice in America has sharpened black class consciousness, and religious life has mirrored the social divisions. In Chicago, for example, middle-class blacks gravitated toward African Methodist Episcopal (AME) and Baptist churches, while working-class blacks—including migrants from the South—were more likely to join pentecostal, or "sanctified," congregations. Middle-class black denominations modeled their worship customs on white churches: in the latter 1920s, the choirs at two of black Chicago's largest Baptist congregations were singing sacred music by the likes of Handel and Mendelssohn. The ministers of these churches favored a restrained preaching style and avoided traditional black worship music, except for arranged, notated Negro spirituals. A different spirit was found in pentecostal denominations such as the Church of God in Christ: congregational hymns were "gospelized" and the mood ecstatic, with jubilant singing to drums and tambourines (or even pots and pans), hand clapping and foot stomping, shouting and fainting, as in the days before Emancipation.

Modern black gospel music took shape before World War II as mainstream denominations brought pentecostal musical styles into their worship. A key step took in August 1930 at a convention of black Baptists in Chicago when a singer stirred the delegates with *If You See My Savior*, composed in 1928 by Thomas A. Dorsey. Sometimes called "Georgia Tom," Dorsey was an active Chicago musician and songwriter whose performing credits included a stint as pianist for blues singer Gertrude "Ma" Rainey and who, from the early 1930s on, devoted himself entirely to sacred music.

In 1931, Chicago's Ebenezer Baptist hired a new minister from Alabama, who hoped to introduce songs like those he had heard in the South. So in early 1932, a new choir was formed, accompanied by Dorsey himself. Later that year, Dorsey joined with others to form the National Convention of Gospel Choirs and Choruses, dedicated to teaching the gospel style. And 1932 also saw the founding of the Dorsey House of Music, the first publishing company devoted to black gospel music. Dorsey's ability to compose, improvise, and notate music, his command of blues-based rhythmic drive, commitment to the church, and understanding of sacred and secular music as two sides of the same coin make him the very model of a black gospel musician. At a time of cultural tension in Chicago's churches, Dorsey came forward with music that was authentically Southern yet urbanized enough to counter the Northern culture's push for European anthems.

LISTENING GUIDE 61

Talk About Jesus (Dorsey, sung by Marion Williams)

For several generations, Thomas A. Dorsey's gospel songs have offered black gospel singers an attractive body of sacred performers' music: songs in standard forms, with straightforward melodies and harmonies. The richness and excitement are supplied neither by the music nor the words, which tend also to be simple, but by the performers. *Talk About Jesus* is a good example: a verse followed by a chorus, which is then repeated with different words, and an approach to the subject more down-to-earth than elevated. As seen by Dorsey, Jesus is no distant icon but a "friend of mine," a comrade described as "mighty fine." In this 1986 recording, Marion Williams provides her own piano accompaniment. Starting quietly, Williams is soon caught up in the spirit of her praise. By the start of the chorus, she has established a powerful rhythmic groove, using her large, supple voice and an arsenal of techniques—blue notes, bent notes, off-beat melodic phrasings, register shifts, and even a growl (when "the tears come rollin' out")—to express religious devotion in an inventive, heartfelt way.

Fifty-nine years old when she made this recording, Williams later became the first singer to receive a "genius" grant from the MacArthur Foundation; she died a few months after winning the award.

Gospel music offered rich opportunities for women as well as men, including solo singers Sallie Martin, Marion Williams, Clara Ward, and Mahalia Jackson. Jackson, born in New Orleans and raised chiefly in Chicago, won fame during the 1950s and 60s through recordings, tours, and broadcasts. Her voice and artistry made her the world's leading gospel singer, a judgment that still stands today.

Roberta Martin's career in gospel music proved that singing was not the only role open to women. Born in 1907 in Arkansas, Martin moved with her family at age ten to Chicago, where piano study gave her a solid musical background. At Ebenezer Baptist in the early 1930s, she worked with Dorsey and accompanied a choir of youngsters. She also began showing a knack for leadership. In 1933, Martin recruited several male singers to form the Frye-Martin Quartet; gospel groups then consisted either of male quartets in business suits or female choruses in choir robes. By 1936, she was adding her own alto voice to the group, now called the Roberta Martin Singers, which she accompanied on piano. In the mid-1940s, she added two women singers, marking the first combination of male and female voices in one ensemble. By then, Martin and her singers were also making records. The group spent part of the year in and around Chicago,

The Roberta Martin Singers, a Chicago-based gospel ensemble, photographed in 1969.

singing in churches, meeting halls, and religious revivals. They also toured by car from January to June, beginning in either California or Florida.

Roberta Martin sang, played, and traveled with her singers until the late 1940s. From then on, she concentrated more on writing and arranging for them, and running her own publishing business. For as well as a performing style, gospel was also a musical repertory, and new songs boosted the music's appeal for singers and congregations. Martin composed some fifty gospel songs and arranged many more, putting her stamp on gospel's entry into a written tradition. Between 1939 and her death in 1969, she published nearly three hundred pieces of gospel sheet music. Unlike Dorsey, who issued only his own compositions, Martin published the songs her group sang, regardless of the composer. Alone among musicians of her era, she seems to have recognized gospel music as an endeavor that could link spirituality, music making, and commerce in a single enterprise. (The example of the musician-businessman Lowell Mason in the 1830s and 40s comes to mind.)

Roberta Martin's funeral has been seen as a symbol of black gospel music's place in American life: a blend of acceptance and obscurity. When she died in January 1969 at the age of sixty-two, fifty thousand Chicagoans passed through Mount Pisgah Baptist Church, where she was music director, to view the body, although no national newspaper or journal covered the event. Across the United States, gospel fans heard the news through word of mouth and on the radio.

Gospel music's roots in the heritage of spirituals, ring shouts, and the blues have made it the wellspring from which other African-American musical traditions have flowed. Many who have excelled in jazz, blues, rhythm and blues, and soul have served their apprenticeship in the black church. And partly because gospel music making has been widely accessible to black Americans, its influence has been broad as well as deep. Gospel music was responsible for much of what came to be considered emblematic in American culture of the 1960s: from rock and roll's beat, drama, and group vibrations to the hymn singing at sit-ins and freedom marches and the "brother and sister" fraternity of revolution.

36

Jazz, Broadway, and Musical Permanence

IF GOSPEL MUSIC WAS A WELLSPRING THAT NOURISHED POPULAR music making, jazz was the most highly regarded distillation to come out of the African-American reservoir. As we saw in Chapter 34, jazz was the one popular genre that earned consistent critical attention. Rooted in blues and gospel, jazz also attracted musicians who pushed the boundaries of technique and expression. Modern pioneers such as Charlie Parker and Dizzy Gillespie were received from the start as virtuosos who were saying something new, in an idiom often called "bebop." And historically minded critics placed their music in a tradition starting in New Orleans and developing in Chicago, New York, and Kansas City, leading into the big-band music of the Swing Era, from which modern jazz was born.

Charlie Parker, born in Kansas City, Kansas, in 1920, was a musician whose rhythmic originality, harmonic complexity, virtuoso technique, and inventiveness as an improviser helped to bring about changes in style that much of the popular music audience disapproved. Parker's saxophone playing was geared not to pleasing swing-band fans but to a musical logic of his own, and to listeners who liked the result. In making a style change that reduced the audience's size, Parker seized an artistic freedom that few earlier jazz musicians had enjoyed. But that freedom imposed a burden: how to survive as a popular artist who played music that only a fraction of the jazz audience would accept.

When the war ended and the big bands began to break up, a corps of players remained who were eager to emphasize the listening side of jazz. In the early postwar years, the musicians' artistic originality sparked excitement. Though pared down to a small fraction of the Swing Era's scale, New York's modern jazz scene blossomed: uptown in Harlem, downtown in Greenwich Village, but most of all in midtown, on 52nd Street between Fifth and Sixth Avenues. Tenor saxophonist Dexter Gor-

Famed trumpeter John Birks "Dizzy" Gillespie standing with friend at
New York's 52nd Street and Sixth Avenue.

don later described "The Street," where the top jazz clubs were located, as "the most exciting half a block in the world. Everything was going on—music, chicks, connections . . . so many musicians working down there, side by side"—a milieu, in other words, where women who liked jazz musicians could be found, and so could drug dealers. (Parker had been a heroin user since his teenage years and was also a heavy drinker. Many others followed his example, partly in the belief that drug use sparked Parker's creative imagination.) Fans of the music made up in passion what they lacked in numbers. Those who "dug" modern jazz gloried in being "hip" to the music's freedom, intensity, and young performers, chiefly black, who radiated independence of spirit.

Some white commentators suggested parallels between bebop and modern music in the classical sphere. The black writer Albert Murray, however, has seen the music differently. Rather than trying to turn dance music into concert music, Murray wrote, Parker "was out to swing not less but more." "Sometimes he tangled up your feet but that was when he sometimes made your insides dance as never before."

LISTENING GUIDE 62

Parker's Mood (Parker)

Parker's Mood, a blues number recorded in 1948, contains four improvised choruses: two by Parker, one by pianist John Lewis, and a final one by Parker. (Drummer Max Roach and bass player Curly Russell are also heard.) A typical modern jazz performance begins and ends with the "head" (composed melody); but this work presents only a two-bar introductory figure that returns after the last chorus as a tag. Yet the lack of a twelve-bar head does not leave *Parker's Mood* short on tunefulness, for the saxophonist fits plenty of melody into his decoration of the harmonic scheme. Each chorus begins with a melodic statement that is hard to forget. In the first, Parker opens with a pair of complementary two-bar phrases. In the second, he offers a shorter statement that, ignited by a bold upbeat octave leap, lands with a turning gesture on the downbeat and then, following a brief stutter on B-flat, dissolves into a long descending cascade. After Lewis' lyric third chorus, Parker returns with a new statement, outlining the tonic triad (B-flat) in bar 1 and the subdominant (E-flat) in bar 2—separated by another B-flat stutter.

Alto saxophonist Charlie "Bird" Parker and trumpeter Dizzy Gillespie, with bassist Tommy Potter (1950).

For all the disorderliness of Parker's personal life, contemporaries recognized his superior talent and musicianship, and by 1950 jazz already bore clear signs of his influence. Some of his compositions were by then standards. His recordings were widely known, and saxophonists were not the only players who wore them out with repeated listening, trying to learn from his dense improvising style. Finally, Parker's bold artistic spirit, ready to follow musical logic wherever it might lead, inspired other musicians to push the boundaries further, distancing modern jazz even more from the center of the popular sphere, on which it relied for economic support.

Another part of Parker's legacy was the recognition that high technical skill was needed to perform modern jazz. Yet those who dominated the music's second decade (1955–65), such as Thelonious Monk, John Lewis, and Miles Davis, did not emphasize virtuoso technique. Monk's roots as a pianist lay in the Harlem stride school. As the first major jazz composer since Ellington, however, Monk developed a performing style that made the piano sound more percussive than singing. And the rhythm of his lean-textured compositions is even more asymmetrical than Lester Young's or Charlie Parker's.

John Lewis, like Monk a pianist-composer, made his mark as leader of the Modern Jazz Quartet (MJQ, with piano, vibraharp, bass, and drums), formed in the early 1950s. Instead of relying chiefly on improvising, Lewis combined composition and improvisation in ways that repaid close listening, as in a concert hall. In doing so, he brought order and form to the materials that brilliant first-generation improvisers like Parker had discovered. The Modern Jazz Quartet, with its relatively soft, "cool" sound, opened the concert hall to a kind of jazz akin to classical chamber music. And Lewis explored that link further by composing Baroque-style "suites" and jazz fugues for the MJQ.

Miles Davis, another key second-generation master, emerged in the latter 1940s with an introspective lyric approach that contradicted the image of modern jazz as virtuoso music. By 1954, he had discovered an intensely personal trumpet sound that was often heard in tightly muted playing, close to the microphone. During the 1950s, silence and space became basic to Davis's musical vocabulary. In 1959, on the album called *Kind of Blue*, Davis pursued simplicity and directness in another way, basing the thirty-two-bar structure of *So What* not on a chord pattern but on an eight-note Dorian, or modal, scale. And in 1965, in a group with tenor

Trumpeter Miles Davis (1926–1991) was a magnetic presence on the jazz scene from the mid-1940s through the 1980s.

saxophonist Wayne Shorter and drummer Tony Williams, Davis again found the cutting edge of jazz innovation with a set of his own unusual compositions, including *Circle*.

By the early 1950s, jazz recordings were appearing in the 33 1/3-rpm format developed for classical music. The flexibility that LP recording offered jazz musicians influenced the content of their music as well as boosting its prestige. An LP offered the possibility of longer pieces. The relatively high price encouraged repeated listening, which helped fans absorb unfamiliar styles. LPs also came with liner notes by a writer who might suggest a frame for listening. Thanks in part to LP recordings, fans of modern jazz began to include more concertgoers and readers of the journals for which jazz critics now commonly wrote. Growing numbers of white college-age youngsters embraced jazz as their own. And in the summer of 1954, the Newport Jazz Festival, modeled on classical festivals, was founded in Newport, Rhode Island. Jazz was finding a new place on the American scene.

To widen their audience, then, jazz musicians made records, and writers on jazz treated them as an artistic legacy. Indeed, writers shaped that legacy into a *body of work* that, with its great figures, canonic recordings (such as *Parker's Mood*), and style periods, paralleled the tradition of the Western classical sphere. And they did so long before most classical musicians and music lovers showed interest in jazz as an art form. In a day when such labels as "new music" and "contemporary music" pointed to a Europe-centered classical sphere, jazz musicians lacked the prestige to convey their own artistic ideas beyond the circle of jazz fans. Therefore, even though modern jazz musicians scorned the popular sphere's emphasis on easy accessibility, their informal customs of training, repertory, and notation—and the general tone of the music itself—held more in common with the commercial marketplace than with the classical concert hall.

In the 1960s, as a larger cultural community finally began to recognize the contributions of black musicians, jazz became accepted as a Western art conceived and transmitted by black Americans. The view took hold that jazz artists, in their own way, are no less accomplished, diverse, or aesthetically knowing than classical composers. Tenor saxophonist Sonny Rollins, for example, was seen as a master of large-scale improvisation. Pianist Horace Silver, champion of a mid-1950s trend toward "funk" that emphasized the rhythmic groove, was described as a dedicated professional craftsman. Pianist Bill Evans was credited with an unusual willingness to explore his own emotional vulnerability. Bass player and composer Charles Mingus was cited as an artist whose public pronouncements "seemed to offer us himself . . . as part of his music," in the words of jazz writer Martin Williams. Saxophonist John Coltrane, considered by many listeners to be the dominant figure in the history of jazz, was hailed for his originality, virtuosity, and inventiveness. And saxophonist Ornette Coleman is credited by Williams with "the first fundamental reevaluation of basic materials and basic procedures for jazz since the innovations of Charlie Parker."

Billie Holliday and Ella Fitzgerald were well-known featured singers with big bands, the only role readily open at the time to women. The singer Sarah Vaughan, who had been on the scene since the 1940s, was recognized for the exceptional range, sound, and variety of her voice, as well as her excellent control and near-perfect sense of pitch. Her achievements may be summed up in a pair of challenges she met: (1) adapting her vocal technique to the demands of rhythmic swing, and (2) capturing the mood of a song and sustaining it without giving up vocal and musical freedom.

Sarah Vaughan (1924–1990), a remarkable singer by any standard, could use her capacious voice as a jazz instrument or a vehicle for words, or both.

Jazz Writer Martin Williams on John Coltrane

Like all true artists, he spoke of matters of the spirit, not of society and politics. . . . Indeed, the deeper purpose of the incantatory sections in his music has to be—as with any incantation—to evoke the gods and the demons whose ways are timeless and yet always contemporary. Perhaps, if his music does not quite reach me and satisfy me as it has reached some others, the answer is that the gods he sought to invoke are not my gods.

In any case, Coltrane was bold enough to state his message so that the future must acknowledge that he has been with us.

CD 3
13

LISTENING GUIDE 63

Welcome (Coltrane)

Saxophonist John Coltrane is renowned for his virtuosity as a player and for carrying the art of jazz into new expressive territory. Coltrane also increased the length of individual numbers. In 1965, he recorded *Ascension,* a composition of his own, in versions that lasted 38'37" and 40'31"—a remarkable development in that until the early 1950s, jazz recordings had seldom run beyond 3'30" (one side of a 10-inch, 78 rpm single). When working club dates in the 1960s, Coltrane would often start a set with the melody of a waltz in his band's repertory and then step aside, letting the rhythm section (pianist McCoy Tyner, drummer Elvin Jones, and bassist Jimmy Garrison) take over for fifteen or twenty minutes. When a tumultuous climax was reached, Coltrane would return, his sax "sailing in like an ecstatic release," as one of his producers described it. From there he might start a new buildup that brought the intensity to an even higher level.

Welcome, recorded by Coltrane and his quartet in 1965, shows the leader-composer in a mood more lyrical than tumultuous. Melodically and harmonically, the composition is little more than an embellishment of a C major chord. Yet the sound and scale of the performance demonstrate the independence and animation of Tyner and Jones; the leisurely unfolding of the saxophone melody, simple and brief as it is; Coltrane's expressive, effortful tone; and his purposeful avoidance of the tonic pitch, around which the music revolves. Blending energy with spiritual gravity, this five-and-a-half-minute musical greeting manages to be straightforward, spacious, and modern sounding, all at the same time.

The rising status of jazz encouraged some musicians to focus their energies on the common ground held with the Western classical tradition. The classically trained composer Gunther Schuller, a French horn player long involved with jazz, coined the term "third stream" for music that brought jazz techniques into the classical sphere, or vice versa, through improvisation or written composition. John Lewis and the Modern Jazz Quartet were already working that territory. And Schuller himself explored third-stream possibilities in such works as *Transformation* (1957), for jazz ensemble, and *Variants on a Theme of Thelonious Monk* (1960), recorded with Ornette Coleman and Bill Evans among the performers.

Around 1960, then, jazz musicians were borrowing classical forms, classical musicians were cultivating jazz fusions and intersections, and critics were debating the merits of such blendings. But even as modern jazz was being pulled toward the classical sphere, a counterpull was taking place, led by black musicians and activists, toward its African traditions. Spurred by the black struggle for social equality, these men and women believed that some modern jazz performers were working out a characteristically black mode of expression whose deepest spirit was inaccessible to whites. Music like Coltrane's, they argued, was best understood from a black perspective, and white critics lacked the background and experience to judge his work (though Coltrane himself never made any such claim). The rise of black nationalism during the 1960s brought ideas into the discourse on jazz that would influence its creation, presentation, and reception deeply in the years to come.

Meanwhile, another genre outside the classical sphere was also being touted for higher intellectual respect.

BROADWAY MUSICALS
IN THE POSTWAR ERA

On October 7, 1956, the thirty-nine-year-old composer and conductor Leonard Bernstein surveyed the American musical theater in a national television broadcast. "For the last fifteen years," he told viewers, "we have been enjoying the greatest period our musical theater has ever known." Bernstein supported his statement with a list of classic Broadway shows: *Pal Joey, Annie Get Your Gun, Oklahoma!, South Pacific, Guys and Dolls, Kiss Me, Kate.* And he illustrated the talent of these shows' creators with examples from Rodgers and Hammerstein's *South Pacific.*

The shows Bernstein called young classics all belonged "to an art that arises out of American roots." As he saw it, the best recent shows were neither opera nor light entertainment, but a new form somewhere between the two. "We are in a historical position now similar to that of the popular musical theater in Germany just before Mozart came along," he

Composer and conductor Leonard Bernstein (1918–1990) made a strong impact on the public with television appearances that took up serious musical matters in an engaging way.

announced. American musical theater needed only for its own Mozart to arrive, which might happen "any second." Less than a year later, Bernstein himself stepped into that role. In September 1957, *West Side Story*, with lyrics by Stephen Sondheim set to Bernstein's music, opened in New York to the acclaim of critics and audiences.

The high value Bernstein placed on American musicals seemed calculated to surprise 1956 viewers. Musicals before that time were largely ignored by music critics, who saw the classical and popular spheres as separated by a firm barrier. If a new opera was performed, for example, both its quality and its connection to earlier operas received critical discussion. The Broadway musical, however, needed no such go-betweens. Authors and composers submitted their work directly to the judgment of audiences, whose verdict, registered at the box office, was equally direct. Aesthetic decisions were made to trigger positive public responses. If the audience seemed pleased, the decision was right; if not, changes were made. A tryout run preceded a show's Broadway opening so that out-of-town audience response could be used to identify problems, but the makers of musicals took the public pulse even earlier. Alan Jay Lerner, the librettist and lyricist of *My Fair Lady*, wrote that when he and composer Frederick ("Fritz") Loewe finished a song, "we would dash around the neighborhood, looking for 'customers,' as Fritz would say, meaning neighbors for whom to play it. Naturally, our captive audience was complimentary, but somehow we could always tell if the compliments were because of the song or because of the friendship. Very often it influenced us and made us aware of a weakness."

In his 1967 book *The American Musical Theater: a Consideration*, Lehman Engel, a composer and conductor of Broadway shows, made up his own list of classic musicals from the years 1940–57. The list included the six Bernstein praised in 1956, plus *Brigadoon*, *My Fair Lady*, *West Side Story*, *Carousel*, and *The King and I*. To Engel, what set these musicals apart was not the music, choreography, scenery, or acting, but the more realistic stories and better-rounded characters. And in musicals, as in opera, personal traits only hinted at in the dialogue could be revealed in a song.

All the shows on Engel's list succeeded as dramatic wholes. At the same time, like shows of the earlier Golden Age, they contained hit songs that circulated independently. The list leaves no doubt that Rodgers and Hammerstein were supreme masters of the form. It also testifies to the creative powers of two leading composer-lyricists of an earlier day who flourished in the postwar era, when they found the right book. One was Irving Berlin, whose *Annie Get Your Gun* was the leading hit of 1946. The other was Cole Porter, whose *Kiss Me, Kate* (1948) took Shakespeare's *The Taming of the Shrew* as its starting point.

LISTENING GUIDE 64

Where Is the Life That Late I Led (Porter)

Petruchio, the leading man of the Shakespearean play-within-a-play staged in Act II of Cole Porter's *Kiss Me, Kate*, has been locked out of his bride's bedroom on their wedding night. Pulling out an old address book, he remembers some of the women he has loved in his travels through Italy. Petruchio's song, *Where Is the Life That Late I Led* (a line from Shakespeare), starts as a tarantella: an Italian folk dance in 6/8 time and verse-and-chorus form that supports the manly baritone of Alfred Drake, who created the role, while helping to place the action in olden times. Marriage may be okay, he says, "But raising an heir / Can never compare / With raising a bit of hell." To this stock image of the frustrated groom, however, Porter adds another dimension: a chorus-ending flashback section where Petruchio recalls earlier love affairs. Sung in free tempo, with a cheesy-sounding mandolin in the background, this section parodies travel-poster images of Italy. Most of all, the virtuoso wordplay of Porter's lyrics turns a macho grievance into a hilarious mockery of romance.

Lerner and Loewe's *My Fair Lady* (1956) was the most popular musical of the 1950s and also one of the shows that Engel studied with care. Lerner's book is based on George Bernard Shaw's *Pygmalion*, a play inspired by the classical legend of a sculptor who fell in love with his own statue. In the opening scene, set in a London market, Henry Higgins, a phonetics expert, encounters Eliza Doolittle, an uneducated flower seller. Lerner later explained: "What Shaw wanted us to know about Higgins was that he was passionate about the English language, believed it to be the principal barrier separating class from class, and that he was a misogynist." These traits are established immediately. After overhearing Eliza's speech, Higgins scolds her for its coarseness and launches into his first song: *Why Can't the English (Teach Their Children How to Speak)?* Before leaving the stage, he bets an acquaintance that he can turn Eliza into a lady, simply by improving her speech. And now, music is used to fill out the character of the woman who has aroused Higgins's ire. In *Wouldn't It Be Loverly?*, sung with other market folk, Eliza imagines a life of comfort to replace the harsh one she knows. The song's quiet charm shows another side of Eliza. Thus, two conflicts are laid out: Will Higgins turn this girl into a speaker of proper English? and how could romance bloom between such an ill-matched pair?

The first conflict is resolved before the second, which is heightened by Higgins's anti-female harangues. Act I revolves around Eliza's language study. Late one evening, a crisis is reached as Higgins tries to teach her the long "a," as in "take instead of tyke." Neither bullying nor endless repetition has worked, so he tries persuasion.

> HIGGINS: Eliza, I know you're tired. I know your head aches. But . . . think
> what you're dealing with. The majesty and grandeur of the English lan-
> guage. . . . The noblest sentiments that ever flowed in the hearts of men are
> contained in its extraordinary, imaginative and musical mixtures of
> sounds. That's what you've set yourself to conquer, Eliza. And conquer
> you will. . . . Now try it again.
> ELIZA: The rain in Spain stays mainly in the plain.

The line, delivered haltingly at first, then repeated with more confidence, marks a breakthrough. Eliza's ear has finally caught the sound of correct

As Professor Henry Higgins in Lerner and Loewe's *My Fair Lady*
(1956), Rex Harrison coaches Julie Andrews (Eliza Doolittle) on English pronunciation while Robert Weede as Col. Pinkerton listens.

pronunciation, and her tongue has matched it. The magic of the moment is celebrated in a song based on Eliza's properly pronounced line. Heroine and hero finally discover common ground; the tango rhythm of *The Rain in Spain* allows them to revel in singing, dancing, and the joy of shared achievement.

From this point on, Eliza proves herself a brilliant student, and Higgins passes her off at a formal ball as a person of high birth. But now the drama moves into deeper waters. Eliza, who has won the audience's heart, is in love with a man so self-absorbed that he remains oblivious to her feelings. In the end, however, Higgins, who claims full credit for Eliza's transformation, realizes that he has "grown accustomed to her face" and feels lonely without her. And when she appears unexpectedly at his house, he delivers the show's last line to a character who hears it as the equivalent of "I love you too." "Eliza?" he asks. "Where the devil are my slippers?" With irony instead of a romantic speech, Higgins preserves his character, Eliza gets the man she fell in love with, and the audience is invited to assume that the gulf between them has been dissolved.

Musical comedy revolves around the blossoming of romance. Once the heroine and hero declare mutual love, the adventure is over, and so is the show. Even the near-operatic *West Side Story*, the only tragic example in Engel's canon, which ends with the hero being shot dead, seems the exception that proves the rule. Modeled after Shakespeare's *Romeo and Juliet*, the story turns on love at first sight. While most musicals end with the hero and heroine poised to begin a life together, Maria and Tony are denied that chance by a hate-filled society. Yet before he dies, they enjoy their moment of bliss, musical-theater-style.

Although stories and characters grew more realistic, reliance on an old-fashioned view of romantic love persisted in the midcentury years. Convinced that audiences came to the theater to watch two lovers find their way into each other's arms, the makers of musicals held to that time-tested formula, showing little inclination to explore beyond it.

37

Melting Pot or Pluralism?

POPULAR MUSIC AND ETHNICITY

OSCAR HIJUELOS'S *THE MAMBO KINGS PLAY SONGS OF LOVE*, A PRIZE-winning novel published in 1989, tells the story of the Castillo brothers, Cuban-born musicians who immigrate to New York in 1949. Forming a group called the Mambo Kings, they win modest success, disbanding in 1957 after one brother dies in a car wreck. In the 1970s, Cesar Castillo is working as an apartment building superintendent who still performs occasionally with Cuban bands around New York.

Hijuelos's portrayal of fictional characters catches the flavor of a working musician's life. Castillo and his band members, like most popular musicians, are part-timers with day jobs; even in a city like New York, many such performers work outside the official structure of unions and taxable income. Another theme is the matter of costume and its effects on the performer-audience connection; Castillo's careful grooming is intended to set him apart as a debonair figure. Yet another is the range of skills that Castillo has developed as an entertainer: master of ceremonies, trumpeter, graceful dancer, and singer. Finally, the book answers the question of what popular singers think about when they are performing by having Castillo, from behind a face "radiant with sincere, love-drenched emotion," coolly reflect on the gaze of a prospective sexual partner.

Oscar Hijuelos's Fictional Portrayal of a Cuban Musician in New York

First, cologne behind his ears and neck; then talcum powder under his arms and on his hairy chest, with its scar over the right nipple. Clean pair of striped boxer shorts, then high silk socks with garters. On with his flamingo-pink shirt and fading white suit, tight around the middle. . . . Then on with his sky-blue tie and silver tie clip. He rubbed slick Brylcreem into his hair, put a little Vaseline under his eyes to help disguise the wrinkles, then applied a wax pencil over his wisp of a mustache, like Cesar Romero's in the old movies. Then he put on his white golden-buckled shoes and spit-polished the soft leather with a chamois cloth. When he finished that, he looked himself over. Satisfied that he had not left a stitch out of place, he was ready to go. . . . As he had for years and years, the Mambo King sang that bolero, his vocal cords quivering, his face radiant with sincere, love-drenched emotion: arms spread wide before his corpulent body, he sang to the women with all his heart. And looking at the crowd, his eyes found Lydia: she had been staring at him, a bent straw dangling from between her cherry-red lips. He sang the last verse of the song to her, and only her. While navigating the melancholic beauty of that melody, he had thought to himself: There goes that young chick again, looking at me.

_____

The Mambo Kings offers a glimpse of music making in one of America's many ethnic groups. Castillo represents foreign-born musicians who reach maturity in their homeland, emigrate to the United States, join a network of musicians with similar backgrounds, and spend much of their musical life in that network. The tradition of Castillo and his compatriots, chiefly Cubans, boasts a history of commercial appeal, as shown by the mambo's appearance in mainstream (English-speaking) popular music during the 1950s. Twenty years later, the impact of the mambo could still be felt in celebrations such as the 1977 post-wedding party described by Hijuelos: an event held at a club in a Latino neighborhood whose owners are Puerto Rican, honoring a bride, groom, and guests of Latino extraction, and featuring the sounds of Latino musicians grounded in a Cuban blend of Hispanic and African influences. Yet while Spanish speakers in New York hold cultural turf in common, separate communties of Cubans, Puerto Ricans, and Dominicans exist in the city, each with its own music and dances. Boosted in New York by recording and broadcast media, these Latin traditions also enjoy a strong presence in southern Florida, especially Miami. And to the west, many other Spanish-speaking Americans from Texas to California are involved in Mexican musical traditions.

LISTENING GUIDE 65

Oye como va (Puente; performed by Santana)

Since the 1930s, Latin music has served Spanish-speaking communities in the United States and also formed an ethnic strain within mainstream popular music. In earlier days, that strain often focused on dances—the rumba, the samba, and the mambo—performed by such Latin-born musicians as Xavier Cugat, Carmen Miranda, and Desi Arnaz. But music with a south-of-the-border flavor has also won popularity via other routes, including Tin Pan Alley and Broadway songs and arrangements.

Rock has also been influenced by Latin music, as *Oye como va*, introduced by Cuban-born drummer Tito Puente on a 1962 album, illustrates. Not really a song with conventional lyrics, this number is more an easy-going celebration, on instruments, of the joys of making music or hearing it. (The words sung on this recording, "Oye como va, mi ritmo, / Bueno pa' gozar, mulata," may be roughly translated as "Listen to how the music goes; / It's good for savoring the experience.") Recorded in 1970 by the long-lived rock group Santana (winner of a Grammy Award in 2000), Puente's number became a major crossover hit. Indeed, Santana's performance is still widely played on the radio over Spanish-speaking and black stations and those that emphasize rock.

Oye como va is built on an eight-bar cycle grounded in one striking chord change: A minor (the tonic) moving to D major, where a D-minor chord might be expected. Percussion instruments provide a hard-to-resist rhythmic perk, while solos by Carlos Santana's guitar and a bluesified organ bring more variety to the sound, keeping listeners pleasantly engaged.

Latin-based traditions are only one example of the ethnic musics that have flourished in America. Our chronicle began with American Indian tribes, and we have returned often to African-American traditions. But many other ethnic groups, including eastern, western, northern, and southern European ones, Caribbean immigrants from outside the Spanish-language orbit, and Asians (especially Chinese), have also carried on

Tito Puente (1923–2000), Latin band leader and percussionist, pictured at a 1998 festival in the Bahamas.

their own musical practices. Where do such traditions belong in American music history?

Few symbols of national identity are more potent than music. While some ethnic groups adapted traditional repertories to New World situations, others maintained music orally that in the Old World had been abandoned much earlier. Non-English-speaking groups have tended to be more conscious of their folk heritage than native-born Americans, and music has helped these immigrants keep the cohesion of their group while also gaining the respect of mainstream society. Many have promoted their folk heritage through modern means, with books and cassette tapes replacing oral tradition.

The oldest music preserved by such groups as the Amish is mostly religious. In contrast, Jewish-American traditions are chiefly secular and wildly eclectic. French Cajun–American music of southern Louisiana, also secular, can claim roots reaching as far back as the mid-eighteenth century, when Acadians were deported from Nova Scotia to the southern colony. Slavic and Polish-American music has also taken root. And the 3.5 million Asian Americans, including Chinese, Japanese, Koreans, Indians, Pakistanis, Filipinos, and recent arrivals from Vietnam, Cambodia, and Laos have preserved their native customs while also assimilating into American society. Reflecting the contrary pulls of ethnicity and the melting pot, immigrants are likely to feel both a desire to adapt to their new environment and a drive to maintain their ethnic heritage. Singing societies and theaters have furthered ethnic music in America, as have the record industry and the commercial media.

This brief overview leads back to one of our chronicle's main premises: that the history of music in America revolves around performance. Only after studying performance contexts can we come to grips with the role of composition, written or oral. All the ethnic traditions named so far, chosen from among many possibilities, could have appeared earlier in our story. We mention them now because of the way these traditions have been perceived in America (and keeping in mind that not until the 1960s did the word "ethnicity" come into common use).

YOUTH, ETHNICITY, AND THE FOLK REVIVAL IN THE EARLY 1960s

Before the 1960s, most Americans recognized a patriotic duty to place the national interest above the wishes of their own faction. When President John F. Kennedy urged people in 1961 to "ask not what your country can do for you; ask what you can do for your country," patriotism seemed alive and well. Yet by 1970, the notion of "your country" lost much of its power to command allegiance. And group identity challenged the melting-pot ethos, which was rooted in patriotic feelings of an earlier day.

Though not universal, the shift away from a collective American identity was widespread among ethnic groups. Some African-American leaders called for racial separation as an alternative to the civil rights movement's drive for integration. American Indians banded together to claim political rights lost in the settlement of North America. Mexican Americans formed a "Chicano" movement that took pride in Mexican culture and in the Spanish language. And then there was the generation gap, which divided Americans by age.

We have seen how white teenagers in the mid-1950s distanced themselves from their parents' generation. Over the next couple of decades, baby boomers bought into the notion that their parents had not managed the country well. An ethnic issue lay at the heart of this verdict. The civil rights struggle proved that African Americans were still being denied basic rights of citizenship, especially in the South. By 1960, a few white college students had begun to join in the campaign for equality under the law. Opposition increased sharply after 1965, when, in a bid to stop the spread of communism, the United States entered a long-simmering civil war in Vietnam. By the end of the decade, the student generation's quarrel with its elders had erupted on many campuses into open revolt.

College-age activists of the early 1960s were idealistic young men and women for whom the folk music revival provided a source of identity. Rejecting commercial mass culture, they became singers and players, borrowing, performing, and reshaping music from the traditional sphere to address concerns of their own. By learning these songs and mastering the styles of traditional performers, revivalists saw themselves as renewing connections with a strain of democratic experience that modern life was threatening to destroy.

Having claimed common ground with music makers in traditional cultures, revival musicians mixed with them more often as social equals. This approach was encouraged by the rise of ethnomusicology, an academic field centered on the study of traditional music. Personal contact led some revivalists beyond Anglo-American and African-American traditions, which had so far dominated the revival. By the 1990s, folk styles from Latin America, Africa, Indonesia, eastern Europe, and the Middle East would turn the traditional sphere into a continuous, spiraling process of musical globalization. The blendings, and the commercial negotiations involved, called older notions of folk purity and authenticity into question. During the 1960s, however, performers in ethnic traditions, from Latino salsa players in New York City to Chinese opera singers in San Francisco, were sometimes claimed as allies by those with a political agenda.

The folk revival used old and new forms to comment on current issues. One who provided a link to the political heritage of the 1930s was Bob Dylan. Born in 1941, Dylan learned to play the guitar in high school and briefly attended the University of Minnesota. In 1960, he made a New York pilgrimage to the bedside of an ailing Woody Guthrie (father of performer-songwriter Arlo Guthrie). Donning the mantle of Guthrie, who a generation earlier had written topical folk songs with political messages, Dylan in 1963 recorded *The Times They Are a-Changing*, an anthem to the generation gap that threw down the gauntlet to older Americans. Set in 3/4 time, the words declare that parents cannot really know daughters and sons who have already joined other young comrades in rejecting older values. Dylan accompanies himself on acoustic guitar. His voice—nasal, a bit thin, uncultivated in sound but with clear declamation of the words—evokes Guthrie's spirit.

By the time Dylan wrote this song, he had already made a mark as a folk-revival musician. Yet Dylan did not fit comfortably into the revival movement. He showed a special affinity for love songs whose bitter tone was tied neither to folk tradition nor any apparent social cause. Using the folk revival's acoustic guitar accompaniments, and singing in a somewhat strident voice, Dylan offered songs that showed a high standard of professional skill, challenging audiences rather than offering them easy listening pleasures.

We can recognize Dylan as an artist in transition from his appearances at the Newport Folk Festivals of 1963, 1964, and 1965. In the 1963 festival's first evening concert, he sang a set of his own topical songs to an appreciative audience. The concert ended with Dylan, Joan Baez, Pete Seeger, and others joining together on *We Shall Overcome*, the anthem of the civil rights movement. In August of that year, the same performers gathered to sing during a march on Washington, which culminated in the Reverend Martin Luther King's historic "I have a dream" speech on the steps of the Lincoln Memorial.

Dylan's contribution to the Newport Festival of 1964 consisted of two new songs that could have been topical only to him: *It Ain't Me, Babe* and *Mr. Tambourine Man*. And the subpar quality of his performance at an

The final concert in the 1963 Newport Folk Festival ended with the singing of the spiritual *We Shall Overcome* by many of the participants, including (left to right): the group Peter, Paul, and Mary (Paul Stookey, Mary Travers, Peter Yarrow), Joan Baez, Bob Dylan, Rutha Mae Harris, Charles Neblett, Cordell Reagon, Bernice Johnson, and Pete Seeger. Standing at Seeger's left but not visible in this picture was actor-folksinger Theodore Bikel.

evening's concert was noted. But the festival that year also included musicians and styles outside the usual folk circle. One was the country singer
Johnny Cash. Another was Muddy Waters, a bluesman from the Mississippi Delta who performed with amplified instruments. These two musicians, plus Dylan's own determination to move beyond topical songs,
pointed the way to elements that the young singer would soon integrate
into a fresh personal idiom.

Dylan's performance with rock-and-roll backing at the Newport Folk
Festival of 1965 has long been recognized as a landmark event. Yet "electric songs" were more a return than a departure, for he had grown up listening to and playing rock and roll. Dylan later admitted to having latched
on to folk singing when he got to New York City "because I saw a huge
audience was there." Constructing a folk singer's persona, he won both
artistic and commercial success, but without sharing the folk revival's devotion to musical boundaries.

When Dylan appeared onstage with the Butterfield Blues Band and
an electric guitar, the audience registered its disapproval. And when he
led the band into *Like a Rolling Stone*, the outcry grew noisier: "This is a
folk festival! Get rid of that band!" Pete Seeger is said to have turned pur-
ple, perhaps even to have threatened to destroy the stage wiring system.
After one more number, Dylan and his musicians left the stage. Returning alone with an acoustic guitar, he was able to calm the crowd. But in
effect, Dylan was bidding farewell to the folk audience.

Dylan's performance at Newport '65 did much to carry him from the
traditional into the popular sphere. This move freed him from the folk revival's tendency to view human affairs as a struggle between honorable
friends and evil enemies. As folk singer Dave Van Ronk once put it, the
danger of a protest song was that it served to "dissociate you and your
audience from all the evils of the world"—a naive position in his view,
and in Dylan's too, for both understood good and evil to be intertwined
in ways that involve everyone.

By 1965, social change was opening the realm of popular song to the
complexities and ambiguities that filled Bob Dylan's imagination. As well
as Woody Guthrie, Dylan had also been drawn to poetry by the French
symbolist Arthur Rimbaud and such beat poets as Allen Ginsberg and
Jack Kerouac. And now he deepened his engagement with the grotesque
and the absurd in art, with existentialism, and with dreams and halluci-
nations. In an earlier day, such mental terrain would never have inspired
popular songs. But never before had the popular music audience included
so many educated young people who were avidly looking for messages.

Dylan's *Like a Rolling Stone* (unavailable for use in this record set), in

Bob Dylan sings at the piano with harmonica
at the ready.

which he sings caustic words to a joyous, almost hymnlike accompaniment, shows the power of his fresh approach to songwriting and performance. Electric guitars, piano, and organ play over a foundation of bass guitar, drums, and tambourine. Dylan's voice slices in over the rolling tide of electrified sound, as amplification allows players to relax while still projecting adequate volume. Too free in form, repetitive in material, and scarce in vocal melody to pass as a standard pop, country, or folk song, this number from 1965 is an early example of a rock song. (A trade paper proclaimed it in 1976 the top rock single of all time.) In the chorus, the instruments sound as if they are playing responses to Dylan's vocal calls: driving, bluesified figures over which a short, patterned organ melody soars.

Like a Rolling Stone lasts six minutes, unusually long for a pop single. The subject is also unusual: an overprotected person being forced out into a cruel world. But even as his song lays out a scenario of existential loneliness, Dylan offers a counternarrative in sound: the undisguised camaraderie of musicians who are having a wonderful time playing together.

BLACK-WHITE INTERACTIONS

"Little Richard" Penniman, a black rock and roller of the 1950s, once confided: "I believe my music can make the blind see, the lame walk, the deaf and dumb hear and talk, because it inspires and uplifts people. . . . it regenerates the heart and makes the liver quiver, the bladder splatter, the knees freeze." These words by a star performer testified that the new popular music was capable of exploding into the realm of the spirit.

Rather than a style, rock and roll has been called a culture that grants musicians access to a broad range of music, and that allows them to be rebellious. The notion that rock and roll is a music with an attitude helps to explain why it found a willing audience in the 1960s. The year of Bob Dylan's *Like a Rolling Stone* (1965) was also the year the U.S. government began sending troops to Southeast Asia. Many younger Americans saw the war in Vietnam as a symbol of national failure, and rock musicians helped fans hone a vocabulary of disrespect for elders and the status quo. Their personalities, costumes, and hair styles seemed calculated to widen the generation gap. Ear-splitting volume, harsh singing, raucous guitar playing, and a fondness for repetition signaled that these musicians meant to overturn musical refinement. Song lyrics, behavior, and the publicity surrounding the new breed called "rock star" flaunted restrictions on sex and on drug use. A young writer of the day commented in 1971: "There was a fantastic universal sense that whatever we were doing was *right*, that we were winning. . . . We were riding the crest of a high and beautiful wave."

But politics has probably not been uppermost in the minds of most people who over the years have listened and danced to rock and roll. Behind the cutting edge of unruliness, an expressive territory has opened up in which singers, players, and songwriters have found almost limitless possibilities in styles, moods, and persuasions. The rock-and-roll musician Robbie Robertson remembered the mid-sixties as a charmed musical age, with Bob Dylan, the Beatles, and the Motown and Stax record companies all breaking exciting new ground. "Everything was changing, all these doors were being opened, and it made you think, 'I could try *anything, right now.*'" It was an era when a young musician could aspire to being artistically serious *and* commercially successful.

New patterns of black-white exchange powered these revolutionary times. Until the 1960s, white control of the music business had been taken for granted. During that decade, however, star performers won more independence, and the balance of power began to shift. Racial interaction changed too. More white singers and players tried to match the emotional intensity of black gospel and blues performers, and more white listeners became their fans. Two record companies in particular flourished in this climate.

Founded in Detroit in 1959 by black songwriter Berry Gordy Jr., the Motown record company in the 1960s came to be one of the most influential in the history of popular music. Motown's records, with performers drawn chiefly from Detroit's black community, combined elements from rhythm and blues, gospel, blues, and rock and roll with the aim of attracting white listeners as well as black. The Motown sound relied heavily on mainstream pop trappings, including orchestras with string sections. At the same time, the recordings boasted a vital rhythmic core, supplied by a jazz-oriented rhythm section sometimes called "the Funk Brothers." The company's blend of pop lushness with rhythmic bite and imaginative harmonies proved appealing to white and black listeners alike. In the racial climate of the 1960s and after, white teenaged audiences were ready to respond to black performers. Such Motown stars as Diana Ross and the Supremes, Smokey Robinson and the Miracles, Marvin Gaye, Stevie Wonder, and the Jackson Five enjoyed great success in the marketplace.

Meanwhile, white-owned Stax/Volt Records in Memphis was making rhythm-and-blues hits with black singers backed by Booker T. and the MGs, a racially mixed rhythm section. In 1962, the label released its first record by Otis Redding, a singer from Macon, Georgia, who soon became Stax's best-selling artist. In 1965, Jerry Wexler of New York's Atlantic label, traveled to Memphis with Wilson Pickett and other Atlantic artists and recorded them with Stax's Booker T. and the MGs. The link with Wexler and Atlantic allowed Stax to improve its distribution. Thus a Memphis firm's combination of black singers, Southern white ownership, national marketing network, and mix of white and black instrumentalists gave rise to "soul" music, which by the latter 1960s was being marketed as quintessentially black.

The career of singer-songwriter-dancer-bandleader James Brown, raised around Augusta, Georgia, reflects another kind of black-white interaction. As a teenager, learning piano to supplement his drumming and guitar playing, Brown "got all the Hit Parade books and learned all the pop tunes," admiring especially numbers by Bing Crosby and Frank Sinatra. Another inspiration came from the black church, whose atmosphere impressed Brown deeply. He remembered one revival service featuring a preacher who screamed, stamped his feet, and dropped to his knees. "The people got into it with him, answering him and shouting and clapping time." The experience stuck with Brown, who from then on studied preachers closely and imitated them.

James Brown (at the microphone) and the Famous Flames perform in 1967 with the James Brown Orchestra.

Brown's first big break came in the mid-1950s, when he began recording for King Records in Cincinnati. Having scored a national hit with *Please, Please, Please* (1956), he and his group hired a touring band. By the early 1960s, the James Brown Show was an evening-length revue, built around the star's energy. According to Brown, he was now performing as many as 350 days a year. Billed as "the hardest-working man in show business," Brown took a blue-collar approach to his profession. "When you're on stage," he wrote, "the people who paid money to get in are the boss, even if it cost them only a quarter. You're working for them." Brown developed a charismatic presence, not only as a singer but as an accomplished, athletic dancer who mesmerized audiences with splits, leaps, and other exuberant steps.

By 1964, James Brown was moving away from conventional song structures and toward a new emphasis on movement and dance. For example, *Papa's Got a Brand New Bag* (1965), more than four minutes long, devotes less than half its length to a sung delivery of the lyrics, which celebrate dancing.

LISTENING GUIDE 66

Papa's Got a Brand New Bag (Brown)

Papa begins with the briefest of intros: a sustained blast from a band that plays with fierce precision from start to finish. Brown sings a pair of vocal choruses in twelve-bar blues form, followed by an eight-bar bridge and another two choruses. But at this point, the blues structure disappears to be replaced by a vamp—here a repeated four-beat unit built on a rhythm in the bass: ♩. ♪♫♫ The melody instruments interlock with that figure by attacking the second beat with an explosive accent: ♪ ♫♫ ♪ ♪. The drummer accents the backbeats (two and four) regularly. This lurching, effortful vamp churns ahead for the next two and a half minutes to the final fadeout, overlaid by a long tenor sax solo and Brown's shouts of encouragement. (In live performance, the singer danced this part of the number.) Brown's commitment to rhythm is made unmistakable by *Papa*'s two-part form, which uses song to introduce the vamp instead of the other way around. By this time in his career, Brown later said, "I was hearing everything, even the guitars, like they were drums."

In *Papa's Got a Brand New Bag* and other recordings that followed, Brown virtually invented the style we now call "funk," and in the process became the best-selling rhythm-and-blues artist of the day. He was the only 1950s rhythm-and-blues singer to bridge the gap successfully to soul artist in the 1960s and funk artist in the 1970s. Echoes of Brown's techniques were inescapable on black radio of the 1980s. And his influence has proved international, extending to European new wave music, West African Afrobeat, and West Indian reggae.

38

The Beatles, Rock, and Popular Music

BY THE LATE 1950s, ROCK AND ROLL ENJOYED A PROMINENT PLACE in the youth culture of the United Kingdom as well as the United States. A few British youngsters encountered African-American styles through recordings by Southern blues artists. Many more took in the sounds of Chuck Berry, Fats Domino, and Elvis Presley. By around 1960, the city of Liverpool and its environs alone boasted almost three hundred rock-and-roll clubs and as many local bands, including one that began there in 1956 as the Quarrymen. The group, founded by singer and guitarist John Lennon—rhythm guitarist Paul McCartney joined the same year, lead guitarist George Harrison joined in 1957, and drummer Ringo Starr was added later—was reincarnated as Johnny and the Moondogs and finally as the Beatles. In their early days, the group played rough-and-tumble clubs in Hamburg, Germany, as well as the Cavern Club in Liverpool.

In 1962, after several other companies had rejected their demonstration tape, the Beatles won a recording contract with EMI. George Martin, the producer who signed them, admitted that neither the group's singing nor their original songs impressed him much at first, but he was taken with their engaging personalities. Martin was more impressed after traveling to Liverpool for a performance at the Cavern Club. The Beatles "sang all the rock-and-roll numbers that they'd copied from American records, and it was very raucous, and the kids loved every minute of it." Martin spotted at once "the total commitment of the Beatles" in front of an audience, "which somehow got down to the very roots of what the kids wanted." During 1963, featuring more original songs by Lennon and McCartney, the Beatles won such ardent popularity in Britain that their reception earned its own label: "Beatlemania." The group's twelve successive number-one singles hits in 1964–65 had no precedent. In those years, Martin recalled, "the question was not whether a record would get to number one, but how quickly. In the end, it was happening in the first week, with advance sales around the million mark."

The Beatles' impact in the United States was sudden, far-reaching, and at first dependent on adolescent girls. American Beatlemania began in 1964 with the group's appearance on the Ed Sullivan television show. The screaming teenagers recalled Frank Sinatra's performances in the 1940s and Elvis Presley's in the 1950s. And their enthusiasm helped to enrich the record industry's coffers through a remarkable sales development: the Beatles' first LP, "Meet the Beatles," outsold the group's first single by a margin of 3.6 million to 3.4 million, the first time an album had ever sold more copies than its single counterpart.

The Beatles' American reception, a subject that received wide attention in its own day and after, may be boiled down to a chronology:

1964   Appearance on "Ed Sullivan Show" on February 9 wins highest Nielson rating in TV history, with an audience of 73 million. *I Want to Hold Your Hand* becomes No. 1 record in United States. Eight other Beatles recordings are top sellers for the year. The movie *A Hard Day's Night* released.

1965   Beatles concert fills New York's Shea Stadium on September 16.

1966   Last live Beatles concert given in San Francisco on August 29.

1967   *Sergeant Pepper's Lonely Hearts Club Band* recording released; *Magic Mystery Tour* album released, tying in with TV movie of same name.

1968   Total record sales calculated at more than 200 million worldwide.

1969   John Lennon marries Yoko Ono on March 20.

1970   *Abbey Road* recording released, the Beatles' last LP; Paul McCartney announces his departure from the group.

1975   Beatles partnership legally dissolved.

These events outline a fairly clear path: immediate acceptance on a grand scale; a retreat from public life; a new burst of artistic growth; a continuing appeal to record buyers; and the growing pressures of wealth and fame, leading to a breakup. From an artistic standpoint, the 1966 entry marks a basic shift in the life of the group. The Beatles' audience had grown so enormous that touring and live performance lost their appeal. Therefore, the group concentrated on the recording studio, experimenting with new textures, forms, and sounds.

If the Beatles' impact was remarkable in the 1960s, it came to be even more so for the way the music outlived the group itself. Beatles recordings are still heard on the radio and are readily available in record stores. Music and book stores carry the songs in sheet-music folios and fake books; and in 1989, *The Beatles: Complete Scores* appeared in print, a huge volume containing full transcriptions of 213 songs recorded by the group. Chronicles, biographies, and discographies document the Beatles' career, and critical interpretations of their music abound. Today the Beatles can claim many devoted fans who were not yet born when their partnership dissolved. In pursuing the popular sphere's goal of accessibility, the Beatles created a body of recorded music that now seems on the brink of achieving artistic transcendence. While the Beatles are not the only rock-and-roll musicians to approach this position, their matchless success, breadth of appeal, and slant on the issue of social class did put them in a category by themselves. To understand what made the Beatles different, we also have to look overseas.

The Beatles' musical roots have been traced to Little Richard's hard-edged rocking and Motown's softer call-and-response style, two approaches that had never before been combined. And the way they treated the British class system was especially crucial to their success. Many novels and films of the latter 1950s took the perspective that working-class life was more honest, real, and interesting than life in the middle class. Coming from working-class backgrounds themselves, the Beatles might have made perfect spokesmen for that attitude. Instead, they undermined it, reveling in wealth and fame. Their image of working-class youth was irrepressibly playful, showing no more respect for the notion of class-based virtue than for the older aristocratic hierarchy. And audiences found their expressions of hedonism charming. Indeed, both male and female audiences seemed to love the Beatles, one of very few groups who turned out to be as musically interesting as they were fun to watch.

Three points need to be kept in mind in any discussion of the Beatles' music. First, the group's appeal to teenage fans formed the cornerstone of their career. Second, the originality and freshness of their songwriting help to explain their staying power. And third, the Beatles' claim to artistry owes much to their use of the recording studio and the idea that an LP album can make a unified statement through related songs.

In 1964, Lennon and McCartney's *Can't Buy Me Love* appeared as a single record, quickly earning number-one hit status on both sides of the Atlantic. The end of each verse repeats the song's message: "I don't care too much for money / For money can't buy me love." And the title line also forms the basis of the chorus, though sung to a different tune (do-mi-sol-*sol*-mi). The tempo is quick, the singing youthful and exuberant. The verses follow the twelve-bar blues chord progression, but this is not a song about a problem. Rather, it enacts the spirit-lifting, joyous feeling of being in love, which makes jewelry, cash, and other possessions seem trivial. In *Can't Buy Me Love*, the Beatles were working out of the straightforward approach they developed while absorbing American influences during their years in Liverpool and Hamburg.

A more musically adventurous side of the group appears in *You're Going to Lose That Girl*, written for the movie *Help!* (1965). The song blends unconventional and conventional elements from the start: a statement of the chorus with no instrumental intro. The chorus text consists of the title line, sung by the lead and backup singers as a call and response, over a familiar harmonic progression (I-vi-ii-V in E major). But the chorus is unusually short (four bars) and open-ended, sounding more like half a statement than a whole one.

Next comes an eight-bar verse sung by Lennon and echoed by McCartney and Harrison.

> If you don't take her out tonight
> She's going to change her mind,
> And I will take her out tonight
> And I will treat her kind.

After more verse and chorus alternation, an extension of the chorus pulls the key level into G major and a stomping new statement:

> I'll make a point
> Of taking her away from you,
> (What would you do?) Yeah!
> The way you treat her
> What else can I do?

From there to the song's end, earlier sections are repeated often enough to make the harmonic shifts sound less strange, though still offbeat and fresh.

The thirteen musical numbers of *Sergeant Pepper's Lonely Hearts Club Band* could be called a song cycle. According to George Martin, the idea of a unified album came from Paul McCartney. After writing one song about a band led by a mythical character named Sergeant Pepper, McCartney suggested: "Why don't we make the album as though the Pepper band really existed, as though Sergeant Pepper was making the record? We'll dub in effects and things." Martin recalled: "I loved the idea, and from that moment it was as though *Pepper* had a life of its own." Looking back in 1979, Martin remembered *Sergeant Pepper* not only as their top seller but as the album that turned the group "from being just an ordinary rock-and-roll group into being significant contributors to the history of artistic performance." In his view, *Sergeant Pepper* used record-

The cover of the Beatles' album *Sergeant Pepper's Lonely Hearts Club Band* is one of the enduring icons of the 1960s.

ing techniques to create "a valid art form: sculpture in music, if you like." Having taken over 900 hours of studio time to put together, the *Sergeant Pepper* album is unperformable in a live setting.

Lennon and McCartney's *A Day in the Life*, "the major piece of the whole album" according to Martin, cannot be summarized as if it were an independent number. For it was the last of a series of songs in an album intended to make a cumulative impression. All of the song lyrics are included with the record; so are many color photos of the Beatles, dressed in fancy band uniforms. The cover shows the Beatles as bandsmen surrounded by effigies of several dozen historical figures, living and dead, including Karl Marx, Marilyn Monroe, W. C. Fields, Oscar Wilde, Marlon Brando, Bob Dylan, Mohandas K. Ghandi, Shirley Temple, Karlheinz Stockhausen, and Albert Einstein. And the ways the lyrics of the thirteen songs are connected with each other are no more straightforward than are the links among this assortment of characters.

A Day in the Life, which begins with the voice of John Lennon singing, "I read the news today, oh boy," meditates on life in the modern world. Sounding a bit bewildered, the singer notes a few of a single day's experiences: hearing news of a traffic fatality, seeing a war film, and reading about the nation's deteriorating roads, sandwiched around the problem of getting to work in the morning. Lacking rock and roll's usual catchiness and rhythmic drive, the music is more discontinuous, less tuneful, and built around studio effects. The song's only direct statement of personal feeling, the line "I'd love to turn you on," which Lennon sings near the middle and again at the end, is answered both times by a long, slow, somewhat discordant *crescendo*, filling twenty-four bars and played by a symphony orchestra, which George Martin hired and conducted for this recording. Once recorded, this passage was spliced into the final version, illustrating what Martin meant when he called the album a "sculpture in music."

One critic compared *A Day in the Life* to the poet T. S. Eliot's masterpiece *The Waste Land*. Another likened the song to Picasso's *Guernica*, the monumental 1937 painting that depicts the horrors of the Spanish Civil War. This writer heard echoes of nuclear disaster in the orchestra *crescendo* and the reverberation of the last chord (which, thanks to George Martin's sound sculpturing, takes almost a minute to die away). Such judgments would have been unimaginable for a popular song in an earlier day. But during the 1960s, the work of Dylan, the Beatles, and other popular stars suddenly seemed worthy of critical treatment, and a new breed of writer, the rock critic, appeared on the scene. The periodical *Rolling Stone*, begun in 1967, was one of several journals founded in the latter 1960s to celebrate the countercultural spirit, including the work of rock musicians, in all their varied styles.

Subgenres of rock abounded: hard rock, soft rock, folk rock, progressive rock, rockabilly, heavy metal, jazz rock, acid rock, and others. The rapid growth of the popular-music audience brought influence and power increasingly into the hands of a select group of performers. Yet fame and wealth could be dangerous. The example of such stars as Jim Morrison of the Doors, Janis Joplin of Big Brother and the Holding Company, and guitarist Jimi Hendrix, all of whom lived hard and died young, embodied the destructive side of success. But those like Elvis Presley, who eventually outlived his early fame, faced the risk of growing so rich and reclusive that they might lose the edge that had made listeners' livers quiver in the first place. Thus punk rock, a mid-1970s genre in which inexpert but passionate performers offered a radically nihilistic view of society, was an attempt to purge rock of greed and musical professionalism; such genres have allowed rock and roll to maintain a rebellious edge despite its grounding in the commercial marketplace.

So far in this chronicle, "rock and roll" and "rock" have been treated as if they were synonymous, but it is now time to distinguish between them. Until the middle 1960s, the term "rock and roll" had been applied generally to post–Tin Pan Alley popular styles. By 1967, however, when such San Francisco–based groups as Big Brother and the Holding Company, the Jefferson Airplane, and the Grateful Dead gained national attention, the term "rock" was coming into use for their music. In addition to a heavy reliance on electricity (for amplification and the mixing of instruments and voices, which requires manipulation in a sound studio), the new style featured a wider variety of instruments, more flexible song forms, and intensely subjective lyrics. While rock and roll was a working-class idiom that appealed to working-class people *and* teenagers across the economic spectrum, rock was tailored for white suburban youth. By the early 1970s, members of the rock audience might be found embracing such varied styles and artists as the classical Indian music of Ravi Shankar, the fusion of jazz and rock by Miles Davis, Joan Baez's folk revival songs, organist Virgil Fox, who sometimes superimposed a light show on his performances of J. S. Bach, and avant-garde composer John

Janis Joplin (1943–1970), one of the 1960s' outstanding female rock singers, onstage.

Cage—if for no other reason than because many listeners outside the rock community would find something incomprehensible or offensive in the music of each of them.

In the late 1960s, Americans were placing a new emphasis on personal identity, growing out of the generation gap, the civil rights movement, the rise of ethnic pride, the gay rights movement, and a women's movement that was just getting started. And rock music, with its concern for individuals and knack for getting at serious issues, offered a ready means for expressing identity and trying out new ones. In the following decades, rock has defined the popular sphere's commercial mainstream. Many Americans continue to find its populist stance authentic and engaging. Moreover, the exclusion of nonfans lends a provocative edge to the rock experience. As long as a sizable audience believes in the sensation of a community favoring "rebellious" personal identities and ready to scorn those outside the tribe, the music seems likely to maintain its place in the popular sphere.

39

Trouble Girls,
Minimalists, and The Gap

THE 1960s TO THE 1980s

AS MALE-FEMALE RELATIONS HAVE CHANGED IN LATE TWENTIETH-
century America, women have explored a widening range of identities.
Music has been involved in that exploration. In the early 1960s, for example, popular vocal ensembles made up of women ("girl groups") spoke
powerfully to girls and female teenagers, who were bombarded with contradictory messages from parents, teachers, and the mass media. The
songs of girl groups allowed teens to play at being the defiant rebel as
well as the docile girlfriend. *Sweet Talkin' Guy*, by the Chiffons, a recording from 1960, offers an example. The song is about a deceitful, irresistible
male charmer. Its message is that it's normal to want to yield to such boys
as well as try to resist them.

Also in the early 1960s, movies, literature, and fashion proclaimed a
new openness about sexuality. That openness followed a breakthrough
in biology: the 1960 appearance on the market of the birth-control pill.
Women could now engage in sexual activity without worrying about un-
wanted pregnancies. With fertility under control through contraception
and abortion, growing numbers of married women pursued careers outside the home, and family roles changed accordingly. This development
had many causes, from economic (the desire for a higher standard of living) to personal (the wish for a more stimulating life). Since the 1970s, it
has been supported by the women's movement, which has challenged the
idea that women are truly fulfilled only through child care and house-
work.

As we saw in Chapter 32, songwriters in the 1920s began celebrating romantic love between free individuals. But rock-and-roll songs
introduced other views of love. For young men and women of recent
generations, sexuality was no longer an undercurrent but a realm of self-
assertion. Where the characters in earlier love songs longed for connec-

496

tion, those of rock songs also perceived that male-female connections involved power. Though women may have been freed from earlier stereotypes, they were assigned new ones, still subordinate to men, including the flower child, earthmother, and idealized prostitute. The tension between sexual freedom and restraint persisted.

Whatever the balance of power between males and females today, there is a strong tendency to picture young modern women as independent, even untamable, rejecting the view that their identity revolves around duty. That tendency is found throughout *Trouble Girls: The Rolling Stone Book of Women in Rock* (1997), written and edited entirely by women. The cover features P. J. Harvey, a British rock-and-roll performer, repre-

British rock singer P. J. Harvey graces the cover of this publication of 1997.

senting the spirit of modern womanhood. Harvey's image, caught in motion, invites the male gaze while at the same time repelling it. ("Stare all you want," the image seems to say, "but try to touch me, and I'm outta here.") Harvey glories in her attractiveness, aware of the power that looks like hers can wield. But the image seems to signify that this cover girl needs no one—especially not a man who might try to take her under his wing.

In the final essay, the book's general editor celebrates Harvey's emotional authenticity. The singer's "hard-headed songs," "full of slash-and-burn exuberance," are praised. And Harvey's second album (1993) is called "a raw-throated, mud-soaked woundfest" whose songs form "a brilliant miasma of tortured love and fractured fables," as well as "a roiling ball of gorgeous aggression."

Trouble Girls, which returns often to the theme of suppressed rage, reads like a 1990s time capsule touting the need for women to speak their mind and to confront misogyny. In the preface, a prominent female rock critic of the 1960s endorses truth telling, wherever it leads: "Music that boldly and aggressively laid out what the singer wanted, loved, hated— as good rock & roll did—challenged me to do the same, and so, even when the content was antiwoman . . . the form encouraged my struggle for liberation." The responsibilities of marriage and motherhood are seldom mentioned. A woman's right to live life in accord with personal priorities and wishes is assumed, free from any program dictated by earlier social custom or even by biology.

Rock and roll, at first a male enterprise, saw its expression broadened by such 1960s pioneers as Carole King, Aretha Franklin, Diana Ross, Laura Nyro, and Grace Slick. And the women who followed them broadened it even further. From blues-based performers (Janis Joplin, Bonnie Raitt) to the cabaret, theater, and screen (Bette Midler); from writers of their own material (Raitt, Joni Mitchell) to interpreters of the songs of others (Midler, Linda Ronstadt); and from black-influenced (Raitt, Joplin, Tina Turner) to Mexican and Hispanic (Ronstadt), these women dramatize rock's diversity. For several decades, rock music has been an arena where modern identities for women are being proposed and constructed.

WOMEN IN CLASSICAL MUSIC

Opportunity for women in the classical sphere has been limited until recent years. Before World War II, almost all performers in major symphony orchestras were male; although separate women's orchestras also existed, they disappeared almost entirely after the war, and since then integration has been the pattern. In 1947, female employment in orchestras stood at 8 percent; by 1982, that figure had risen to 26.3 percent. Such changes indicate that women's past exclusion was based on prejudice.

Women also made small gains in classical composition, a field long monopolized by men. Commissions and prizes awarded by foundations have overwhelmingly favored men, though a pattern of more inclusiveness could be found in the Guggenheim, Koussevitsky, and Fromm Foundation awards to composers after the mid-1960s. By the 1980s, female composers were working in a wide range of styles: serial music (Louise Talma, Joan Tower, Barbara Kolb), sound-mass (Kolb, Nancy Van de Vate), sonic exploration (Annea Lockwood, Lucia Dlugoszewski, Darleen Cowles Mitchell, and Julia Perry), performance art (Pauline Oliveros, Laurie Anderson, Joan LaBarbera, Meredith Monk), electronic and computer music (Emma Lou Diemer, Jean Eichelberger Ivey), symphonic music (Ellen Taaffe Zwilich), and a synthesis of old and new elements (Elaine Barkin, Libby Larsen, Joyce Mekeel).

Women have often been said to approach music making differently from men. In a 1984 essay, Pauline Oliveros describes contrasting creative modes: "(1) active, purposive creativity, resulting from cognitive thought,

Composer Pauline Oliveros (b. 1932) has pioneered the exploration of musical sound and the presence of women in avant-garde musical circles.

deliberate acting upon or willful shaping of materials, and (2) receptive creativity, during which the artist is like a channel through which material flows and seems to shape itself." According to Oliveros, society has valued the first mode—analytical and "identified with aggression and masculinity"—more highly than the second, which she calls intuitive. Women, she believes, are more likely than men to recognize the intuitive mode as an alternative to the analytical.

Oliveros has been called the female counterpart of John Cage, with each of her works a kind of meditation on sound itself. During the 1970s, she composed a series of *Sonic Meditations*: collective improvisations that can involve the audience ("My feeling was that if somebody wanted to participate they were welcome, but if they didn't there was no obligation"). Compositions of this kind are attuned toward intuition and receptivity and away from analytical modes. Oliveros has tried to make audiences more aware of sound and its sensuousness, while at the same time raising consciousness about women as creators of music.

Pauline Oliveros is also recognized for helping to found a new genre: so-called performance art, linked chiefly with female composers who came on the scene in the 1970s. Women—the dancer-filmmaker-singer-composer Meredith Monk, for example—have shown more inclination than men to consider their own bodies and voices as material for the making of music. Born in 1942, Monk was one of a number of younger Americans who developed alternative approaches to music and sound. Reversing the postwar trend toward the analytical mode, their work offers fresh notions of what it means to be an American composer.

THE GAP AND THE IDENTITY OF AMERICAN COMPOSERS

Perhaps no twentieth-century condition has done more to fragment the world of classical music than the gap between composer and audience. Since the 1910s, exploring new musical territory has often been considered a higher artistic goal for a composer than communicating with general audiences. Commenting wryly on "The Gap," the author of a 1997 study has written: "We pretend to lament its existence, but actually, we have become so proud of it that, when music doesn't put up barriers to the audience's comprehension or patience, we accuse it of not being authentically twentieth-century." The writer is composer Kyle Gann, born in 1955 in Dallas. As he sees it, the rise of academia after World War II widened The Gap even further. Favoring the intellectual side of composition, it put a damper on expression and ignored audience response. In recent years, more accessible approaches have attracted new audiences—especially to so-called minimalism. Another approach ("totalism") combining complex twentieth-century systems (e.g., serialism) with a beat while engaging listeners' emotions, holds out promise for a classical sphere in the new millennium that is not so sharply divided against itself.

Keeping in mind that many more composers exist today than ever before, and that their range of styles is enormous, we can identify seven conditions that divide the musical world of American composers born in the 1950s (and after) from that of older composers:

1. European music of the 1700s and 1800s (Bach to Debussy) has lost much of its privileged position.

2. If Americans have a common musical culture, it comes from the radio.

3. Because so much music is now made directly on a computer screen, musical notation is fading in importance.

4. Few scores are published today, but recorded music is easy to distribute; therefore, new music is more likely than ever before to be judged by how it sounds.

5. Thanks to sound samplers, which can record any sound and play it back at any pitch level, the most elemental musical unit, which used to be the individual note, may now be a complex of sounds or a quotation.

6. Because the experience of rock music is almost universal, composers who hope to reach a live audience rarely write without referring to rock's musical conventions.

7. Today's audience for classical music has splintered into many different groups, each increasingly cut off from the others.

In general, younger classical composers are inclined to accept the world as they find it and to ground their work in conditions they encounter in everyday life. Influence seems to be passing away from composers who see themselves as champions of quality in an age of quantity. Traditional barriers of nationality, culture, and economics are wearing down, and the supply of music grows increasingly out of proportion to the demand. An almost limitless capacity exists to gather, record, reshape, and circulate musical sound. In a culture of such abundance, the idea of composing as a private activity, walled off within the classical sphere's contemporary wing, seems more parochial than praiseworthy.

Three distinct kinds of composers dominated the New York classical scene in the mid-1960s: the composer as intellectual, the composer as experimentalist, and the composer as creator of works for the concert hall. Serial (intellectual) composers dominated academia. Composer Jacob Druckman remembered that "not being a serialist on the East Coast of the United States in the sixties was like not being a Catholic in Rome in the thirteenth century." Though their audience was small, serialists dealt with artistic issues in a way that ensured support for teaching and composing. Cage and his fellow experimenters challenged the very idea of an artwork; these composers tapped patrons who supported modern dance and avant-garde painting. Finally, a number of composers including George Rochberg, George Crumb, Jacob Druckman, William Bolcom, Lukas Foss, and David del Tredici, took an approach—sometimes called the New Romanticism—that harked back to the European past. They, and more recently Christopher Rouse, Ellen Taaffe Zwilich, John Harbison, Joseph Schwantner, and Joan Tower, among others, have benefited from the resources that orchestras and opera houses can place at a composer's disposal.

LISTENING GUIDE 67

Violin Concerto in D Major,
Third Movement (Bolcom)

William Bolcom's *Violin Concerto in D Major* (1984) harks back to a European past stretching from Vivaldi to Prokofiev, but the third movement could only have been written by a composer on this side of the Atlantic. "Few serious-music violinists show much interest in the jazz-fiddle tradition," Bolcom has said, but Sergiu Luca, for whom this work was composed, proved an exception. In the 1970s, the composer recalls, "I was delighted when Sergiu began to play with Joe Venuti," veteran jazz fiddler, "appearing with him several times in public (including a session at New York's Michael's Pub, during which my wife Joan Morris and I did a set with Joe's trio—a wondrous experience for us!)." This recollection points to Bolcom's longtime involvement as a performer, especially as Morris's piano accompanist in their recitals of American popular song. Bolcom's drawing on the jazz tradition in this concerto comes out of a sensibility akin to that of George Gershwin—also a pianist and, we may recall, a composer who admired and mastered a wide range of Old and New World styles.

Tonal clarity, rondo form, and the demand for solo virtuosity link the movement to European traditions of concerto writing. But the character of the melodies is unmistakably American. The main theme's square-cut, syncopated swagger is drawn from ragtime, and so is a stiff, marchlike figure that follows. Most remarkable, though, is a slower lyric section whose bassline recalls the pop song *Heart and Soul.* Over this familiar four-bar loop, a broad new melody is heard, plus a soaring countermelody from the soloist. Grounded in the humblest of formulas, this section memorably embodies the sensuous lyricism of high-register string sound.

THE RISE OF MINIMALISM

By 1965, LaMonte Young and Terry Riley, both from the western United States, were writing lengthy works based on small amounts of musical material that would point the way for Philip Glass, Steve Reich, and other young composers who fit none of the three composers' niches. Two generations ago, it has been said, when composers were asked what one piece had made them most want to be a composer, many named Stravinsky's *The Rite of Spring.* But when composers born after 1940 are asked the same question, many point to Terry Riley's *In C* and Steve Reich's *Come Out.* Written in San Francisco in 1964, *In C* became in some ways the minimalist movement's anthem.

Questioned about his work's origins, Riley, a California native, has described improvisation as one of its main influences. The fifty-three short motives that make up *In C*—repeated constantly over a fast pulse high in the piano—must be played in order, but the performers decide how long each one is played and therefore how they fit together. Having grown up playing jazz, Riley was comfortable with the idea of on-the-spot creation. Technology was another influence. *In C* is written for live performers playing an unfixed number of unspecified instruments, but its repetitions sound much like tape loops. A third influence was Riley's outlook on life. "I was a beatnik, and then I turned into a hippie," he told an interviewer. "For my generation," the mid-sixties provided "a first look towards the East, that is, peyote, mescaline, and the psychedelic drugs which were opening up people's attention towards higher consciousness. So I think what I was experiencing in music at that time was another world. Besides just the ordinary music that was going on, music was also able to transport us suddenly out of one reality into another." *In C* was premiered in November 1964 at the San Francisco Tape Music Center by an ensemble of thirteen, including Riley and Steve Reich playing keyboards and Pauline Oliveros accordion.

Reich's role in the premiere also belongs to the story of minimalism's beginnings. Though not a jazz musician himself, Reich has paid tribute to the impact on his music of trumpeter Miles Davis, drummer Kenny Clarke, and saxophonist John Coltrane. "The jazz influence that's all over my work is not so specific," he said in 1987, "but without the rhythmic and melodic gesture of jazz, its flexibility and nuance, my work is *unthinkable*." He also remembered learning "a tremendous amount from putting [*In C*] together, and I think it had a very strong influence on me."

Reich has described how he stumbled onto the process behind his own breakthrough piece, *Come Out*. In 1965, he made tape loops from a short passage of a street preacher's sermon he had recorded in San Francisco. The loops were intended as a way of superimposing one phrase upon another for musical effect, with the help of two tape machines.

> I put headphones on and noticed that the two tape recorders were almost exactly in sync. The effect of this aurally was that I heard the sound jockeying back and forth in my head between my left and right ear, as one machine or the other drifted ahead. Instead of immediately correcting that, I let it go. . . . What happened was that one of the machines was going slightly faster . . . because the left channel was moving ahead of the right channel. I let it go further, and it finally got to precisely the relationship I wanted to get to. . . . It was an accidental discovery.

Come Out (1966) is based on what Reich discovered from his experiments with tape loops. From an interview with a victim of a police beating in Harlem, who had been told he could only receive hospital care if he was bleeding, Reich chose a single sentence: "I had to, like, let some of the bruise blood come out to show them." Then he tape-looped the last five words. Repeated for more than twelve minutes, and *very* slowly pulled out of phase on several channels, the words are gradually transformed into a new kind of sound material: short, blurred melodic gestures impossible to recognize as human speech. Reich has likened performing and listening to a gradual musical process such as this one to "pulling back a swing, releasing it, and observing it gradually come to rest." And he adds: "While performing and listening to gradual musical processes, one can participate in a particular liberating and impersonal kind of ritual. Focusing in on the musical process makes possible that shift of attention away from *he* and *she* and *you* and *me* outwards towards *it*."

Composer-percussionist Steve Reich performs in New York, 1971.

Reich has also explained that while fond of the possibilities of taped speech, he preferred live instrumental performance. Early in 1967, he organized a pair of concerts at the Park Place in New York, a cooperative gallery associated with the geometric, nondecorative "minimal" art of such painters and sculptors as Ellsworth Kelly, Sol LeWitt, and Richard Serra. The concerts were part of an effort by the gallery to promote interchange among experimental artists in different media. The featured new work was a version of *Piano Phase* for four electric pianos, played by Reich and three colleagues, an outcome of the composer's experiment in playing live against a tape loop.

After one of these concerts, Reich crossed paths with Philip Glass, and before long, the two, along with several other musicians, had formed an ensemble to perform music by its members. Composers have long complained that standard ensembles such as symphony orchestras do a poor job with new music. Forming one's own group ensures not only adequate rehearsal but sympathetic interpreters ready to pour their heart and soul into the music and its performance. In 1971, Reich and Glass split up to form separate ensembles. Containing between five and eight players, these groups sounded more like an orchestra than chamber music, for players doubled each other's lines, and, especially in Glass's works, the music was amplified by the use of synthesizers and microphones. The clear-cut lines of that sound, together with the music's tonal simplicity and rhythmic interest, proved a key to the public appeal of minimalism. (The term, borrowed from the visual arts, began in the 1970s to be applied to music based on a radically reduced amount of musical material. Static harmony, patterned rhythm, and reliance on repetition are key traits of minimalism.)

Glass has described the Philip Glass Ensemble as the cornerstone of his career. He supported the ensemble by working as a cab driver, plumber, and furniture mover rather than teaching. From the first concert on, he paid his players, which kept the ensemble together, while guaranteeing concerts of high quality. Glass also bet on his music's appeal by refusing to let anyone else perform it. "I felt that if I had a monopoly on the music, that as the music became known there would be more work

The Philip Glass Ensemble, with the composer at the left, plays at New York University, 1971.

for the ensemble." He committed the group to twenty concerts a year after discovering that this would qualify his players for unemployment insurance. Glass worked day jobs until 1978, when grants and commissions finally allowed him to concentrate on composition.

Comfortable with the idea of making art that makes money, Glass has also argued that he and his compatriots restored something valuable to American musical life by returning to "the idea that the composer *is* the performer." He has also claimed a long-standing desire to transcend The Gap. "I personally knew that I didn't want to spend my life writing music for a handful of people. . . . I wanted to play for thousands of people; I was always interested in a larger audience."

LISTENING GUIDE 68

Einstein on the Beach, excerpt (Glass)

In November 1976, *Einstein on the Beach*, a "portrait opera" and collaboration between Glass and theater director Robert Wilson, was staged in New York. Wilson's concept was to wean theater away from narrative, reorienting it more toward visual imagery and spectacle. As a result, the opera offers neither a plot nor any singing characters. Singing is prominent in the work, but the soprano soloist and the chorus sing only numbers and solfege syllables. According to Glass, people who attended performances could be counted on to bring their own story with them.

Einstein on the Beach's penultimate scene features a bar of light, earlier used to represent a bed, that is suddenly transformed into a spaceship. Over a six-minute interval, the bar gradually rises, as if lifting off into space. The plot summary reports: "The sense of an atomic explosion is overwhelming. A curtain descends, cutting off the scene. It bears Einstein's equation for atomic energy: $E = Mc^2$." The music is delivered at full volume and rapidly, with a chorus chanting numbers to keep the rhythm. A five-chord progression—one heard earlier in the work at slower tempos—harmonizes the choral singing, sounding like a cadence formula but never finding harmonic resolution.

The effect of all this activity, speed, and volume is static and in-cantatory. Glass has said that only when audiences shed their usual listening habits and become free from memory and antici-pation will they "be able to perceive the music as a 'presence,' freed of dramatic structure, a pure medium of sound." These words apply well to the scene described here. Convincingly and precisely articulated in performance, the gyroscopic energy of its music, driving performers and listeners obsessively around the same loop, succeeds by sheer weight of sound and accumulation in achieving a grand solemnity.

Glass's opera has turned out to be historically significant. For one thing, while opera has long enjoyed a prominent place in American mu-sical life, few American-composed operas have caused much excitement. *Einstein* was different. The Wilson-Glass collaboration introduced a brand of theatricality that, while reflecting a contemporary spirit, was also mu-sically accessible. At the same time, the idea of a new American opera drew audiences, sparked debate, and made the opera house a center for artistic ferment. Commissions for other composers followed, including John Adams, who had written such minimalist instrumental works as *Shaker Loops*. In 1987, the Houston Grand Opera premiered *Nixon in China*, in which Adams collaborated with librettist Alice Goodman and stage di-rector Peter Sellars. That work established Adams as a composer with an international reputation and a distinctive musical style.

More generally, the public attention given the music of Riley, Reich, Glass, and Adams reflects a broader Gap-closing trend that has acceler-ated during the 1990s, reflecting the growth of mutual interest between the concert hall and living composers. While minimalists have pioneered this trend, composers with other stylistic approaches have also con-tributed: the so-called New Romanticists, for example, a group of "post-minimalists," and the younger group referred to earlier as totalists. All have worked to find a place in the mix of institutions that make up the present-day concert hall: an environment where the preferences of pay-ing customers, scorned by some in the postwar era, are treated with respect.

America has been blessed with a wealth of composers and musical traditions; the problem lies in the amount of attention any composer may hope to claim. The choices of so-called leisure activities are legion: mu-sic, drama, literature, dance, and the visual arts; television, radio, movies; sports as participation and spectatorship; travel; cookery and restaurant-going; even shopping. Within the field of music, the popular sphere over-shadows the classical with the sheer weight of its presence. And since classical performance remains focused on the European past, the corner devoted to contemporary composition is little known even to many avowed music lovers. A new work in an unfamiliar idiom has only a tiny chance of winning attention beyond a small circle of connoisseurs. Still, composers continue to write music, knowing that posterity has often judged artists more truly than their own contemporaries, and present-day indifference may not be fatal to the life of one's work.

The image of exclusiveness, idealism, and a long view of history has inspired many composers in the past and will doubtless sustain more in the future. But that image has lost its appeal for many other composers, who were raised in America's consumer culture and are unashamed to declare it their own. They have explored ways of writing music that appeals to the public—not in some indeterminate future, but *now*. For them, the question of how much time a listener must spend to connect with their music is crucial. Therefore, composers may use a regular beat, synthesized sound, and amplified volume in their music to quicken connections with listeners.

Minimalism reaffirmed an axiom out of favor during much of the twentieth century: that composers may honorably seek common ground with nonspecialist listeners. By reducing the amount of musical material a listener had to digest, minimalist composers moved the focus of listening toward the experience of sound in the moment and change on an expanded time scale. That scale invited a contemplative response that could connect with spirituality, ritual, and, in Riley's case, an expanding consciousness linked to drug use. Each of these possibilities opened up common ground with the youthful counterculture of the 1960s and helped mold the tastes of younger listeners. By performing music as well as writing it, and by seeming as concerned with their work's reception as with the way it was composed, these musicians seemed readier than many of their Gap-observing colleagues to embrace the spirit of their own place and time. And by incorporating into their work what they had learned from vernacular (especially jazz) and non-Western music, they made it more widely accessible. The minimalists were not the only agent in the Gap-closing process. But the impact of their presence and their music, like a warm wind thawing barriers that had sometimes seemed frozen into place, has helped to instill a new spirit of excitement into the classical music scene today.

40

Black Music and American Identity

OUR TOUR OF AMERICAN MUSIC HISTORY HAS LED IN THESE FINAL chapters to the subject of identity: personal and group identity, ethnic identity, generational and gendered identity, and the artistic identity of American composers. And therefore it seems fitting to note an aspect of African-American identity that has not been stressed so far: a spirit of cooperative interplay that has helped make black music irresistible to listeners and musicians outside black culture. Ring shouters, congregations, and work crews are just three groups in African-American culture noted for collaborative musical expression. But as black musicians have moved into more professional settings, writers about their music have tended to take group interaction for granted or even to ignore it. Jazz criticism and history, for example, have stressed individual achievement. Singling out such greats as Louis Armstrong, Art Tatum, Charlie Parker, and John Coltrane, writers have tended to stress originality, virtuosity, and structural imagination, each a trait valued in Western art music.

We get a different perspective from Michael Carvin, a jazz drummer who holds forth on the drummer's function in a five-man ensemble. "A drum is a woman," Carvin announces, picturing a scene in which four children come home from school at once, each in a different mood. The mother is obliged to deal

> with *all* of them at the same time and cool each one of them out for the energy level that they are *dealing* with. And that's why they say the drum is a *woman* . . . cause that's the same thing a drummer has to do. You come to the gig, the trumpet player's *up*, boy he feel like playing it. The saxophone, you know, he don't feel too good. The piano player say, "Aw, man, I shouldn't have ate so much, man, I'm feeling a little sluggish." It's the

same thing. And . . . they all coming to you at the same time, so you're getting the news from all four of them at the same time. Right? Cause you're the bandleader, right? And you have to say, "Aw, man, damn you ate too much? Why, man, you big as a house." And you got to try to get him happy and the other guy that's *already* stretching, then you want to kind of cool him *down*, cause he's stretching *too* much. He got too much energy. And then the guy that is not feelin' so good, then you got to [give him] a pep talk . . . before you go play. And they never ask you, "How do *you* feel?"

These remarks, made to jazz scholar and trumpeter Ingrid Monson, underline the sociability of jazz improvisation, a striking trait of black musical identity. In interviews with the rhythm section's bass players, piano players, and drummers, Monson has pressed them to talk about the near-telepathic communication that can occur when chemistry and sociability are right. Veteran pianist Sir Roland Hanna tells us: "We train ourselves over a period of years to be able to hear rhythms and anticipate combinations of sounds before they actually happen."

The drummer is a key to creating a sociable environment for playing jazz. Jazz drumming has been described as a musical exercise for four limbs, each with a separate function. The right hand keeps time on the ride cymbal; the right foot tends the bass drum pedal, chiefly for punctuation and accents; the left hand is free for hits and "fills" on the snare drum, tom-tom, or cymbals; and the left foot is on the pedal controlling the high-hat cymbals, usually played on beats two and four of a four-beat measure. Thus the drummer forms a complete ensemble. In performance, each limb's prescribed function serves only as a starting point. Just as a mother balances tensions among family members whose emotions are all over the map, a drummer seeks to unite individual musicians (sometimes by guiding an out-of-sync player back on track with a foot or hand) in a spirit of sociable interdependence that promotes creative improvising.

But no drummer can do that alone. When the bass player Cecil McBee tells what can happen when the interactive spirit takes hold, he starts with a point often taken for granted. Jazz performance depends on each player having something unique to contribute *and* a willingness to let the exchange guide individual effort. Since no member of the group knows, when a piece begins, how long it will last, or what notes he or she will play in the course of it, or the rhythmic effect, harmonic voicing, or sound quality that any particular moment will demand, the musicians must make those choices as the piece unfolds—on the spot, and according to cues from each other. That process is the history that is about to be made.

The next part of McBee's testimony comes out of his performing experience. When the band plays, he says, a new entity may come into being. McBee personifies this new force as "energy," and he gives it a voice that promises to guide the musicians. The players' job is to recognize energy when it appears and to keep it going. But that calls for discipline and delicacy, because if any player ventures outside the zone of collaboration, energy will most likely disappear. The musicians create something rare and valuable together; each of them engages with it, and then they "get out of the way."

Cecil McBee Describes the Interactivity of Jazz Improvisation

We are all individuals. . . . When we approach the stage . . . we are collectivized there. . . . the band begins to play, history is going to take place. This energy proceeds to that area and it says, "All right, I'm here, I will direct you and guide you. You as an individual must realize that I am here. You cannot control me; you can't come up here and say, 'Well, I'm gonna play this,'" unless you're reading [from a written arrangement]. . . . You can't go there and intellectually realize that you're going to play certain things. You're not going to play what you practiced. . . . Something else is going to happen . . . so the individual himself must make contact with that and get out of the way.

While most of Monson's jazz musicians had extensive training in music theory (chords, scales, and harmonic progressions), they usually turned to metaphors when discussing aesthetic issues. McBee's was "energy," but a more widespread term is "groove" (synonymous with "swinging" or "cooking"). One clarinet player called grooving "a euphoria that comes from playing good time *with* somebody." And a piano player described it "as a type of personal and musical chemistry." The term signifies an emotional response as well as a rhythmic one; in fact, the groove can be said to lie in the tiny discrepancies between musicians (or between a drummer's hand and foot) playing to a strict beat. Moreover, the feeling of oneness is all-important to performers and listeners alike.

The connection of jazz to African-American ethnic identity is a broader question, complicated by the economic and social inequalities between whites and blacks. In 1963, the black writer Leroi Jones (Amiri

Baraka) argued that the roots and the meaning of blues and jazz lie in "the social and political struggles of black Americans to escape slavery and oppression," that "white Euroamerican hegemony has robbed African-Americans of their culture," and that only black solidarity and black control of independent cultural and economic institutions will allow black musicians to express the true ethnic identity of African Americans. Yet if white control had been so thorough, why had so many African musical techniques flourished and performers such as Bessie Smith, Billie Holiday, Lester Young, and Miles Davis achieved such artistic excellence? Responding to Jones's analysis, the novelist and critic Ralph Ellison saw in black music a remarkable triumph: the story "of enslaved and politically weak men [and women] successfully imposing their values upon a powerful society through song and dance." And for another black intellectual, Albert Murray, the blues tradition has managed to balance the bewildering array of contradictions and complexities of Africans in America, and turn painful experience into a "near-tragic, near-comic lyricism" that celebrates life. The music humanizes the conditions in which people lead their lives. Singers, players, and listeners (dancers) are drawn together by the power of the rhythmic groove.

Bassist Cecil McBee in his role as teacher in the jazz program at Boston's New England Conservatory.

JAZZ SINCE THE 1960s

As artistic recognition of jazz blossomed during the 1960s, the music splintered into a widening range of styles. Earlier ones, from New Orleans to bebop, were maintained; and new styles also came to the fore, including free jazz (Ornette Coleman), modal jazz (Miles Davis, John Coltrane), fusion with rock elements (Davis, John McLaughlin, Herbie Hancock, Chick Corea), intersections with non-Western music (Art Ensemble of Chicago, Coltrane, Keith Jarrett), and connections with the classical avant-garde (Anthony Braxton). At the same time, as more and more young listeners turned to rock, jazz's economic base declined. New organizations were formed, chiefly by jazz musicians themselves, to promote and sustain music making that could not support itself in the marketplace.

Another symptom of jazz's changing place in American culture was the spread of formal instruction. In the latter 1960s, schools and colleges began to set up programs of jazz study. Ten years later, a quarter of a million people were studying jazz formally. Moreover, in a move unprecedented for any music in the popular sphere, musicians and institutions devoted to jazz began receiving grants from government agencies and private foundations. The idea of grants for jazz musicians is a double-edged commentary on the music's new position: recognized as artistically important but largely overlooked by the popular-music audience.

Schools were not the only institutions to embrace jazz. The Smithsonian Institution set up a jazz program in 1970. Important record reissues followed, and so did Smithsonian-sponsored concerts by "repertory" ensembles, reconstructing jazz performances of the past. In 1991, a jazz department was created at New York's Lincoln Center for the Performing Arts, the nation's flagship classical-music institution. The 1997 Pulitzer Prize in music composition was awarded for the first time to a jazz work: *Blood on the Fields*, an oratorio for jazz ensemble and vocalists by Wynton Marsalis, trumpeter, composer, and director of Lincoln Center's jazz program.

CD 3
19

LISTENING GUIDE 69

In This House, on This Morning, excerpt (Marsalis)

In This House, on This Morning is an instrumental depiction of a Sunday worship service in a Southern black church. Commissioned by the Jazz at Lincoln Center program, it was composed by Marsalis for a seven-person ensemble: trumpet, alto sax, tenor (and soprano) sax, trombone, piano, bass, and drums. The work was premiered in 1992, recorded, and released in 1994 on a two-CD set.

Our excerpt presents the beginning section, called *Devotional*: the first of the twenty-one sections that make up this three-part (almost two-hour-long) work. Many of these sections draw on the expressive power of the jazz tradition's rhythmic groove, but this section's tempo is free. *Devotional* also introduces musical material that will be heard in later sections: especially the wide-ranging six-note figure played first by the soprano saxophone, then the double bass, then the trumpet, and finally again by the soprano sax as the section nears its end. This figure, containing a minor seventh and a ninth (which may be contracted into major seconds), is used in *Devotional* as a blues-like call, which draws varied responses from the other instruments: a bluesey eighth-note piano figure, three (or two) bell-like piano chords, and hushed chords from the rest of the players. Only twice does the drummer join the ensemble, as if an in-tempo section is about to start. Both times, after a brief polyrhythmic moment, the unifying call returns and the beat again becomes flexible. While *Devotional* is not intended as a freestanding piece, it provides an example of nonswinging jazz elements being used to introduce a large-scale musical structure.

New York's Lincoln Center Jazz Ensemble, directed by trumpeter-composer Wynton Marsalis, performs music from all periods of jazz history.

New Orleans native Marsalis, born in 1961, has taken the view that, as well as an African-American inheritance, jazz is also a broader reflection of American character. Backed by a pedigree that includes professional training at the Juilliard School and performances of many classical works, Marsalis has presented himself as an artist working within the jazz tradition's strict standards—that is, the evolutionary stream beginning with ragtime and blues and followed by such styles as New Orleans, Chicago, New York (the dance orchestras of Duke Ellington and Fletcher Henderson), Kansas City swing, bebop, and more recent spinoffs from the bop mainstream of the 1940s and 50s.

In a milieu full of strong-minded individuals, it is no surprise that Marsalis's stance has drawn criticism, especially since he has become a dispenser of patronage through Lincoln Center. Many musicians have disagreed with his historical approach to a tradition that since the 1950s has evolved into a broad range of musical styles, linked chiefly by improvisation. Some have also challenged his image of jazz musicians' identity. As clarinetist Don Byron has put it: "One of the fallacies of the Wynton era is that jazz cats don't listen to rap." For trumpeter Lester Bowie, the tradition is much more diverse than Marsalis has granted. Jazz, Bowie says, is "not simple music anymore. So it does belong in the concert hall. But it also belongs in the street, on the farm, it needs equal access everywhere, the same as country western, rap, anything. Because jazz is all of these."

Marsalis told an interviewer in 1984 that a society's ultimate achievement "is the establishment of an art form . . . indigenous to that society." He explained that during the 1940s, jazz musicians, including Armstrong, Parker, Ellington, and Monk, "introduced an entire range of mood and emotion into the vocabulary of Western music, an entirely new way of phrasing, an entirely new way of thinking in the language of music" that "perfectly captures the spirit and tone of America." Their contribution, however, went unrecognized. For one thing, racism and economic inequality had marginalized jazz. For another, improvisation was thought to rely more on intuition than on intellect. And for yet another, cultural standards had slipped to the point that "anything can pass for art." Marsalis blamed the mass media for promoting a popular culture with everything reduced to the lowest common denominator. And he challenged his colleagues to fight for standards: "We musicians should never forget that it is our job to educate people, to stand up for excellence and quality." In his view, the excellence and quality of jazz were democratic and characteristically American because the music combined a vernacular base with a hunger for artistic exploration. "To me," Marsalis declared, "the test of true greatness in an artist is the ability to write or perform music that is on the very highest level but can also appeal to common people. That's the problem Beethoven, Stravinsky, Charlie Parker, and Louis Armstrong all faced."

In a published piece from that year, Marsalis used the rhythmic groove to illustrate the intellectual control a jazz musician had to possess:

> When you don't have words or images to communicate with people, your logic has to be so strong that the rhythm of the notes makes sense to them. When you can do that while improvising like Pops [Armstrong] or Bird [Parker] could do, it should be obvious that some mother wit didn't get them by. Or when you can use harmonies like Duke or Monk did, and get all those precise colors out of the piano, you can't just throw that up to soul.

Marsalis's comments reveal a belief in hierarchy: jazz deserves to be part of an educational agenda; Ellington's artistry places him on an equal footing with such European composers as Beethoven and Stravinsky. But perhaps the most striking notion of all is that *no music is more thoroughly American than jazz*—that is, the blues-based strain championed by Marsalis—whose civilizing force has provided a much-needed boost to the nation's sense of humanity.

The artistic recognition that jazz has received in recent years testifies not only to its new position among American music's three spheres but also to the way the music's elements cut across those categories in the first place. For jazz, rooted in black folk music, has also relied on the popular sphere for repertory and forms; the careers of jazz musicians are still mostly carried on in the popular sphere's marketplace, but some have identified with the traditional sphere (chiefly African) and others more with the classical concert hall. Finally, once jazz is recorded, it is likely to be analyzed historically, culturally, or technically with the help of approaches developed in the classical sphere. Works that pass muster may then be treated as part of a transcendent musical legacy. Thus a music that was once socially controversial, linked in the minds of many white Americans with unsavory conduct and a lack of schooled musicianship, enjoys today the respected status due a full-fledged art form.

 IDENTITY AND HIP-HOP CULTURE

While jazz matured in a climate of segregation, the newer form of black expression known as hip hop took shape during the 1970s and 80s as the American economy was moving away from its industrial past. In the new global economy, resources were transferred away from local business into the hands of international corporations; as these corporations gained power in the marketplace, manufacturing jobs were moved out of cities to locations where labor was cheaper. As a result, many Americans who lacked education and technical skills found themselves consigned to low-paying jobs in the service sector. In a time of generally rising prosperity, the gap between rich and poor widened. For those at the lower end of the economic scale (mostly Hispanics and blacks) the industrial fall-off brought low-paying jobs, joblessness, and rising crime rates, often linked to the use of drugs.

The South Bronx area of New York City was hit especially hard by these developments. And hip-hop culture was born there in the late 1970s to resist them. Hip hop sprang from the tension between postindustrial oppression and the positive bonds of black expressiveness. Both sides of the ledger are reflected in *The Message*, a rap number about life in the ghetto, recorded in 1982 by Grandmaster Flash and the Furious Five:

> Got a bum education, double-digit inflation
> Can't take the train to the job, there's a strike at the station
> Don't push me cause I'm close to the edge
> I'm tryin' not to lose my head
> It's like a jungle sometimes it makes me wonder
> How I keep from going under.

The words of this number register the destructive effects of unequal opportunity: poor schooling, unreliable public services, and a feeling that the jungle of urban life is about to claim another victim. On the other hand, rap's combining of rhythmic word delivery with a reverberating beat allows it to draw on preaching and music, two of the most potent black cultural resources. Further, the words suggest an analogy with blues singers, who keep painful experience alive in their consciousness by placing it in an artistic frame, though *The Message* is less a lyric statement than an angry diatribe. That *The Message* was heard by outsiders at all was a tribute to the resourcefulness of Grandmaster Flash and his cohorts, who, working in a blighted part of the city, found a local company willing to record and distribute their music.

Rather than being performed live, the musical background to *The Message* is a collage of excerpts from earlier recordings, a technique Grandmaster Flash perfected on two turntables that would lead eventually to the use of "samplers": computers able to duplicate any existing sound digitally, play it back at any speed or pitch, and loop it endlessly. People growing up in the South Bronx in the 1970s, we may assume, had little contact with standard musical instruments. Yet many were avid listeners, and a few learned to "play" electronic devices—turntables, then tape decks, synthesizers, mixers, drum machines, and samplers—with expert control. Like other early rappers, Grandmaster Flash came to this branch of music making not as a musician in the traditional sense but as a disk jockey with a charismatic line of talk.

LISTENING GUIDE 70

It's Like That (Run-D.M.C.)

From the early 1980s comes *It's Like That*, by the three-man group Run-D.M.C., reputed to be the first political rap number. This recording gains force and authority from its square-cut form and simplicity. Over what sounds like a synthesized background, chiefly a drum machine, the rapping voices declare hard truths about the realities of modern life. The lines are delivered in paired sixteen-bar stanzas: three lines of specifics about society, politics, jobs, or education, and then the fourth line: "It's like that, and that's the way it is." The rhythm of this stanza-ending punch line is invariable: ♩ | ♩ ♩ ♪ ♪♫ | ♪♩ ♪♩ ♪ |. The number starts with a synthesized "instrumental" background and ends with a long tag and a gradual fadeout, over which the rappers repeat the fourth line. In between, six pairs of stanzas are heard, separated by wordless interludes that vary in length and sound but are always in four- and eight-bar sections.

From the 1980s on, the themes of rap videos have centered on local neighborhoods. Asked to define the three most important themes in representing rap visually, an experienced video director answered: "Posse, posse, and posse"—in other words, setting the action in the artists' locale and feeding off the sense of tight connectedness with their sidekicks. To be grounded on one's home turf and in the company of a "posse" of like-minded cohorts is a source of strength and confirms the musicians' unambiguous identity. At the same time, rap's competitiveness stimulates the energy and assertiveness that go into a rapper's performance, boosting its appeal for some listeners in part because the sound, tone, and stance are offensive to others.

Rap music has been criticized for its content: the often obscene language, images of violence against women and authority (especially the

The rap group Run-D.M.C., pictured in 1988 after winning a Grammy Award (left to right: Joseph Simmons, Darryl McDaniels, Jason Mizell).

police), and thinness of musical interest. The story of the music's evolution in the marketplace is one of local entrepreneurship, unexpected commercial success, and an appeal to audiences far beyond ghetto communities. It is also a story of growing diversity. Since 1990, together with gangsta rap and such familiar subjects as sexual boasting, Afrocentric emphases, and protest raps, rap music has embraced the experience of blacks in the South, jazz samples, live instrumentation (including folk guitar), introspective lyrics, and even New Age/soul rap fusions.

Young white males from the suburbs are among rap's most avid fans. Perhaps part of the appeal has to do with the fantasy of downward mobility that earlier made rock music so widely appealing: white youngsters geared for success in competitive settings seeking temporary release from those responsibilities. It is probably fair to say that what these fans appreciate most about rap is its "edge," its sense of entitlement and open defiance. But from a historical point of view, rap may also be seen as the latest in a line of African-American styles that have broadened the world's idea of music. For whatever the words may be saying, the *sound*—the cranked-up dominance of the bass drum machine, the pulsating rhythmic grooves, the sense that modern technological power is being tapped, the high volume at which the music is played, the ranting, in-your-face tone of the voices—testifies to an ever-broadening conception of what music is and does, continuing an expansion in which twentieth-century America won pride of place.

Acknowledgments

The publishers have made every effort to contact all copyright holders. If proper acknowledgment has not been made, we ask to be contacted.

Music

DIMINUENDO AND CRESCENDO IN BLUE, by Edward Kennedy Ellington. Used By Permission of Famous Music Corporation. All Rights Reserved—p. 399.

DIPPERMOUTH BLUES. By Joe Oliver © 1923 (Renewed) Universal—MCA Music Publishing, a Division of Universal Studios, Inc. All Rights Reserved. Used by Permission. WARNER BROS. PUBLICATIONS U.S. INC., Miami, FL 33014—pp. 386–87.

EINSTEIN ON THE BEACH, by Philip Glass © 1976 Dunvagen Music Publishers, Inc.—p. 507.

THE HOUSATONIC AT STOCKBRIDGE, by Charles Ives © Copyright 1954 by Peer International Corp. All rights reserved. Reprinted by Permission—p. 317.

LESTER LEAPS IN, by Lester Young © 1940 (Renewed) WB Music Corp. All Rights Reserved. Used by Permission. WARNER BROS. PUBLICATIONS U.S. INC., Miami, FL 33014—p. 404.

THE MAN I LOVE, by George Gershwin and Ira Gershwin © 1924 (Renewed) WB Music Corp. All Rights Reserved. Used by Permission. WARNER BROS. PUBLICATIONS U.S. INC., Miami, FL 33014—p. 414.

THE MESSAGE, by Grandmaster Flash © by Sugar Hill Music Publishing. All Rights Reserved. Used by permission.—p. 518.

MY HEART STOOD STILL, Words by Lorenz Hart, music by Richard Rodgers © by Williamson Music and The Estate of Lorenz Hart administered by WB Music Corp. International copyright secured. All rights reserved.—p. 412.

MY FAIR LADY, by Lerner and Loewe © 1956 Alan Jay Lerner and Frederick Loewe. © Renewed Chappell & Co. owner of publication and allied rights throughout the world. All Rights Reserved. Used by Permission. WARNER BROS. PUBLICATIONS U.S. INC., Miami, FL 33014—p. 473.

RHAPSODY IN BLUE, by George Gershwin © 1924 (Renewed) WB Music Corp. All Rights Reserved. Used by Permission. WARNER BROS. PUBLICATIONS U.S. INC., Miami, FL 33014—p. 353.

ROUND AND ROUND HITLER'S GRAVE, Words and Music by Pete Seeger © copyright 1951 Universal-MCA Music Publishing, Inc. a division of Universal Studios, Inc. (ASCAP). International Copyright Secured. All Rights Reserved—p. 381.

THIS LAND IS YOUR LAND, Words and Music by Woody Guthrie. TRO-©-Copyright 1956 (Renewed) 1958 (Renewed) 1970 (Renewed) Ludlow Music, Inc., New York, NY. Used by Permission—pp. 378. NOTE: The excerpt used in this book was taken from Woody Guthrie's original manuscript and the lyrics are different from the published words.

YOU'RE GOING TO LOSE THAT GIRL, by John Lennon and Paul McCartney. Copyright © 1965 Sony/ATV Songs LLC. All rights administered by SONY/ATV Music Publishing, 8 Music Square West, Nashville, TN 37203. All Rights Reserved. Used by Permission—p. 491.

Books and Articles

Browner, Tara, "American Indian Music and Dance," from the *Grolier Multimedia Encyclopedia,* 1999 Edition. Copyright 1999 by Grolier Incorporated. Reprinted by permission.—p. 247.

Duckworth, William, *Talking Music: Conversations with John Cage, Philip Glass, Laurie Anderson, and Five Generations of American Experimental Composers,* Schirmer, 1995. Reprinted by permission of The Gale Group.—pp. 500, 503–4, 506–7.

Gann, Kyle, *American Music in the Twentieth Century,* Schirmer, 1997. Reprinted by permission of The Gale Group.—pp. 500, 504.

Guralnik, Peter. *Last Train to Memphis: The Rise of Elvis Presley.* Copyright © 1994 by Peter Guralnick. By permission of Little, Brown and Company (Inc.).—pp. 441–42, 444.

Harjo, Joy, "Anchorage," from *She Had Some Horses,* by Joy Harjo. Copyright © 1983, 1997 by Thunder's Mouth Press. Appears by permission of the publisher, Thunder's Mouth Press.—p. 248.

Hijuelos, Oscar, *The Mambo Kings Play Songs of Love.* Excerpt from Side A: "In the Hotel Splendour 1980" and "Toward the End, while Listening to the Wistful 'Beautiful Maria of My Soul" from THE MAMBO KINGS PLAY SONGS OF LOVE by Oscar Hijuelos. Copyright © 1989 by Oscar Hijuelos. Reprinted by permission of Farrar, Straus and Giroux, LLC. © 1989 by Oscar Hijuelos. Used by permission of HWLA, Inc.—pp. 475–76.

Ives, Charles, *Selected Writings,* reprinted by permission of the American Academy of Arts and Letters, copyright owner.—pp. 312–14, 316, 318–19, 324.

Monson, Ingrid, *Saying Something: Jazz Improvisation and Interaction,* University of Chicago Press, 1996, © 1996 by the University of Chicago. All Rights Reserved.—pp. 510–11.

Illustrations

p. 5: Collection of Wiley L. Housewright; p. 37: Courtesy Congregational Church, South Dennis, Massachusetts; p. 38: Library of Congress; p. 39: From the collection of the Moravian Historical Society, Nazareth, Pennsylvania; p. 49: Library of Congress; p. 50: From *New York Statesman,* September 24, 1824; p. 52: © Christie's Images; p. 53: New York Public Library, Music Division; p. 62: Corbis; p. 67: © Collection of The New-York Historical Society; p. 72: Corbis; p. 75: Abby Aldrich Rockefeller Folk Art Center, Williamsburg, Virginia; p. 78: Maryland Historical Society, Baltimore, Maryland; p. 78: Maryland Historical Society, Baltimore, Maryland; p. 83: (top) Library of Congress, (bottom) Library of Congress; p. 96: New York Public Library, Music Division; p. 102: From *White Spirituals in the Southern Uplands,* Dover Publications, Inc., New York; p. 116: New York Public Library, Music Division; p. 118: New York Public Library, Music Division; p. 119: New York Public Library, Music Division; p. 125: From *Popular Songs of Nineteenth-Century America,* edited by Richard Jackson, Dover Publications, Inc., New York; p. 129: From *Popular Songs of Nineteenth-Century America,* edited by Richard Jackson, Dover Publications, Inc., New York; p. 130: Corbis; p. 133: From *Stephen Foster Song Book,* selected by Richard Jackson, Dover Publication, Inc., New York; p. 136: © Collection of The New-York Historical Society; p. 139: Library of Congress; p. 141: New York Public Library, Music Division; p. 145: Culver Pictures; p. 148: © Collection The New-York Historical Society; p. 150: New York Public Library at Lincoln Center; p. 153: Warder Collection; p. 155: From *Popular Songs of the Nineteenth-Century America,* edited by Richard Jackson, Dover Publications, Inc., New York; p. 157: Corbis; p. 159: New York Public Library, Music Division; p. 161: Corbis; p. 164: Photograph by permission of the Buffalo & Erie County Public Library, Rare Book Room; p. 165: From *The Civil War Songbook,* selected by Richard Crawford, Dover Publications, Inc., New York; p. 170: Library of Congress; p. 176: © Collection The New-York Historical Society; p. 179: Corbis; p. 183: © Collection The New-York Historical Society; p. 184: © Collection The New-York Historical Society; p. 186: Courtesy of the Harvard University Archives; p. 189: Corbis; p. 191: Cincinnati Museum Center; p. 195: Warder Collection; p. 199: Daguerreotype Collection, Library of Congress; p. 201: The New York Philharmonic Archives; p. 207: From *Piano Music of Louis Moreau Gottschalk,* Dover Publications, Inc., New York; p. 211: Corbis; p. 212: From *The Banjo in the Music of Gottschalk,* ed. Richard Jackson, Dover Publications, Inc., New York; p. 217: Courtesy New England Conservatory; p. 220: Courtesy of the heirs of George Whitefield Chadwick; p. 223: Library of Congress; p. 225: Corbis; p. 229: Corbis; p. 239: National Museum of American Art, Smithsonian Institution, Gift of Mrs. Joseph Harrison, Jr. Photo: National Museum of American Art, Washington, D.C./Art Resource, NY; p. 240: National Museum of American History, Smithsonian Institution, Washington; p. 242: Nebraska State Historical Society; p. 244: Idaho State Historical Society, #3771; p. 247: © Joel Gordon, 1995; p. 250: Abby Aldrich Rockefeller Folk Art Center, Williamsburg, Virginia; p. 258: Corbis; p. 261: Charles L. Blockson Collection; p. 263: Harvard Theatre Collection, the Houghton Library, Frederic Woodbridge Wilson, Curator; p. 269: Courtesy of the Southwest Museum, Los Angeles. Photo #24536; p. 270: Courtesy of the Southwest Museum, Los Angeles. Photo #42036; p. 275: New York Public Library, Music Division; p. 282 (top) State Historical Society of Wisconsin, WHi(X3)38436, (bottom) State Historical Society of Wisconsin, WHi(X3)12673; p. 285: New York Public Library, Music Division; p. 290: U.S. Marine Archives; p. 293: (detail of photo) © Collection of The New-York Historical Society; p. 295: Charles W. Stein Collection; p. 296: Daniel C. Harter Collection; p. 297: From *Favorite Songs of the Nineties,* edited by Robert Fremont, Dover Publications, Inc., New York; p. 303: From *Favorite Songs of the Nineties,* edited by Robert Fremont, Dover Publications, Inc., New York; p. 305: Warder Collection; p. 311: The Charles Ives Papers, Yale University Music Library; p. 313: The Charles Ives Papers, Yale University Music Library; p. 315: Corbis; p. 324: Yale University Music Library; p. 326: The New York Public Library, Music Division; p. 329: New York Public Library, Music Division; p. 331: Warder Collection; p. 332: Corbis; p. 337: Baldwin H. Ward/Corbis; p. 341: Frank Driggs Collection/Corbis; p. 346 (top). Frank Driggs Collection/Corbis; p. 348: Warder Collection; p. 351: UPI/Corbis; p. 357: Hulton-Deutsch Collection/Corbis; p. 358: Corbis; p. 361: Corbis; p. 365: Warder Collection; p. 371: Courtesy English Folk Dance and Song Society; p. 374: Frank Driggs Collection/Corbis; p. 375: Smithsonian Institution, Courtesy of the Alan Lomax Archive, New York; p. 377: Frank Driggs Collection/Corbis; p. 380: Courtesy of the Woody Guthrie Archives; p. 383: William Ransom Hogan Jazz Archives, Tulane University Library; p. 385: William Ransom Hogan Jazz Archives, Tulane University Library; p. 388: Corbis p. 391: Corbis; p. 394: Warder Collection; p. 395: Corbis; p. 396: New York Public Library, Music Division; p. 403: Frank Driggs Collection/Corbis; p. 409: Warder Collection; p. 411: New York Public Library, Music Division; p. 411: UPI/Corbis; p. 416: UPI/Corbis; p. 418: Corbis; p. 419: Photofest; p. 423: Corbis; p. 426: © 1999 Nancy Crampton; p. 429 (top) Corbis, (bottom): Warder Collection; p. 433: Hulton-Deutsch Collection/Corbis; p. 435: Archive Photos; p. 437: New York Public Library, Music Division; p. 437: New York Public Library, Music Division; p. 440: Photofest; p. 443: UPI/Corbis; p. 446: Courtesy Retna, Ltd., Photograph by David Redfern; p. 449: Penguin/Corbis; p. 451: Courtesy Country Music Hall of Fame; p. 455: © Frank Driggs/Archive Photos/PNI; p. 459: *Chicago Defender;* p. 462: © Bill Gottlieb; p. 464: Frank Driggs Collection/Corbis; p. 465: Corbis; p. 467: Corbis; p. 470: Corbis; p. 473: Cecil Beaton Collection, Sotheby's, London, Print Division; p. 478: David Allen/Corbis; p. 481: © Copyright David Gahr; p. 483: New York Public Library, Music Division; p. 486: UPI/Corbis; p. 492: Photofest; p. 494: New York Public Library, Music Division; p. 497: Courtesy Random House, Inc., New York and Visages, Los Angeles; p. 499: Photograph: © Paula Court; p. 505: © Richard Landry. All rights reserved; p. 506: © Richard Landry. All rights reserved; p. 513: Courtesy New England Conservatory, Boston. Photograph by Paul Foley, p. 515: © Carol Friedman/Courtesy Jazz at Lincoln Center; p. 520: UPI/Corbis.

Index